Citizen Strangers

Stanford Studies in Middle Eastern and Islamic Societies and Cultures

Citizen Strangers

PALESTINIANS AND THE BIRTH OF
ISRAEL'S LIBERAL SETTLER STATE

Shira Robinson

Stanford University Press
Stanford, California

Stanford University Press
Stanford, California

Printed in the United States of America on acid-free, archival-quality paper

Library of Congress Cataloging-in-Publication Data

Robinson, Shira, 1972- author.
  Citizen strangers : Palestinians and the birth of Israel's liberal settler state / Shira Robinson.
     pages cm--(Stanford studies in Middle Eastern and Islamic societies and cultures)
  Includes bibliographical references and index.
  ISBN 978-0-8047-8654-6 (cloth : alk. paper)--ISBN 978-0-8047-8800-7 (pbk. : alk. paper)
  1. Palestinian Arabs--Civil rights--Israel. 2. Palestinian Arabs--Legal status, laws, etc.--Israel.
  3. Citizenship--Government policy--Israel. 4. Land settlement--Government policy--Israel.
  5. Jews--Colonization--Palestine. 6. Arab-Israeli conflict--1948-1967. 7. Israel--Politics and
  government--1948-1967. I. Title. II. Series: Stanford studies in Middle Eastern and Islamic
  societies and cultures.
  DS113.7.R56 2013
  323.1192'74009'045--dc23   2013021486

  ISBN 978-0-8047-8802-1 (electronic)

Typeset by Bruce Lundquist in 10/14 Minion

For my mother, Lenore Annette Robinson

CONTENTS

ILLUSTRATIONS

NOTE ON TRANSLATIONS AND TRANSLITERATIONS

This book is intended for specialist and nonspecialist readers alike. The text follows modified versions of the Arabic and Hebrew transliteration systems according to the *International Journal of Middle Eastern Studies* (*IJMES*) and the Library of Congress, respectively. I have eliminated all diacriticals and long-vowel markers except for the *ayn/ayin* (' in both languages) and *alif/aleph* with *hamza* ('). Names with common English spellings (for example, Gamal Abdel Nasser) are preserved as such.

The spelling of place names in Israel and Palestine requires more deliberation, both because of the differences between Modern Standard Arabic and local pronunciations, and because in many cases choosing between the Arabic and Hebrew is a political act. With the occasional exception when I offer both spellings, I have used common English renderings for well-known places such as Acre, Nazareth, Jerusalem, and Beersheba. For the spelling of Palestinian villages and towns that appear frequently in the text or in an oral interview, I have used the colloquial form. Thus *Rama* becomes *Rame*, *'Arraba* becomes *'Arrabe*, and *Shafa 'Amru* becomes *Shafa 'Amr*. In transcribing interviews I also spell the Arabic word for "mother," *Umm*, as *Imm* (as in *Imm Mahmud*). Some of the authors cited publish in two or more languages. I have deferred to the spellings they have chosen for their English-language publications (such as Elias Shoufani and Emile Habibi) but have maintained the *IJMES* system for the works they have published in Arabic (such as Ilyas Shufani and Imil Habibi).

On occasion, Arabic- or Hebrew-language books include an official English translation in their front matter. Otherwise, and unless noted, all translations are my own. For the sake of brevity, I have translated but not transliterated article titles from the Arabic- and Hebrew-language press. Because the rules for Arabic and Hebrew differ, I have used the same capitalization style (only the first word of a headline) for both languages.

ACKNOWLEDGMENTS

This project has been a long time in the making. It is also the fruit of critical engagement, inspiring argument, and unwavering friendship. It is with a heavy dose of humility that I recognize the institutions and individuals who ushered me through the journey.

I am deeply grateful for the generous financial support that made it possible for me to research and write this book. Fellowships and grants from the US Fulbright Institute for International Education, the Social Science Research Council, the Palestinian American Research Center, the Mellon Foundation, and Stanford University's History Department and Taube Center for Jewish Studies provided crucial assistance during its initial incubation period. A stimulating year at the Davis Center for Historical Studies at Princeton University, coupled with numerous research grants and invaluable course reductions from the University of Iowa and the George Washington University (GW), contributed to the book's development at later stages.

I used a good deal of this funding to mine the Israel State Archive, the Israel Defense Forces Archives, the Jewish National and University Library, the Lavon Institute, Givat Haviva, the Kafr Qasim municipality, and the Israeli Communist Party Archives at Yad Tabenkin. I would like to thank the librarians and reading room staff in all of these places for allowing me to make the most of my time there. Other funds enabled me to hire wonderful research assistants, including Doaaʿ Elnakhala, Kate Walters, Courtney Freer, Madelyn Yribarren, and Justin Marcello. Shir Alon, Alissa Walter, and Diab Zayed saved me from making mistakes in both translation and transliteration. When I wasn't writing full-time, doctoral students Andrea O'Brien, Shaadi Khoury, Julia Sittman, Jason Hushour, and Martin Margolis made my day job in the classroom immensely easier and more fun. My deepest gratitude goes to Bill Becker, my department chair; Ed Berkowitz; and all of my colleagues at GW's History Department and the Elliott School of International Affairs, for enabling me to write the book that I wanted to write.

Most of the oral interviews in the book were conducted between 2001 and 2002, at the height of the second Palestinian Intifada, or uprising, against Israel's ongoing occupation of the West Bank and Gaza Strip. It was a frightening and dispiriting time for Israeli citizens working to end the 1967 occupation and to combat racism and inequality inside Israel's 1949 armistice lines. I am forever indebted to all of the older Palestinian women and men—many of them leading activists in their day, some still going strong—who spent hours sharing their recollections of military rule, as well as to everyone who introduced me to others willing to do the same. Without the enthusiastic help of 'Umayma Abu Ra's, Rose 'Amr, Issam Aburaya, Jehad Abu Raya, 'Adil Budayr, Leena Dallasheh, Hazzar Hijazi, Ya'qub Hijazi, Suha Ibrahim, Zuhayra Sabbagh, and Marzuq Shufani, not to mention the unparalleled hospitality of their families, my understanding of this period would have been significantly impoverished. Most of my interlocutors were happy to be identified by name. Here I would like to thank those individuals who wished to remain anonymous.

Over the past decade, conversations with colleagues and friends have directed me to sources, answered detailed queries, pushed me to hone my arguments, and offered critical feedback on small and large portions of the text. Special thanks go to Lori Allen, Nemata Blyden, Oren Bracha, Michelle Campos, Daniel Cohen, Hillel Cohen, Elliott Colla, Jonathan Cook, Ahmad Dallal, Leena Dallasheh, Rochelle Davis, Gil Eyal, Ilana Feldman, Geremy Forman, Khaled Furani, Michael Gordin, Neve Gordon, Aziz Haidar, Shay Hazkani, Adina Hoffman, Rhoda Kanaaneh, Dane Kennedy, Linda Kerber, Laleh Khalili, Dina Khoury, Alina Korn, Jessica Krug, Peter Lagerquist, Chris Lee, Zachary Lockman, Ussama Makdisi, 'Adil Manna', Melani McAlister, Ed McCord, Joel Migdal, Maha Nassar, Marcy Norton, Tom Pessah, Mouin Rabbani, Laura Robson, Catherine Rottenberg, Johanna Schoen, Sherene Seikaly, Tamir Sorek, Rebecca Stein, Bob Vitalis, and Lora Wildenthal. Na'ila Naqara and 'Issam Makhoul generously shared their photo collections. Last but not least, the manuscript benefited greatly from the readings of two anonymous reviewers at Stanford University Press, where editor Kate Wahl, Frances Malcolm, and Mariana Raykov worked with grace, patience, and speed.

Over the past sixteen years, Joel Beinin has been an unflagging mentor, interlocutor, and friend. While I bear sole responsibility for the failings of this book, he deserves much of the credit for its strengths. No one deserves more credit for the project's completion than Amy Robinson, Tresa Grauer, and Chris Toensing. At three crucial stages, their editorial interventions made it both possible and rewarding to keep writing. I continue to be touched by the way Avi, Elya, and Maayani made me feel at home during my extended stays in Philadelphia.

Although at times it seemed like life outside my head and my office did not exist, the companionship of friends and family consistently pulled me out. At home in Washington, Andrew Z., Elliott, Ilana, Johanna, Julia K., Marcy, Mona, Chris T., Melani, Sara, and Tyler nourished me regularly with their food, solidarity, and wit. Lifelong friends Amy S., Andrew P., Anne, Danielle, Deb, Jen, Jess, Jessi, Esther, Peter, Pnina, Sarabeth, Shosh, and their families kept me laughing, singing, and sane. Farther away, Amy R., Michelle, Lisa, Max, Rebecca, and Sherene cheered me on. The loving encouragement of my father, Larry; his partner, Julia; and my brother, Noah, has sustained me in more ways than they realize. Above all, what kept me aboveground over the past four years was the unflinching support and good humor of my husband, Josh. I thank him for opening his heart to me, for reminding me what a big world we live in, and for bringing his precious, sweet boy into my life. Without Caleb, I would not have known just how compelling cherry pickers and stuffed puppies could be.

I had originally planned to dedicate this project to my mother's mother, Batsheva Naimer (née Stern). Although she died before I was born, I have always attributed to her part of my long-standing interest in the history of Palestine, where she was born and raised at the end of the Ottoman Empire, and where I was born six decades later. Today I dedicate this book to my mother, Lenore Annette Robinson, who passed away unexpectedly and prematurely in April 2004. My parents met on a bus during the 1969 teachers' strike in New York City. Both union members, they opposed the strike because they believed it was racist. From an early age my mother instilled in me a commitment to fight for social and economic justice. If, in the last years of her life, she struggled to understand some of my conclusions about the past and future of Israel/Palestine, she took pride in the strength of my convictions, and in my ability to communicate them to others.

Citizen Strangers

INTRODUCTION

TAWFIQ TUBI HAD EXPECTED LITTLE FROM THE MEETING. It was an unseasonably warm morning in late October 1966 and the elected deputy was just months shy of entering his eighteenth year of service in the Israeli parliament.[1] Until that day, the Palestinian communist had confronted "the Old Man," as former Prime Minister and Defense Minister David Ben-Gurion was known, only in the Knesset chamber. Starting when he was just twenty-six years old, the young Arab activist from Haifa quickly rose to the helm of the struggle to end Israel's systematic discrimination against the roughly 150,000 Palestinians who had managed to stay in or return to the country after its war of independence in 1948. During Tubi's time on the floor, it was not uncommon for his fellow deputies—many of whom were immigrants from Eastern Europe—to shout him down. In the 1950s and 1960s, most Knesset members treated any political opposition from "an Arab" as a sign of impudence toward a nation that had been magnanimous enough not to deport him.

Although he had followed Tubi's public statements over the years, Ben-Gurion had refused to meet with his junior colleague privately while in office. If there was one conversation the former leader had wanted to avoid, it was the demand to end the military administration that he personally had insisted on maintaining in the roughly 104 Arab villages and towns that had survived the *nakba,* or catastrophe, as Palestinians refer to the wartime ethnic cleansing campaign that wiped their country off the map and rendered those who remained a sudden minority in the new state.[2] Since then, Israel's Palestinian citizens had come overwhelmingly to despise the military regime for its despotism, its contempt for due process, and its Big Brother-like insinuation into their lives

1

and communities. They reviled it most, however, for its draconian restrictions on their movement and its role as the handmaiden of the colonization of their land by Jewish settlers. Ben-Gurion had been the regime's most loyal champion, but three years had passed since his resignation. Why, Tubi wondered as he approached the door of the former leader's apartment in Tel Aviv, had the Old Man summoned him now?

Tubi had been wise to have low expectations, for his host's paternalism was as fresh as ever. Although Ben-Gurion began by expressing his desire to discuss "the problems between Jews and Arabs," he proceeded instead to fixate on the question of whether Tubi was a first name or a family name. When the Palestinian deputy politely but firmly steered the conversation back to the matter at hand, the former leader, now eighty years old, expressed surprise that Tubi had served in the Knesset for the previous two decades. For the next several minutes Ben-Gurion's deflection persisted. With each charge that Tubi leveled about Israel's maltreatment of Palestinians since 1948, the Polish-born settler and founding father of the Jewish state feigned incredulity: "We expelled people?" he asked. "From which village did we expropriate land?" "Is it true that our universities reject Arab applications en masse?" Exasperated, Tubi at last gave up and invoked the historic comparison between Israel and Western colonial powers that the Jewish public had long vilified him for suggesting. "I do not wish to insult [you, Mr. Ben-Gurion], but [we are treated] like 'natives' [*yelidim*]. This is the sort of relationship that has been created." The official transcript of the encounter between the two men does not indicate whether Ben-Gurion looked uncomfortable or paused to reflect on Tubi's indictment, but it is unlikely. "Under the British," he averred, "we were all 'natives.'"[3]

This brief exchange—the charge of colonial dispossession and its disavowal—is at the heart of the puzzle that drives this book. What does it mean for a democratically elected representative of a sovereign parliament to identify himself as a colonial subject? Ben-Gurion was, of course, correct that in 1948 the Jewish settler community in Palestine had proclaimed its liberation from the yoke of the British Empire. Under the British Mandate, individual Jews in Palestine had been colonial subjects no less than their Arab counterparts. It was also true, however, that Zionist leaders had lobbied aggressively for the Empire's sponsorship of their collective settler project, and that their patron, with the blessing of the League of Nations, had done much to facilitate the development of a Jewish national home at the direct expense of a people who in 1922 comprised 90 percent of the land's inhabitants.[4] But this was not

Tubi's point. What concerned him, as the Old Man knew full well, was that, for the Palestinians, the settler-colonial yoke had not just remained in place since 1948, but had grown immeasurably heavier.

. . .

This book explores the contradictions that emerged from Israel's foundation as a *liberal settler state*—a modern colonial polity whose procedural democracy was established by forcibly removing most of the indigenous majority from within its borders and then extending to those who remained a discrete set of individual rights and duties that only the settler community could determine. Jewish settler leaders seized the rights *to* the state, granting the newfound Arab minority only a handful of rights *within* it. My choice of language is deliberate. Although Jewish citizens today are largely native-born, they continue to enjoy an array of social and political privileges relative to their Arab co-citizens. These privileges date back to the historical status of Israel's founders as a minority of foreign nationals in Palestine whose separatist political aspirations required them to secure a favored legal position over the indigenous non-Jewish majority. In contrast to conventional wisdom, my argument is that Israel's attainment of sovereignty did not alter fundamental status of the local Jewish population as settlers. By grappling with the paradoxical status of the Arab minority during the first two decades of independence—as citizens of a formally liberal state and subjects of a colonial regime—my analysis aims to restore empire to the history of post-1948 Israel, and post-1948 Israel to the history of modern imperialism.

IN SEARCH OF A BLACK HOLE

For years the birth of the Jewish state in Palestine was celebrated as the fulfillment of an ancient dream of national liberation; as the outcome of hard work and humanitarian sacrifice; and ultimately, as a miraculous victory for David against Goliath. The indigenous Arab majority of Palestine figured only in the shadows of this narrative, which chronicled the Zionist movement through a carefully selected recounting of the movement's declared intentions. In May 1948, so the story went, duplicitous Arab leaders over the border ordered Palestinians to flee the country so that invading Arab armies could drive the Jews into the sea. These leaders—and no one else—were responsible for the sudden and mass exodus of the Palestinian population from the territory that became Israel. For decades following their dispersion and the destruction of their social, economic, and political institutions, Palestinians lacked the archival evidence and institutional backing to counter this narrative—with its ethical and political burden—to any effect.[5] Outside the confines of Israeli fiction, a handful of inaccessible Hebrew-language studies, and the muted memories of Jewish war veterans, Palestinian accounts of massacres, systematic expulsions, and village destruction hit an iron wall of denial.[6]

In the mid-1980s, in the aftermath of Israel's widely unpopular invasion of Lebanon, a handful of young Jewish Israeli scholars seeking to reconcile these competing accounts availed themselves of newly declassified archival material on the 1948 war. Their findings confirmed the basic parameters of long-standing Arab claims about how the Yishuv, as the settlement movement called itself, had marshaled its prewar intelligence and overwhelming military superiority to drive most Palestinians out of their villages and towns.[7] Unintentionally, their research also catalyzed a transformation in the study of Israel/Palestine as a whole. Whereas earlier accounts had depicted Zionist settlers and Palestinian Arabs as isolated, monolithic, and pre-formed groups that came together only in war, new studies shifted attention to the rich and multiple sites of their social, cultural, and economic encounters.[8] By demonstrating the mutual formation of Jewish and Arab societies since the 1880s, the new accounts overturned the long-held belief that the separation of the two peoples had *caused* the Zionist-Palestinian conflict. Instead, it was the conflict's result.[9]

The new literature also succeeded in undermining the exceptionalist origin story of the Zionist movement. In particular, a growing body of work that situates the movement within the broader context of European imperialism and settler nationalism has done much to normalize a parochial field of inquiry long burdened by idealism and essentialism.[10] Today, across the ideological spectrum, few historians dispute the social, economic, and cultural ties between the early Zionist settlement project in Palestine and the more "classical" European settler-colonies in North America, South Africa, and Australia. (In terms of land policy, the German colonization of Posen at the turn of the twentieth century was another important model.)[11] Although Jewish settlers lacked an imperial patron until the end of World War I, they were determined to make Palestine their home while maintaining European living standards. To rationalize their demands, many embraced the claim that they were doing their part to bring "civilization" to the putatively backward peoples of Asia and Africa. Like other European settler movements, the Zionists often touted the uniqueness of their mission in world history. Notably, this assertion did not stop them from drawing links with other "pure settlement" colonists—those who, for reasons of economic survival or fear of racial contamination, sought to displace rather than exploit the indigenous majority.[12]

For all the advances of the "imperial turn" in the historiography of Israel/Palestine, perhaps its most vexing characteristic has been its cursory and static coverage of the early state period.[13] Outside of pathbreaking socio-legal histories of land expropriation, most archive-based narratives cease abruptly before the start of the 1948 war or after its formal cessation in the spring of 1949.[14] The story resumes occasionally in 1967, with the inauguration of Israel's settlement project in the surrounding Palestinian, Egyptian, and Syrian territories that it occupied during the June war.[15] This nineteen-year breach in our account of the identifications and disavowals of Zionism as a settler-colonial project defies basic evidence, including the intimate political and ideological ties that Jewish settlement leaders fostered with British imperial officials, as well as Israel's nearly wholesale adoption of the British legal system within days of declaring independence. It also flouts basic methods of historical reasoning by perpetuating an image of the post-1967 settlement enterprise as emerging in a vacuum, closing down an investigation of continuities in legal systems, intelligence gathering, disciplinary tactics, cultural practices, and actual personnel, precisely when scholars should be prying this case open.[16]

For many decades, the black hole in our account of Zionism as a settler-colonial movement resulted from a popular nostalgia for the first two decades of statehood as Israel's golden age of majority-rule democracy and the rule of law—a "high point of universalistic, civic, and liberal fulfillment."[17] According to this fantasy, which emerged shortly after the 1967 war and has surged since the collapse of the state's political negotiations with the Palestine Liberation Organization in 2000, it is fanatical settlers and a reactionary strain of Jewish nationalism that bear responsibility for undermining Israel's international legitimacy and for bringing its "political culture to the brink of an abyss."[18] This fantasy has always been predicated on "forgetting" the violent dispossession and destruction that created Israel's Jewish majority, and on sidelining the post-1948 military regime as an anomaly in the state-building process. Looking forward rather than back, adherents to this narrative suggest that an end to the Occupation would bring about a return to a fundamentally different political project.[19]

BEYOND THE CONCEPTUAL STRAITJACKET

The popular proclivity for burying uncomfortable historical truths endures. Yet, the misplaced yearning for the "small and beautiful Israel" (*erets yisra'el ha-ktana ve-ha-yafa*) of the past can no longer explain the elisions in our account of Zionism as a settler-colonial movement.[20] Research over the past three decades has produced an unassailable body of evidence pointing to the state's deliberate policies that aim to alienate indigenous Palestinians from their land while keeping them economically dependent and politically divided.[21] Although many archives remain sealed, the opening of thousands of formerly classified records since the 1990s has yielded a host of innovative studies on nationalism, state power, and the relationship between Palestinians and Jews in the early state period. In the meantime, Palestinian personal memoirs have proliferated, and it has become easier than ever to review old runs of the Arabic- and Hebrew-language press.[22]

Today, the nostalgia that informs the prevailing tendency to ignore these continuities has been reinforced by our failure to recognize that the history of Israel/Palestine is part of the global history of liberalism. As elsewhere, liberalism in Israel was never a prepackaged bundle of rights to dignity, representative democracy, and the rule of law. Fraught with contradictions since its emergence in eighteenth-century Europe, liberal thought has always been predicated on exclusions of gender, religion, race, and class in the name of public order, while the idealistic pursuit of the "common good" has served regularly to justify coercion against individuals or groups who do not fit its definition.[23] The point is not simply that liberal ideas have produced a wide range of political forms, but that their very oscillation between freedom and compulsion, universalism and particularism, has helped to fuel Western imperial conquests in Asia, Africa, and the Pacific, where the same tensions have infused the techniques and rationalizations of rule.[24] Appreciating this history is critical if we are to grapple with Israel's extension of citizenship to Palestinians under a regime that even many Jews viewed as a colonial administration, a system of rule whose laws and practices shared commonalities with French rule in Algeria and white rule in South Africa.

A similarly myopic treatment of colonialism has perpetuated our inability to make sense of the coexistence of liberal citizenship and colonial rule in post-1948 Israel, and to wrestle historically with the complexity of Palestinian experiences within it. In recent years, for instance, historians have paid growing attention to the unique legal and social dynamics that have distinguished colonialism of settlement from colonialism of extraction.[25] Nonetheless, we continue to carry an image of colonies as clearly demarcated, overseas possessions whose conquerors openly and proudly affirm them as such.[26] The hazard in relying on such affirmations is that colonial administrators and proponents of imperial expansion have long disavowed their intentions and past violence. Instead, more often than not they have insisted on the unprecedented universality, enlightenment, and benevolence of their missions—claims that some sincerely believed.[27]

Professions of exceptionalism can be traced back to the entangled rise of liberal nationalism and imperial expansion in nineteenth-century Europe, but it is instructive to see how they assumed new forms over time and space. Middle East historians, for example, have examined the contradictions spawned by the European "mandates" over the new states created in the region after World War I—a reconfigured imperial system that pledged to prepare its inhabitants for self-rule on the premise that they would eventually be "capable" of realizing their right to self-rule.[28] Meanwhile, studies of the US occupations of the Philippines, Hawaii, and the Mariana Islands (among others) have shown how the purportedly unique ambivalence of Americans toward the idea of empire was more the imperial norm than the exception at the turn of the previous century.[29] So was the US propensity to present itself as non-imperial (if not anti-imperialist) by inventing new designations such as "trusteeships" and "unincorporated territories," and by creating what one scholar has described as "sliding scales" of sovereignty and rights.[30]

The attempt of Western imperial states to write themselves out of colonialism reached a fever pitch in the decade after World War II, the same period in which Jewish settlers attained sovereignty. As colonized peoples in Asia and Africa became more militant in their demands for national independence, they pressed the United Nations to enforce the principles of human rights and national self-determination outlined in its 1945 Charter. They drew particular attention to Chapter XI, which called on the "administering powers" of "non-self-governing territories" to effect a gradual transition to self-rule in those territories and to report regularly on their progress. Not surprisingly, the imperial powers involved in drafting the UN Charter had signed off on this language only because they had banked on the exemption of their territories from eligibility. Indeed, the Charter failed to specify what constituted a non-self-governing territory, much less a "people" with national rights. It also declined to list the criteria by which to measure if and when self-rule had been achieved, or to impose any enforcement obligations on the UN or the administering powers.

It was in this legal vacuum that Britain, France, Portugal, the United States, and others responded to indigenous demands by pledging to "integrate" or "assimilate" their subjects, and by offering them full or partial citizenship status and suffrage rights as a way to remove their colonies from the list of territories eligible for independence.[31] The game was largely over by the late 1960s, with the critical exception of the indigenous minorities of former landlocked settler colonies in Australia, New Zealand, and the Americas. As with the Palestinians who remained in Israel after 1948, the UN's respect for the sovereignty of existing member states and its commitment to "international security" would consistently trump the rights of their native inhabitants.[32]

Just as the question of empire is absent from our accounts of Israeli society before the 1967 war, the history of pre-1967 Israel is absent from histories of settler-colonialism and late imperialism. It is true, as a recent volume points out, that the Zionist project in Palestine was the only twentieth-century settler movement to attain majority status and internationally recognized statehood.[33] It is also true that Israel's particular fusion of procedural rights with settler sovereignty was unique. The question that few scholars have asked is *why* and *in what way* Israel became a historical outlier, and how its unique political form shaped its ongoing colonial project.

LIBERAL SETTLER SOVEREIGNTY

The chapters that follow chronicle Israel's formation as a liberal settler state within, rather than outside, changing global norms of republican sovereignty after 1945. The entrenchment of the colonial relationship between Jewish settlers and native Palestinians after 1948 *in tandem with* the provision of citizenship and suffrage rights to the newfound Arab minority is the argumentative thread that ties them together. Drawing on multiple archives, memoirs, oral histories, film, music, and an extensive reading of the Arabic and Hebrew press, the book also weaves a far messier tale than other works that have characterized the period of military rule as a more or less orderly program of displacement, exclusion, and repression.[34] It is a tale, in fact, woven of contradictions: Israel's citizenship law was formulated ultimately not to enfranchise the Jewish majority but to combat the unanticipated determination of Palestinians to remain in or return to their homes from exile. Palestinians were not only neglected and marginalized. They were also actively recruited into the state's public culture in order to reassure Jewish labor leaders, school principals, commanders, and civil servants that they had internalized their defeat, and that they were grateful for it as well. Whereas the government viewed the military regime as the single most important tool in the continuation of the Zionist struggle to conquer Arab land, the army thought it was a joke and refused to allocate it any resources. And the crack of political maneuver that Palestinian activists and intellectuals courageously forced open as citizens all but sealed their fate as colonized subjects.

These and other discrepancies etched into the foundation of the Israeli state grew, I contend, out of two originary seeds. The first was the unprecedented colonial bargain that the Yishuv was forced to accept in order to gain international recognition of its sovereignty in 1948. Israel was not the first state in history to emerge from a settler-colony that extended citizenship and voting rights to its indigenous inhabitants, but it was the first to do so in the midst of its ongoing quest for their land. Whereas the United States, for instance, spent two centuries attenuating the land base of Native Americans before offering them citizenship in 1924, the norms of self-determination, republican citizenship, and human rights that rose from the ashes and hypocrisies of the two world wars precluded the possibility that Israel would enjoy the same luxury. The Palestinian national movement is a case in point. Although it crystallized only in the 1920s, it posed a formidable challenge to Zionism with which earlier European settler projects did not have to contend. This challenge would culminate in 1947, when the United Nations recommended that Palestine be partitioned into two states for the "two peoples"—a category defined in positivist racial terms—who inhabited it.

My use of the term *race* may surprise some readers. Correctly, many will point out that the Zionist leaders—unlike, say, the architects of the original US Constitution, with their "three-fifths of all other persons" clause, or the authors of South Africa's apartheid policy—neither developed nor drew upon a specific biological theory to justify its political claims. But the search for scientific racism alone can obscure other forms, particularly in the context of settler societies and nationalist movements in the early twentieth century.[35] The term *race* appears here in two senses. The first is the near impossibility of Arab religious conversion to Judaism, which has made birth (that is, blood) the sole path to membership in the settler community. Second, and more salient, is the way the construct of race (as a category of difference) and the charge of racism (as a moral indictment) took root in local law and the public imagination during the decades leading up to and following the establishment of Israeli statehood. As in colonial Algeria, the juridical concept of nationality in Israel both complemented and reinforced a preexisting racial logic.[36]

The second, and related, root of these contradictions is the Yishuv's distinction as the first modern settler-colony to reverse its minority status through the mass displacement, but not annihilation, of the native majority.[37] Because most Palestinian refugees were scattered along the ceasefire lines of the new state and clamoring to return home, and because for many years there were not enough Jews willing or able to farm their lands, Israeli officials worried that the permanence of their wartime conquests was imperiled. Compounding their fear was the fact that 90 percent of the Palestinians who managed to stay put or return to land inside Israeli lines during and after the war were concentrated in areas designated for the Arab state of Palestine whose establishment the UN had endorsed—regions where Jewish settlers had barely made a dent during the course of the Mandate.

Israel's dilemma, in short, was how it could secure its wartime gains while sharing political power with the very people who—by virtue of their desire to hold onto their lands and bring home their relatives, friends, and compatriots—would want to reverse them.

In reconstructing this history, we can see how and why military rule helped to contain the contradictions of liberal settler sovereignty, at least at first. Israel's regime of checkpoints, travel permits, and other restrictions on Palestinian freedom of movement, for instance, impeded the ability of its Arab citizens to mount direct challenges to the state. However, in large part *because they were citizens*, Palestinians soon developed subtler means of contesting power within the Israeli polity and highlighting the injustices of the liberal settler state before a global audience. By the mid-1960s, the political costs of maintaining military rule would prompt Israel to abolish the outward manifestations of the regime in Palestinian towns and villages—but not their legal basis or the other pillars of the state's "sliding scales" of citizenship.[38] Those contradictions have never gone away; they have only been elided and disguised from view by the conquests of the 1967 war, which, in the eyes of the world, created a larger paradox whereby Israel was both a democracy and a belligerent occupying power.

1 FROM SETTLERS TO SOVEREIGNS

THE STRUCTURAL CONTRADICTIONS OF THE ISRAELI STATE and the paradoxical status of the Palestinian Arabs who managed to remain in or return to the country after 1948 are rooted in the struggle for sovereignty over the six decades that preceded its creation. Drawing largely on secondary sources, this brief chapter examines how the development of the Jewish settler movement, British Mandatory law, and Arab nationalism converged in such a way as to harden the political and legal identities of Palestine's inhabitants. It also traces how and why the League of Nations, and its post-World War II successor, the United Nations, singled out the Zionist movement for exceptional treatment in comparison to the European settler populations that it sought to constrain in Africa—a status that shifted over time from a privilege to a burden. At no time did the contradiction between popular democracy and Jewish statehood haunt Yishuv leaders more than in November 1947, when the section of Palestine that the UN had voted to allocate to them included nearly as many Arabs as Jews. Thanks to years of political and military preparation, the rapid descent into war enabled the Zionist movement to reverse the minority status of Palestine's Jews.

. . .

Zionist settlement in Palestine began in 1882, the first political expression of a tiny proto-nationalist movement emerging in Eastern Europe in response to waves of anti-Jewish attacks and a mounting socioeconomic crisis.[1] Although, at the time, Ottoman Palestine was divided into two administrative districts, it had for centuries featured as a single, discrete place in the minds of its inhabitants and neighbors.[2] An estimated twenty-four thousand Jews already lived there, comprising 5 percent of the total population. Concentrated in four major cities, they consisted of a small class of Arabic- and Ladino-speaking merchants and a large community of Yiddish speakers who had come during the previous centuries to live and die in the Holy Land. Palestine's indigenous Jews lived alongside half a million Muslim and Christian Arabs, whose production and export of textiles, olive oil, soap, tobacco, and citrus fruits wove intricate social, economic, and political networks between city and countryside and across provincial borders.[3] In 1914, roughly 10 percent of the native Arab majority belonged to various Christian denominations; of the rest, most were Sunni Muslims.[4]

The first Zionist colonies established in Palestine consisted of a handful of farms modeled on the racial division of labor in Algerian vineyards, where Eastern European Jewish planters oversaw underpaid local Arab employees with capital from Western European Jewish philanthropists. Because living conditions were tough and settlers could not compete with the abundant supply of low-paid farmers, their farms failed to turn a profit. By the turn of the century, at least one-third of the new immigrants had left. The growing depletion of the Yishuv prompted many leaders of the nascent national movement to fear the demise of their ultimate goal of statehood. Over time, they gradually changed strategies and adopted a program of national and "pure" colonial settlement. Instead of coercing or exploiting the labor of indigenous Palestinians, the Zionist leaders would work to displace them.[5]

One of the first institutions created by the Zionist Organization (established in 1897 in Basel, Switzerland) to implement its new colonial strategy was a body to coordinate all land purchasing and settlement work. The founding charter of the Jewish National Fund prohibited "non-Jews" from leasing (and soon, working on) any holdings it acquired. The Fund's creation in 1901 quickly escalated tensions between foreign settlers and indigenous Palestinians because it changed the rules of the game. Since the 1880s, conflicts had erupted whenever the contracts of Jewish land purchases (usually from absentee owners) included a proviso to evict the existing Arab tenant farmers. These tensions usually subsided, however, when planters hired the farmers to work on the colonies or allowed them to lease back certain parcels. The new mission to "conquer" the land and labor market from indigenous farmers and workers foreclosed these options. Indeed, despite exhortations to cultivate "brotherly relations" with Palestinians in subsequent decades, labor and settlement leaders came quickly to view their project as a zero-sum game.[6]

Over the next few years, reports of peasant dispossession began to capture the attention of Arab urban elites, communal authorities, and Palestine's budding professional class. The concerns they expressed were not entirely new. Since the 1880s a handful of notables had been petitioning the Ottoman authorities about the ruinous intentions of Jewish settlers, but new outlets for popular opposition opened up after 1908, when the Young Turk Revolt restored the constitutional parliament in Istanbul and lifted repressive press restrictions at home.[7] In the final years before World War I, denunciations of the settler movement in the local Arabic (and in some cases Ladino) press, along with political appeals by elected Arab deputies in Istanbul, began to make it harder for Zionist leaders to sustain the fiction that Palestine was for all intents and purposes an empty land.[8]

Like the European colonists in North America, Africa, and Australasia with whom they often identified, Zionism's luminaries believed that their rights to Palestine exceeded those of its "natives."[9] Although the movement's leadership could not deny that the land was full of people, it portrayed Palestinians as a "mixture of races and types," a "multitude" distinguished not by their shared history or national character but by their inferior human "quality."[10] This belief, which enabled them to see the local population as merely another part of the landscape to be tamed, enabled movement leaders in Palestine to blind themselves to the political conflict that their project was likely to sow. Among them was a young activist named David Ben-Gurion, who rose to the top of the social-democratic Jewish Workers' Party shortly after he immigrated from Poland in 1906. As he told an audience of potential immigrant recruits in New York in 1915, the Yishuv needed more pioneers to fight "wild nature and wilder redskins."[11]

THE PURSUIT OF PRIVILEGE

Early on in World War I, as the European Allies began to deliberate over the future dispensation of the Ottoman provinces they hoped to conquer, Zionist leaders close to the British government lobbied intensively for its patronage. They had chased this prize for nearly two decades, enlisting several prominent evangelical parliament deputies along the way.[12] It was not until the Ottomans appeared to be on their last legs, however, that enough policymakers were persuaded that the cost of sponsoring a European settler community in Palestine was in the geostrategic interests of the British Empire. Six weeks before British troops marched into Jerusalem in December 1917, the Foreign Secretary announced the government's pledge, in the eponymous Balfour Declaration of November 2nd, to facilitate "the establishment in Palestine of a national home for the Jewish people." The Balfour Declaration prompted immediate demonstrations and petitions throughout the Middle East. As Lord Balfour would later admit, Britain's commitment to the Zionists contradicted its prior (and secret) pledge to support the postwar independence of most of Ottoman Arabia, Mesopotamia, and Greater Syria. "Zionism," he explained in 1919, "be it right or wrong, good or bad, is . . . of far profounder import than the desires and prejudices of the 700,000 Arabs who now inhabit that ancient land."[13]

For the Arabs of Palestine, the problem with Britain's endorsement ran deeper than its diplomatic duplicity. More important was that it violated the lofty principle of national self-determination that US President Woodrow Wilson had unwittingly popularized in Asia and Africa after introducing the concept during his famous congressional address in January 1918.[14] In particular, Arabs in Palestine pointed to the Balfour Declaration's express delineation between the national rights that Britain would accord to Jews (still a tiny, and largely foreign-born, minority) and the nonpolitical "civil and religious" rights of the "non-Jewish communities" (the overwhelming native majority, defined in the negative and more diminutive plural), whom Britain would strive "not to prejudice." As Ben-Gurion acknowledged at the time, this formulation ran counter to democracy and negated their national existence.[15] Warning that the Yishuv sought to drive them out of the country, Palestinian leaders forecasted the bloodshed this mission would produce at home and the instability that Muslim resentment would wreak in British-ruled South Asia.[16]

Arab stakes in convincing the Great Powers that calamity would strike the region if Jewish colonization were to gain broader Western sanction rose sharply at the end of the war, when the Ottoman Empire relinquished all future claims to its provinces outside of Anatolia. As urban notables, secular nationalists, and communal figures pressed for united sovereignty with their neighbors in Syria, Zionist leaders lobbied for a British administration in Palestine that would fulfill Balfour's pledge. This debate took a sharp turn in 1919, when the Allied war victors announced their plan to establish a new colonial formation in the territories now severed from Ottoman and German control. Because, they claimed, the inhabitants of these areas were "not yet able to stand by themselves under the strenuous conditions of the modern world," the fledgling League of Nations would "mandate" selected Western powers to tutor them in the ways of self-rule.[17] Suddenly, after working to establish a constitutional republic based in Damascus, the most the former Ottoman citizens of Greater

Syria (of which Palestine was a part) could hope for was a choice among a handful of imperial overlords.[18] In July 1919, an American commission traveled to the Eastern Mediterranean to survey their wishes. Apart from the Zionists themselves, the overwhelming majority of those polled reiterated the demand for unified independence and an end to Jewish colonization. If immediate sovereignty was off the table, the only mandatory power they would accept was the United States, which lacked the stain of imperial interference in the region.[19]

As peace talks continued in Paris, Zionist boosters worked to dismiss Arab prophesies of national dispossession. Before the war, their promotional literature had generally avoided mention of Palestine's indigenous population, but the patent contradiction between Jewish colonization and the Wilsonian slogan of self-rule was rendering this silence untenable. For this reason, movement emissaries adopted a two-pronged strategy. In public forums, they began to highlight the humanitarian burden they were undertaking to bring prosperity and civilization to the backward peoples of the Holy Land.[20] Behind the scenes they lobbied aggressively to block the formation of a US mandate—their fear of which derived from a simple numerical formula. Despite the near doubling of their demographic ratio since the 1880s, Jews still comprised less than 10 percent of Palestine's population.[21] As the Zionist Organization in London explained at the time, the possibility that the United States might facilitate the birth of a constitutional republic in Palestine anytime soon would make "the task of . . . developing a great Jewish Palestine . . . infinitely more difficult."[22] As it turned out, their fears were overblown. The final report of the American commission was quickly buried and forgotten.

Racializing a People

Over the next three decades, the conflict between democratic principles and demographic realities dogged Zionists leaders, Palestinian nationalists, and Britain, which inaugurated its colonial administration in Palestine in 1922. The inclusion of the Balfour Declaration in the Palestine Mandate's preamble and second article imposed a uniquely challenging mission on the colonial administration from the outset. Quite simply, British officials did not know how they would balance their obligation to shepherd the people of Palestine to self-rule against their simultaneous duty to facilitate the creation of a Jewish national home. Of course all of the postwar Arab successor states were haunted by the inherent conflict between colonial occupation and national state building. Access to their new parliaments was limited to wealthy and conservative male elites, whose own power was severely circumscribed by their imperial overseers.[23] Still, it mattered that the European mandatory regimes in the Middle East were expected to "trade ... in words and not arms"; to offer more legitimacy than the ferocious violence they unleashed to quash early uprisings; and that they were obliged, in theory, to guarantee the well-being and national development of their subjects. Because of these constraints, the legislatures in Lebanon, Syria, Iraq, and Transjordan all created narrow wedges of maneuver that nationalist politicians and local citizens managed occasionally to pry open.[24] In Palestine, the contradiction carved into the edifice of the administration made this task much harder.

The central impediment to Palestinian state building during the interwar years was the Mandate's recognition trap. The Arab Executive, for instance, the committee of Palestinians who assumed the leadership of the national struggle in the 1920s, refused to participate in any forum that would signal consent to their inferior legal status or recognition of a regime that refused even to mention them by name.[25] Other Palestinians, such as businessmen and municipal authorities, adopted a more flexible stance toward agencies and bodies when they believed their participation would make a difference to the public's well-being by providing much-needed technical expertise or bureaucratic experience. Ultimately, however, Palestinians' unequal access to the colonial administration as a result of its partnership with the Zionist movement sharply limited their impact.[26]

Not surprisingly, the recognition trap that gridlocked Palestinian political efforts served the Yishuv's effort to build national institutions that could steer government policy in their favor. Most important was the *Histadrut*, established in 1920 as a federation of Jewish trade unions attached to a fledgling underground settler militia called the *Haganah* ("defense" in Hebrew). Under the leadership of Ben-Gurion and other labor leaders, by the end of the decade the organization transformed itself into the Yishuv's single largest banker, employer, insurance agent, manufacturing engine, and provider of housing and social services. Until 1929, when the Jewish Agency was established as the Zionist movement's official representative to the administration, the Histadrut was the Yishuv's most powerful mediating agency in Jerusalem. Throughout the twenty-five years of the Mandate, it labored tirelessly to pressure public- and private-sector employers to hire more Jews and to pay them "civilized rates," as opposed to what Palestinian Arabs earned.[27]

The insistence of Zionist labor leaders that Palestine's European working class was culturally entitled to privileged wages had an explicitly racial overtone. Although Jewish settlers were not identified formally as belonging to a distinct "race" before the Mandate, Britain's dual imperative gave birth to a subtle yet fatal shift in the way the government classified them—and in turn the indigenous Arab majority. This process began with the Mandate itself, which, in order to facilitate the naturalization of Jewish settlers, became the only colonial regime in the region to include a specific nationality clause. Three years later, Palestine earned another distinction as the sole post-Ottoman mandate whose citizenship law was enacted in the metropole. That statute also made Palestine one of just two Arab successor states where native-born residents living abroad could acquire automatic citizenship even if they "differ[ed] in race from the majority of the population."[28]

In international law at the time, the terms *race* and *culture* often appeared interchangeably with *nation* and *people*.[29] The slippery boundaries between these categories reflected the prominence of race thinking in European liberal thought and imperial expansion since the late eighteenth century.[30] Notably, the practice of tying political citizenship to an imagined cultural essence had no Ottoman precedent until the early twentieth century. The imperial state had no citizens per se until 1869; before then, the only political ties that had bound all subjects were their fidelity to the sultan and their payment of taxes. Although the empire had privileged Muslims in certain spheres of social and political life, its system of "institutionalized difference" had not been rooted in notions of biological destiny. Not only had the sultan granted substantial autonomy to non-Muslim communities, but he had also made no demands on them to speak a single language, to assume a singular identity, or to assimilate to a "majority" culture. Unlike the French or British approach to emancipated Jews, for instance, the Ottoman state had not needed to "tolerate" non-Muslims because there had been no norm from which they had appeared to depart.[31] There had been, to be sure, periodic eruptions of violent communal conflict, but these had been exceptions to the norm.[32] Overall, the Ottoman Empire's laissez-faire approach to culture had enabled group boundaries to remain relatively fluid and had been the key to its survival for five centuries.[33]

This fluidity disappeared under the post-Ottoman order, when the victors of World War I set out to ensure that international sovereignty would now reside in "the nation"—the people—instead of the dynast. The idealization of national homogeneity within state borders was nearly a century in the making, but the Allied Powers created new mechanisms that reinforced the presence of ethno-religious pluralism as a problem to be solved, if not removed.[34]

In the defeated territories and new states of Central and Eastern Europe, they imposed the Minorities Treaties to protect the safety and cultural autonomy of groups deemed outside the core of the "nation" alongside whom they lived. In Ottoman Anatolia and the Balkans, they endorsed the mass "exchange" between Muslim Greeks and Orthodox Turks in order to "repatriate" them to their purported homelands, and other forms of what then British Foreign Secretary Lord Curzon called "ethnic unmixing."[35] The Allies' emphasis in the Arab world was on nation-state building, in which the construction of new identities had similarly productive and destructive legacies.[36] Only in Palestine, however, did this process take on an explicitly racial cast. As the conflict stemming from the Yishuv's effort to conquer the land and labor market intensified in the mid-1920s, Zionist leaders and their local backers in Jerusalem began to promote a conception of the Jews in Palestine as a racial rather than an ethnic or religious community.[37]

evidence?

Once again, the rub was the conflict between democracy and demography. For the same reason that they opposed the American Mandate, Zionist leaders were reluctant to join the legislative council, or "joint" parliament, that the British had proposed early on. Whether the franchise would be territorial (one person, one vote) or communal (allotting an equal—much less proportional—number of seats to Jews, Christians, and Muslims), the Yishuv would be outnumbered and thus politically stymied. For this reason they made clear that their cooperation would be contingent upon the establishment of "racial parity," or the allotment of an equal number of seats to Jews as to Arabs.[38]

The talks to establish the legislative council collapsed permanently in 1936, but the racialization of Palestinians became a creeping reality in mandatory statistics. The Jewish Agency was responsible for this shift only in part. In the early 1930s, British officials in Jerusalem and London began to concede that indigenous opposition to Jewish settlement crossed sectarian, class, and urban-rural divides. As the Colonial Secretary concluded, commitment to the creation of a Jewish national home had produced a racial conflict akin to those in colonial Kenya, Ceylon, and India.[39] The League of Nations drew the same lesson, stating years later that the classification of Palestine's population as members of two races "had become a political necessity."[40] In the meantime, prominent figures in the Yishuv continued to embrace the racial mission of European empire. "Never before," wrote Berl Katznelson, founding editor of the Histadrut daily, *Davar*, "has the white man undertaken colonization with that sense of justice and social progress which fills the Jew who comes to Palestine."[41]

The Blessing and Burden of Special Treatment

In the 1930s some Mandate officials began to complain that their mission in Palestine was both impossible and contrary to "the spirit of the twentieth century."[42] Fortunately for the Yishuv, London was not the Zionist movement's only patron. Most important in this regard was the Permanent Mandates Commission (PMC), established by the League of Nations to supervise the progress of its charges in preparing their subjects for eventual self-rule. The PMC was a toothless oversight body staffed with liberal imperialists who occasionally used their power to call the mandatory administrations to task for failing to fulfill their obligations. Despite its conservative politics, the Geneva-based commission became an unwitting forum for political agitation by Arab nationalists throughout the region, who quickly learned how to exploit its public petition process—except, that is, for Palestinians. As with the mandate-supervised legislatures, Palestine stood out from the political space opened by the PMC because of the recognition trap imposed on its indigenous Arab majority by the League of Nations. Because the Mandate charter did not recognize them as a national community, the commission simply denied them legal standing.[43]

Even starker was the difference between the PMC's treatment of Palestine and its treatment of the other settler colonies under its jurisdiction. In the mandates of central and southern Africa, commission members urged local governments to rein in settler violence and to limit the alienation of indigenous farmers from their lands. In Palestine, where 30 percent of Arab peasants were landless by 1930 and 80 percent of the rest lacked enough for subsistence, the commission chastised British officials for failing to provide enough support to settlers and for deploying too little violence to crush the Arab rebelllion that began in 1936.[44] Revulsion against the mounting anti-Semitism in Europe was one reason for the exceptional treatment that Jewish settlers enjoyed from the commission. Equally decisive, however, was the effective lobbying by Zionist emissaries of the already sympathetic commissioners with whom they had ties, and the general perception in Geneva that the Jews were patently more deserving of self-determination in Palestine than the Arabs. Not only were the Jews equally indigenous, it was argued, but the Palestinians also had six other "Arab homelands" from which to choose.[45]

Yet, the Yishuv's treatment by the League of Nations as a *sui generis* settler community was not always to the Yishuv's benefit. As popular Arab opposition to colonization grew, Zionist leaders felt compelled to promise equal living standards, cultural autonomy, and political equality to the native Arab inhabitants of their future state.[46] Such a move was unprecedented in the history of settler-colonialism, and it is hardly surprising that the Jewish Agency had no vision of how it would contend with a sizable voting base certain to block its efforts to displace them.[47] Not only had its Labor Zionist leaders spent the previous two decades consolidating the Agency's power around the strategies of separation and exclusion—in land ownership, the urban labor market, residential patterns, bus lines, health care, education, and culture[48]—but they had also worked to deepen existing wedges within Palestinian society and its incipient national movement in order to undermine Arab resistance to their project.

In the 1920s, the Yishuv expanded its practice of paying willing informants and land agents and placing sympathetic opinion pieces in the Arabic press; during the 1936–1939 Arab Revolt, it sponsored counterinsurgents to form a network of undercover and in some cases armed collaborators.[49] Political representatives and intelligence operatives of the Jewish Agency also worked to cultivate native allies among religious, ethnic, and cultural minorities in order to establish what one official referred to as "spots of light and inspiration inside the dark Arab sea all around us."[50] They reached out to specific Bedouin leaders in the south and to tiny sects such as the Circassian Muslims, Maronite Christians, Ahmadi Muslims, and Persian Bahá'ís in the north. Above all, they courted the Druze, an Islamic sect that broke away from Isma'ili Shi'ism in tenth-century Egypt. Numbering twelve thousand or so people and comprising an estimated 1 percent of the Palestinian Arab population during the Mandate, the Druze community was largely cut off from the urban elite nationalist movement.[51]

The Yishuv's efforts to pit Palestine's Arabs against one another bore substantial fruit, facilitating clandestine land purchases and contributing to the crushing defeat of their anti-colonial revolt in 1939.[52] However, neither these measures nor the near tripling of the Jewish demographic ratio through legal and illegal immigration were enough. By the end of World War II, Jews held an estimated 5.8 percent of Palestine's land and remained outnumbered by Arabs two to one.[53] In the meantime, the founding charter of the United Nations, which succeeded the League in 1945, had introduced new slogans such as "equal rights" and individual "human rights," as well as a more concrete pledge to support the self-determination of the colonized world. As Zionist leaders understood it, the lip service paid to these principles in the wake of the genocide in Europe made even more distant the prospect of attaining recognition for a state ruled by a racial minority.

Apparently Britain drew the same conclusion. In early 1947, as the British government prepared to leave India, London decided that it was no longer willing to try to square the circle of its mission in Palestine. One year after the last of the Arab mandated territories attained independence, the Crown asked the UN General Assembly to study the "Palestine question" and recommend a practical solution to the conflict at its upcoming session. Delegates from the Arab states and representatives of Palestine's Arab Higher Committee (AHC) rejected the need for an investigation, demanding the immediate declaration of an independent, democratic Palestinian state on the basis of the UN's founding principles. Their proposal was quickly voted down, and in June the members of the UN Special Committee on Palestine (UNSCOP) established their head-quarters in Jerusalem. They had hoped to hear testimony from representatives of the country's Jewish and Arab communities; but in a redux of 1922, Pales-tinian political leaders refused to cooperate because the very terms of the com-mittee's mission—a source of considerable contestation in Geneva—privileged Zionist aspirations. In addition to leaving out any reference to Palestine's future independence, the final instructions issued to the committee empowered it to survey the wishes of the Holocaust survivors still languishing in Europe's dis-placed persons camps.[54] *Bunce*

UNSCOP members regretted the AHC's decision to boycott their hearings but proceeded with their work. By August 1947, the testimony it collected from Jewish Agency executives, labor leaders, party activists, and prominent intellectu-als formed the outlines of two different proposals. Those who supported the idea of partition, such as Jewish Agency Chair David Ben-Gurion, argued that the key to peace in the region was the creation of a Jewish-majority state.[55] To justify this claim, his second in command, Moshe Shertock, invoked the language of human rights to rail against the "racial discrimination" that the Yishuv was enduring as a result of the government's restrictions on land sales to Jews and the AHC's on-going boycott of "Jewish products."[56] Other speakers who testified to the com-mittee argued against partition on the grounds that the demographic imbalance and minimal Jewish land ownership in Palestine made it practically impossible. Instead, they advocated for a "binational" or federal state with a UN-guaranteed constitutional provision to secure Jewish political "parity." During the hearings, UNSCOP members struggled to understand how any of these options could be reconciled with democratic principles, and a few times pushed speakers to ex-plain it to them.[57] The failure, however, of anyone to formulate a clear answer to this question turned out to be less decisive than the consensus among committee members that the Jews were now an unmistakable "people," or race, in Palestine, and as such had earned the right to self-rule there.[58]

UNSCOP's final report threw this tension, and the anomalous treatment of Palestine over the previous three decades, into relief. On November 29, 1947, a narrow majority in the General Assembly voted in favor of the committee's proposal to partition the country into two states, with a small international administration over Jerusalem and Bethlehem.[59] Resolution 181 allocated 51 percent of the territory to a third of its inhabitants, a largely foreign-born community whose national development owed much to the combined muscle of the British military and the League of Nations.[60] During the two months of debate preceding the vote, AHC representatives from Palestine and delegates from other Arab states emphasized the overwhelming regional opposition to partition. The UNSCOP proposal not only violated the principles enshrined in the UN Charter and sparked further fears of Palestinian dispossession, but also unjustly punished the Arabs of Palestine for Europe's war crimes against the Jews. Britain, looking to the catastrophe it had just helped to unleash in India and wanting to commit fewer troops rather than more, also opposed partition. It warned that because the proposed borders of the two states failed to encompass demographically homogenous territories, partitioning Palestine would almost certainly lead to war.[61] Skillful diplomacy by Zionist delegates, Western guilt over the failure to save more Jews in Europe, and the budding American and Soviet desire to increase the size of their footprint in the region all served to drown out these arguments.[62]

Resolution 181, which contains the Partition Plan, marked the triumphant cap on six decades of diplomacy and colonization to secure international backing for Jewish statehood in Palestine. Still, from the vantage point of Yishuv leaders, its fine print was far from ideal. The Plan included a host of provisions that guaranteed the property, political equality, and cultural autonomy of the "national minority" that would inhabit each state. To gain a seat among the "community of nations," as the exclusive club of UN members defined itself, each state would have to hold democratic elections for a constituent assembly to draft a bill of rights based on universal suffrage and citizenship. The resolution also barred the future governments from confiscating privately owned land, except when necessary for "public use." These clauses meant little for the proposed Arab state, whose Jewish community was projected to comprise 1.3 percent of the total citizenry. Where they mattered was in the future Jewish state, whose Arab citizens were projected to number just a hair less than their counterparts.[63] The barely 51 percent Jewish majority that UNSCOP's cartographers had managed to carve out of the country was a far cry from the 80 percent minimum that Ben-Gurion believed was crucial for the state's long-term survival. Indeed, the patent hurdle that the minority provisions would place in the way of further colonization seemed to vitiate the purpose of partition.[64]

If Yishuv leaders felt singled out by these requirements, it would not have been unwarranted. The stark incongruity between the dream of a "pure" Jewish nation and the binational future laid out in Resolution 181 seemed to negate the postwar understanding in Europe that it was impossible to "reconcile national rights and national minorities."[65] Prior to World War II, the statesmen of Western Europe had assumed that the international rules of war protected their continent—the birthplace of "civilized law"—from ethnic irredentism, unprovoked occupation, and unilateral annexation. Hitler's abuse of the Minorities Treaties during the interwar period to justify these depravities in the name of racial purity had shattered this assumption, but the lesson that the Allies drew from their experience was ironic.[66] Despite their rejection of the eugenics that the Nazis had espoused, their decision to sanction the forced removal of more than twelve million "minorities" across Europe and the Soviet Union immediately after the war affirmed the German chancellor's belief that political stability was predicated on ethnic, or racial, homogeneity.[67]

The United States, for its part, did not question this conclusion, even though it had been spared the cataclysmic upheavals that had ravaged Europe. The White House had its own "minority" problems to contend with, and it was eager to keep the world out of them.[68] Indeed, the anxiety surrounding minority rights was so powerful among the war's Allied victors that it became the only League of Nations mission that did not carry over into the UN's 1945 Charter or any of its other founding conventions.[69] That the Charter already included so many clauses on the states' rights of noninterference that it rendered the language of human, or individual, rights meaningless indicates just how desperate the Allies were to bury minority rights as a normative ideal.[70]

Neither UNSCOP nor the General Assembly appears to have offered a formal explanation as to why Palestine became an exception to the vision of national minorities as a problem to eliminate: why, for that brief moment in the fall of 1947, the international community committed itself to preventing the ethnic cleansing that they had actively or passively endorsed in the rest of the war-torn world. There are, however, at least two obvious clues. The first, which we can glean from UN protocols, was that Latin American and European delegates sought to ensure the maintenance of and access to the multiple sites of Christian pilgrimage and devotion that dotted Palestine's landscape. (They expressed far less concern about the political rights and well-being of local worshippers.[71]) A second concern was the credibility of the UN itself, whose Charter had outlined the organization's allegiance to the universal right of self-determination more forcefully than its predecessor.[72]

India's position is instructive. Along with Iran, it was the only state outside of Europe and Latin America that attained UNSCOP representation. Although the delegates of both countries would ultimately agree that the Jews of Palestine deserved some form of collective political rights, in May 1947 India's ambassador to Washington, Ali Asaf, described "a general feeling among Asiatics [including the peoples of the Middle East and North Africa] . . . that Palestine is a test case of the sincerity of the United Nations." In a personal warning, he suggested that the sovereign states of these regions would consider forming an "Asiatic" counterpart if the UN violated its own Charter by blatantly disregarding the demands of Palestine's native majority for democratic self-rule.[73]

WORDS AND DEEDS

Popular demonstrations erupted in Palestine the day after the Partition Plan was announced, and within a matter of weeks a series of attacks and counterattacks escalated into a burgeoning civil war. To label the subsequent five months of fighting as lopsided would be an understatement. On one side were no more than ten thousand poorly equipped veterans of the Arab Revolt against the Mandate. Their efforts were hampered not only because most of their leadership remained exiled by the British, but also because—as Zionist intelligence consistently reported—they were operating within a society that was exhausted from the previous decade of war and sought to avoid another fight that they had no chance of winning.[74] On the other side were fifty thousand Haganah fighters, who enjoyed the general backing of their community, and whose leading commanders had been drawing up plans to take over the country since 1937. Half of them had been trained by the British during World War II.[75]

The other parties to the conflict were the national armies that bordered Palestine. Although the Haganah was smaller than these forces, the neighboring countries were woefully unprepared and their political leaders not nearly as motivated for a fight. Notwithstanding their bellicose warnings following the UN vote, the member states of the Arab League were also deeply divided and mistrustful of one another's intentions—a fact of which the Yishuv was well aware. For Egypt, Saudi Arabia, and above all Syria, the Zionists posed less of a threat than Transjordan's King Abdullah, who had made no secret of his expansionist aims in the region and whose ostensibly sovereign military remained under British command. (Indeed, the Hashemite king had already negotiated secretly with the Jewish Agency to divide Palestine between them in the event of a war.) Rather than call up their respective armies, then, League members established the Arab Liberation Army (ALA), a regional force comprising a few thousand volunteers provided with "rudimentary training" before beginning to cross into northern Palestine in late January 1948.[76]

The Yishuv was far from invincible or free of internal power struggles, but it looked like the opposite of the Palestinian national movement and the Arab states in terms of its military readiness, its relative political cohesion, and its clarity of purpose. The fact that the Jewish Agency announced the mobilization of its human and economic resources nearly two months *before* the UN vote is indicative of this point.[77] As throughout the Mandate period, its organization was also superior. Resolution 181 called for the leadership of each future state to form a provisional government to prepare for Britain's withdrawal, scheduled initially for August 1948. The Agency did so immediately after the resolution passed, and the new government, headed by Ben-Gurion as provisional prime minister and defense minister, embarked on two parallel projects.

One of the new government's first orders of business was to draft a constitution for future approval by a democratically elected assembly.[78] Prominent intellectuals in the Yishuv embraced the constitutional project, particularly for the dialogue they hoped it would start about the ethical foundation and public mission of the nation.[79] No such idealism guided the Old Man and his confidants. Their appointment of some of the Yishuv's brightest legal advisors to the job was dictated by the assumption that failing to do so would jeopardize their future UN membership application. It certainly did not signal a change in their concern that the immediate establishment of a popular democracy posed an existential threat to their political project. On November 2, 1947, just weeks before the UN vote, Ben-Gurion warned his colleagues at the Jewish Agency about the irredentism they would face with such a large Arab population if the rest of the region remained hostile to the state. If Israel granted the Arabs citizenship, he explained, it would be unable to deport them in the future. "It is better to expel [them] than imprison them," he urged.[80]

Ben-Gurion's operational prescription would have surprised few in the room. By the early 1940s, the idea that the creation of a Jewish majority state would require a large-scale removal of Palestine's Arab population had reached close to a consensus among Zionist political leaders.[81] Although historians continue to debate whether the Yishuv entered 1948 with a master plan to achieve this task, it is clear that the descent into guerilla warfare following the UN partition vote—a confrontation for which the Haganah had been preparing for close to a decade—propelled such a plan forward.[82]

Several developments contributed to the finalization of Plan D (short for "Dalet"), a document that amounted to an expulsion blueprint, in March 1948. During the prior three months, tens of thousands of middle and upper class Arab families had fled the fighting in the cities they co-inhabited with Jews, seeking temporary shelter with relatives or in their winter homes over the border. Almost immediately, Ben-Gurion and a handful of commanders and intelligence officers began to contemplate how they might encourage this movement and widen it.[83] The Haganah's confidence grew following the success of its early attacks and its expulsion, or provoked flight, of the inhabitants of between thirteen and eighteen Palestinian villages. The militia had deemed some, but not all, of these communities threatening: both because they sat in between Jewish settlements, and because of the dearth of soldiers to police them once they were conquered.[84] Plan D also emerged alongside the rising toll of Jewish casualties, due largely to Arab mortar and sniper attacks in urban centers, but in a few cases to the success of Palestinians and ALA troops in besieging certain settlements by cutting off the roads to them and attacking the convoys that tried to bring them supplies.

Technically speaking, Plan D was a military plan. Its objective was to secure not only the territory earmarked for the Jewish state, but also a safe corridor between Jerusalem and Tel Aviv, and the vast territory surrounding the small number of Jewish colonies in the Central Galilee—a region designated for the Arab state. Yet Plan D was also decidedly political in its allusion to the one million Palestinians who inhabited the "enemy settlements" located in the territory designated by the UN for Jewish sovereignty.[85] On the one hand, the Haganah explicitly instructed field officers to destroy and depopulate any village whose residents resisted conquest. At the same time, it offered no guidelines by which to measure if a village had surrendered. After implementation began in early April 1948, only an explicit order to halt expulsion or the defiant moral conscience of a commanding officer on the scene would stop the depopulation, or *tihur* (literally, purification), of an occupied Palestinian village.[86] Indeed, by the time Israel announced its independence six weeks later, the Haganah had conquered most of the territory allocated to the Jewish state, as well as some land that the UN had designated for the Arab state. Its forces had also depopulated at least two hundred additional villages and the majority of the Arab neighborhoods in the seven major cities they now occupied.[87]

To be sure, the battle to secure the Jewish state was draining and costly for the Yishuv. Some 1 percent of the population died, consumer prices rose more than 35 percent, and the food supply had to be carefully rationed.[88] During the three weeks between the government's declaration of statehood on May 14, 1948, and the start of the first truce on June 11, the newly organized Israeli army faced invasions from all four of the Yishuv's neighbors plus Iraq, and it suffered from a significant deficit of arms. Yet this period of vulnerability was fleeting. The expeditionary units of the Arab armies that arrived with the ostensible aim of blocking Palestine's partition were poorly coordinated and in some cases sought actively to sabotage each other. Unlike Israel, they also failed to bypass the UN Security Council's arms embargo on the region. As a result they spent most of their time holding down separate defensive positions inside the territory allotted to the Arab state.[89]

The patent dysfunction of Israel's enemies and the mutual distrust that the Yishuv had helped to sow among them enabled the army to push back each front and expand beyond its designated borders. By December 1948, while most of the British and UN forces tasked to protect the well-being and property of civilians stood by, Jewish forces had conquered nearly 78 (instead of 51) percent of Palestine and pushed an estimated 750,000 Arab refugees over the battle lines.[90] This figure amounted to a staggering 85 percent of the Arabs who inhabited the part of Palestine that became Israel, and half of the entire Palestinian Arab population.[91] Against their will, Palestinian refugees left behind an estimated 425 villages and eleven cities and urban neighborhoods, many of which stood fully or partially intact.[92] In the meantime, Transjordanian and Egyptian forces occupied the remaining 22 percent of the Mandate territory. Within a year of partition, Palestine had been wiped off the map, and the designated Arab state fell into virtual oblivion.

.   .   .

Incredibly, the tumultuous events of the spring and summer do not appear to have distracted the committee of jurists assigned to drafting Israel's constitution. Although the final version they submitted to the new government in October 1948 reflected their failure to reconcile Jewish statehood with popular democracy, it was not for lack of trying. The committee recommended the announcement of a state of emergency that would permit imprisonment without charge or trial, declared Israel the "national home for the Jewish people," and mimicked the Balfour Declaration's refusal to identify Palestinians by name. It also called, however, for a "democratic republic," citizenship for all those in the country on May 15, equal political rights, and an indivisible justice system with judicial review and habeas corpus.[93]

No such effort informed the final wording of the Israeli Declaration of Independence, which was drafted hurriedly in the midst of Plan D's execution and carefully purged of the word *democracy*. Instead, both its lofty pledge to establish equality and freedom and its "invit[ation to] the Arab inhabitants of the State . . . to preserve peace and participate in the upbuilding of the state on the basis of full and equal citizen rights and due representation" were added to placate the United Nations. According to Israeli historian Yoram Shahar, Ben-Gurion and his associates approved these clauses only after watering down the language so as to preserve the "superiority and Jewishness of the Hebrew community."[94]

2 THE FORMATION OF
THE LIBERAL SETTLER STATE

*We are not the first people to be ill treated . . . yet the ill-treatment to
which we have been exposed over the length of the past years is of a
strange kind. By means of the law our lands have been seized . . . and
by means of the law Military Government has been imposed on us . . .
and nevertheless, by means of the law we can speak . . . and protest . . .
and by means of the law we can complain to the . . . governor . . . and
by means of the law we can write . . . and cry out . . . and demonstrate
against all this. It is a strange situation. Whenever I think about it, I
keep on smiling.*

Rashid Husayn, Palestinian poet[1]

DURING THE FIFTEEN MONTHS OF FIGHTING that erupted after the announcement of the UN's Partition Plan in November 1947, the Yishuv managed to bypass the liability of minority rule by expelling and coercing the flight of most of
the Palestinians who inhabited the territory it conquered. Yet the end of the war
would raise more questions than it answered. One of the nascent government's
priorities in the fall of 1948 was to join the United Nations without having to
repatriate the Palestinian refugees or relinquish the territory its army was continuing to capture beyond the partition lines. Even after successfully joining the
elite club known by its members as the "community of nations" in May 1949,
concerns over sovereignty and international law would continue to haunt Israeli
leaders. Palestinians in a position to undertake open political action were even
more compromised. The recognition trap that had confronted nationalists over
the previous three decades had now assumed a new form, and activists who remained were conflicted about how they should relate to the new sovereign. But
the urgent material needs of the remaining Arab population left no time for a
studied consideration of these questions. The decision of a small cadre of Palestinian communists to work within Israel's political and legal system would give

them crucial room for political maneuver after 1948—to run for office, publish a newspaper, hold open meetings, and form a youth movement, among other things—if always under duress. But recognition for the sake of civil equality as individuals would emerge as a Faustian bargain, one that would hamper their resistance to the very settler project that aimed to dispossess them.[2]

THE TRIUMPH AND TRIAL OF SOVEREIGNTY

Compared to Palestine's demographic reality in November 1947, it was considerably easier to ensure the political dominance of Jewish settlers by the time the last shot of the formal war was fired in the spring of 1949. The arrival of 350,000 immigrants between May 1948 and the end of 1949 increased the Jewish population by nearly 50 percent, and the ratio of indigenous Arabs inside Israel plummeted from the 49 percent projected in 1947 to just 14 percent.[3] By the end of 1952 the population of the Yishuv had doubled in size, and the percentage of the new "minority" had dropped to 12 percent.[4] What remained of the Palestinian people inside the nascent state was a poorer, more rural, less educated, and largely leaderless shadow of its former self. When all was said and done—after Israel had conquered the Central Galilee against the Arab Liberation Army in late October 1948; wrested the Naqab, or Negev, desert from Egyptian control in January 1949; and annexed the Little Triangle, a narrow sliver of Jordanian territory that hugged its new armistice line to the east, in May—Palestinians inhabited only one hundred villages, one town (Nazareth), and fragments of five cities: Haifa, Ramla, Lydd (Hebraicized as Lod), Acre ('Akka in Arabic, Akko in Hebrew), and Jaffa.[5] Israel systematically denied responsibility for the creation of the refugee problem and deployed its public relations machine to convince the world that the Palestinians had fled of their own accord, at first because they could not bear the humiliation of living under Jewish rule, and later because the Arab armies told them to clear the way for the annihilation of the Yishuv. If anything, the government claimed, Jewish leaders had begged the Arabs to stay.[6]

This message did not preclude Israeli leaders from rejoicing over the demographic achievements of the war. David Ben-Gurion, who was elected Israel's prime minister (and appointed himself defense minister) after the first Knesset elections in January 1949, minced no words in making this point. On occasion his public remarks even threatened to undermine the official line. In April, shortly after Israel signed its armistice agreement with Jordan, the veteran leader of MAPAI (Mifleget Poalei Erets Yisrael), the ruling Workers' Party of the Land of Israel, explained to his more maximalist Knesset opponents from Herut (the Freedom Party) why he had not fought harder to conquer the remaining 22 percent of Palestine and the land east of the Jordan River that the Zionist movement had always coveted. As Ben-Gurion had maintained over the previous three decades, it still came down to a question of numbers: "Do you want a democratic state of Israel throughout the Land of Israel in 1949," he challenged his opponents, "or do you want a Jewish state throughout the Land of Israel from which we will drive the Arabs out?"[7] Remarkably, the prime minister acknowledged one of the atrocities that had become the very condition of possibility for a liberal democracy within the state's armistice lines. Invoking the slaughter of more than one hundred Palestinians in the Jerusalem-area village of Dayr Yasin that had triggered mass flight from Palestine one year earlier, the Old Man reminded his opponents that, "a Jewish state without Dir Yassin [sic] can exist only by the dictatorship of the minority."[8]

Ben-Gurion's liberal assurances must have been cold comfort to the three Palestinian Arab deputies in the chambers that day, as well as to the two Jewish representatives of the Israeli Communist Party—known as MAKI, or *ha-Miflaga ha-Kommunistit ha-Yisra'elit*, in Hebrew and *al-Hizb al-Shuyu'i al-Isra'ili* in Arabic—a critical and uniquely non-Zionist political force to which I will return. Of the roughly one hundred thousand Palestinians who managed to remain in Israel before the annexation of the Little Triangle, between 15 and 20 percent had been displaced during the war and were now barred from returning home by the authorities, who coveted their property and rich farmlands.[9] In April 1949, refugees comprised half of the Arab inhabitants of Acre and more than 30 percent of the population of Nazareth, which had also witnessed "a flash flood of desperate, coursing humanity" during the war.[10]

In fact, the army had frozen the movement of all Arabs inside the state's tentative lines. In the countryside, it forcibly confined them within the residential sections of the small town of Nazareth and the villages still standing, where it placed them under a curfew that began as early as 2 P.M.[11] The tiny minority of Palestinians who remained inside the mixed or newly mixed towns were barred from exiting the urban ghettos that the army had erected upon conquest. The nightly curfews and blackouts imposed on them were not imposed on their Jewish neighbors, even where they lived on the same street.[12] In the eyes of Israel's ruling establishment, it seemed, the war had obviated the need for a dictatorship of the old minority (the Jews), but not over the new one (the Arabs).

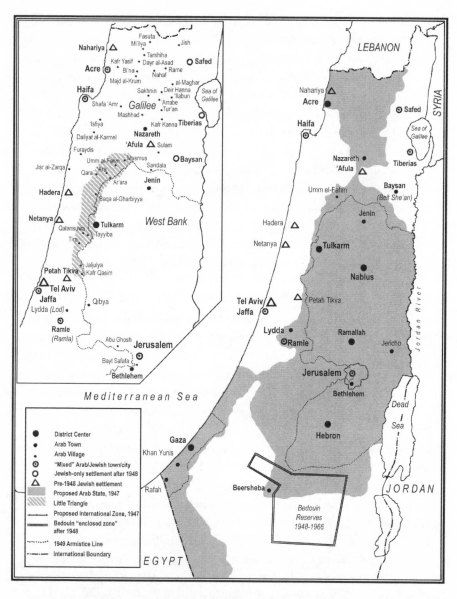

Right: British Mandate Palestine, with the borders of the 1947 UN Partition Plan, the 1949 Armistice Agreements, and the "reserves" where Israel forcibly concentrated the remaining Bedouin population of the Naqab (Negev) Desert after 1948. *Left*: Palestinian villages and Jewish settlements in the aftermath of Israel's establishment, along with the District Centers and towns that were repopulated partly or completely by Jews after the war.

Created by Hamdi Attia based on UN maps; Emanuel Marx, *Bedouin of the Negev* (New York: Praeger, 1967); and Adalah's "Interactive Map and Database on the History of the State of Israel's Expropriation of Land from the Palestinian People" (Adalah—The Legal Center for Arab Minority Rights in Israel [adalah.org/features/land/flash]).

At the heart of the government's conviction that it needed to rule over (rather than with) the Palestinians who remained after 1948 was its zealous territoriality, a propensity that historian Patrick Wolfe has called "settler-colonialism's specific, irreducible element."[13] Although troops and settlers had seized millions of acres during the war, the nascent state lacked both a constitutional framework and a sufficient mass of bodies to colonize them.[14] Indeed, from the day the Yishuv declared independence, its single greatest fear was that refugees both within and outside its lines would try to return and resettle on their property, perhaps with international support. As Israeli leaders would reiterate over the next two decades, the attainment of sovereignty thus inaugurated only the next phase in the Zionist enterprise of "coloniz[ing] the frontiers and the filling of blank spaces"—a "project of colonization far greater than all of the last seventy years."[15] To quote Wolfe, it is easy to imagine how those Palestinians still in the country had merely "to stay at home to get in the way."[16]

Normalizing Emergency

Seven months before Ben-Gurion's remarkable tribute to the Dayr Yasin massacre, Israel's Provisional State Council, or cabinet, had established a formal military regime (*mimshal tsva'i* in Hebrew, *al-hukm al-'askari* in Arabic) to administer any area that the army had occupied, or might still occupy, outside the territory that the UN had slated for the Jewish state.[17] Although its tribunals would not open for prosecution until January 1950, two monumental ordinances draped the regime in legal garments from its inception. The first, which the cabinet issued on May 15, 1948, announced the wholesale absorption of all mandatory laws until the Knesset replaced them with its own statutes. (There were two key exceptions: the regulations that had restricted Jewish immigration and land purchase were both repealed.[18]) Critically, these laws included the 1945 Defense Emergency Regulations (DERs), which had delegated effective sovereignty to the military within a specified territory and authorized its commander to suspend all basic constitutional liberties, including the property and habeas corpus rights, of its inhabitants.

Britain's emergency legislation had a rich history of its own. Since the 1830s, political theorists and imperial civil servants such as John Stuart Mill had justified colonial rule overseas on the grounds that some peoples (those of color, in particular) were not yet sophisticated enough to handle legal mandates—that they understood only the language of force.[19] This belief was widely accepted among London's legally minded liberal elites, but their ability to reconcile imperial rule with their constitutional values was tested in the mid-nineteenth century as the army responded brutally to expressions of popular dissent in Britain's Asian and Caribbean dominions.[20] Seeking assurance that the military's conduct had a legal basis, they were discomfited when the Crown's most decorated commander defined "martial law" as "a kind of legal anti-matter . . . neither more nor less than the will of the general," a system designed not to punish a specific crime but to restore the sovereign's prestige and moral authority.[21] Their anxiety only intensified in the early 1880s, when the royal army demanded permission to apply martial law against whites during the Land War in Ireland, and then again in 1899 during South Africa's second Boer War.[22]

In 1914, fear that the rule of "no law at all" might someday come home to roost led British parliamentarians to codify emergency legislation that would prevent the use of excessive force (a term never defined) and delimit its geographic scope and duration.[23] India became the testing ground of their first attempt, known as the Defense of the Realm Act (DORA), and it did not go well. In the spring of 1919, to restore their political and moral authority following protests against the suspension of civil liberties, British commanders in Punjab deployed these powers: opening fire into peaceful crowds, forcing students and professors charged with no crime to march in the hot sun following the defacement of government posters, and ordering Gandhi sympathizers to report to the police station three times a day. Back in London, a Committee of Inquiry expressed concern about the Amritsar massacre, which killed some 380 people and injured thousands more, and about the "fancy punishments" carried out in Lahore. Nonetheless, the British government continued to enforce DORA there and in Ireland, where the Colonial Secretary had already exported it.[24]

In the late 1930s, Britain adapted DORA's provisions in order to quell the Arab Revolt in Palestine. From among the numerous provisions included in its (Defense) 1937 Order in Council, or executive decree, the High Commissioner made particularly extensive use of its powers of administrative ("preventative") detention and house arrest, collective punishment such as curfews and home demolitions, banishment within and outside the country, random searches and seizures, censorship and prohibition on public assemblies, and the "closure" of designated roads and areas to anyone who did not have a permit.[25] When World War II began, London suspended its emergency powers in order to "quiet the Empire," but it authorized their restoration and update in Palestine when a Zionist paramilitary insurgency began in 1945.[26] Suddenly, Jewish attorneys who had said nothing when the High Commissioner enforced emergency powers against their Arab neighbors were outraged when he unleashed the same laws against the Yishuv. Only then did they identify Palestine as "an occupied country," pointing to the privileges they had enjoyed for the previous three decades of mandatory rule. Repudiating their patron's claim that the newly renamed DERs targeted only criminals and terrorists, the leading counsel of the Jewish Agency testified indignantly at the time that "it is too much to ask a citizen to respect a law that outlaws him."[27]

Fast forward eighteen months to May 15, 1948, Israel's first day of sovereignty. In addition to absorbing the DERs, Israel's Law and Administration Ordinance No. 1 empowered cabinet ministers to issue specific "emergency regulations" of their own, and to suspend or amend any law passed by a democratically elected body for reasons of defense or public security. Although the Knesset would have to renew the regulations, as a whole, every three months, it would have no oversight over their individual content.[28] Four days later, the cabinet reinforced its constitutional immunity by declaring a national state of emergency. The declaration authorized the Knesset chair to delete any passage from the official record and, in the event of a threat to state security, empowered the defense minister to issue, suspend, or amend any statutory legislation. Unlike the emergency regulations that derived from Ordinance No. 1, these administrative edicts would expire only when the Knesset legislated the end of the emergency itself.[29]

The government quickly availed itself of this wide room for legal maneuver. On October 21, 1948, perhaps in anticipation of its upcoming operation to conquer the all-Arab Central Galilee, the Defense Ministry established the Military Government to replace the ad hoc administrations that the army had established in the districts of the country that continued to be home to significant Arab populations.[30] To lead the regime, Ben-Gurion appointed veteran Haganah commander Elimelekh Avner. During the Arab Revolt, Avner had authored the first precursor to Plan D, whose implementation had set in motion the formal ethnic cleansing of Palestine earlier that year.[31] Of the 147 statutes of the 1945 DERs that Avner was tasked to enforce, he made immediate use of two in particular: No. 125, which allowed local governors to declare any area of the country closed to the public without a permit, and No. 124, which empowered them to impose a curfew in any area for any length of time.

That same month the cabinet also issued an emergency regulation that authorized the agriculture minister to allocate all lands depopulated of their Arab inhabitants—now labeled "absentee"—to Jewish settlers. Cynically named the

Cultivation of Fallow Land Act, the regulation offered retroactive validation to the wildcat land grabs that settlers had undertaken following the expulsion and flight of their neighbors over the previous nine months. On December 2, the cabinet issued a follow-up regulation that shifted the designation of "absentee" status from land to people and applied that label to anyone who had left his or her village or neighborhood of residence and entered "enemy territory" for any reason or duration between November 29, 1947 (the day the Partition Plan was announced) and September 1, 1948. With the stroke of a pen, the government then transferred the property of all "absentees"—including the tens of thousands of Palestinians who were physically present—to a "custodian" tasked with determining its status.[32]

Addressing International Concerns

The timing of these regulations was inauspicious, to put it mildly, for the interim Foreign Ministry, whose emissaries were gearing up for the review of Israel's application to join the United Nations. One week before the December 17 vote in New York, the General Assembly passed Resolution 194, which called on Israel to repatriate all Arab refugees wishing to return and willing "to live in peace with their neighbors . . . at the earliest practicable date."[33] The text of the resolution had no political teeth, and General Assembly resolutions are nonbinding in any event. Nonetheless, Israel's first membership bid was easily derailed by a combination of other factors, including its categorical rejection of any sizable repatriation, its refusal to delimit its borders, and its failure to sign armistice agreements with its neighbors.[34]

During the December 1948 deliberations, UN delegates had made scant mention of the small number of Palestinians still living inside Israeli lines. This silence made sense at the time, given the immediate humanitarian crisis created by the arrival of 750,000 refugees, now scattered across the neighboring states.[35] Still, Israel's South African-born UN delegate, Abba Eban, reiterated his government's willingness to protect "positive minority rights" despite the fact, he claimed, that Arab rejection of the Partition Plan had nullified its legal obligations to the future Arab minority. In practice, the Foreign Ministry was deeply concerned about this question, especially now that the conduct of Israel's upcoming elections in January might play a role in its second application to the UN. In order to avoid a second rejection, the cabinet felt, it had no choice but to extend suffrage rights to the roughly seventy thousand Palestinians under Israeli rule since the previous summer.[36]

Israel's precarious global standing was, however, short-lived. Despite broad diplomatic support for the right of Palestinian refugees to return to their homes, restoring political stability in the region was the highest priority. The government resubmitted its application to the UN the day after signing its final armistice agreement with its Arab neighbors, and although Israel still refused to declare its borders, the bid passed easily through the UN Security Council in March 1949.[37] To mollify the fence-sitters in the General Assembly, and under pressure from the United States, Foreign Minister Moshe Sharett also announced a tentative commitment to repatriate one hundred thousand refugees, subject to Knesset approval. His pledge was disingenuous, as we will see, but it was enough to tip the vote in Israel's favor.[38]

The language of the May 1949 resolution admitting the nascent state to the United Nations gently recalled Israel's prior obligations under Resolutions 194 and 181 (the Partition Plan). It also invoked the promise made by thirty-four-year-old Eban that the current restrictions on "the liberty of persons [and] property" belonging to Israel's "minorities" would be lifted as soon as peace was restored.[39] Yet any leverage the international community may have had before the admission vote was now lost. In their refusal to impose preconditions on borders, refugees, or constitutional equality, or even a concrete plan to monitor Israel's fulfillment of those commitments, the prevailing member states endorsed the Yishuv's crowning wartime achievement—the transformation of Palestine's Jews into a racial majority—as an irreversible fait accompli. Widespread acceptance of Israel's claim that the Arabs had brought the calamity on themselves was certainly crucial to their decision, but it was also easier for the world's leading statesmen to accept that version of events than to take on further "troublesome minority problems." Already by October 1948, even those European diplomats who were most critical of Israel's refusal to repatriate the refugees began to consider a "consensual population exchange" a more realistic solution. If anything, wrote one observer at the time, "the sentiment in the UN was more favorable to the completion than to the reversal of the process."[40]

Israeli officials appreciated the significance of the UN decision in May 1949, but they were not content to rest on their laurels. Their fear was not that the world would interfere on behalf of Arab minority rights per se; instead, because it would be harder to carry out mass expulsions now that the fog of war had cleared, they worried that the country's postwar racial geography would threaten the permanence of Jewish sovereignty over all of the territory they had conquered.[41] Most of the Palestinians who remained inside Israeli lines inhabited communities that were occupied during the final stages of the war or (in the case of the Triangle) annexed shortly thereafter.[42] These communities fell primarily inside the 45 percent of Palestine that the UN had slated for the "Arab state," including the Galilee and the Triangle, regions that contained few Jews.[43] Israeli diplomats vowed publicly that they would never return to the partition borders, but they worried that Palestinians and their international sympathizers would demand secession in accordance with Resolution 181 and the general principle of self-determination before the state could permanently settle these regions with Jews. No less frightening was the prospect that Palestinians might instead use their suffrage rights to overturn Jewish privilege and the ban on the return of their family, friends, and compatriots suffering in exile.

Israel took various steps to mitigate this possibility in the late 1940s and early 1950s. When questioned by foreign journalists, ministers and their spokesmen would tout the democratic rights that the state had promised to extend to its new "non-Jewish minorities."[44] Mostly, however, they worked to remove the Arab population from the global spotlight: downplaying its size in order to overstate the country's homogeneity,[45] reminding their visitors that minorities themselves had become "a throwback" in the modern era,[46] and chastising their "Christian" peers for expecting Israel "to improve on their own precedents."[47] The government also phased out the international humanitarian relief provided to internal refugees.[48] In subsequent years, it also used the state's General Assembly seat to block the issue of Palestinian citizens from appearing on the agenda.[49]

ESTABLISHING MILITARY RULE

By far the most important step that Zionist leaders took to ensure absolute Jewish rule over the Palestinians who remained in Israel was to entrench rather than abolish the military regime they had established after the formal end of the war. In addition to enforcing the British DERs, the regime made extensive use of one of the cabinet's own emergency regulations, issued in February 1949. This decree authorized the defense minister to designate any area along the border a "security zone," forbidding access to it without a permit and empowering the minister to expel its inhabitants.[50] By the end of 1950, the Security Zones Ordinance had legalized the eviction of the residents of at least eleven Palestinian villages, thus enlarging the internal refugee population. It also enabled Israel to turn nearly each Arab village, town, and tribal community into its own "closed zone" that residents could not exit without a permit.

Life changed overnight. By early 1949, the Military Government had divided the Galilee alone into fifty-eight separate ghettos, severing Palestinians from their relatives, their commercial markets, and the urban centers where they had worked, studied, sought medical treatment, taken care of their administrative affairs, and enjoyed an evening out.[51] After the annexation of the Little Triangle in May 1949, roughly 90 percent of the Palestinians in Israel lived under military rule. That figure dropped to 88 percent in June 1951, when Acre became the last "mixed" city to enjoy a "sufficient" number of Jewish settlers to allow for civilian rule.[52] Despite the transfer of jurisdiction, "systematic" segregation continued within the mixed cities,[53] and the Interior Ministry assigned "minorities officers" to handle the Arab population's administrative affairs.[54] Meanwhile, Palestinians were forbidden to move to another village or town without permission from their local governor. Informally, they were also barred from living in any Jewish colony or town, including those depopulated of their all-Arab communities and now inhabited solely by Jews.[55]

The sense of lockdown was felt most acutely in the south. Between 1948 and 1953, the government forcibly concentrated the eleven thousand Palestinian Bedouin farmers and pastoralists who had managed to remain in or return to the country—a shadow of the ninety-five thousand who had lived in Beersheba (Bir al-Saba' in Arabic, Beersheva in Hebrew) and the surrounding desert before the war—into an area that comprised 10 percent of their ancestral lands.[56] The military regime called this area the _syag_—a term whose technical translation is "enclosed zone" but that was formally rendered in English as "reservation" or "reserves."[57] The authorities then confiscated the remaining 90 percent, including the most fertile lands between the district capital, Beersheba, and the de facto border with Gaza, for settler use. Farmers and herders were allowed to lease back some of their land from the state but were forbidden to build stone homes on it, in order to make it easier to expel them later.[58] Tribal leaders, recognized as such only on account of their cooperation with Israel during and after the 1948 war, wielded extraordinary power as the mediators between the regime and the general population, which was allowed to apply for a travel or work permit at the closest army post only two times a week. The regime institutionalized their role in part by listing the tribal affiliations of residents on their identity cards.[59] Until 1958, just 3.5 percent of the male working population had permits to work "outside the reservation."[60]

In the Galilee and the Little Triangle, where the overwhelming majority of Palestinians in Israel lived, virtually every aspect of daily life required a military pass: to open or maintain a shop, to harvest one's land or graze one's animals on it, to find work in a nearby quarry or town or in the fields and orchards expropriated from refugees and now contracted out for cultivation by the Custodian of Absentee Property, to fish or bathe in the sea, to seek medical treatment, and to visit family.[61] These permits, which were printed in Hebrew, specified not just the date but also the specific destination, span of time, and precise route permitted. To apply for such a permit, applicants typically had to reach the governor's headquarters at daybreak, sometimes walking several kilometers from their homes because not every village had an office. Upon arrival, they then had to wait in line for several hours, often while permit officers subjected them to humiliation, terror, and physical abuse.[62]

Permits were extremely difficult to obtain, particularly for anything unrelated to work or a meeting with an attorney or government official. In the early years, work permits were usually granted for periods lasting between a few days to a few weeks. Each application required clearance from the Arab Division of the Shin Bet, the state's internal security service, which over time developed a network of informants in nearly every village and town. Between December 1948 and January 1949, intelligence officials issued permits for less than one third of 773 applicants, most of them for work; they rejected the rest without explanation.[63] Years later, this figure would seem high compared to the six years of mass unemployment that followed. In addition to working with the Shin Bet, the military regime protected Jewish jobs by coordinating the number of permits it issued with the Labor Ministry and the MAPAI-controlled Histadrut. The federated trade union—or what then Labor Minister Golda Meir would later call "a great colonizing agency"—continued to bar from membership Palestinians who remained after 1948.[64] This decision resulted in rampant unemployment and provided an excuse to deny the Arab population coverage by the country's largest health care provider. It also enabled employers to pay "illegal" Palestinian workers an average of just 40 percent of the wages that "organized" Jewish workers could command.[65] Statistics are sparse but revealing. In the spring of 1949, fewer than 7 percent of the thirteen hundred people in Nazareth who had worked in Haifa before the war had permits to return to their jobs in the public and private sectors.[66] In April 1956, permits were held by just 13 percent of the six thousand residents of Umm al-Fahm, the largest Palestinian village in the Little Triangle and a community that had lost 80 percent of its land to government expropriation immediately after the war.[67]

THE LAW OUTSIDE THE LAW

Israel's decision to maintain military rule after the completion of the armistice agreements it signed with its neighbors was contentious from the start. Paradoxically, the army viewed the military regime as a superfluous body that added nothing to public security. It was widely recognized that Palestinian society was devastated and "in shock" after the war, and that the police could enforce the emergency regulations.[68] For this reason, the Israel Defense Forces (IDF) refused outright to allocate any resources to the regime. "It is no business of the army," Chief of Staff Yigal Yadin told Commander Emmanuel Mor in November 1949, when Mor asked his boss for more personnel and higher-ranking officers.[69] Yadin was not saying anything that Mor did not already know. In September 1948, a small group of government Arabists had decided that governors would handle the *civil* affairs of the population under their jurisdiction, leaving military affairs to the other branches of the army.[70]

Some cabinet ministers also opposed the continuation of the regime in peacetime. Bechor Shitrit, who headed simultaneously the Ministry of Minorities (until June 1949) and the Ministry of Police, objected on principle: The imposition of martial law on the Palestinians who remained would be incompatible with the political equality promised in the Declaration of Independence, and the regime's low-caliber officers had already engaged in looting, theft, rape, and murder.[71] Other ministers worried about how it would look to enforce a group of laws that in 1945 the Yishuv had characterized as a "police state" that was "worse than the Nazis."[72]

These concerns would continue to haunt the government, but higher priorities eclipsed them for the time being. In March 1949, Ben-Gurion tasked Jaffa-born Joshua Palmon, of the Arab division of the Haganah's intelligence unit, along with several governors and the army's legal counsel, to determine when and where to end the regime. Two months later, the men recommended lifting martial law only in the "mixed cities," those co-inhabited by Jews. Otherwise, they concluded, military rule was the best mechanism at the state's disposal to block the return of Palestinian refugees (from both inside and outside the country) to their lands; to depopulate other Arab villages whose lands they sought to expropriate immediately; and to bring in Jewish immigrants to replace the original residents. As the committee saw it, Israel needed a governing apparatus "not subject to the rules of normal procedure."[73] Thanks to the British mandatory regulations the government had inherited, and to a few emergency decrees of its own, the military regime offered a ready-made system that did not have to pass parliamentary approval and would not be subject to its scrutiny.[74]

Like all colonial regimes predicated on maintaining the privilege of the settler population, the enforcement of administrative (non-statutory) law was at the core of Israeli military rule. The permit system was not merely bureaucratic. Rather, it created a culture of racial profiling and served to criminalize the Palestinian public at large. Officers from the military police and the Border Guard regularly patrolled the "closed zones" and erected both "fixed" and "flying" checkpoints where they stopped pedestrians and bus passengers and demanded to see the permits of "any Arabs."[75] In cities under civilian rule, the police routinely stopped anyone who wore a white headcloth or appeared to have a darker complexion (often stopping Yemeni Jews by mistake).[76] In at least some Jewish towns, officers had to meet monthly quotas for the number of Palestinians they arrested on permit infractions, and they were rewarded for exceeding them.[77]

This task was not difficult. Palestinians were desperate to harvest their crops, graze their animals, market their produce, look for work, and take their relatives to the doctor, and they often could not afford the bus fare to travel to the permit office. For these reasons, many soon found themselves entering a revolving door of summary military tribunals that were closed to the public and were headed by military officers with no legal training, and that deprived defendants of the basic due process rights they would otherwise receive in the civil court system.[78] Although the army's general prosecutor could choose to try violations of the emergency regulations in Israel's civil courts, he sent only 2 percent of the cases to them.[79] Instead, inside the makeshift tribunals, justices offered no leniency for shepherds whose animals grazed off-pasture, for travelers who returned after the expiration of their permit because their buses had been delayed, for village women who took the bus into town to sell yogurt so they could feed their children, for old men who violated the evening curfew to pray at the mosque, for a permit holder found at the edge of a Jewish settlement even though it was located along the assigned route, or for anyone who veered from the route specified on his permit to buy a loaf of bread.[80]

Rather than protecting the state from physical assault or a threat to public security, the permit system was designed to keep the Arab population dependent on the regime for its basic means of survival.[81] Through 1967, an estimated 95 percent of the convictions issued by Israel's military tribunals were for administrative offenses, such as carrying an expired permit or "trespassing in a

Umm al-Fahm, April 18, 1956. Inside a makeshift military tribunal. *Top*: Young women await their sentencing. *Bottom*: Defendant argues his case. Courtesy of the Israel Defense Forces and Defense Establishment Archives (IDFA).

closed zone"—often on the land still owned by the defendant or her relatives now in exile.[82] Although the law provided for the imprisonment of a convicted offender for a maximum of one year, 60 percent of the offenders were fined and 30 percent were allowed to choose either a fine or detention that typically lasted between one and two weeks.[83] These numbers speak to the utterly political nature of the rulings. It was precisely because the authorities did not view those convicted on administrative violations as security risks that parents were permitted to serve out the jail sentences of their children, and young adults often sat in detention on behalf of their elderly parents.[84] Those convicted often chose detention, either on principle or because they could not afford the fine, which often amounted to between one and two months' worth of wages. This is one reason that detentions quickly accumulated.[85] In the 1950s, the number of Arab citizens detained in Israel was triple their total ratio in the population, and six to seven times the number of Jewish inmates.[86]

In addition to preventing Palestinians from accumulating independent economic power, senior policymakers used the permit system and the collective dependence on the regime that it fostered to try to render the public's suffrage and (after 1952) its citizenship rights meaningless. Governors and their staff drew extensively on the powers of punishment delegated to them: censoring the media, preventing political gatherings, closing small businesses, and issuing banishment and home arrest orders against anyone who campaigned against the ruling party or who was otherwise suspected of criticizing the status quo. The regime's careful distribution of enticements was equally critical, particularly because of the minimal resources the army allocated to it.[87] Taking advantage of the postwar devastation of Palestinian society, the Yishuv's ties with local collaborators under the Mandate, and pre-existing patriarchal structures in the countryside, the authorities offered travel permits, store licenses, weapons, and university admissions to compliant *mukhtars* (village heads), clan leaders, and local informants, many of whom came from the social and economic margins of pre-1948 society and were grateful for the opportunity to bolster their status.[88]

Similar rewards were offered to anyone willing to work openly on the governor's local staff or to campaign during election seasons for the "Arab lists" of the ruling MAPAI party—political fictions that enabled the government to show off headdress-donning Knesset deputies while denying them any meaningful access to the party's decision-making process.[89] Between the mediating powers the regime extended to the men who cooperated with them, the population's economic dependence created by the permit system and the mass confiscation of Palestinian land, and the ongoing fear of expulsion, MAPAI had little trouble securing solid election returns for two decades.

Public Complicity

In 1957, the prime minister's advisor on Arab affairs explained to an American researcher the government's philosophy behind maintaining military rule:

> Ben Gurion always reminds us that we cannot be guided by the subversion [that] the Arab minority has *not* engaged in. We must be guided by what they *might* have done if they had been given the chance. . . . If we cancelled the restrictions the Communist Party would invite Arab refugees to squat on their ruins, demand their lands back . . . [and] the return of the refugees. They will form organizations, parties, fronts, anything to make trouble.[90]

Such candor was rare during the first decade of statehood. Through the mid-1960s, the seemingly neutral idiom of security that infused the regime made it easier for Israeli Jews to turn a blind eye to what one scholar has called the "dirty war" that the authorities were unleashing in the Palestinian communities around them.[91] Backed by the state of emergency and the British DERs, which a Knesset majority renewed every three months, the government struck unwanted comments from the parliamentary record and granted wide license to the military censor.[92] When a handful of critical Knesset members managed to raise questions about specific cases of murder, abuse, and neglect, or about national policy toward the Arab minority more generally, ministers frequently denied the charges or simply refused to answer them.[93]

Israel's High Court of Justice, whose founders preached the importance of safeguarding universal protection under the law, also contributed to the silence and indifference of the Jewish public. Although its justices were keen to establish their independence from the executive branch, they were also close to MAPAI's political establishment, which held steadfast to its insistence on the military regime's necessity until the mid-1960s. More important, they viewed the court as an integral arm of the Zionist mission to settle as much of the land with as many Jews (and as few Arabs) as possible.[94] So, although the justices did, on occasion, challenge the Military Government on technical and procedural grounds, they did not question the security rationale for the Court's wide operational powers. Instead, they systematically declined to evaluate the constitutionality of the emergency regulations (and subsequent statutory laws that further stripped Palestinians of their rights) and ruled in 1950 that the Declaration of Independence (with its explicit provisions for equality) lacked constitutional authority.

In theory, Palestinians could petition the civil court system for redress of bureaucratic neglect, police abuse, property theft, land confiscation, and the violation of their civil equality. However, few Palestinians had the money needed to hire an attorney, and most were unfamiliar with Hebrew or with the judicial system.[95] The High Court, for its part, rejected most of the petitions from those who managed to submit them.[96] As a result, military officers, the Shin Bet, and the police enjoyed virtual carte blanche in their exercise of a wide range of "fancy punishments" designed to reassert Jewish sovereignty: ordering citizens to walk several kilometers three times a day to report to a police station, or to stand under a tree from sunrise to sunset for a six-month period;[97] opening fire on striking workers and invading the homes of members of the Arab Workers' Congress, a leftist labor union that had survived the 1948 war;[98] and beating Arab citizens to the point of hospitalization for failing to present their permits "politely and modestly."[99] Palestinians as young as sixteen were insulted, taunted, and clubbed during random ID checks in their markets and orchards—apparent punishment for not greeting the local governor or commander as he saw fit, or for refusing to carry out cruel and humiliating orders, such as fornicating with a donkey.[100] According to MAKI's Hebrew-language newspaper, Kol ha-'Am (Voice of the People), children as young as eight were interrogated about their political views.[101]

Most of the Jewish public was predisposed to accept the government's claim that military rule along Israel's frontier—a construct defined as any land not settled by Jews, and projected as the nation's symbolic center—kept them safe.[102] The conflation of Arab land ownership with physical danger was already well established in the pre-state period. This association only intensified after the Holocaust and the ethnic cleansing of Palestine in 1948, particularly for Jewish youth, whom government schools were educating to prepare for conscription. Government fear mongering around the security threat posed by the insufficient numbers of Jewish settlers in the Galilee and the Negev likely resonated with older citizens as well. This was especially true for poorer immigrants, whom the state had sent to live in depopulated Arab villages along Israel's porously guarded armistice lines, where, along with occasional physical attacks, theft and small acts of sabotage were common.[103] Through the early 1960s, Ben-Gurion and those closest to him exploited the physical vulnerability in which the authorities responsible for immigrant absorption had knowingly placed these newcomers, arguing that the military regime was necessary to prevent an inevitable culture clash between them and their Palestinian co-citizens.[104]

Above all, the racialization of security provided settlers outside Israel's urban centers with a moral alibi for further dispossessing the Arab minority of their land.[105] Two Knesset laws that retroactively legalized the seizure of "absentee" property and landholdings that the state had first used its emergency laws to undertake illustrate this point. In March 1950, the enactment of the Absentee Property Law rendered permanent the ostensibly temporary expropriation, through all the emergency regulations it had issued since 1948, of more than 10,000 shops, 25,000 buildings (housing 57,000 family dwellings), and nearly 60 percent of all fertile land in the country. These holdings, which included 95 percent of existing olive groves and nearly one half of all citrus groves, increased the land available for Jewish settlement by 250 percent. The law dealt a ruinous blow to many villages in the Little Triangle and Galilee. Although their residents had stayed put during the fighting, much of their land had fallen under Jewish control. The government thus counted them among Israel's "present-absentees."[106]

Three years later, in March 1953, the Knesset's Land Acquisition Law targeted the holdings of citizens who were not "absentee" by legalizing the seizure of any land uncultivated since 1948, or cultivated but untitled by April 1952, for the purpose of settlement, security, or "improvement." The law did offer compensation to affected landowners, but the options were pitiful: alternate plots that were either uncultivable or belonged to refugees in exile, or a "purchase price" at 1950 rates—a fact that caused a modest outcry even among some in MAPAI. (Foreign Minister Sharett called the compensation offering "a scandalous robbery.") Unlike the Palestinians and their Jewish allies who tried to overturn the law, no one on the Zionist left questioned the legality of the original seizure or the movement restrictions and convenient bureaucratic technicalities that rationalized it.[107] Within a matter of months, the state had expropriated another 40 percent of the land owned by Palestinian citizens.[108] All told, 350 of 370 new settlements created between 1948 and 1953 were established on Arab-owned land, and by 1954 more than one-third of Israel's Jewish population lived or worked on Arab "absentee" property.[109]

Jurisdictional Fictions

Paradoxically, what most enabled the government to avoid censure for creating the conditions for the mass confiscation of Palestinian land was the fact that the emergency regulations applied theoretically to territory rather than people. Of course, anyone who lived in, neighbored, or passed by Nazareth or the roughly one hundred Arab villages that survived the war knew that the reality was otherwise. Unlike Palestinians, both Jews and foreign tourists traveled freely in and out of the new colonies built on expropriated Arab land, as well as on the roads that took them there.[110] All of these settlements were located ostensibly within the "closed zones," or what both civil and military officials labeled privately as "the minorities regions" and "the pure Arab areas" of the country.[111] As Palestinian attorneys and activists would document over time, these zones encompassed not only rural colonies along Israel's de facto borders, but also Tiberias and Safad, cities whose historic Arab majorities had been driven out in their entirety by British and Haganah forces in April 1948.[112]

Most, if not all, Knesset deputies knew that military rule was imposed solely on Palestinians and that the permit system was racially enforced. It was, after all, they who had determined the policy. Starting in July 1949, both the justice minister and several parties outside of MAPAI proposed bills either to replace the notorious British DERs with slightly less restrictive Israeli equivalents, or to annul them altogether. Public support for the repeal of the DERs peaked in May 1951, when the police placed fifty-three ultra-Orthodox anti-Zionist Jews in administrative detention on suspicion of stockpiling weapons, smuggling explosive devices into the Knesset building, and planning violent acts against the state. The consensus that the colonial regulations violated the basis of a democratic state, coupled with the fear that they might be deployed against the Knesset opposition, resulted in a vote of fifty-three to one (with forty abstentions), which gave the Law and Constitution Committee two weeks to submit a new bill to cancel the DERs. Two months later, with the assent of the parties represented on the committee, the proposal was buried. The utility of the DERs to further the dispossession of Palestinian land and property owners was simply too valuable. When the debate finally resurfaced in February 1952, a majority in the Knesset voted to extend the regulations, with the quiet understanding that the government would no longer enforce them against Jews.[113]

A combination of forces perpetuated the myth of territorial jurisdiction.[114] First were the army's refusal to publish the maps of its closed zones, the silence of the High Court, and the self-censorship of the dominant press.[115] Then there was the collective lockdown on most Palestinians in the country and their vast concentration outside the country's coastal strip and urban centers—areas the Haganah had successfully cleared of their compatriots even before Israel declared independence. Together these factors enabled Jewish citizens, of whom 75 percent lived in Jerusalem and along Israel's coastal plain, to look the other way.[116] In the meantime, official minders accompanied foreign journalists and tour groups seeking to enter the territories under military control.[117]

As it did with foreign tourists, the army cautioned local Jews against visiting all but a handful of "friendly" Palestinian villages and designated tribal encampments in the south.[118] But this admonishment was not about law enforcement, and it did not derive from concerns for the visitors' safety. Instead the objective was to police the social boundaries between native Arabs and immigrant Jews lest they develop political alliances,[119] romantic attachments, or any relationships that could call into question the rationale for Jewish privilege.[120] Some officials worried considerably about this prospect, because more than half of the Jews who immigrated to Israel in the 1950s and early 1960s came from elsewhere in the Middle East and North Africa.[121] Not only did many of the new immigrants grow up speaking the same mother tongue, reading the same literature, and listening to the same kind of music as the Arabs of Palestine.[122] Some of them, particularly those from Iraq and Egypt, also shared leftist sensibilities and a history of political activism back home.[123] Even those who filled a large number of faculty slots in Arab schools during the first decade consistently proved to be "weak" and unreliable as informants; this was one of the reasons they were gradually removed.[124]

COLONIAL SPECTERS

That military rule could coexist with Palestinian voting rights served only to bolster the government's claim that the regime did not discriminate between Arabs and Jews within the "frontier" regions in which it operated. As the 1950s unfolded, this assertion became central to Israel's refutation of the charge by Arab states that it was a foreign implant whose survival was predicated on the same policies of racial privilege and dispossession employed across the colonized world. Israel was not alone in its effort to disavow the colonial nature of its policies. Toothless and vague though the United Nations' commitment to human rights and decolonization may have been in 1945, it quickly became something that European imperial leaders could ill afford to ignore. After World War II, both Britain and France were forced to introduce modest programs of social welfare and economic development and "measured doses" of procedural democracy in select possessions as a way to forestall emboldened demands for independence in their African colonies.[125] A discursive shift accompanied this process, as evolutionary rationales for racial discrimination gave way to the celebration of ethnic coexistence and the dynamic possibilities for African progress.[126]

Both Arabists and government spokesmen in Israel were attuned to these shifts, and they recognized the need to strike a balance between repression and reform. Some language was off limits. Critically, they never referred to the Arabs who remained after 1948 as Palestinians; doing so could serve as an unwanted reminder of their collective history, culture, and ties to the land. Instead, the Palestinians in Israel became the "non-Jewish minorities," "Israel's Arabs," "the Arabs, Druze, and Bedouin," and even "our Arabs."[127] At the same time, Israeli officials generally avoided the word *natives* as well as other charged terms that might have implied a colonial relationship between Jews and Arabs, a bond that could be broken only through a change in sovereignty. Labor leaders, radio broadcasters, newspaper editors, and educators in Israel's newly named "Arab sector" regularly invoked their efforts to foster coexistence (*du-kiyum*), mutual understanding and recognition (*havanah ve-hakarah hadadit*), and "the coming together of the hearts" (*kiruv levavot*)—an improved relationship between groups alternately indexed as races, peoples, and religions.[128] Like the pre-state language on which it built, the official discourse of coexistence after 1948 was understood privately as contingent upon absolute Jewish domination.[129]

Despite this general semantic vigilance, the racial and colonial consciousness of Israel's ruling elite, its Military Government personnel, and the public at large always hovered close to the surface. This sensibility found multiple expressions, ranging from exoticism to the seemingly neutral affirmation of difference, unmitigated contempt, and the projection of a civilizational burden.[130] In early 1951, for instance, a Foreign Ministry official responded with concern to a journalist's draft article on "the Arabs in Israel" that questioned the necessity of military rule now that the war had ended. Lifting the regime now would be "premature," the official advised, because it was the state's primary tool to modernize "the backward areas" and "educate its residents in self-rule."[131] Later that year a government committee decided to continue the regime because of the "Arabs' social situation."[132] In the case of at least some high-ranking officials, this kind of thinking appears to have been heartfelt.[133]

National elections and demands for local self-government became triggers for more brazen outbursts, especially when the ruling party lost Knesset seats to MAKI—the military regime's most consistent and vocal opponent, and the only parliamentary bloc where Arabs and Jews enjoyed equal membership from the start. During the second Knesset elections in July 1951, MAKI captured a fifth seat (representing 4 percent of the total Israeli electorate) after most Galilee residents became eligible to vote for the first time. Shortly thereafter, some in MAPAI proposed a suspension of campaigning among Arabs on the grounds that they lacked "experience with the lustiness of democratic procedures."[134] Joshua Palmon, who now served as the prime minister's senior advisor on Arab affairs, echoed this sentiment two years later at a press conference in Tel Aviv. Questioned about popular agitation for democratic municipal elections in Nazareth, he explained that the predisposition of Arabs toward family feuds and sectarian strife rendered them "unsuited" for self-government.[135]

Even Palmon, who would subsequently defend the provision of lower wages and food rations to Palestinian citizens on the grounds that they "needed less" than Jews, kept some thoughts to himself.[136] Only decades later would he acknowledge the worldview he shared with H. F. Verwoerd, South Africa's prime minister from 1958 to 1967 and one of the principal architects of its apartheid regime. In 1986, historian Tom Segev asked Israel's former senior Arabist why he had supported the prolonged continuation of military rule. Palmon explained that he had always "preferred separate development" to "integration," above all because it had enabled Israeli Jews to enjoy a democracy for themselves.[137] It is not surprising that Palmon had refrained from using such charged language during his tenure. In the aftermath of the Nazi genocide, such overt endorsement of scientific racism would have offended many in the Jewish public. Israeli leaders were also keen to develop trade relations and political alliances with the emerging independent states of Asia and Africa, so as to compensate for their regional isolation.[138]

But the affirmation and accusation of a shared cultural foundation between Israel and South Africa did surface in the early 1950s. In June 1953, when Prime Minister D. F. Malan became the first "European" head of state to visit Israel, Ben-Gurion reportedly praised his "contribution to mutual understanding between the races."[139] Malan's visit fell three years after the parliament in Cape Town passed the Group Areas Act, which designated all residential areas as belonging to a specific "race" and led to the forced removal of all those living in the "wrong" areas (primarily blacks and those of multiracial ancestry, known as "coloreds").[140] It is hard to imagine that correspondents from the dominant Hebrew press were unaware of this tribute, which coincided with growing public attention to the National Party's policies of *hafradah* ("apartheid" in Afrikaans, "separateness" in English). Thousands of readers had already picked up the internationally acclaimed exposé of apartheid, Alan Paton's 1948 *Cry, the Beloved Country*, which had been translated in 1951 by Israel's most prominent publishing house and was already in its third edition.[141] That spring, hundreds also flocked to the stage adaptation of the book at Israel's national theater, ha-Bima, in Tel Aviv.[142]

Six months after Malan's visit to Israel, the independent *Ma'ariv*, the country's most widely circulated daily newspaper, published a searing op-ed headlined with the title of Paton's book. Writing under his regular pseudonym, the newspaper's iconoclastic founder and editor, Azriel Carlebach, denounced the hypocrisy of his compatriots who silently reaped the fruits of native dispossession at home while canting about the policies of white superiority and land theft in "faraway Africa." "Za'aki, erets ahuvah" took the form of a letter of apology to the author's young daughter in which he described his shame in watching the Jewish settlements flourish on "stolen land." Invoking the myth of "Arab flight" that he himself had helped to manufacture, Carlebach confessed that "we took the lands" belonging not only to those "who fled . . . a great miracle that happened to us," but also to those who stayed.

> "How can we take land that belongs to someone else who is here, who lives and works on it?" Ah, my daughter, there is no technical difficulty in this. . . . If you hold the reins of power, you declare, for example, that these lands are a "closed zone." And you forbid anyone to access them without a permit. You give permits only to your cronies [*mekoravim*], the people of the neighboring kibbutzim who had set their sights on this land. And you don't give permits to the Arabs, to whom the land belongs. The matter is simple.[143]

The appearance of Carlebach's op-ed coincided with a large MAKI-led conference aiming to convince the Knesset to repeal the Land Acquisition Law that it had passed earlier in the year. A large section of the piece focused on the irrelevance for Palestinians of Israel's touted rule of law, which Carlebach, who had escaped Germany in 1933, compared to the 1935 Nuremberg Laws that had denaturalized Jewish citizens and facilitated the seizure of their property. Israel's offer to compensate Arab farmers for the lands it was expropriating from them was a joke, he told his daughter: the plots were either uncultivable or belonged to refugees over the border, and the cash alternative was based on 1950 market rates. Carlebach, as we have seen, was not the only mainstream public figure to criticize the compensation provisions of the law. Nor was his intervention a call for solidarity with Israel's Arab citizens—whom he viewed as hopelessly primitive.[144] Nonetheless, his critique stood out for its moral censure of Israel's settlement enterprise in the aftermath of the war. Since 1948, he explained—when the government "declared the end of colonialism, the end of racist land laws, the end of discrimination, and the start of human rights and the sanctity of democracy"—"the original owners of the land have not been allowed to access it."[145]

Carlebach's words seem to have fallen on deaf ears, perhaps confirming for him the inability or unwillingness of the general public to rectify their sins—the same crimes that elsewhere they condemned righteously in the name of "the brotherhood of man."[146] This silence had precedents. For years Palestinian leftists in Israel had already been drawing comparisons between the apartheid policies of racial classification and their own experiences since 1948. In June 1950, for instance, Pretoria submitted a bill mandating all South Africans to carry identity cards denoting them as white, black, or colored, and requiring blacks to carry a "passbook" in order to travel outside their designated "homelands." Noting the parallel designation of Israeli identity card holders as either Jewish or Arab—terms that the Jewish Agency had successfully persuaded the British to conflate with race in the late 1920s—the editors of Israel's Communist Party Arabic-language organ, *al-Ittihad,* "congratulate[d] the government of Ben-Gurion, the teacher from whom the fascists learn the methods of racial discrimination."[147] Two years later they compared the prime minister's legislative effort to criminalize Israel's Communist Party and Malan's 1950 Suppression of Communism Act.[148] "Birds of a feather flock together," they charged, and would continue to charge over the next two decades.[149] A handful of Jewish intellectuals had also begun to document widespread "racist attitudes" and a "sense of superiority" among the Jewish majority toward their "minority citizens," a phenomenon that foreign observers had also described.[150] For some, this trend was both a symptom and a cause of what they branded as Israel's "colonial administration."[151]

Between the 1948 war and the trajectory of Zionist-Arab relations in Palestine prior to it, it is difficult to imagine how a discourse of colonial racism could not have permeated the zeitgeist, or spirit, of the day.[152] Early Zionist leaders in Palestine had imagined themselves following in the footsteps of European settlers in Africa, Australia, and the New World. During the Mandate, most of the Yishuv's political and legal elite had identified with local British colonial officials,[153] a sensibility consistent with the dominant view of Palestinians as backward, parasitic, and responsive only to the language of force.[154] The identification with imperial Europe was equally, if not more deeply, entrenched within the Yishuv's paramilitary brass. In 1945, after gaining invaluable training while helping Britain to crush the 1936–1939 Arab Revolt, the Haganah's leading journal of military science, *Ma'arakhot* (Campaigns), began to translate essays on the theory and practice of counterinsurgency by senior European commanders in Asia, Africa, and the Arab world. It is telling that Israel's Defense Ministry, which took over the journal in 1948, continued to publish these pieces until the mid-1950s.[155]

In the meantime, state leaders instilled within the Jewish public at large the idea that all Palestinians, including their co-citizens, were marauders and savages until proven otherwise: exotic at times, perhaps, but fundamentally part of the "desert and unknown" that continued to threaten the nascent state's survival.[156] On national holidays, at military parades, and in Knesset addresses, Ben-Gurion urged Jewish audiences to understand that they stood only "on the edge of [their] colonization"—to see themselves as bearers of a historic mission even more difficult than the "conquest of the Wild West" (ostensibly because Palestinians had a modern national consciousness).[157] Once again, this image had a history. Since the 1930s, the cultural identification of Zionist settlers with the mythology of America's westward expansion had become deeply embedded in the icon of the *haluts ha-Erets Yisra'eli*, the Jewish settler-warrior in the Land of Israel. For sociologist Uri Ben-Eliezer, the two "were alike in that both were pathfinders who showed others the way":

> Their shared motif was the conquest of the "wilderness" by establishing agricultural settlements—the farther from the center the better—in order to realize the national idea, bring progress and civilization, and confront the dangers inherent in primitivism, backwardness and wilderness in the form of Indians or Arabs.[158]

The fascination with cowboys and Indians in 1950s Israel reverberated beyond stump speeches and nationalist pep rallies. Jewish schoolchildren flocked to magazine stands to purchase dime-novel translations of German storyteller Karl May's turn of the century adventures in the Wild West and the Orient. They soaked up the burgeoning genre of Hebrew-language comics that melded Tarzan and Buffalo Bill-like characters into heroes who fought Africans and Arabs alike.[159] Tourist guides and travelogues reflected this cultural climate as well as its popular currency in the English-speaking world. Their American and German authors romanticized Palestinians, particularly Bedouin tribal leaders who had collaborated with Jewish forces in 1948, as all-powerful Indian chiefs.[160] One 1955 guide, for example, characterized the encampment of Shaykh Sulayman Huzayl as "Israel's 'Red Indian Reserve,'" adding that "the tourist who stops here is sure to take some really swanky pictures home."[161] The same author also applied the analogy of the American pioneer to remote colonies established in the Upper Galilee, the site of mass expulsions in late October 1948 that resulted in the dispersion of more than fifty thousand refugees—well over half of the region's population—to Lebanon.[162] Readers learned that Kibbutz Sa'sa, the collective agricultural colony founded by ninety American Jewish settlers who adopted the name of the depopulated Palestinian village whose lands they now enjoyed, "combin[ed] the features of a Texan frontier post with those of a roadside inn on an oriental caravan route."[163]

DILEMMAS OF LIBERAL SETTLER SOVEREIGNTY

Compared to the years that followed, in the early 1950s, racial outbursts and colonial self-identifications were still a relatively marginal problem for Israel and its public image. Having lost their place on the map, Palestinians in general were largely invisible to the world, except as hapless objects of humanitarian intervention.[164] In the meantime, European leaders were clinging desperately to their own colonial possessions, much of Israel's adult population did not read Hebrew, and foreign tourists were limited to businessmen, relatives of Jewish citizens, and a small number of Christian pilgrims.[165] A more formidable challenge emanated from the structural contradictions of the state: between the separatist imperative of settler rule and the more incorporative expectations of liberal democracies after the Second World War. Above all, Israel's dilemma stemmed from the unprecedented colonial bargain that its government believed it had to strike in order to gain international recognition in 1949—to grant Palestinians the right to vote in the midst of its ongoing quest for their land.

As we have seen, Israeli policymakers decided early on to classify the areas of Palestine that the UN had designated for the Arab state as "frontier zones" in order to justify suspending the civil liberties of their Palestinian residents. But the extension of the Zionist strategy of separation after 1948 through the imposition of a colonial police state could also backfire. Some mid-level Arabists warned early on that the heavy-handedness of the military regime, combined with the absolute racial segregation that it helped to enforce, would drive Palestinian citizens—who had "torn up too few of our flags and spied too little"— to do just that.[166]

On occasion, even Ben-Gurion and Palmon drew distinctions between what they identified as acceptable harassment versus excessive abuse perpetrated along Israel's racial and spatial frontiers. If acts of rape, looting, property theft, and mysterious deaths in police custody offended the ethical sensibilities of the two men, they did not dwell on it in the paper trail they left behind.[167] Instead, what concerned them most was that unrestrained despotism would lower the standing of both the regime and its collaborators, push Palestinians into the arms of the communists—"the only body fighting their fight" (*ke guf ha-rav et rivam*), to quote one intelligence report—and invite unwanted public scrutiny of what was happening inside the ghettos and reservations of the regime.[168]

To head off this threat, leading officials pressed for the continuation of the divide-and-rule strategy that the Jewish Agency had developed over the previous three decades: to maintain a "desired tension between the various segments of the population."[169] One expression of this policy was the constant search for new informants and collaborators. Another was the active effort to "divide and subdivide" the population by politicizing the ethnic and religious divisions within it and institutionalizing the ties that the Yishuv had fostered with those communities whose leaders had decided to throw in their lot with the state.[170] The reliance on these strategies was particularly important after the IDF chief of staff reduced the number of military regime personnel from fifteen hundred to two hundred low-ranking soldiers.[171]

The experience of the Druze is the most prominent illustration of this phenomenon. During the war, the Haganah used the Yishuv's overwhelming military superiority, the Jewish Agency's ties with a handful of sympathetic families, and its own ability to offer critical economic incentives to bring the entire Druze community under its wing. In exchange for the decisive military assistance provided by its volunteer auxiliary units in the Galilee, the army chose not to expel the residents of a single Druze village; this included two communities that initially tried to resist Israeli occupation in October 1948. By the end of the war, the ratio of the Druze to others within the Arab population had increased tenfold, from 1 to 10 percent.[172] In January 1949 the IDF created a Jewish-led Minorities Unit comprising four hundred Druze, two hundred Bedouin, and one hundred Circassian soldiers, tasking it with ambushing Palestinian refugees who tried to cross the armistice lines to return home. The unit's first swearing-in ceremony was held at Nabi Shu'ayb, a minor Druze shrine under the control of the Tarif family. Their patriarch, Shaykh Amin Tarif, worked with the Ministry of Religions over the next few years to transform the shrine into a mass pilgrimage destination of the Druze community.[173]

The chief of staff agreed that the Minorities Unit contributed nothing to national security, but he continued to maintain it, and to support the 1952 conscription agreement with a small group of Druze patriarchs for the Unit's service as "the sharp blade of a knife to stab in the back of Arab unity."[174] The isolation of the Druze from the Sunni Arab majority was also institutionalized in the bureaucracy. After the government closed the Ministry of Minorities in June 1949, each ministry created a separate division to administer "Arab and Druze" affairs. Six years later, the government would entrench this cleavage further by embarking on a process to recognize the Druze as a separate "nationality," to be marked as such on their identity cards. In addition to creating a separate Druze scouts movement, Ben-Gurion also reportedly encouraged Druze to stop speaking Arabic.[175]

Yet the Zionist policy of divide and rule was more complicated than it had been in the pre-state era, because liberal sovereignty brought with it new burdens. Already in 1952, some Druze demanded the dismissal of Shaykh Amin Tarif as guardian of the Nabi Shu'ayb shrine after he consulted the minister of religions on whether the community should celebrate the popular Muslim holiday of 'Id al-Fitr. The conscription agreement itself was the result of the army's effort to break the resistance of young men in the community to volunteering.[176] Some Druze opposed the military draft on political and religious grounds, but even those who might have been more open to it resented the professional glass ceiling they faced—including the refusal to integrate them with Jewish units, and the fact that for many years their service earned them no reprieve from the general movement or labor restrictions imposed on other Palestinians.[177] In short, it seemed unclear to many young Druze why they should cooperate with a regime that claimed to offer them favored status when it still treated them as unwanted natives—as Arabs—on the fundamental issues of land and labor.[178]

Even before the fault lines in Israel's policy to isolate the Druze from other Palestinians began to surface, some Arabists worried about the lack of policy direction toward the other 90 percent of the Palestinian citizenry. Under British rule it had sufficed for the Yishuv to recruit individual informants and land agents to facilitate Jewish colonization. Having attained their sovereignty but determined to maintain Jewish privilege, state officials now asked themselves whether, and how, they should try to transform the feelings of the Arab public at large—whether, and how, to enlist them into Israel's "community of sentiment" while excluding them from the national community.[179]

Until the mid-1950s, the question of Arab "sentiments" (*hilkhe ruah*) was driven especially by the fear that Arab citizens would abet Israel's neighbors in the latter's ostensible quest to destroy it. Some officials believed that this alienation was inevitable because Arabs would always be "humiliated" by living under Jewish rule. Others, such as the Russian-born editor of MAPAI's Arabic-language daily, *al-Yawm* (Today), argued that although the Arab public might never "love" the state, any sedition on their part would result directly from the state's maltreatment of them. "It is natural that Israeli Arabs do not love the State of Israel and are not devoted to it," explained Mikhael Assaf in the biweekly policy journal, *Beterem* (Before); but it was also possible—indeed crucial—to reduce the population's "active non-love" to a "passive" state.[180]

Another contradiction that government officials strove to manage was the separation of military and civilian powers in the area under military rule. Unlike the colonized subjects of overseas territories such as India and Ghana, but also unlike the indigenous peoples of settler colonies such as Algeria and Kenya, the Palestinians in Israel lived under two sovereigns. One was a military governor, who ruled through a body of colonial emergency laws and whose commander answered only to the cabinet. The other was a national parliament, to which they had limited—but, as we will see, not irrelevant—access.[181]

The legal ambiguities created by the reality of dual sovereignty in the Galilee, the Little Triangle, and the Negev do not appear to have been discussed openly in the judiciary. One of the founding theoretical precepts of the international rules of war is that civil and martial law cannot overlap in the same territory. The justices of Israel's Supreme Court appear to have accepted this view, but only by blinding themselves to the facts in front of them. In February 1958 the court ruled on a case pertaining to the justiciability of military infractions committed by Israeli police officers during Israel's four-month occupation of the Gaza Strip from 1956 to 1957. Writing for the majority, Justice Moshe Landau cited the 1905 principle of renowned University of Cambridge legal scholar L.F.L. Oppenheim that martial law applied only when "a state sends its army outside its borders and conquers additional territory without extending sovereignty over it."[182] "Every civilized state" that is sovereign over a territory applies its civil laws there, wrote Landau. If that state merely occupies a territory, as Israel had done in Gaza—"a place in Palestine outside the area where [Israeli civil] law ... applies"—it must apply military law.[183]

The willingness of Landau's colleagues to sign off on this ruling demonstrated their refusal to acknowledge the reality that military law already applied within nearly a third of the territory over which Israel had declared independence. For more than two years after the UN recognized Israeli sovereignty within its armistice lines, the IDF continued to designate the zones under military rule "Occupied Territories" (*shtahim muhzakim*),[184] and to refer to its Arab citizen-subjects as "foreign."[185] At least through 1956, the army continued to differentiate between the "Arabs of the state"—in Jaffa, Lydd, Ramle, and the handful of the remaining villages located within Israel's original UN-allocated borders—on the one hand, and "the Arabs from the reserves"—referring to Negev but also the Little Triangle, whose residents lived under a nightly curfew until August 1962—on the other.[186]

The members of the High Court were not the only civil authorities who ignored or wished to erase these distinctions. Already by 1950, mainstream Arabists had started to complain that the absence of parliamentary oversight inside the zones of military rule was fueling corruption and profiteering.[187] As the decade wore on, jurisdictional turf wars and attacks rose from Zionist parties who resented MAPAI's monopoly over the Arab vote.[188] Ben-Gurion himself recognized that the refusal to clarify the separation of military and civilian powers inside the zones of military rule was a problem, but the alternatives seemed worse. Lifting martial law would encumber Jewish colonization, but delegating exclusive authority to the governors in their districts would be "inappropriate in a democratic regime" and harm Israel's image abroad.[189] The result of this predicament was a political stalemate that half a dozen official commissions formed to clarify the separation of military versus civil powers within its "Arab regions" would fail to break.[190]

BETWEEN EQUALITY AND SOVEREIGNTY

If the contradictions of liberal settler rule posed challenges for Israel's Jewish officials, they were exponentially more fraught for the Palestinians who managed to remain inside or return across state lines after 1948. The flight and expulsion of more than 80 percent of their compatriots, including most of the middle and upper classes, had all but eviscerated Palestine's educational, economic, and political infrastructure. In the weeks and months after Israeli occupation commenced, homelessness, hunger, illness, and unemployment preoccupied the shadow of the intelligentsia, the labor movement, the clergy, and the urban community leaders who remained. Along with the rest of the population, they spent the summer and fall of 1948 negotiating with military officials and the Ministry of Minorities to retrieve their property and gain access to their fields, ensure the distribution of food rations and supplies, and secure short-term government jobs harvesting the crops from refugee-owned fields. They also took the lead in protesting harassment and looting by vigilante settlers and soldiers, and in demanding the release of the thousands of boys and men detained in so-called prisoner of war camps.[191]

These efforts were conducted almost entirely on the local level, where people focused on their immediate needs of survival and recovery. Although Israel's Declaration of Independence had promised to treat Arabs and Jews equally, it was difficult, if not impossible, to imagine what the long-term political future would bring. Between the military's isolation of each community behind checkpoints, the internal political fissures that the Yishuv had exploited and exacerbated during the war, and Palestinians' limited knowledge of Hebrew, the likelihood that the population would organize itself on a national scale was nil.

Communism Versus Nationalism Before 1948

MAKI was the one, and only partial, exception to this vacuum. In October 1948, the Communist Party became heir to a political movement that had experienced several factional splits and ideological recalibrations over the previous two decades.

Communism first came to Palestine in the early 1920s by way of a small group of Eastern European Jewish émigrés who concluded that their commitment to socialist internationalism was incompatible with the ethnic nationalist project for which they had originally signed up. In 1924, as a condition of their recognition by the Comintern (Communist International), the Palestine Communist Party (PCP) renounced Zionism as an illegitimate settler-colonial movement aligned with Britain, which sought to mask its imperial project under the guise of class struggle.[192]

Despite the PCP's disavowal of Jewish nationalism and its repudiation of Zionist separatism, it was not until the escalation of anticolonial violence and British repression in 1929 that the party, on marching orders from Moscow, began actively to recruit Arab members. Expanding its ranks forced Jewish members to grapple with fundamental questions about the party's relationship with the Palestinian national movement that had crystallized a decade earlier, and about the future status of Jewish settlers, which until then they had failed to confront: Were all Palestinian factions allies by virtue of seeking to throw out the colonizer? After how many years in the country would settlers (including themselves) count as "natives"?[193]

Answers to these questions unfolded gradually, and partly on an individual basis. In 1936, for example, some Jews left the party after it threw its support behind the Arab Revolt and some Palestinian members joined the armed struggle.[194] Despite the PCP's formal support for the Revolt, tensions began to fester over the equivocation of Jewish party members in their opposition to Zionism. It was against this backdrop, and the dissolution of the Comintern, that a cohort of young, urban, and largely Christian intellectuals broke away from the PCP in 1943 and joined members of the noncommunist League of Arab Intellectuals—originally a Bethlehem-based student group, established in 1938—to form their own faction, the National Liberation League (*'Usbat al-Taharrur al-Watani*). Although the NLL identified itself as a national rather than a communist party, it welcomed Jewish members, differentiated between the Zionist leadership and the Jewish working class, and continued to attack the Palestinian nationalist leadership for their reactionary and "racialist" positions toward Jews. Nonetheless, it now sat firmly under the Palestinian national umbrella. By 1945, some twenty thousand workers had joined the affiliated Arab Workers Congress, and its weekly newspaper, *al-Ittihad* (The Union), had established a strong presence in the Galilee and in the coastal port cities.[195]

Whereas the 1936 to 1939 Arab Revolt had tested the internationalist commitments of Palestine's Jewish communists, a different sort of test confronted their Arab counterparts in October 1947. That month the Soviet Union announced its support for partition as the only practical solution to the deteriorating situation in Palestine and the first step toward an anti-imperialist struggle in the Middle East. The reversal of its position put the NLL in a difficult position. After decades of arguing that the Arab national liberation struggle in Palestine was analogous to other indigenous anticolonial movements throughout the world, the Soviets were now calling on Arab communists to accept Jewish settlers as a legitimate national community with equal rights to self-determination.[196]

NLL leaders were divided in their response to this volte-face. Some, such as Haifa's Tawfiq Tubi and Emile Habibi, argued that Palestinians' subordinate power relative to the Yishuv required them to accept partition as the lesser of two evils (the other being the continuation of the Mandate). Many more leaders, such as Emile Touma and the majority of those who attended the party's Central Committee meeting in Nazareth in December 1947, continued to reject partition, but their ideological perseverance could not withstand the growing political and military reality. It took just two months, after which Palestine's civil war erupted in earnest, for most committee members to declare their support for two states until the long-term goal of democratic unity between them could be realized.

Shortly after the Nazareth meeting, the British revoked the license of *al-Ittihad*, and the party's ability to meet and organize became strained under the chaos of the war. Palestinian communists in the north continued nonetheless to propagate their message through the distribution of mimeographed leaflets. Starting in early May they warned the Arab masses not to be duped by their enemies: the British, who sought to foment racial hatred between them and Jews; King Abdullah and his "liberation" army, which he was using to annex the portion of Palestine allocated to the Arab state; and the nationalist leadership, whose support for the killing of Jewish civilians and the flight from Haifa and Jaffa was as much to blame as the Zionist leadership and (what the leaflets referred to as) "Jewish extremist groups" for the tragedy that had befallen the Palestinian people. Although these leaflets did not directly recognize the Yishuv's right to self-determination, their call for the expulsion of all foreign (British, Arab, and Zionist) armies from the territory allotted to the Arab state so as to realize the Palestinian right to self-determination signaled an awareness among party members that their dream of a unified democratic state had become a dead letter.[197]

The NLL's formal recognition of the Yishuv as a national community became more explicit as Israel's expulsions and its occupation of the Ramle, Lydd, and Nazareth districts—all slated for Palestinian sovereignty—continued over the summer. In September the Central Committee issued a "correction" to its earlier support for a majority-rule democracy in all of Palestine. Specifically, the statement noted the party's "mistake" in failing to appreciate that a "separate Jewish nationality" had emerged over the course of the Mandate, and that the nationalist split of Arab communists from the PCP had constituted a "rightist deviation" that had only weakened Arab-Jewish understanding and the two groups' joint ability to expel the British.[198] Having offered this self-criticism, the Central Committee went on to condemn Israel's maltreatment of the Arabs who remained in the country, and to affirm the right of all refugees to return to their homes. Finally, it called on NLL members living within the UN-allocated Jewish state to join the members of the former PCP, now renamed MAKI, and the only legal non-Zionist secular political party in the nascent state.[199]

The NLL's "correction" paved the way for the reunification of Jewish communists with their Arab counterparts living within Israel's proposed 1947 borders. Desperate to find work for their affiliated unionists, to ameliorate the living conditions of their compatriots, and to resume the publication of *al-Ittihad*, what remained of the NLL leadership decided that it was in the interests of those based in Haifa and Jaffa to struggle from within their new reality rather than try to resist it altogether. Their decision, which culminated in the Haifa Unity Meeting on October 24, 1948, marked a watershed in the political relationship between Jews and Palestinians.[200] Never before had the two peoples had an opportunity to participate on equal footing in a political bloc with access to a self-governing legislature. Never before had the Zionist movement been compelled to reckon with a group of Arabs and Jews who could pose a democratic challenge to the pillars of separatism and native dispossession that had formed the basis of the Jewish nationalist enterprise in Palestine.

For nearly two decades it had been easy for the MAPAI-dominated Jewish Agency to ignore the antinationalist politics of the PCP's small and mostly underground membership.[201] Until the Soviet delegate to the United Nations announced his reluctant support for partition in October 1947, the party had continued to oppose any "dismemberment" of the country on the grounds that it would vitiate the interests of the country's two peoples.[202] Developments turned quickly, however, following the UN vote. The party's enthusiastic embrace of their patron's support for partition, its procurement of vital military aid from Eastern Europe, and its decision to stop referring to the Palestinian state whose establishment it theoretically still supported all forced the Yishuv's political tent to offer Jewish communists a modicum of shelter.[203] More pointedly, the party's newfound "Jewish national tilt"[204] would make it much more difficult for Prime Minister Ben-Gurion, who identified the reunified party as MAPAI's most threatening political rival precisely because of its agitation against military rule and the policies of racial separatism, to outlaw it.[205]

Communism Versus Nationalism After 1948

After the reunification, the Communist Party stood alone on all matters relating to the basic rights of the new Palestinian minority. This stance included its demand for the immediate end of military rule and the repeal of all emergency legislation, the return of all Palestinian prisoners and refugees, and the establishment of a Palestinian state based on the right to self-determination in accordance with UN Resolution 181. Until 1954, MAKI was also the only legal party in Israel that Palestinians could join and lead as equal members, a fact it made much of during the first elections.[206] Yet the old questions regarding the PCP's relationship to Zionist colonization in the early 1940s quickly resurfaced, and now in starker form. Young NLL leaders such as Tawfiq Tubi, who became MAKI's first Palestinian Knesset deputy in January 1949, and Emile Habibi, who would join him after the next election in 1951 (and later become one of the world's most celebrated Palestinian novelists), understood that the party's new-found legitimacy, and the need to continue to win Jewish votes, would come at a cost. In those unstable and uncertain times, however, they could not have predicted precisely what or how great that cost would be.

One of the first tests of MAKI's stated commitment to Palestinian state-hood and adherence to the UN Partition Plan came less than a week after the Unity Meeting, when Israeli troops occupied the Western and Upper Galilee. In the weeks leading up to the event, NLL leaders in Nazareth had supported the parties' reunification within the partition borders of the Jewish state on the grounds that MAKI would continue to recognize them as representing the Communist Party of the Palestinian state-to-be. But MAKI's lone insistence on withdrawing from the Galilee, as well as from Jerusalem and the other parts of the country that Israeli troops had occupied outside the UN-allocated lines, soon waned. In April 1949, following the conclusion of the regional armistice agreements, references to the NLL disappeared from the pages of both *al-Ittihad* and MAKI's Hebrew organ, *Kol ha-'Am*. The party's de facto acceptance of the "territorial status quo" was confirmed six months later at MAKI's Eleventh Congress. In deference to the overwhelming Jewish consensus to retain all the territory within the new ceasefire lines, party leaders resolved that Israel's final borders should be agreed upon "by the two states," referring to the future Palestine.[207]

Veteran NLL leaders now within the MAKI fold appreciated the significance of the party's concession to the Zionist consensus in Israel but viewed it as a temporary setback. In an interview four decades later, Habibi explained their thinking that the only way Palestinians could effectively combat expulsions, which had continued throughout the spring and summer of 1949, and attain the equality that Israel's founding document had promised, was by accepting the application of Israeli law within the territories that the UN had allocated to their state. Given the absolute odds against them—Israel's crushing defeat of its Arab neighbors, King Abdullah's expansionist agenda, and the UN's prioritization of regional security and the sovereignty of existing states above all else—the only real choice they had was between doing something or nothing at all.[208]

This gamble would pay off in the short-term. Along with their compatriots in MAPAM (*Mifleget ha-Po'alim ha-Me'uhedet*, the Labor Zionist United Workers' Party) after 1954 (though to a lesser extent), Palestinian communists and their Jewish allies stubbornly exploited the fact of their suffrage rights—

and after 1952, their citizenship—to raise the political and diplomatic costs of maintaining the status quo. They did so in the Knesset, in the courts, and on the streets. Critical to these efforts was their work in the press, which—in the case of al-Ittihad—villagers often had to smuggle in under their hats or clothes in order to avoid confiscation by the local governor.[209] As the 1950s wore on, both Communist Party newspapers systematically shed light on the violence and abuse against Palestinians by the authorities as well as by individual Jewish citizens. (MAPAM's 'Al ha-Mishmar and al-Mirsad, and the small independent Hebrew-language muckraker ha-'Olam ha-Zeh [This World], joined them, though less consistently.)

All of this exposure would play a critical role in undermining Israel's efforts to keep the reality of military rule hidden from the general public. It also became a way for Palestinians—most of whom were isolated from one another by the military's restrictions on their movement—to discover and heed lessons from what was happening elsewhere in the country. Al-Ittihad's editors were particularly effective at using the newspaper, as well as its 1953 literary spinoff, al-Jadid, to fill the cultural vacuum created by the Arab world's commercial embargo on Israel and the resultant absence of new Arabic fiction and poetry not written through a Zionist filter.[210] Aside from the thirteen newspaper issues that the explicitly anti-Zionist al-Ard (The Land) movement—in contrast to MAKI's less-forceful non-Zionism—published between 1959 and 1960, after which it was outlawed, MAKI's Arabic press quickly became the primary home not just for communists but for all Palestinian poets, essayists, short story writers, and other intellectuals who wished to express themselves in their native tongue.[211]

In the struggle for racial equality, MAKI, MAPAM, and the unaffiliated Palestinian activists who worked with them would eventually lose more fights than they won. We can appreciate their successes, however, in light of the extraordinary efforts of all the dominant Zionist parties to render meaningless the rights that Israel had been forced to concede to them.[212] Leading the charge was Ben-Gurion's MAPAI party, which enjoyed (along with its successor, the Labor Party) effectively uncontested control of the government, the Histadrut, and the economy until the mid-1970s. Their campaign took multiple forms, including electoral coercion and the cultivation of a corrupt patronage system that rewarded anyone willing to do favors for the regime.[213] Its punitive dimension was more extensive, including the deprivation of travel permits, store licenses, employment, university admission, and—before 1952—identity cards to any families with members known or suspected to have MAKI sympathies.

As open Palestinian civil resistance stepped up in the mid-1950s, the military stepped up its enforcement of those DERs that provided for administrative detention, censorship, home arrest, and banishment.[214]

The long-term results of the NLL's decision to unite with MAKI and to work within the legal system were more ambiguous. By the end of the first decade, it was clear that Arab suffrage rights had become a double-edged sword—that the struggle for civil rights would make it difficult, if not impossible, for Palestinians to attain their national rights. One reason for this paradox was the already marginal position of Israeli communists within the national political landscape, and the compromises that party leaders chose—and in some cases felt obligated—to make in order to maintain their majority Jewish base. Within the dominant Zionist consensus in the mid-1950s, it was already threatening enough that a party in which Arabs did not serve as "yes men" to their Jewish bosses made relentless demands for citizenship, civil rule, equal access to jobs, and democratic municipal elections for the small minority of them who remained after 1948. It was an entirely different matter for that minority to demand the repatriation of the refugees, the restoration of their stolen land and property, and the right to national self-determination within the UN partition lines. After 1954, the return of Palestinian refugees and lands to their owners would have left the state with one four-hundredth of the available land on which housing officials could settle new immigrants; it also would have severely weakened Israel's economy. The formation of a Palestinian state within the borders allocated by UN Resolution 181 would, moreover, require secession. Israel would surely crush such a move with military force, a reaction the United Nations would likely support for the sake of preserving regional stability.

Palestinian communists thus faced a catch-22. Between the party's need to stay in the political game if it wanted to have any impact and the growing unwillingness of Jewish communists since the late 1930s to confront Zionism's settler-colonial mission, it is not surprising that MAKI's formal platforms would offer increasingly vague demands for the realization of Palestinian collective rights.[215] To be fair, the party would never formally deny Israel's colonial status. As we will see, some of its Jewish leaders would draw explicit ties between the segregationist policies of Israel and South Africa in the early 1950s. More frequently, however, and especially as the Partition Plan became easier to forget over time, Israeli communists would skirt the national—and thus the colonial—question. By parroting the standard Soviet refrain that Israel was merely a lackey of the imperial West (and its stepchild, hireling, and so on), most Jewish communists managed to avoid reflecting on the expulsions of 1948 and their indirect endorsement of its colonial logic.

.   .   .

Formally, Palestinian party leaders, and indeed most Palestinian intellectuals in the 1950s, toed this line, but they would struggle deeply with its contradictions and the way it compromised their ability to address the fundamental questions of sovereignty, land, and refugees that were at stake. To start, how could they convince the United Nations that they were a colonized people deserving of self-determination if they were already voting citizens of another state? How would the organization's leading members reconcile the principle of decolonization with its prior recognition of Israel's wartime territorial conquests and its tacit approval of Israel's refusal to repatriate the 750,000 Palestinian refugees now dispersed on the other side of its armistice lines? It is to the first major confrontation over these questions—the struggle over who was eligible to gain permanent legal status in the nascent state—that we turn next.

3 CITIZENSHIP AS A CATEGORY OF EXCLUSION

In 1948 we lost a country and gained citizenship.

Former Knesset Member Azmi Bishara¹

ON JUNE 14, 1949, the cabinet devoted a few minutes of its daily meeting to address a seemingly minor diplomatic crisis that the Arab-Israeli armistice agreements in April had failed to resolve. The holdup of basic nationality and immigration laws in the new state had delayed the printing of passports, and Jewish residents traveling abroad on personal or official state business were being hassled and turned away at many airports because their *laissez-passer* travel documents reflected a status, and a country, that no longer existed.

> Moshe Sharett (Foreign Minister): Why is it that when a person from Israel goes abroad, his travel document states, "Palestinian *netinut* [literally, subjecthood] until this very day?
>
> Moshe Shapira (Interior Minister): I must look into this.
>
> David Ben-Gurion (Prime Minister): I propose that we write "Israeli citizenship" there.
>
> Shapira: There is no such thing.
>
> Ben-Gurion: No such thing exists in reality, because no decision has been made. I propose that we decide to write "Israeli citizenship," and then it will exist. . . .
>
> Pinhas Rosen (Justice Minister): The experts say that there is no Israeli citizenship; nor is there any such thing as Land-of-Israel citizenship.
>
> Ben-Gurion: I'm not interested in what the experts say. There are no experts when it comes to this! Laws like this are created by agreement, and in the whole world there are no experts on this matter.

Ya'akov Shapira (Director General, Justice Ministry): Might I suggest that we call the thing Israeli *ezrahut* [citizenship] and not *netinut?*

Ben-Gurion: I accept that.

Decision: From now on [travel documents] issued by the Israeli government will specify citizenship as "Israeli"—instead of "Land-of-Israel" or "Palestinian."[2]

Such a swift pronouncement belied the legal and political turmoil that enveloped the nascent regime and its ability to survive under the conditions it desired, for the contents of "Israeliness" and its citizenship had yet to be filled in. Since 1925, when the British Mandatory Government issued the Palestine Citizenship Order, all Jews and Arabs living in the country for at least two years could choose to identify themselves legally as "Palestinian." In order to clarify their legal inferiority to full English nationals in the metropole, the Order's official Hebrew version had translated "citizenship" as *netinut*, a derivation of the biblical term *natin*, or "subject." In the Old Testament, the legal status of a *natin* stands between that of an *ezrah*—a homeborn, native citizen—and a *zar*—a foreigner, alien, or literally, a stranger.[3] Two decades later, it is no surprise that, having thrown off the imperial sponsorship they had once desperately pursued, the new sovereigns in the land sought to assert their status as bona fide nationals of a country with a name of their choosing.[4] In the scope of international law, however, it was an entirely different matter to proclaim a largely immigrant society to be "homeborn," to the exclusion of most of its actual legal natives.[5] Indeed to call the Arabs of Palestine *zarim*—strangers, aliens—as Israeli leaders so often did, reflected a political and cultural aspiration rather than a legal reality.[6]

Since November 1947, Zionist leaders had pledged repeatedly to promulgate a democratic constitution that would guarantee the provision of universal citizenship, in accordance with their obligations under the UN Partition Plan. If their reiteration of that promise had been halting in their Declaration of Independence on May 14, 1948, it seemed even more distant by the end of the summer, as the Jewish state was preparing its application to join the international body and the Partition Plan's proposed Arab state had become a dead letter. Few Israeli officials relished the prospect of extending suffrage and other rights to the country's "non-Jewish residents,"[7] who continued to own or hold a large portion of the land in the country.[8] The contradiction at the heart of their policy objectives thus could not have been starker: uphold the universalist ideal of a constitutional republic, join the community of nations, and at last afford the Jewish people a transition to a "normal existence," or maintain the racial privilege at the heart of their ongoing settler project and live in indefinite isolation.[9]

To be sure, the long-wished-for demographic cataclysm precipitated by the war made the extension of equal rights to the Palestinians who remained in the country somewhat easier for the government to swallow. Thanks to the coerced flight and direct expulsion of some 750,000 Arabs who lived in the territory that Zionist forces captured, the number of Palestinians in the Jewish state had plummeted to well under one-third of the 49 percent envisioned in the Partition Plan. Reflecting on the sudden emergence of the first Jewish majority in Palestine, at least since the Zionist settler movement began in the late nineteenth century, Foreign Minister Moshe Sharett rejoiced in the "wholesale evacuation" of an overwhelming portion of Palestine's Arabs as an event "more spectacular than the establishment of the state."[10] The provisional government wasted no time in working to consolidate the new status quo. In mid-July, backed by sustained appeals from settlers and the army, the cabinet announced an official ban on the return of the refugees, as well as its intention to lease their lands to Jews.[11] In subsequent months and years, Israeli officials would labor to explain to the public that anything less than an overwhelming Jewish majority was tantamount to national suicide.[12] Not only would the nation refuse to be "depleted"[13] or "strangled" by native Arabs wishing to "live . . . work . . . and share the economy,"[14] but Jewish immigration would trump all other imperatives, including the pursuit of peace in the region.[15] As a former Israeli foreign minister put it, the ban on Palestinian return became the conflict's "defining moment."[16]

Yet Palestinian refugees—most now destitute, hungry, and in many cases sleeping in donated tents or under the open sky on the edges of Lebanese, Egyptian, and Jordanian-held territory—had their own ideas.[17] Stuck in makeshift camps and reliant on charity for just one meal a day, many resolved to return to their homes, their small businesses, and their crops, which would soon need harvesting; and for all of Israel's fiery rhetoric, the army seemed remarkably inept at stopping them. Already by August 1948, the dearth of soldiers to patrol the frontiers of the new state had enabled thousands of Palestinians to take advantage of two brief truces to return to Nazareth, Acre, and the surrounding villages of the coast and Lower Galilee.[18]

The decision of these refugees to vote with their feet only reinforced the mounting sense among world leaders that Israel would have to repatriate at least some of those wishing to go home, a fact that deeply concerned the Foreign Ministry. Its staff understood that the longer this unregulated movement into the country continued, the more it threatened to undo the new demographic reality and enable more Palestinians to gain residency status, voting cards, and ultimately full citizenship. But if such a prospect imperiled the very sovereignty of the state of which they had dreamed, they had to balance their confrontation of the problem with their defense of Israel's fragile image abroad. With the army unable physically to seal the borders, ministry officials fixated on the need to distinguish between two groups of Palestinians: those who had managed to stay in the country during the fighting, whose legal status would be difficult to contest, and those who had recently returned, whom the authorities would now deem "illegal." Only an immediate census and registration of the entire Arab population would enable the government to identify and deport those Arabs residing in the state without its permission. Only in this way could Israel minimize the number of those who could claim their legal rights as citizens before further international pressure for repatriation emerged.[19]

The situation turned out to be even more complicated than ministry officials had imagined. As we have seen, by mid-1949 Israel had yet to define who counted as a citizen, or even a legal resident. Behind the holdup was the prime minister himself, who feared that any universal law that treated Arabs and Jews uniformly would enable refugees abroad to claim Israeli residency and citizenship by virtue of their prior nationality as "Palestinians"—the same status that Jews in Palestine had enjoyed since 1925. For more than a year already, Ben-Gurion had persuaded the cabinet not to send its draft citizenship bill to the Knesset for consideration,[20] but the delay on the bill proved to be a double-edged sword. Without defining who was legally permitted to reside and claim rights in the country, the government also lacked a legal framework to prohibit returning refugees from doing just that. Even the army's orders to conduct "sweeps for infiltrators"—roundup and expulsion operations against Palestinians suspected of having returned home without permission—were compromised by the uncertainty regarding those whom it could not legally (or feasibly) expel.

In the years before the Knesset passed its citizenship and entry laws in 1952, the consequences of the absence of legal citizenship and residence in Israel were much more grave for Palestinians than for Jews. The possibility of being deported without reason or recourse was high, creating a climate of fear, abuse, and corruption that would shape Palestinians' long-term relationship to the state in profound ways. At the same time, the fact that the state lacked an established legal basis on which to expel Palestinians and nullify their prior citizenship also inspired panic among Jewish officials, who spent four years devising new but repeatedly flawed bureaucratic mechanisms to prevent refugees from crossing the border and then retroactively obtaining the necessary papers to stay.

This chapter traces the protracted, muddled, and violent process of resolving this legal ambiguity in order to make sense of the paradox at the heart of Israel's history as a liberal settler state: that the juridical and social content of Israeli citizenship was determined not by an ideal vision of whom to include but rather by the stark imperative of whom to keep out. The story chronicles the determination of Palestinians to make permanent, in the face of a vast military, administrative, and ultimately legislative apparatus designed to stop them, the state's recognition of their legal claims of belonging. Starting with the first census and the distribution of a chaotic array of identity papers, it follows the increasingly desperate efforts of the authorities to rationalize their system of demographic regulation with a special identity card known as the Temporary Residency Permit (TRP). Although this stopgap measure was no substitute for a democratically approved legal framework, and in many ways exacerbated the crisis of paperwork, the TRPs bought the government more time before having to send a draft universal citizenship law for a vote. In the interim, politicians and state attorneys bypassed the threat of universalism by drafting what amounted to two different nationality laws: the 1950 Law of Return, for Jews, and the so-called 1952 Nationality Law, for Palestinian Arabs.

As Israel enters its seventh decade as a sovereign nation-state, it continues to be marked by the enduring weakness of citizenship as an institution and its attendant refusal to establish a singular nationality that encompasses all citizens. The nature of both of these legal categories—citizenship and nationality—is the historical outcome of Israel's resistance to the determination of thousands of Palestinian Arabs to remain in or return to their homes and seize the equality and democratic rights they believed the state was bound to grant them. To escape the subordinate status of "refugee," many risked their lives to obtain the "right to have rights" as legal citizens.[21]

COUNTING AND "SWEEPING"

Israel's first census was held on Monday, November 8, 1948, in order to serve urgent practical needs in the realm of population management: to administer the construction of new housing and the provision of food rations for the tens of thousands of new, and largely destitute, Jewish immigrants flooding into the country each month; to establish a system of national conscription; and to distribute voting cards in advance of the first parliamentary elections in January 1949. Except for ultra-Orthodox anti-Zionists, Jewish communities around the country reportedly experienced the census as a celebration, happily enforcing the seven-hour curfew as a symbol of their newfound political sovereignty.[22]

In all likelihood, at least one-third of the Palestinians under Israeli rule heard nothing about the census that day and, in any event, were still reeling from the terrifying and life-altering events of the week before. In late October, Israeli forces had carried out a deadly blitz to conquer the Central and Upper Galilee pocket against the Arab Liberation Army (ALA), whose volunteer forces had been holding the region since January 1948. Inhabited exclusively by Arab villagers and town dwellers, the region had been designated for inclusion in the Partition Plan's projected Palestinian Arab state. In three short days, the Israeli military's aerial bombings, executions, and ethnic cleansing of between fifty and sixty thousand Palestinians turned the region into a devastated and decidedly less Muslim shadow of its former self.[23]

Census officials had neither the staff nor the resources to conduct the census in the remaining Palestinian villages of Israel's newly occupied territory on November 8, but there were additional reasons why tens of thousands of Arabs located inside the new state were left out of the final tally of sixty-nine thousand "minorities." For starters, they chose not to register between thirteen and fifteen thousand Bedouin in the south in order to make it easier to expel many of them before international organizations noticed.[24] Another five to eight thousand boys and men between the ages of fifteen and sixty years were interned in labor and prison camps and left uncounted. Although the overwhelming majority had taken no part in the fighting, conquering IDF troops detained them as "prisoners of war" (POWs) simply because they were of military age.[25] Camp officials reportedly offered many of them cash and transit to emigrate with other family members still inside the country, but most refused.[26] Finally, census takers also failed to count between thirty and forty thousand Galilee residents, primarily but not only from the villages just occupied.[27]

Over the next two months, registration clerks made their way slowly across the north to count the communities they had missed. In the meantime, the failure to complete the census and to patrol the borders effectively renewed the Foreign Ministry's alarm. By late December the army reported that between three and four thousand refugees had managed to return in the previous two months, and complaints were beginning to surface about the absence of a uniform policy regarding whom to expel and whom to leave in place.[28] Compounding the confusion was a dizzying assortment of papers that were already circulating among Palestinians, documents that the army, police, intelligence services, and rations inspector had distributed in the villages and towns occupied since May.[29]

The likelihood that Palestinians would take advantage of this documentary disarray to claim proof of legal residence was particularly disconcerting to the government in light of Israel's precarious standing in the international community. Earlier that month, concern over the ongoing state of war alongside Israel's refusal to repatriate Arab refugees or even define its borders had helped to derail the state's first bid for UN membership.[30] In truth, the fate of the new Arab minority that remained under Israeli control received little attention in the Security Council's deliberations.[31] But officials at the Foreign Ministry feared that Israel might jeopardize its second application if it openly denied suffrage in the upcoming elections to those Palestinians who claimed to be legal residents. Thus Ya'acov Shim'oni, in the ministry's Middle East Department, warned that a further delay in completing the census would "put us in danger and cause complications."[32]

With their hands tied by the state's tenuous international status, Israeli leaders resolved to complete the count of the Arab population while simultaneously working to reduce its size.[33] To this end, Ben-Gurion launched in early January what he called the "War on Infiltration," a massive bureaucratic, military, and ultimately legal campaign against Palestinian return, resettlement, and overall presence. For the next seven years, this campaign, more precisely named the "War on Return," became a frightening and fate-altering staple of Palestinian daily life in Israel.[34] Together, the Military Government and the Shin Bet, along with the new Border Guard and IDF Minorities Unit created specifically for the occasion, waged their battle on two fronts: along the edges of Israel's territorial holdings, and within the remaining Arab population centers now under martial law.[35] In each of these regions, Israeli forces regularly conducted surprise identity checks along the roads and sweeps inside villages and urban neighborhoods.[36] Accompanied by intelligence agents and Arab informants, armed troops would cordon off an area before dawn, wake up residents by loudspeaker, and summon them to the central square. Soldiers would then separate them into two holding pens—one for men, the other for women and children—and then check each person for their ID and expel or detain those who did not have proper papers.[37] The operation could last anywhere from seven to forty-eight hours, forcing residents to endure extreme weather conditions and go for hours without food or water. They often faced callous and undisciplined troops for whom physical abuse, plunder, and in some cases "pleasure" killing had become the norm over the previous year.[38]

As the War on Return unfolded, panic spread among tens of thousands of Palestinians who either had yet to be registered or had not yet received the documentation to prove that they had.[39] One reason for their dread was that census clerks had still not completed the count and registration in many communities. The panic stemmed from other reasons as well. Unlike Jews, most Palestinians experienced a significant lag between the actual count and the distribution of their IDs. On the day of the census, clerks issued "registration receipts" to all the Jewish adults they counted; these tiny paper stubs contained nothing but the name, number, and birthplace of their holders. They were difficult to verify and easy to lose, but between December and mid-January, the authorities completed the distribution of IDs to all Jews who had been registered.[40] Few Palestinians, by contrast, received receipts at the time of registration; they had to wait weeks, often months, and in some cases years before receiving first their receipts and then their blue-colored civil ID cards. Anyone without this ID was denied the rations books associated with the government's new austerity regime[41] and thus forced to pay high prices for food and clothes on the black market.[42] Palestinians without IDs, whose access to their farmlands was barred in most cases, could obtain neither a permit to leave their community nor a legal job through the government-run labor bureau.[43] They were also denied licenses to drive, to marry, and of course to vote.[44] Even worse was lacking the flimsy receipt that constituted the only evidence of their authorized presence in the country and to which Galilee residents reportedly "clung the way sweat clings to the body."[45] With living conditions already dire throughout the region due to the devastation wrought by the war, delays in the registration process left tens of thousands of Palestinians even more vulnerable to hunger, isolation, and banishment.[46]

The holdup in distributing the paperwork that Palestinians needed in order to live in relative safety was not the result of a master plan. There was, undoubtedly, a deliberate effort to thin out as much of the Arab population as possible, and the sweep operations offered an excellent cover to achieve that goal.[47] But technical problems with printing Arabic forms, inadequate resources to fund the registration bureaus, and the absence of political will to discipline troops played important roles as well.[48] For all of these reasons, the operations cast a

wide and more arbitrary net that drew in far more than the unauthorized returnees they were designed to catch.

Certain categories of people were especially vulnerable during the sweeps,
and the Border Guard expelled hundreds of individuals, families, and entire
communities from each group. First, in numerous villages, the clerks failed to
register the population for almost a year after the War on Return began.[49] Elsewhere they ran out of forms but failed to return to finish the job.[50] Also at risk
were thousands of Palestinians who did not yet appear on the registration rolls
but whose presence the local authorities had authorized after they missed the
census for reasons outside their control.[51] Prominent in this group were former
POW camp detainees and their wives, who were sometimes denied receipts in
order to pressure the couple to leave permanently.[52] University students abroad
whose parents had stayed in the country, the hospitalized, and some farmers
were also affected.[53] Rumors from neighbors about the wartime conduct of
those who were waiting for their IDs were enough to get them expelled.[54]

Many other Palestinians were endangered during the sweeps while waiting, and often pleading, for their receipts. A combination of enmity toward
Muslims, the thirst for revenge, and simple bad luck account for why troops
expelled only selected individuals and families from this group.[55] This was especially true in villages where residents had actively opposed Zionist colonization or cooperated with ALA units to defend their communities during the
war.[56] More calculated was the targeting of internal refugees, who had been
deported or otherwise displaced from their homes, and who numbered between 15 and 20 percent of the total Arab population that remained inside Jew-
ish-held territory after the war. The army barred the overwhelming majority
of these Palestinians from returning to their homes and lands. Although the
census staff registered these refugees wherever it found them, in many cases
it stalled on issuing their paperwork in order to facilitate their expulsion or
to pressure them to leave voluntarily.[57] But nonrefugees were also vulnerable.
Throughout the Galilee, sweep units deported hundreds of Palestinians from
their home villages and towns despite their possession of receipts and in some
cases after physically tearing them up.[58] Finally, several thousand Palestinians
carrying blue ID cards were driven within and across armistice lines. Some of
these expulsions became high-profile cases because they involved entire communities whose appeals reached the High Court of Justice,[59] but hundreds of
other ID holders, long forgotten, were expelled in order to deter their refugee
spouses from returning, and for other unknown reasons.[60]

OBSTACLES TO THE WAR ON RETURN

There is no doubt that the sweep operations that began in January 1949 contributed to the reduction of the Palestinian population in Israel and instilled terror throughout Arab communities in the Galilee and Negev. In the first four months alone the army expelled some two thousand people in the north, and those numbers would continue to rise.[61] Rather than dwell on the "success" of these operations, however, I want to consider their failures—to account for how refugee resettlement appears to have increased the Arab population in Israel by as much as 30 percent by the early 1950s.[62] Although no regime ever operates as the unified and omnipotent agent it claims to be, it is especially important to recall that in those early years, the institutions of the new Israeli state were under development and continual reconfiguration on the ground.[63] Examining this process up close enables us to demystify policies and laws that originated not from a rational, calculated plan but rather from a series of makeshift responses to unexpected challenges, internal struggles, and structural contradictions.

In fact, during Israel's first years of sovereignty, several factors worked in favor of Palestinian attempts to reverse their forced exodus. First, the disorganized and phased execution of the census made it easier for some people to return to their villages before the count.[64] A bigger problem was the army's scanty intelligence, poor coordination, and dearth of troops to patrol Israeli lines.[65] In the Galilee, Jewish settlers who might have supplemented this manpower were in limited supply, because the Zionist movement had failed to make a sizable dent there before the war.[66] Still, planters and town dwellers did not hesitate to ignore national ideological imperatives when they were desperate for working hands or simply had something to gain.[67] Throughout the country, police investigated and worked to try Jewish women and men suspected of harboring Arab returnees in exchange for cheap (and occasionally free) labor or smuggled cloth and foodstuffs.[68]

Of course the ultimate obstacle to the War on Return was the sheer determination of thousands of Palestinians to come home, to remain, and to protect others from capture. Returnees were hidden in attics and holy places.[69] Registration receipts were forged or passed on following the death of a relative or neighbor.[70] According to local lore, some men spent the little money they had to buy weapons on the black market in order to turn them in and gain leniency during the sweeps.[71] Women also went to great lengths to keep their families intact. Some who were engaged to men without papers managed to obtain speedy marriage licenses from Muslim and Christian personal status courts without proof of their fiancés' residency status.[72] At times, new mothers under similar circumstances took opposite tacks: some tried to procure IDs for their husbands after registering their newborns with the Interior Ministry; others hid their infants from the local governor in order to conceal the whereabouts of their paperless returnee husbands.[73]

Military officials seemed continually astonished by the negligible impact of their "psychological war on the Arab public,"[74] in particular the refusal of Palestinian families to cooperate with search units looking to rout out their unauthorized relatives and friends.[75] In September 1949, for example, the Western Galilee governor was flabbergasted that harboring did not abate after he issued an emergency regulation criminalizing the practice and personally plastered its announcement on community walls throughout the region.[76] Israel's failure to eliminate these "underground railroad stations," as one spokesman called them, was fueled in no small measure by the propensity of many Palestinians to return within days or weeks of their expulsion—often to be deported, and then return, once again.[77] As if infected with "return fever," or what the army dubbed "chronic infiltration," an average of a thousand refugees crossed into Israel each month, a flow that continued even after a free-fire policy issued in April 1949 turned the country's truce lines into killing fields that left a thousand dead by the end of that year.[78]

As spring turned into summer, Palestinians safely inside Israel began to test the limits of the government's pledge to liberal equality by protesting against the sweeps with petitions, critical reportage, street demonstrations, and Knesset inquiries. In these early and uncertain years, however, they faced a strategic and moral dilemma regarding the language of their opposition: was it more effective to focus on the principle and legality of the War on Return, or on the methods and brutality of its execution? And which of these choices was more true to their expectations and experience in the new state?

It is noteworthy how many private appeals and public petitions alike utilized the language of democratic citizenship to express their authors' discontent, revealing at least a strategic decision to hold Israel accountable for its claim to be exercising the rule of law. Many people spoke of the sweeps as a violation of their collective moral economy and conveyed their incredulity at the state's despotic treatment of legal citizens, as they saw themselves.[79] Complaints were also raised about the hours and days that people were forced to waste waiting in long lines to obtain the registration papers they needed.

Many questioned—in apparent earnestness—why the government was not doing more to help its citizens, precisely as the demand to carry receipts at all times was so high.[80]

The Galilee clergy became particularly vocal following the army's repeated damage to churches in depopulated locales, in addition to its humiliation of local priests and unauthorized church raids. In their petitions, the clergy repeatedly invoked the clauses of Nazareth's July 16, 1948 surrender agreement regarding the military's promise "to treat the residents of Nazareth [district] like all other residents [of Israel]." As one letter explained, their purpose in writing was "to inquire as to the army's powers to violate the law, as well as your own conscience and orders." On other occasions, they adopted the discourse of communal rather than civic rights. Questioning Israel's status as a democratic republic and positioning themselves as colonized subjects, the priests compared the sweeps to

> all these acts of terror that have been carried out in various parts of Africa, especially against Christians. These acts are growing day by day, and there is no escape from them. Fear has entered into the hearts of the residents, and everyone wonders if the government of Israel wants to . . . remove them from their homeland, even if they have an ID in their hands.[81]

The fact that the region's leading bishops and priests spent nine months sending unanswered letters to the military suggests the value they placed in holding it accountable to its agreements and professed principles. It was not until June 1949 that they finally recognized the futility of petitioning the army and redirected their complaints to Jerusalem, "denounc[ing] the [army's] shameful conduct, which stands in total violation of the promises, orders, and morality of the Israeli government."[82]

Throughout the War on Return, the public voice that most consistently decried the abuses of the authorities and vigilante settlers was that of the Communist Party: its four elected deputies (two Palestinians, two Jews), its activist base, and its weekly organs in Arabic (al-Ittihad) and Hebrew (Kol ha-'Am). For al-Ittihad in particular, the relentless, detailed coverage of collective sweeps, home invasions, and expulsions "without legal order or justification" cast light on what often appeared to be a blurry line between official and unofficial actions.[83] Although the military censor frequently removed lines and even whole paragraphs from its stories, news of the traumas resulting from the sweeps and relentless checking for IDs reached the public on a regular basis. In August

1949, *al-Ittihad* covered a series of violent home raids in Haifa that city residents believed were being carried out unofficially "to increase the pressure" on them.[84] In the months that followed, recurrent cases of arbitrary beatings and ID confiscations led editors to question the sincerity of the police's promises to investigate and punish the offenders. To the extent that its reports doubled as indirect petitions, *al-Ittihad* often invoked the Declaration of Independence and its pledge to equality regardless of race or creed. Following the post-sweep arrest of twelve receipt holders in al-Maghar, for example, the editors solemnly pronounced that "the expulsion of people carrying registration documents violates the most fundamental of rights enjoyed by all citizens of Israel" and asked where those "sacred rights . . . [had] gone."[85]

In the summer of 1949, outrage over large and brutal sweeps erupted into the first mass protests and petitions against the War on Return. Hundreds of people in Eastern Galilee villages and the central towns of Ramle and Lydd attended open meetings and cabled signed telegrams that detailed the soldiers' "aberrant" and "wanton" behavior and demanded the cancellation of "the military laws that anticipated them."[86] Some Palestinians were permanently radicalized by the acts of civil disobedience undertaken by older communist activists during the sweeps themselves. Watching them confront soldiers and lie on the ground to block the transport trucks from driving their neighbors and family to the border led scores of women and men to swell the party's ranks.[87]

Grassroots resistance on the ground escalated in tandem with formal protestations in parliament. Month after month, the young MAKI deputy, Tawfiq Tubi, demanded that Defense and Prime Minister Ben-Gurion clarify the legal basis of the expulsions without trial of registered residents, and that he release POW detainees whose families were still in the country.[88] Tubi's pointed questions lay bare what was in fact the lawless foundation of the War on Return and forced the revered Zionist leader to address the fundamental contradiction of the liberal settler state: between equality and the rule of law for all citizens, and the illiberal measures necessary to colonize the country for one group at the other's expense. Tubi and his colleagues scored a victory in August, when Ben-Gurion finally responded to his query about the case of seven men deported in March after soldiers tore up their registration receipts. Asked whether the authorities would reissue the men's papers upon their inevitable return, the prime minister announced that Israel would indeed allow back any Arab resident who was expelled while carrying a verifiable ID or receipt.[89] As I discuss later, the Military Government would experience these words as a blow. For although the expulsion of Palestinians who had never left the country continued, Ben-Gurion's pronouncement created a platform for further investigations and hundreds of successful appeals to the High Court.[90]

Although MAKI was alone in the Knesset in its opposition to the principle of the War on Return, complaints about its methods surfaced slowly from within Zionist parties as well. To the chagrin of the military and the Foreign Ministry, Western media coverage and complaints from foreign diplomats prompted open parliamentary as well as closed party debates—on the army's free-fire policy, the expulsion of paperless women and children, and the mistreatment of Palestinians on the way to deportation.[91] In June 1949, some in the left-Zionist MAPAM party—whose settler base had planted mines to keep Arab refugees from returning to the lands it had seized from them—voiced regret over the expulsion of some returnees from Abu Ghosh, near Jerusalem.[92] Villagers there had famously aided Jewish settlers and troops during the war, and until then the authorities had been treating their gradual return as an "open secret."[93]

The case of Abu Ghosh and the ambivalent blind eye that some authorities cast on its returning residents reflected a broader structural challenge to the War on Return. For all of its doomsday warnings, Israel's crusade to crush the tenacity of aspiring returnees was beset by a degree of quiet equivocation. In August 1949, the foreign minister admitted to charges raised on the Knesset floor that the government's resolve to combat infiltration had lapsed earlier that year. Apparently a few officials in the ruling MAPAI party had reconciled themselves to the inevitability and even "reasonableness" of some return,[94] especially as nuclear families sought to reunite and as diplomatic pressure to repatriate refugees intensified after the UN General Assembly passed Resolution 194 in support of that principle in December 1948.[95] In some cases, the regime may also have looked the other way as unauthorized returnees were hired to harvest their old crops on behalf of the less experienced, less willing, and at first unavailable (still conscripted) Jewish settlers who had taken their lands.[96] A much thornier problem was the unspoken conclusion that Israel could not safeguard its wartime gains without enlisting considerable numbers of Palestinians to help: as informants and cross-border spies to gather intelligence and seal migration routes;[97] as authorized smugglers to supplement the inadequate meat supply in the country;[98] as intermediaries to pressure remaining Arab landowners to sell their property;[99] and as imams to preach to congregants against sheltering returnees lest the entire community be expelled.[100]

The debate over the strategic advantages of selective return was inaugurated just weeks after the proclamation of independence. Joshua Palmon, the Haganah's chief handler of Palestinian informants and land agents in the waning years of the Mandate, was its most loyal advocate. Following a deluge of personal repatriation appeals from former residents of Jaffa and Haifa, Palmon argued that it might be "useful" in the future to allow back a select group of largely non-Muslim Arabs willing to sign a loyalty oath.[101] His proposal was vehemently opposed in the cabinet and rejected in favor of a blanket ban. Nonetheless, many Jews quietly embraced the return of particularly "friendly" or "peace-loving" Arabs, a label they applied mainly to religious and ethnic minorities such as the Druze, Circassians, and to some extent Christians, but also (as with Abu Ghosh) to select Arab Muslims who had provided economic or military aid to the Yishuv.[102]

Along with extending this latitude to "friends," the desire to mollify church officials abroad also led the foreign minister to authorize the return from Lebanon of Catholic refugees from 'Ilabun and Kafr Bir'im in late 1948 and early 1949.[103] Even the prime minister, who at first opposed any exception to the comprehensive ban on return, came around in the weeks leading up to his decision to launch his War on Infiltration. In November 1948, Ben-Gurion found himself in the unlikely position of trying to persuade his colleagues to repatriate nine thousand people from select Bedouin tribes who had taken shelter in the Jordanian-held West Bank. Not only would they guard the border effectively, he explained, but "we'll never work the land like they do, and there's plenty of room."[104]

High-level discussions of this sort were the exception during the first year of statehood, however, and many officials, operatives, and land agents had their own ideas about precisely which Palestinians the state should make room for.[105] Both on their own initiative and in response to Arab queries, each began to arrange the return or right to stay of certain families, employees, and acquaintances with whom they had contact.[106] The chaos resulting from the lack of oversight over this process came to a head in the spring of 1949, when officers in charge of sweep operations found themselves impotent to expel hundreds of Palestinians carrying unfamiliar certificates from various state agencies for temporary or permanent resettlement.[107] Over time, other tensions emerged as informants recruited for a designated period began to outstay their welcome or were caught smuggling contraband, as well as their own friends and family, over the border.[108]

EFFORTS TO MANAGE RETURN

Several initiatives adopted in the early summer of 1949 brought equal measures of order and confusion to the management of selective return. In May the government established a committee alongside the Immigration Ministry to oversee the handling of return requests from refugees who had "served the Yishuv and its authorized agencies" in the past or who were "likely to be of political, economic, or other use to the government of Israel in the present and future."[109] Spymaster Palmon was named as its chair, and in June he was promoted to the position of prime minister's senior advisor on Arab affairs. The creation of this position marked a turning point in Israel's approach to governing the Palestinian population. The former handler and his tiny staff of aides replaced the entire Ministry of Minorities, whose modest efforts to ease the plight of the population had earned the wrath of the prime minister and the army.[110]

The fact that the primary expertise of the leading government official now responsible for Arab affairs lay in the recruitment and management of Arab collaborators was to have enormous policy consequences moving forward. Palmon's commitment to this work was the legacy of a long-standing philosophy shared by British and Zionist leaders that the best way to govern the Palestinian Arabs was to foster internal divisions and bolster communal structures so as to inhibit the formation of united, secular-nationalist opposition to their dispossession.[111] The flight and expulsion of the Arab political elite during the war eased that task considerably, but it also created a political vacuum that the Communist Party—with its call for democratic unity with Jews on the basis of a common rule of law—was best primed to fill. Indeed, shortly before the first elections in January 1949, Ben-Gurion warned that the real danger in granting suffrage rights to Arabs was that Jews, who comprised two-thirds of the party's base, would elect them to office.[112] Thus, six months later, when the premier asked his new advisor to "concentrate all powers to *allow* infiltrators to enter or stay in the country,"[113] Palmon set his sites on potential strongmen in exile who could help to combat MAKI's influence.[114]

He did not have to wait long. On June 10, 1949, Palmon signed a secret agreement with Maximos V (George) Hakim, archbishop of the Galilee, a deal he hoped would simultaneously eliminate the scourge of Palestinian return, reduce international pressure on Israel, and combat the region's MAKI supporters with a large base of quietists. Hakim, born in Egypt to Syrian parents, had been a vocal opponent of both Jewish immigration and partition in the 1940s, and at the start of the war he formed an armed militia to defend Galilee Christians before fleeing to Lebanon.[115] He was also a renowned anticommunist. In February 1949, Israel permitted him to return in his capacity as a church official, but probably also as part of a political understanding.[116] Hakim immediately began to put out feelers to the authorities in the attempt to secure the release of church property and the repatriation of as many Greek Catholics from northern Palestine (now Israel) as possible. In the end, Palmon agreed to a maximum of seven thousand returnees, including up to two thousand people who were already in the country. Each "candidate" would have to be personally recommended by Hakim and cleared by the Shin Bet; refugees from depopulated villages, towns, and neighborhoods were excluded. In exchange, Hakim pledged to help "stop ongoing Christian infiltration"; end all clerical opposition to the War on Return; speak favorably in church forums about the treatment of the Arab minority; and conduct propaganda abroad to dissuade other refugees from trying to return.[117]

The active role of Arab Catholics in the Palestinian nationalist movement and their formation of defense militias in the Galilee would have made such a deal inconceivable only one year earlier.[118] But times had changed, and Hakim knew that the desperation of largely peasant families to reunite and to avoid the poverty and humiliation of exile would trump their political opposition to Zionism, and that it would likely endear them to him for years to come.[119] Palmon's effort to "promote" Hakim to represent the Arab minority as an antidote to MAKI's urban Greek Orthodox base in Haifa, Acre, and above all, "red" Nazareth, likely dovetailed with his own ambitions.[120]

Days after Palmon quietly shook hands with Hakim, Foreign Minister Sharett announced Israel's consent to the UN-sponsored Family Reunification program and invited "Arab [male] bread-winners lawfully resident in the country" to apply for the return of their wives and children still in exile.[121] Sharett refused to specify how many refugees would be allowed to return in this way, but officials privately expected a maximum of fifteen thousand—a far cry from the hundred thousand he had insincerely offered to accept at the regional armistice talks in April. At the time, Israel had wanted to bolster its second membership application at the United Nations and to placate American officials, who worried about the damage that their silence on the refugee question might do to their nascent diplomatic ties in the Arab world.[122] Two months later, an added incentive to join the Family Reunification program was the army's need to "sweep" the new eastern frontier, a narrow land strip of former Palestine known as the "Little Triangle" that Israel annexed from Jordan on May 1 as part of the armistice agreement signed in February. Since, as the army reasoned, dispersed relatives were the greatest source of infiltration, the Family Reunification program would reduce the army's burden in the north and allow it to redeploy some troops to the Triangle. There it could go about sorting local residents, whom Israel had promised not to harm, from refugees.[123]

As with the census, neither the Hakim deal nor the Family Reunification program got off to a smooth start. In the Eastern Galilee, the Military Government first heard about the closet agreement in July through a vague announcement by Nazareth priests at Sunday Mass, and until mid-September the misinterpretation of a cable from Palmon led to their delaying the expulsion of all Christian returnees.[124] In the Western Galilee, tempers flared as Hakim accused the governor of "illegally" detaining and in some cases expelling "his" people—the names of whom the governor furiously insisted he had not received—after the sweeps.[125] The Military Government's outrage over the damage being done to the War on Infiltration as a result of all the exceptions the government seemed to be making peaked when the commander discovered that local police in Shafa 'Amr had been issuing "infiltrator permits" to the archbishop's returnee candidates. "From now on," he informed Palmon, "I will completely refuse to discuss any recommendation to permit an infiltrator who has come in violation of the law to stay."[126]

Such hotheaded outbursts aside, mishaps in coordination and communication were minor compared to the growing crisis caused by the legal void in which the authorities were executing the War on Return. The Israeli government had intentionally postponed drafting legislation that would establish a universal definition of Israeli "citizen," or even "legal resident," in order first to reduce the number of Palestinians who could claim the future rights that would accompany either status. Paradoxically, it was precisely this holdup that left the authorities bereft of a rational framework to justify whom they could expel and how.

In August 1949, concern mounted at the highest levels of the Justice Ministry after the staff discovered a legal loophole that could enable aspiring returnees to sidestep the requirement to apply for the Family Reunification program from abroad. At issue was the interpretation of the Registration of Residents Ordinance, issued in February, which required the interior minister to register any person who had been "located in the country" already for three consecutive months. Although the original intention of the Israeli ordinance had been to facilitate the flow of the new state's burgeoning Jewish population, no one at the time had considered whether the minister was also obliged to apply this order to Palestinians. Now the question arose: Was the term *located* a mere physical designation, or did it have legal implications that would entitle registered residents to future citizenship?

M. A. Hartglass, staff attorney at the Interior Ministry's immigration desk, impatiently dismissed the hermeneutical handwringing of his colleagues. "The meaning of any law must derive from the social relations that produced it," he argued. "If the law speaks of a 'person located,' it is self-evident that it is intended to refer to a person who is legally located in that place, and not someone hiding from the authorities or *wandering around* in violation of the law. . . ."[127] The counsel's concern with legal location masked, of course, the irony that it was the Jewish state that had transformed Palestine's Arabs into "wanderers" and was now criminalizing their attempt to end that condition by returning home, or even to walk freely in their birthplace and on the land they had tilled. His explanation also did nothing to clarify the ambiguous status of the thousands of Palestinians who had never left the country but still had not been registered. More revealing was Hartglass's contention that jurists had the duty to interpret the ordinance in a manner that was "good for the state and the order that needs to prevail therein"—a reminder of the incompatibility between the Zionist dream in Palestine and the promise of universalism inherent in the rule of law.[128]

Questions of principle fell outside the jurisdiction of the Military Government, which was focused on the need to maximize the impact of the sweeps while shutting down the debate they were continuing to elicit. The army conceded that it could "avoid" some of the "drastic means" it had been using so as to avoid the impression that the state was launching a war against its own citizens.[129] But these reforms offered no solution to the growing influx of returnees, whose estimated number in September more than doubled the monthly average. According to military intelligence, many returnees were driven by the hope that once they reached home they could apply for family reunification and obtain retroactive permission to stay. Rumors circulating in the Lebanon refugee camps that the Red Cross was planning to cease its aid distribution also convinced some families that the danger of crossing into Israel was no greater than the prospect of trying to live under conditions even more insufferable than those they were already experiencing.[130] In the absence of a legislative framework to block this trend, the new returnees threatened to gain what Hartglass referred to as Israel's "imprimatur of legality."[131]

TRPs AND THE POLITICS OF NATURALIZATION

Over the next few months, Palmon hammered out the details of a new system of demographic regulation that would "achieve the concealment of the War on Infiltration."[132] At its center was the resuscitation of a provisional identity document from the Ottoman Empire. The selective distribution of this document would enable the government to freeze the process of extending legal status to its holders without having to deport them.[133] The targets of the TRPs were the tens of thousands of Palestinians in the country who remained unaccounted for in some way: they were either unregistered; in possession of suspicious registration receipts; or in possession of one of numerous provisional certificates issued not only by the police, Military Government, and the Interior Ministry but also by the security services and in some cases foreign consuls. This documentary potpourri made it difficult to distinguish between those Arabs whom the authorities considered legitimately entitled to be in the country and other Arabs who were not. The idea was to streamline the bureaucratic chaos by completing the registration of the Arab population and dividing those registered into two groups: those with state IDs and those with TRPs. The authorities could then invalidate all other papers and deport everyone who had neither.[134]

State and military authorities designed the TRP both to reduce discreetly the number of Palestinians with permanent rights in the country and to deepen the population's dependence on the regime for its basic needs. As was clarified at a planning meeting, "the fact that permit holders will need the military governor to renew or extend his permit will serve to tie them to him and enable him to maintain good relations with the public."[135] The final formulation that appeared in October highlighted the postwar power dynamics and cultural registers in which Israel transformed native Palestinians into "guests" in their own country:

> Completing the distribution of ID cards and TRPs should serve as an opportunity to check and cancel the . . . provisional certificates, to discover all those people located in the state as illegal guests. At the time of the distribution . . . District commissioners and military governors are requested to minimize the number they distribute in order to liberate the state from the presence of people with suspicious pasts or whose present behavior does not ensure that they will be quiet and desirable residents. [They] are called upon to act with extreme caution and to perform a detailed check of those requiring TRPs before issuing the licenses to them; this way only those who are suitable and kosher will be entitled to them. . . .[136]

Eligibility requirements for the TRP were cumbersome and complex. Any Palestinian who did not possess a civil ID was at the mercy of local military governors, who could choose to issue the permits for the duration of one month to one year. That choice was not arbitrary: governors had to justify to a special committee in Jerusalem their decision to issue the provisional permit on the basis of the applicant's "clean past" or his "quiet and straightforward" character, or if he or his children had fought alongside Israeli forces in 1948.[137] When the permit expired, the holder would either be expelled, obtain a civil ID, or have his TRP renewed; in the meantime he was technically safe from expulsion while the governor continued to test his "good behavior," "discipline," "loyalty to the state, and trustworthiness."[138] In creating a substitute for the permanent ID card, Israel produced a new class of thousands of Palestinians, largely Muslims, whose future legal status depended on their willingness to satisfy the whims of local Jewish military governors, police officers, and intelligence operatives.[139]

Although the government introduced the TRP as a way to simplify an already unwieldy bureaucratic process, distribution procedures were widely misunderstood, and there was delay, confusion, and an absence of coordination from the start. Because the bureaucrats charged with executing the system did not understand it, the TRPs ultimately exacerbated rather than eliminated the confusion of the registration process. Some governors, for instance, thought they were supposed to distribute the new permits to internal refugees only, while registration clerks often failed to conduct full security checks on permit applicants. Tensions ran particularly high between the Military Government and the police, who engaged in mutual recriminations in early 1950 when some twenty-five hundred Galilee residents received TRPs without police approval.[140] Technical delays also led the regime to distribute military IDs instead of TRPs in certain regions—precisely what the authorities in Jerusalem had wanted to avoid.[141] In the Negev, where the Interior Ministry was also ambivalent about issuing *any* papers to Bedouin, a hunger crisis emerged because Palestinians could not obtain ration books without them.[142]

Certain patterns surfaced in terms of who received a TRP and who did not, but in most cases individual circumstances defied the neat categories that the system's architects had established. A survey of one unusually detailed report on the distribution of TRPs in the Haifa district between late November and early December 1949 illustrates this point.[143] A handful of the eighty-five recipients named were former POW camp detainees and other residents whose registration receipts had "expired." Others had never been registered before because they had gone to work that day, because they had arrived from elsewhere in the country immediately afterward, or because the clerks had run out of forms. Still other TRP recipients claimed they had returned after the army had expelled them even though they had been counted and had never left the village—either because they were not carrying their papers at the time of a random ID check or because the army or intelligence services had confiscated their IDs. Finally, some TRPs were issued to people who had fled during the war to other villages inside the territory that became the new state and had returned home immediately after the registration. Most people had more unique circumstances, however. The following sample of TRP holders from the Haifa district illustrates not only the upheaval caused by the war and the rules of the new state but also the impossibility of containing human experience within bureaucratic abstractions:

- Man, age sixty. Returned from Lebanon with son's wife, eight months pregnant in February 1949.
- Man. Fled during the occupation and injured by the army during his escape. Carries receipt but no one would vouch for his presence during the census.
- Village imam and his wife. Fled and returned in November 1948. Claims that he was not registered the first time due to lack of forms, and that he missed it the second time because he was at work.
- Couple. Returned on April 1, 1949. Both the Muslim shaykh and Archbishop Hakim submitted special requests on their behalf. Officer Sabaji also recommended them.
- Shepherd. During the war went out to search for his flock. Detained and taken by the ALA to Lebanon. Returned in November 1948. Not counted due to lack of forms.
- Couple from Iʻblin. Fled with their children and lived in the fields. Returned around February-March 1949 and have been in village ever since.
- Man. Lived in Haifa, worked for Shell [Oil Co.] before the war. Fled to Nazareth and then Tamra. Here now for a year.
- Couple from Haifa. Fled to Tamra during the occupation but not registered there due to lack of forms.
- Several people living in area around [depopulated] Kawkab. Returned less than a year ago.
- Son of a Muslim mukhtar. Returned from Lebanon on March 15, 1949.
- Man. Studied at the Bayt Kadduri [agricultural] school in Tulkarm. Returned February 1949 and teaches agriculture in the village.[144]

Each of these cases had to be justified by the official who filled out the application. To the extent that Palmon issued clear guidelines that were supposed to inform each recommendation, the authorities did not always follow them consistently. In some cases, especially with minors who crossed the border alone, it was proposed that the applicants be allowed to stay provisionally, or that the government limit their punishment to a fine.[145] Other times, young children—boys in particular—were hunted down and expelled.[146] Returnees who voluntarily reported themselves to the authorities sometimes fared better, especially if they came before June 1, 1949. But their honesty could also work against them.[147]

More than inconsistency and coordination problems, what most troubled Palmon was that too many Palestinians were receiving TRPs in the first place. Jealously guarding each and every permit, Palmon repeatedly threatened to cancel any permits granted by Interior Ministry officials who had failed to conduct full security checks with the relevant government agencies. Nor did he hesitate to question military governors on their individual decisions.[148] In March 1950, the TRP committee reaffirmed that the permits should be granted "only in the most vital and necessary cases," that is, only "to those whom we do not want to grant IDs (and thus citizenship) and those whom we do not have the ability [read: legal authority] to deport."[149] In order to translate this principle into practice, the committee reduced all future permits to a maximum duration of one month[150] and further narrowed the categories of people eligible for them. No longer would Palestinians who had worked for the security services during or before the war receive automatic residency status, for instance. Instead they would now have to prove that they were still "necessary for, or beneficial to, one of the recognized institutions of the state, the economy, or the public."[151] If these measures removed certain ambiguities, the general disarray of the TRP program continued to create problems, including publicity headaches, for the authorities.[152]

THE POWER OF PAPER: INTIMIDATION, ABUSE, AND CORRUPTION

Accounts documented in memoirs, the military archives, and the Arabic press reveal that the authorities withheld civil IDs and held out the threat of expulsion in order to pressure Palestinians into selling their land, working as informants at home and abroad, and campaigning for the government's ruling party during election seasons. Families who sought to bring their relatives home from exile were similarly squeezed. These threats were not empty, and they served throughout the early years of Israeli statehood to organize daily life around the perpetual threat of expulsion.

The exploitation of Palestinians' vulnerability vis-à-vis the papers they did or did not carry intensified as returnees became increasingly desperate—and determined—to stay. In late 1950, a group of residents from the Central Galilee village of Dayr Hanna hired an attorney after the authorities failed to respond to their complaints of being terrorized by two Military Government officers in their village. The accusations they leveled at the officers included beating, extortion, theft, and various acts of humiliation—such as urinating on residents and bringing a dog to defecate inside the mosque—but the most prominent charge was that the officers had compelled residents to sign documents that threatened either their own legal status or the status of others. One woman, for example, watched an officer beat her husband until she "confessed" to falsifying another woman's ID, and a male refugee living in the village was beaten until he initialed a statement that said he and his family wished to be expelled. Three other residents had their IDs confiscated, and five more were summoned and accused of threatening a sixth man to leave the village.[153]

This kind of cruelty contributed to the general climate of intimidation that was fostered in the hopes of encouraging Palestinians to emigrate. Other forms of coercion were more structural than physical and were tied to the immediate policy aims of the state. Arab landowners were specially targeted, and the authorities often used collective punishment to pressure individual families to consent to their own dispossession. Consider the case of nearby 'Ilabun, a largely Greek Catholic village. As late as July 1951, the village's seven hundred residents signed a petition to the Foreign Ministry in which they protested the government's ongoing refusal to exchange their military IDs for civil IDs, which blocked access to their lands as well as their right to vote in the upcoming parliamentary elections.

The problem in 'Ilabun dated back to October 1948, when the Israeli military unit that occupied their village murdered twelve residents and expelled the rest, who were subsequently invited back as a goodwill gesture to church officials abroad. At issue three years later was the refusal of six farmers to accept the confiscation of their orchards on the basis of the March 1950 Absentee Property Law, which offered a permanent legal seal on all prior "emergency" expropriations since the war.[154] Now the government was trying to force the six 'Ilabun residents to lease their own land back from the state:

> We have already sent numerous cables and petitions that prove our loyalty to the State of Israel and our innocence of any criminal charges in the eyes of

the law. Your Excellency, we do not consider ourselves to be absentees, we do not revolt against the government, and we are famous for our obedience. But this law does not apply to the residents of our village because we stayed in our homes until the army arrived and removed us . . . and we submitted completely to the authority of Israel, hoping that we would live a happy life. . . . [W]e shout and say that we are oppressed, very oppressed, and we seek your mercy to issue orders to stop the implementation of the restrictions on absentee property. . . . We hope you will issue orders to exchange our IDs lest we be prevented from voting in the elections. . . .[155]

While the people of 'Ilabun were using the language of the democratic rule of law to plead their case, the Military Government withheld more civil IDs in order to prevent its implementation. Nimr Murqus, a former teacher, mayor, and MAKI activist in Kafr Yasif, recounts in his 1999 memoir how a high-ranking officer tried to cut a deal with a party comrade named Nicola Farah on the eve of the first Knesset elections in January 1949. In Murqus's account, the officer offered to stop the expulsion orders of Farah's two brothers and to furnish them with civil IDs on condition that Farah set fire to the local party headquarters on the night before the elections.[156] Novelist Hanna Ibrahim tells the story in his autobiography of a young man he knew who was loudly cursing MAKI, to no one in particular, as he walked down the street. When Ibrahim confronted the young man, he quietly explained that he was shouting "in order to guarantee his freedom."[157] Having managed to return home twice with his brother following their post-sweep expulsions, the two men blocked their third expulsion and obtained TRPs from the Acre police chief on the condition that they publicly slander the Communist Party. Still other Palestinians were forced to campaign for the ruling MAPAI party in order to return home from Lebanon or to obtain IDs for their relatives there.[158]

Not everyone agreed to work for the authorities in order to secure their right to stay in the new state. Murqus recounts the case of a certain Dawud from Kafr Yasif, a former employee of the Iraq Petroleum Company in Haifa who was forced to leave Palestine when the firm's offices moved to Beirut during the war. Unbeknownst to Dawud, the relative who helped bring him home to his parents from exile was working for Israeli intelligence in Lebanon. Soon after his return, Dawud was invited by Captain Haim Auerbach, a former Haganah intelligence officer, to perform the same work as his cousin—"to bring us information that we want from our people in Lebanon, and to take whatever we give you to them." When Dawud refused, Auerbach ordered his immediate expulsion. His family never saw him again.[159]

Feasting on the Frontier

By far the best-documented form of abuse and corruption revolved around Palestinian conventions of hospitality. Disguised as a "cultural" and thus apolitical act, the practice of feeding Military Government officials and police officers offered a supple space for material exploitation by the authorities, on the one hand, and for negotiations and bribery by villagers, on the other. Today, few recognize the role that military rule played in fostering the tradition of Jewish consumption and tourism in Palestinian villages and towns—an industry that boomed in the 1990s and that the state has long promoted as a form of "coexistence."[160] In other words, the personal fiefdoms of control created by military governors were also fiefdoms of leisure. In the 1950s, food in general and mealtime in particular became central venues for Palestinian-Jewish encounters, both real and imagined.[161]

In the initial years of Israeli statehood, the frequency with which some governors and other Military Government officials took advantage of Palestinian hospitality imposed an enormous financial and physical burden on their hosts, who often felt obligated to serve meat and other delicacies they could not afford in honor of their guests.[162] Nor was vulnerability to this pressure limited to rural villagers. Shortly before the 1954 municipal elections in Nazareth, Mayor Yusif al-Fahum reportedly moved out of the city and declined to renew his political candidacy in order to escape the weekly and uninvited arrival of the governor and his friends for Saturday lunch. The feasts, which forced the mayor to buy meat on the black market, were ultimately threatening to bankrupt him.[163]

Of course the vulnerability that made these encounters possible could also backfire or carry unanticipated costs. Some Palestinians tried to exploit the temptations of Jewish officers and clerks in order to sweeten their lonely (and to the officers' and clerks' minds, unappreciated) work on the frontier by trying to secure certain privileges and promises in exchange. Thus, in late 1949, the top brass of the Military Government announced its first restrictions on all recreational encounters with Arabs out of fear that low-ranking officers, bureaucrats, and perhaps even civilians were eating too often, and perhaps too much, in Arab homes. The commander also gathered his entire staff to remind them that everyone was required to follow "strict orders on gatherings and meals in

Arab villages" and should "undertake visits . . . without promis[ing residents] to take care of anything."[164]

Yet the phenomenon of mealtime bribery did not disappear. In April 1950, an anonymous Palestinian informant urged the interior minister to investigate the provision of TRPs to ineligible Galilee residents who were offering gifts of hand-carved stone utensils to high-ranking Jewish police officers and military officials. According to the informant, these same officials had informed another group of families who *were* eligible for TRPs that "they had to leave the country" after the families ran out of money to continue the "weekly parties" they had hosted for the officers and their wives.[165] Such practices only increased as Palestinians began to understand the legal insecurity associated with TRPs. Starting in May 1950, the prospect of receiving the dreaded "red IDs," as they were known, led a number of Galilee villages to hold feasts for the clerks who came to exchange residents' registration receipts for blue (permanent) and red (temporary) residency cards. Both the climate of terror under military rule and the seeming capriciousness that characterized the exchange process itself contributed to the assumption that civil IDs would go only to government supporters. One reporter described the scene in Majd al-Krum, where the process began in May 1950:

> A poor and miserable peasant approaches the throne of the clerks as though he is entering God's Last Judgment with the ghost of the "Red ID" hovering over him. First his registration receipt is taken from him, and then the clerks begin to fire a series of threatening questions at him. . . . If he stammers or gets confused in his answer they give him a red ID. An accusation that the person went to Lebanon constitutes an official threat that the investigators level against anyone who applies for an ID, and even the elderly are questioned in a threatening voice about their weapons and the places where they fought the Jews![166]

As it turned out, the villagers grossly overestimated the power of the clerks to decide their fate. However, when a small group began to "lavish food" on their guests, the clerks did nothing to disabuse them of their illusion. As memoirist Hanna Ibrahim recalls,

> They worked at a leisurely pace, taking pleasure in what they imagined to be the villagers' [traditional Arab] generosity, and a system was organized so that each day a different family would take turns feeding them. Every man thought that the future of his family was conditional upon the clerks' feelings and figured that

honoring them would bring something good in return. It would not be an exaggeration to say that every day, lunchtime commenced with a real party, and the clerks would sometimes invite their friends to join them in the fun. But this generosity and sacrifice, offered under dire economic circumstances, was in vain . . . for the people faced the distribution of over 500 TRPs. They were humiliated and angry, and there were attempts to take revenge on th[e] mukhtar. . . . We rushed to clarify [that it was not his fault] and to expose the government's plan.[167]

Although local activists tried to raise awareness about the disaster that had befallen Majd al-Krum, including the distribution of five hundred red IDs, these events repeated themselves as the registration units made their way across the Galilee. Five months later, the mukhtar in nearby Dayr al-Asad announced that the purpose of the "tax" he had collected from all registered villagers was to hold a "party" for the governor and the clerks when they come to distribute IDs.[168] The scandal there peaked two months later, when it was reported that the authorities had distributed TRPs and civil IDs along the lines of local clan politics, such that individuals belonging to families out of favor with the mukhtar who were supposed to receive blue papers received red ones, and vice versa.[169] Nearly one year later, the problem was evidently so persistent that the Military Government issued a new rule barring clerks "from holding meals in Arab locales without prior authorization from the governor." Although some governors believed that the regulation would be "impossible to enforce from a practical standpoint," they decided to require "any clerk who invites himself to meals which seem unjustified" to submit a report of explanation to his supervisor.[170]

Collaborators and Charges of Illicitness

Some Palestinians also found ways to exploit the disorder of the registration process for personal gain. A few village and tribal leaders, for instance, demanded bribes to arrange people's paperwork, nearly always on false pretenses.[171] Others coerced residents into working for them without pay by threatening to tell the authorities to give them TRPs instead of civil IDs, or to report returnees unless the latter, who sometimes carried black-market cloth and cigarette paper, sold them their goods at a pittance.[172]

Ordinary people also used the crisis of paperwork to their advantage—to lighten their criminal sentences, to curry favor with the authorities, and to settle personal scores.[173] The archives are filled with detailed letters from Palestinians who accused others of residing in the country without permission and of illegally marrying off their children, who had the same status as their parents, to civil ID holders.[174] Authorities took these letters seriously even though not all of them were written by hired informants. The complainants often urged the expulsion of the individuals in question and at times questioned Israel's determination to fight the War on Return.[175]

On February 10, 1952, for instance, the interior minister received an anonymous tip accusing the mukhtar in 'Ayn Mahil of bribing the Arab clerks in Nazareth's registration bureau with "cash, cracked wheat, lentils, and a large chicken lunch in exchange for registration forms dated May 13, 1949." According to the report, some thirty families, totaling more than eighty people, had received fraudulent papers in this manner. The mukhtar later denied the charge, which he said was "leveled by someone prepared to use any means of corruption to prevent [the residents] from obtaining IDs."[176]

Other charges of infiltration were more explicitly personal, as this undated letter to the Eastern Galilee governor attests:

> There are infiltrators living in the eastern quarter of Nazareth, Street 711, in a small shack near the home of [named man]. The woman has three children who do not carry ID cards. She has married off her daughter despite the fact that she does not carry an ID. . . . Her sons [named] . . . also do not carry IDs. I am asking you to bring them to court now because she is attracting smugglers to the neighborhood, and the residents are worried.[177]

We have no way to verify whether the author's concern was shared by all residents of Nazareth's most impoverished neighborhood, many of whom were internal refugees and faced the same legal uncertainties. Yet the presence of accused smugglers in an Arab neighborhood *was* likely to attract the attention of the police, something that would expose the community to more frequent home raids and heightened surveillance on the streets. To accuse someone of a crime that could get them deported does not fall into the realm of petty neighborly disputes, but it is noteworthy that the author did not pretend to share the government's political rationale for the War on Return.

LOOKING FOR COVER

Whether the complainants were Jewish or Arab, military or civilian, calls on the government to pursue legal action against Palestinian returnees rested on the false assumption that it had a system in place to do so. In practice, Israeli authorities knew that each and every detention, trial, and expulsion order they issued against an accused infiltrator, each decision to issue one permit or deny another, took place "without suitable legal cover."[178] Fundamental questions and legal vulnerabilities stemming from the absence of Knesset statutes on citizenship and entry, immigration and passports, deportation, and even "infiltration" itself made the execution of the War on Return extremely cumbersome for Palmon and his associates. Could they invoke the British Defense Emergency Regulations (DERs) in order to expel a former citizen who had not acted against state security? What difference did it make, as the prime minister had declared in September 1949 that it would, whether that person carried an ID or proof of registration? Did Palestinians have any right to contest their expulsion, past or future? Could they use their Mandate passports as the basis to demand IDs, as well as future citizenship in the Jewish state? It would take four laws, six years, and multiple court cases to answer these questions.

The Law of Return

The Israeli cabinet first considered a citizenship bill in the midst of its war to secure sovereignty and to expand beyond the borders that the United Nations had allocated to the Jewish state in November 1947. In May 1948, the provisional government had reiterated its pledge to swiftly ratify a constitution that would extend "full and equal citizenship" to the state's Arab residents in accordance with its obligations under the Partition Plan. Separate from the ongoing work to draft the constitution, attorneys at the Justice Ministry set out to draft a citizenship law that would uphold its declared commitment to equality while at the same time providing for open Jewish immigration, which the British had restricted since the 1930s. But the prime minister, who resented the burden of "unnecessary legal procedures," stymied their efforts by rejecting each text they submitted.[179] In his thinking, any citizenship law that did not explicitly distinguish between the rights of Arabs and Jews would make it easier for Palestinian refugees to return.[180]

Ben-Gurion's fear would paralyze the legislative process. In February 1949, he led a successful campaign to suspend the public debate over the constitution, which he threatened would obstruct the "legal flexibility" still necessary for "the mainstays of the state and its future . . . security, Aliyah [Jewish immigration], and settlement."[181] The citizenship bill fared no better. By November, Ben-Gurion had rejected all eighteen drafts presented to him by the three different Knesset committees he had tasked to work on it.[182] In short, none of the state's legal experts could reconcile the contradiction between a state belonging exclusively to one racial or ethnic group and a democratic republic of all citizens.

Although the official absence of citizens in Israel had not endangered the legal security of its Jewish residents, many in the government were losing patience. Their concern, notably, was not that the legislative stalemate had sabotaged the state's second bid for UN membership. In May 1949, an overwhelming majority on the Security Council had voted in Israel's favor. Satisfied with the conclusion of its armistice agreements and its tentative offer to repatriate one hundred thousand refugees, the UN admitted Israel without compelling the new state to reverse its blanket ban on refugee return or—in the face of its military rule over "minority" towns and villages—to demonstrate its commitment to constitutional equality. But the legislative impasse was producing other problems in the international arena, not only encumbering the travel of Jewish residents abroad, as we saw at the opening of this chapter, but also thwarting the state's ability to sign onto various commercial and military treaties.[183] Ironically, the legal void was also causing nightmares at Israeli consular offices around the world, where wealthier Arab citizens of Palestine were showing up to fill out the paperwork to return.[184]

The deadlock finally broke in December 1949, thanks to a proposal from deputy Zorah Warhaftig of the United Religious Front. Deliberately circumventing the nondiscrimination requirement in the earlier drafts of the bill, the Polish-born jurist recommended the creation of a separate legal category, one before and above that of citizenship, that would clarify the parameters of ultimate belonging in the Jewish national polity. The proposed "Law of Return to Zion" focused on immigration and its crucial role in resurrecting the two-thousand-year-old kingdom of the Jewish people. It is best known for endowing all Jews everywhere with the automatic right to move to Israel and become full nationals therein. Crucially, the bill also stipulated that all Jews already living in the country, including its native-born, would count as "immigrants" in order to accord them the same privileges.[185] The only people whose legal ties to the state would remain unresolved by the law were the Palestinian Arabs.

Ben-Gurion jumped on Warhaftig's idea because of the wedge it drove between Jewish rights *to* the sovereign state and the supposedly universal rights *in* that state that could follow. Such a formula posed no dilemma for the veteran leader, for whom the ongoing project of colonization (*hityashvut*) necessarily prohibited the treatment of Jews and Arabs as equals. As a sovereign state, he explained to fellow MAPAI leaders, Israel could grant and deny legal status as it pleased: "There is no automatic citizenship here, and when you forfeit this notion you commit heresy against the entire principle of the state."[186] Modern juridical categories were of little interest to the leader, particularly if they put the individual before the nation.[187] In a private meeting with the justice minister in May 1950, Ben-Gurion argued that citizenship was an "artificial, foreign" concept superseded by the ancient attachment of the Jewish people to the Land of Israel. "We must adapt the juridical form to the national historical content [*ha-tokhen ha-histori ha-le'umi*]," he explained, "and not the reverse."[188] Two months later, as he lobbied for the bill on the Knesset floor, the premier reiterated the legal precedence of Jewish peoplehood even as he paid lip service to the contrary and proclaimed that Jews had "no right of priority over non-Jew[s]" in the state.[189]

In its explicit privileging of the rights of all Jews in the world at the expense of native non-Jews, the Law of Return became Israel's first legal nail in the coffin against the homecoming of Palestinian refugees, and the cornerstone of racial segregation between Israeli citizens. It also buried the constitutional debate for good. Shortly before the law's passage in July, the Knesset changed course and decided to develop the internationally required constitution in stages, one "basic law" at a time.[190] As the first such statute, the celebrated "Charter of Rights guaranteed to every Jew in Israel" was embraced unanimously outside of MAKI.[191] Privately, however, justice officials remained uneasy. Although Israel had joined the United Nations the previous May, they worried that the blatant discrimination contained in what the premier had dubbed the "Proclamation of Zionism" would compromise the country's international standing.[192] (Nor could Israeli diplomats point plausibly to the pledge to equality in the Declaration of Independence as a fig leaf. In December 1948, the High Court had ruled that the document could not serve as a gauge for the validity of other laws because it lacked constitutional status.[193]) Thus Attorney General Haim Cohen urged legislators to frame all future bills in universal terms—that is, without particular reference to Jews.[194]

One week after the Knesset approved the Law of Return, the interior minister presented the draft citizenship bill, now in its nineteenth iteration, to members for the first time. In an opening address that betrayed the precise insensitivity to international opinion against which the attorney general had warned, Moshe Shapira congratulated the government for upholding the biblical commandment to apply "one law, both for the stranger and for him that was born in the land."[195] Not only was the minister openly acknowledging the government's racial understanding of the notion of nativity—virtually all Palestinians in Israel at the time were home-born—but his claim to the law's universalism was also patently disingenuous. As the law was formulated, Israel would grant automatic citizenship to all Jews in the country, by virtue of their "immigrant" status, but only to 63,000 Palestinian Arabs, by virtue of their residence. This figure, which included most of the Arabs who were registered during the first census in November 1948, was estimated to include a minority, between 35 and 50 percent, of the estimated 160,000 Arabs then living in Israel.[196] Everyone else would have to meet a host of conditions in order to naturalize, including proof of their "legal residence" in Israel for at least three of the previous five years, demonstration of their command of Hebrew, and a declaration of loyalty.[197]

The bill was widely debated, with opposition revolving around the restrictions on Arab citizenship and whether Jewish immigrants should be allowed to retain their old nationality alongside their new one.[198] As per procedure, the Knesset returned the draft bill to the legislation committee, where it sat for six months. Then, in January 1951, just as the revised bill was ready to be returned to the floor, the government suspended the process once again.[199]

Court Battles

Palestinians did not stand by passively as this process was unfolding. The religious conversion to Judaism of some refugees willing to seize whatever "right of return" they could get was certainly not a challenge for which Jewish officials had prepared.[200] It was the judiciary, however, and not the rabbinate, that became the primary address for Palestinian resistance within the system. As we have seen, relentless pressure from Tawfiq Tubi and a handful of other Knesset members in the summer of 1949 led the prime minister to concede that any Arab who could prove that he or she had been expelled while carrying an ID or registration receipt should be allowed to return. Ben-Gurion did not specify how this might happen, but the mechanism that attorneys developed was to petition the High Court for a temporary injunction to block the deportation order of a Palestinian plaintiff—usually someone caught after reentering the country following a previous expulsion—and file for either a civil ID or an invalidation of the order. If the Court accepted the petition, it gave the authorities a few weeks to explain the basis of their order and, for example, provide evidence that the plaintiff had not in fact carried valid papers at the time of his or her prior expulsion.

Few returnees under threat of deportation had the material, intellectual, and emotional resources to reach the Court in the first place. Beyond a basic awareness of the appeal process, petitioners needed a formal affidavit, the money to pay the attorney's fee, multiple witnesses, and the courage to persist with their case despite threats from police and military officials.[201] Even then the Court, which prioritized Jewish state building as a "cardinal and supreme value," rejected most petitions outright.[202] Labeling all petitioners a "grave security threat" and a "danger to public order," its justices not only affirmed the normative value of "purify[ing] the country of its undesirable elements,"[203] but also went out of their way to facilitate the project.[204]

Despite the commitment of Israel's leading jurists to Zionism, it was to the advantage of Arab plaintiffs in those early years that Israeli jurists also sought desperately to assert their professional independence—to establish a culture of "legalism" now that the heady days of "illegalist" pioneering and frontier justice were behind them.[205] For this reason, the High Court did accept a considerable number of returnee petitions on technical grounds: for instance, when they believed that an expulsion had been carried out without due authorization or ordered as a way to pressure someone under interrogation.[206] Between 1950 and 1952, the discovery of these and other procedural "defects" led the Court to order the interior minister to issue IDs to at least 865 plaintiffs.[207] Even then, however, justices were careful to underscore the narrow meaning of these rulings. In one of the first such injunction cases, Justice Heshin argued that although the interior minister was required to issue a civil ID to a registered resident, the document offered its holder no legal protection per se because his presence in the country was based on "mercy" (*yeshivah ba-hesed*), not right.[208] Perhaps out of fear of international criticism, in April 1950 the government rejected proposals from Palmon and the Military Government to announce this as official policy.[209]

Beyond the juridical headaches created by the government's violation of its own administrative procedures (for example, expelling people who carried valid papers), the reliance on two problematic legal paths to expel Palestinians constituted a deeper liability in the War on Return.[210] Regulation 112 of the 1945 DERs provided for the deportation of citizens "suspected of treachery" after a signed order from the defense minister. Because this charge would be impossible to sustain en masse, and because the implementation of the regulation was impractical, the High Court justices recommended that prosecutors use it only when other legal instruments were unavailable.[211] Within civil law, the only expulsion tool at the government's disposal was the 1941 Immigration Ordinance still in force since the Knesset had yet to pass a replacement. Covering only noncitizens and nonresidents, this statute had been formulated by the British to restrict Jewish immigration. In July 1949, however, the senior legal advisor to the Interior Ministry cautioned strongly against its use. Technically speaking, he believed, Arab returnees were residents of Israel and still citizens of Palestine.

Jewish jurists were in fact divided over Israel's obligation under international law to recognize the validity of Palestinian citizenship. Unpleasant though it may have been, the question was difficult to avoid in light of Israel's Law and Administration Ordinance No. 1, an emergency measure passed just after the announcement of statehood that rendered all mandatory laws valid in the new state until specific Israeli legislation nullified them. This wholesale legislative transfer produced some unanticipated rulings. In April 1951, the Tel Aviv District Court reversed a previous decision and ruled that until the Knesset passed a citizenship law to replace its 1925 counterpart, the international principle of succession obliged Israel to recognize the ipso facto legal status of all former citizens of Palestine. "Any other view," the judge explained, "must lead to the absurd result of a State without nationals."[212]

Hanna Naqara stood at the helm of attorneys who sued for injunctions against military and government expulsions. Born in the Galilee and admired in the military prosecutor's office as a "fearless warrior" for his clients, he joined the Communist Party in 1949.[213] Himself a returnee of atypical circumstances,[214] Naqara won his first ruling against the government in February 1950, when the High Court blocked the expulsion of a thirteen-year-old boy who had returned from Gaza to his father in Jaffa.[215] But his big break came at the end of that year.

In the summer of 1950, news of the distribution of five hundred TRPs in Majd al-Krum began to embolden neighboring villages, whose residents prepared for a documentary showdown.[216] Thanks to a well-planned grassroots campaign, the hundreds of people in Bi'na who were still waiting to exchange their registration receipts for IDs resolved that they would serve no food or coffee to the registration clerks when they came.[217] More significantly, they agreed that if just one TRP was issued, they would boycott the entire registration procedure, meet with the Acre governor—who had already cut off the travel permits of local organizers and banished the secretary of the local MAKI chapter to another village—and sue for civil IDs in court.[218]

When the clerks arrived in Majd al-Krum in October, villagers stood their ground despite the authorities' circulation of rumors that the entire village would be punished for the insubordination of the boycotters.[219] After four days had passed and not a single ID had been distributed, the registration unit gave up and moved on to other communities, where it met the same resistance. Shortly thereafter, seventy receipt holders in Bi'na and eighty-five of their neighbors from Dayr al-Asad signed over their power of attorney to Naqara, who filed High Court petitions on their behalf. He won civil IDs for every single one of his clients after neither the civil nor the military authorities could provide compelling evidence to deny them.[220] Days later, the people of Bi'na and Dayr al-Asad feted their revered attorney, and for years they continued to chant the songs of their victory:

> Girls of the village, repeat after me:
> May God vindicate the Communist Party.
> Hanna Naqara brought the ID;
> Ben-Gurion's plans met with ignominy.
> Attorney Naqara, we're devoted to you;
> Go to hell—we don't care if it's red or it's blue.
> Hey, Abu Khadr, come drag us from here;
> Of the regime and its rulers we have nothing to fear.
>
> Hey Abu Khadr, take us now, go ahead;
> Go to hell—we don't care if it's blue or it's red.
> May God cause my assailant to grieve;
> Even if he's the governor in Tel Aviv.
> Tubi and Habibi are preparing the fight;
> Along with the Party, the revolt they'll ignite.[221]

Naqara's victory dealt a stunning blow to Palmon and the military prosecutor. Fearful of the precedent the case may have set, they swiftly issued IDs to the plaintiffs who were likely to defeat them in court.[222] Although TRPs did not disappear altogether, the Bi'na and Dayr al-Asad rulings and the boycotting campaign do seem to have ended the distribution of the dreaded red IDs en masse.[223] Over the next year, the Military Government and Interior Ministry were flooded with hundreds of further injunctions on behalf of Palestinians seeking to end the crisis of their paperless status. Palmon and his colleagues divided their time between fighting these cases wherever possible and searching for new administrative measures to block the injunction process altogether. They also knew that such makeshift fixes were no substitute for legislation.[224]

This problem was thrown into relief again in June 1951, when the High Court issued a temporary injunction against the detention of twenty-three Palestinians from Majd al-Krum who had been expelled during a sweep in early 1949. The names of the deportees had been recorded in the Population Registry, but they lacked the receipts to prove that they had been physically present during the census. At the time of the order, five of them had already returned, and the other eighteen were on the way. If Palmon was shocked by the Court's decision to delay the expulsion of "infiltrators" who had been exiled in Lebanon for nearly three years, he was scandalized by its ruling in their favor the following month.[225] In a lengthy memo, he urged his colleagues in the Prime Minister's Bureau to appreciate the hazard of continuing to prosecute the War on Return under conditions of effective lawlessness:

> There is a grave and serious danger because there are several thousand refugees in Lebanon in a similar situation [to that of the Majd al-Krum plaintiffs] who will also wish to return. The success of these Arabs will ... bring ... the return of many people who in fact have not been in the country and were not registered. *This is because the law does not prevent entry on principle.* At the most it prevents them from entering through points outside the recognized border stations, [an offense that] carries a small punishment and does not lead to expulsion. For two years now I have been warning against this grave situation, its history, and its consequences. *The ... Justice Ministry is not achieving the needs of the state. The policies and actions of the government in many cases do not have legal cover.* The state prosecutor is loaded with work and is missing out on trials that are likely to become definitive precedents followed by explosions in the ... law.

Since, as Palmon saw it, the authorities could not rely on the High Court to protect the "needs of the state," he pressed for the government to resume the legislative process that it had suspended seven months earlier. Only the swift passage of what he called "suitable" citizenship and immigration laws would "cover" their campaign to block the permanent settlement and resettlement of more Palestinians in Israel.[226]

Palmon was correct about the government's need for new laws but wrong about the High Court's commitment to the principle of Jewish privilege. In November 1951, shortly after the Majd al-Krum ruling, Israeli jurists ruled that the requirement in the February 1949 Registration of Residents Ordinance that all people record their names in the Population Registry after three months of residence in the country had no bearing on the future citizenship status of those registered.[227] The following month, the High Court applied its decision against six returnees from Kafr Yasif who had appealed for civil IDs on the basis of the three-month stipulation. Military and government officials involved in the War on Return read the verdict as a landmark precedent for the denial of civil IDs to Arab residents on security grounds and circulated the part of the text they found most relevant:

> In these frenzied days—at times when the state is . . . surrounded on all sides by enemy nations that waged brutal war against it in the past and continue to harm it with every step, question, and statement in order to swallow it alive—the very people who abandon and cross over to the enemy camp are returning. They pretend to be loyal residents . . . and dare . . . to demand equal citizenship. . . . [T]hey appeal to the High Court of Justice, concealing the truth . . . [and] insisting on justice. The Court [will not] acquiesce to . . . this custom. Hiding basic facts has, and always will, result in the failure of the plaintiff's request. . . . Nor will [we] . . . provide . . . aid and welfare [to] a *person who wanders willfully and aimlessly without a permit* from the lines of the state's defense to those of the enemy's attack . . . in precisely that struggle which the military is fighting in order to defend the state and its citizens. The Court will not force a civil institution . . . to furnish [such a] person with an ID to prevent the military . . . from prosecuting him for endangering the state.[228]

The emotional language of the December 1951 ruling gave wide license to the government to treat all paperless Palestinians as "willful and aimless" itinerants, hostile and conniving "wanderers," until they could prove otherwise. It was helpful to Palmon and his colleagues on two levels. First, it eliminated any doubt regarding the judiciary's lockstep identification with the government over the fundamental questions of land and people at the heart of the Zionist movement. More important, the ruling bestowed a juridical imprimatur upon the regime's incitement of the Jewish public to regard the remaining Arabs of the country as a security threat and as aliens. The justification for statutory inequality was deepening.

Legislating Inequality

The timing of the High Court ruling was especially helpful to the interior minister, who would mobilize the threat of infiltration and "foreign plots" as a rationale for the restrictions built into the citizenship bill. One month earlier, the cabinet had ended the year-and-a-half-long stalemate by approving the twentieth draft of the law for a second round of Knesset deliberations. As during the first reading, the conditions it imposed on Palestinian Arab residents for obtaining permanent legal status dominated the acrimonious debate. To obtain "automatic citizenship," they would have to provide an ID showing they had been recorded in the Population Registry by May 1951; written proof of their Palestinian (Mandate) citizenship on the eve of statehood (for example, through a birth certificate or marriage license, which many people had lost during the war); and evidence that they had remained continuously in their home residence since May 14, 1948, or had otherwise entered it legally.[229] Anyone unable to meet all three conditions—even if they carried an ID and had voted in the previous Knesset elections—would be considered an "alien" and have to apply to naturalize, a process left ultimately to the discretion of the interior minister.

The one significant revision the government made to the previous draft was the extension of the registration deadline from November 1948, a burden that would have immediately disqualified tens of thousands of Galilee, Little Triangle, and Negev residents from acquiring automatic legal status. The more inclusive nature of the new draft earned the praise of the daily *Ma'ariv*, whose correspondent congratulated the authorities for striking a balance between the particularist exigencies of Jewish privilege and the universalist expectations of nondiscrimination—what he called "the special character of the state of Israel . . . and international [legal] custom."[230] Many parliamentarians disagreed. Several deemed the bill too generous, arguing that most Arabs continued to view the state as the enemy, that they already enjoyed sufficient freedom and equality, or that the proposed provision of automatic citizenship by marriage would encourage Muslim citizens to return from a neighboring state with up to four (gentile) wives.[231]

The more sustained opposition to the citizenship bill came from the Jewish and Palestinian representatives of MAKI and MAPAM, who declared that it would "guarantee blatant and dangerous discrimination against the national Arab minority."[232] First, they claimed that a large portion of the Arab population was still unregistered, whether out of fear of expulsion or because local officials had refused to issue them IDs. Second, they pointed out that the requirement of uninterrupted presence since May 1948 would impose on Arabs the impossible task of proving a negative: that they had not left their home residence for a single day. Not only was this a particularly unreasonable burden on people who did not fall under Israeli control until late October (in much of the Galilee) or May 1949 (in the Triangle), but it also left room for the authorities and their informants to present false claims against people who otherwise had their paperwork in order. Opponents further complained that the Hebrew proficiency requirement for naturalization would deprive applicants of the legal equality promised in the Declaration of Independence. Finally, they condemned the clause allowing Jews to retain "dual citizenship"—a provision designed to encourage the immigration of Jews from Anglo-Saxon countries who had little incentive to leave home—as "an assault on the state's honor."[233] A broader Knesset cohort opposed the power delegated to the interior minister to deny without explanation the naturalization of anyone ineligible for automatic citizenship, and subsequently to revoke that decision if he believed it was in the interests of the state to do so.[234]

The drafting committee spent four months deliberating over the bill before returning it to the Knesset for its final reading in March 1952.[235] Although it further extended the deadline by which Arab residents had to register in order to qualify for automatic status, from March 1951 to March 1952, the requirement to prove former Palestinian citizenship and uninterrupted presence remained.[236] The opposition protested that up to half of the entire Arab population—roughly eighty-five thousand adults and children—could be disqualified from automatic status.[237] Anyone in this group over the age of eighteen would still have to fulfill onerous conditions in order to naturalize. To quote the Communist Party statement read out loud by General Secretary Shmuel Mikunis before the final vote, the law would render tens of thousands of Palestinians "strangers in their land," at the mercy of the interior minister, and at risk of statelessness and eventual expulsion.[238]

Israel's citizenship law was passed on April 1, 1952, despite the "no" vote of nearly one-third of the Knesset's sixty deputies, including every member of the usually passive "Arab lists" of MAPAI.[239] The most trenchant indictment of the statute came from MAKI, which warned that "the people . . . will never agree to allow the state to be controlled by laws like the kind of racist laws in South Africa or like the kind of anti-Negro laws in the American 'democracy.'"[240] On a technical level, it was relatively easy for Interior Minister Moshe Shapira to rebut these charges out of hand. The carefully worded text in fact omitted any mention of Jews or Arabs, instead outlining the two paths to acquire automatic status in seemingly neutral, bureaucratic terms. Section 2, which covers "citizenship by return," extends immediate legal status to "every 'oleh under the 1950 Law of Return." The official English version of the law conveniently leaves the Hebrew term—which translates literally as "one who ascends" and ideologically as a "Jewish immigrant to the Land of Israel"—unexplained, thereby obfuscating its particularist bias. Section 3, which outlines the conditions for automatic "citizenship by residence," refers simply to anyone who does not become a citizen under Section 2.[241]

The authorized English translation of the citizenship law was tweaked in another way to conceal its discrimination. Although its Hebrew name, *Hok ha-Ezrahut*, translates literally as "Citizenship Law," the government called it the Israeli Nationality Law in order to denote the broadest legal meaning of the term as it is understood in English.[242] This was deceptive. In December 1949, Israeli authorities had conceptualized the Law of Return as a way to quietly block the creation of a universal category of citizens. Their aim had been to entrench the legal division between Jews, who would enjoy exclusive national rights *to* the state, and all other residents—the "non-Jewish minorities"—whose civic status they would eventually have to recognize *therein*. This distinction manifested itself most visibly in Israeli identity cards, papers that the population became required to carry at all times. Although state passports designated the citizenship (*ezrahut*, or *jinsiyya* in Arabic) of their holders as "Israeli," internal identity cards marked their holders' nationality (*le'om*, or *qawm* in Arabic) primarily as "Jewish" or "Arab," the racial groupings built into mandatory law and endorsed by the League of Nations.

Translating the name of the 1952 citizenship law as the "Nationality Law," leaving the words *Jewish immigrant* in their original Hebrew (*'oleh*), and insisting that all citizens would enjoy identical rights regardless of their differing paths to their citizenship[243] all obscured from international view the government's active effort to separate the Jewish "nation" from the Israeli state.[244] Yet honest Jewish observers and legal experts could not deny the fact that the law was discriminatory.[245] Unlike Palestinians, not a single Jew would be forced to meet the requirements of prior residency, to naturalize as a "foreigner" and place his fate in the hands of a single man, or to pledge his loyalty to the state.[246] The removal from the bill's final draft of the clause that extended automatic citizenship by marriage, which threatened to break up thousands of Arab families, also posed no risk for Jewish ones. Even Arab children born in post-1948 Israel would not acquire automatic status unless at least one of their parents was already a citizen.[247]

Most analysts tried to downplay these provisions. Some dismissed them as temporary, to be removed as soon as peace prevailed and Israel's presence in the region "normalized." Others invoked the language of social science to explain the inequality built into the law as a necessary response to the "particular sociological problems" and "ethnographical characteristics" of the Jewish state.[248] Such apologies were often buried in the margins of congratulatory studies and opinion columns that celebrated the promulgation of the new law as the culmination of the process to attain international recognition for the Jewish "colonization of Palestine."[249]

In the weeks after the Knesset vote, a small but energetic group of Arab and Jewish activists, politicians, attorneys, physicians, and professors embarked on an unprecedented grassroots campaign to amend the law.[250] Demanding automatic citizenship by marriage and for all Arab residents living in the country until the publication of the law, including all those who returned legally, they held informational meetings in forty-two villages and towns, sent a large delegation to the Knesset, and coordinated a successful half-day work stoppage in Arab communities on July 14, the day the law went into effect.[251] They might have done more had they been able to use the platform of *al-Ittihad*, which the authorities closed down for a month on grounds of "incitement."[252]

Tying Up Loose Ends in the War on Return

After popular opposition failed to formally amend the citizenship law, the government moved to finalize the "suitable legal cover" it needed for its campaign of demographic dilution. Two additional laws, strengthened by a High Court determination that applied the so-called Nationality Law retroactively to the establishment of the state, would fill the remaining holes.[253] In August 1952, the Entry into Israel Law established the first Israeli statutory basis for expelling returnees. The Knesset statute repealed the 1941 British Immigration Ordinance and empowered the interior minister to expel anyone who lacked a residency permit—a status that MAKI warned still applied to thousands of Palestinians. But legal uncertainties continued to stymie the government's campaign. The Knesset had yet to define the term infiltrator, and the police, which had assumed full responsibility for returnee expulsion, feared getting tied down in court over the legality of their detention and deportation orders.[254] It would take another two years before the parliament could agree on that definition. The 1954 Prevention of Infiltration Law also streamlined deportation procedures and ended most civil trials (and High Court injunctions).[255] Although it transferred all "infiltration" cases to a special military tribunal that was authorized to deviate from normal rules of evidence,[256] in most cases the police

January 2, 1956 (location unspecified). Military police inspect the paperwork of Palestinians during a Manhunt for Illegal Wanderers. *Top*: Mother presents her paperwork at a flying checkpoint. *Bottom*: Young man waits while his papers are checked. Courtesy of the IDFA.

continued to expel without trial women, children, the sick, the elderly, and any-one severely injured. The most visible change after the law passed was that the Border Guard began to arrest more returnees than it killed.[257]

For Palestinians, the nightmare of the War on Return continued long after the dust of the legislative debates had settled.[258] The fact that thousands of Arab residents now had or were entitled to legal citizenship did not stop the Interior Ministry from using the registration system to harass them. Foot dragging and negligence in the issuance of replacement IDs, the recording of address changes, the exchange of TRPs for civil IDs, and the registration of newborn children and teenagers who had reached the age of needing to carry their own IDs endangered affected Palestinians during random ID checks. At any given moment, hundreds, if not thousands, of citizens were denied the ability to look for work, collect government food rations, and marry.[259] The situation was more dire for those Palestinians who continued to hold temporary permits or who lived in hiding from the authorities because they lacked any paperwork at all.[260] By the late 1960s, the number of stateless Palestinians in Israel was estimated to have tripled, reaching as many as sixty thousand people—close to one-fifth of the Arab population at that time.[261] The government's decision to sign on to the 1961 Convention on the Reduction of Statelessness prompted the Knesset to revise the law in 1968, but many people remained outside the law.[262] Not until a second amendment in 1980 did Israel extend automatic citizenship to former Palestinian Arab subjects who became residents after 1948 and were registered by July 1952 (or entered legally thereafter), and to their children.

.   .   .

State building is a messy enterprise. The requirements for Israeli citizenship were settled only four years after Israel declared independence, riding on the heels of a makeshift and often violent campaign to minimize the number of Arab residents entitled to that status. Upon its promulgation in April 1952, Israel's "Nationality Law" had little bearing on the country's 89 percent Jewish majority. Their de facto legal identity had been ensured effectively since the first census in November 1948 and even more so following the passage of the July 1950 Law of Return—what I would call Israel's actual nationality law.[263] Instead, the chief purpose of the 1952 law was to resolve the ambiguous status of the nearly 180,000 Palestinian Arabs who had used and would continue to use all means at their disposal to remain in or return to the country. It was their desperate and creative determination along Israel's geographic and legal frontiers that would shape most decisively today's contours of belonging and exclusion in the state.

Today, the terms *nationality* and *citizenship* are interchangeable in most liberal democracies. Israel's decision to sever the nation-state link in the early 1950s was decisive to deepening its settlement project. In order to colonize Palestinian land and property without violating its obligation to serve as the neutral arbiter of its citizens, the state transferred the land it confiscated during and after the war, along with the responsibility for settling immigrants on that land, to technically private, or (Jewish) "national," agencies whose boards it stacked.[264]

The political consequences were also critical. Despite the moderate success of attorneys, parliamentarians, and activists in reducing the eligibility requirements that Palestinians had to meet to gain automatic citizenship, their achievement did not come for free. At MAKI's Twelfth Congress in May 1952, leading Jewish communists retreated further from their commitment to Palestinian self-determination by refusing even to discuss the eventual borders of the future Arab state of Palestine. As Joel Beinin has argued, their desire to stay relevant by refusing to challenge the consensus that Israel's 1949 annexations beyond the partition borders were nonnegotiable would eventually become "the limits of [their] political vision."[265] In the meantime, Palestinian communists were left in the impossible position of having to struggle for individual equality in a state that inscribed their collective subordination into law.

4 SPECTACLES OF SOVEREIGNTY

ON MAY 7, 1949, the mukhtar of the Jerusalem-area village of Abu Ghosh sent an urgent letter to Israel's ministers of religions, minorities, and police. Renowned for their aid to Zionist intelligence and military forces since 1919 and especially during the 1948 war, the people of Abu Ghosh enjoyed a favorable position with the Israeli authorities compared to other Palestinians who managed to remain in the new state.[1] Yet despite their privileged access to daily work and health care, life in the village had not returned to normal. During the fighting in May 1948, the majority of Abu Ghosh's one thousand residents fled from their homes, following the example and advice of their Jewish neighbors. Although several hundred hid in the surrounding hills and returned soon thereafter, many crossed the front lines and landed in Bethlehem, then under Egyptian control.[2] Due to their notoriety as collaborators, they faced "insults, imprisonment, and [threats of] murder—to the point," wrote the mukhtar, that they lived under virtual house arrest. Over the next ten months, numerous families thus risked their lives to cross the new border and return home, where Israeli authorities provided them with permanent identity cards. Suddenly, in early May, this unusual modus operandi—of the Israelis turning a blind eye to the return of Palestinian refugees and even rewarding them with residence papers—broke down. Two days after a new group of women and children returned home, the police arrived and "demanded two of the families . . . and dumped them over the border" in the middle of the night. The police treated the women and children in "heinous and shocking" ways that included "violent pushing." This "horrible spectacle," recalled the mukhtar, had transpired just hours after the village celebration of Israel's "magnificent" Independence

Day. The events were particularly incomprehensible because shortly after these families arrived from their journey they had "joined their relatives in the preparation of victory arches, rejoicing in the holiday and cheering 'Long live the president and prime minister!'" According to the mukhtar,

> The women and children were crying and shouting, pleading with the soldiers to have mercy . . . on them. They began to swear in the name of God and the prime minister, telling the police, "We're in our homes, we're the protected guests of Ibn Gurion! Don't treat us this way! At least hold off until we can rest from our exhaustion . . . after walking twenty hours in one night." Despite this the police shouted and cursed at them until they reached the border. The sounds of the women's cries and the children's wailing were heard that night from the valleys and the mountains, and now we do not know their fate. On top of this, the police in the village continue to use means that violate religion and the law in their treatment of the [other] women and children. They enter their homes day and night . . . and when they find a woman sleeping, they kick her in the leg to wake her up and demand to see her ID.[3]

The tale recounted by the mukhtar highlights the porous borders that characterized everyday life in the nascent Jewish state—not only along the territorial lines established by the Arab-Israeli armistice agreements in the spring of 1949, but also between the notions of loyalty and betrayal, citizens and strangers, hosts and guests. What mukhtar Mahmud Rashid did not know when he urged the civil authorities to stop the unconscionable behavior of the army and the police and help the families resettle in their homes was that the army had been trying for the previous seven months to put an end to the "nuisance" caused by the ongoing return of hundreds of Abu Ghosh residents. The greatest fear of Jerusalem's district commissioner was not that these residents posed a security problem, but rather that "the number of Arabs [in the area] will quickly outpace the number of Jew[s]."[4] Still, the fact that the Interior Ministry had opted not to complete the census in the village testifies to the relative wiggle room that Israel granted initially to those Palestinian Arabs it deemed "kosher."[5]

If the historic alliance between the people of Abu Ghosh and the Zionist movement distinguished them from other Palestinians who managed to stay within Israel's armistice lines, their celebration of statehood and the questions and paradoxes raised by their zealous display of allegiance did not. During the first two decades of statehood, Israeli Independence Day occasioned ritual spectacles of sovereignty performed by and for Palestinian citizens around the country. Blending flag raising with poetic panegyrics, athletic competitions with religious chants, and folk dances with military parades, the events of the holiday juxtaposed Arab cultural forms against visible demonstrations of the modernity and might of the Jewish state.

As the previous chapter shows, the UN demand that Israel extend suffrage and a shared legal status to the newfound 15 percent Arab minority created tremendous anxiety for the leaders of the nascent state. Caught unprepared, their first response was to undertake a military and bureaucratic campaign to reduce further the size of the Palestinian population. Within a few years, they constructed a legal infrastructure that enabled the Knesset to pass a seemingly universal citizenship law while securing the permanent subordination of Arab citizens to Jewish nationals. But the crisis spawned by Israel's promise of native citizenship transcended the law, whose severance of the nation-state link created unanticipated problems of its own. The story of Israel's gradual imposition of Independence Day celebrations on Palestinian communities reveals the way in which liberal sovereignty in an era of revolutionary nationalism over the armistice lines forced the Yishuv to adapt its separatist impulse and complicated its pre-state strategy of divide and rule.

Although the 1950 Law of Return and 1952 (misnamed) Nationality Law formalized Israel's impenetrable borders of belonging, they offered no solution to the territorial concentration of 90 percent of the Palestinians who remained after the war in the regions allotted by the UN Partition Plan to the future Arab state. Jewish settlers had barely made a dent in the Galilee and the Little Triangle before 1948. The time it would take to marshal the resources and bodies to fill these areas with Jews could strengthen local Palestinian claims to self-determination. It was in this context that the attention of policymakers in the new "Arab sector" turned to the problem of Palestinian souls and sentiments.[6] Was it possible to cultivate their affective ties as a way to block the potential challenge to ongoing settler-colonization?

Our story begins with the second anniversary of statehood, when Israeli military and police officers appear to have played on the postwar political vacuum and the fear and isolation of villagers in the southern Triangle to demand three ceremonies that affirmed their national defeat. Jewish policymakers and administrative field staff were unsure at first how to approach these events: the objectives and instructions were unclear, and some feared that instilling a sense of national belonging among Palestinian citizens would eventually undermine the basis of Jewish privilege. In the middle of the decade, unforeseen political challenges to military rule would prompt officials in Jerusalem to cast aside their ambivalence and embrace Independence Day as a strategic opportunity to monitor, foster, and even showcase Palestinian fealty. The first decade of sovereignty thus unfolded alongside growing demands for Palestinians to celebrate their dispossession—to perform allegiance to a community that they necessarily could not join.

Recent memoirs, documentary films, and the oral histories of older Palestinians who joined or watched holiday celebrations during this period reveal the sticks of intimidation and the carrots of opportunity—such as twenty-four hours of free movement—that the regime held out to recruit Palestinians to participate in the holiday. Many jumped at this fleeting glimpse of freedom, combined with the free transportation provided, to head for the beach, watch the parades, or join street festivals in neighboring Jewish towns. Children, whose holiday enlistment was the most systematic, rarely understood the special skits they performed, but they relished the rare sweets to which they were treated and the time off from their overcrowded and underequipped classrooms.[7]

Regardless of their age at the time, Palestinians who remember these events tend to stress the sense of humiliation and demoralization they left behind. Five decades later, they continue to debate the government's ultimate objective in imposing the celebrations, and its success in achieving it: Was the goal merely to ensure their outward obedience, or to change their inner feelings? Their confusion is warranted, for Jewish authorities were themselves deeply ambivalent, divided, and making things up as they went along. To trace how this process unfolded, we must widen our lens from the spheres of physical force and legislated inequality to the realms of discipline and symbolic violence, what philosopher Pierre Bourdieu describes as "that form of domination . . . exerted through the communication in which it is disguised."[8] The story that follows unsettles the long-held wisdom that the Zionist movement only ever sought to displace the Arabs of Palestine—never to win their hearts and minds.[9]

INVENTING TRADITIONS

The process of incorporating Palestinians into the spectacles of Jewish sovereignty began with the first anniversary of statehood in May 1949, when the Knesset passed two laws to ensure the festive nature of the day and the emblems that would represent it. The Law of Independence Day declared the anniversary an official holiday on which all nonessential businesses, public institutions, and nonentertainment services would be closed. It also authorized the prime minister to issue instructions regarding the placement of flags and the preparation of public celebrations, and to determine the "emblems of the state" and their use.[10] A second law stipulated maximum fines and prison sentences for the unlicensed sale and use of state flags and emblems; for the failure to fly flags above government offices, local councils, schools, houses of worship, and other institutions used for public services; and for "insult[ing], or caus[ing] to be insulted, the State flag or State emblem."[11] Despite the operation of a separate legal regime that governed Palestinian villages and towns under military rule, these civil laws applied to all local shops and the few government and public institutions recognized by the new state at the time.

Whose Holiday?

Today our hearts dance joyfully and our feelings tremble with delight. Wherever you look you find people celebrating. . . . Long live our state, bridge of democracy and freedom!

Muhammad Abu Khayt, school principal of Jaljulya

Let us all thank God . . . for granting us safety in our holy country . . . after it became a theater for imperialists and a toy in the hands of their treacherous agents. . . .

Husni al-Salih, school principal of Kafr Qasim

Ask the world and they'll tell you in unison that Israel is heaven on earth.[12]

"Speech for the Holiday of Victory," signature unclear, Kafr Qasim

Uttered in Arabic on April 23, 1950, these encomiums were transcribed by Jewish and Arab police officers in the earliest known transcripts of Palestinian village celebrations on Israeli Independence Day. The meticulous, at times riveting reports described the festivities held that day in Kafr Qasim, Jaljulya, and Tayyibe, three small and impoverished communities in the Little Triangle region, nearly one year after Jordanian King 'Abdullah ceded it to Israel as part of the armistice agreement. In the year prior to the May 1949 annexation, some thirty thousand local residents and eight thousand refugees in the region lived in about twenty villages, hamlets, and open fields under Iraqi military control. During the subsequent summer and fall, the Military Government carried out a sweeping expulsion campaign against refugees, who were easy to identify by the absence of their birth certificates from the custody of local mukhtars, as well as an estimated one thousand native-born residents of six hamlets around Umm al-Fahm in the north. Intelligence officers also interrogated, tortured, and detained in solitary confinement any men accused by informants of volunteering with Iraqi-led units of the Arab Liberation Army; in some cases they employed mukhtars to harass the men into leaving the country.[13] Others were reportedly "disappeared."[14]

Living conditions in the Triangle in those early days were in some ways harsher than in the Galilee. On top of the movement restrictions imposed in all areas under military rule, residents of the newly annexed territory faced an 8 P.M. nightly curfew and were further isolated by the near impossibility of obtaining critical news from *al-Ittihad* or other sources.[15] They also suffered a greater immediate loss of land. After the annexation, the government classified the entire population as "present absentees," refusing to return the massive landholdings that had remained in Israeli hands during the year they were forced to live under Hashemite sovereignty.[16] IDF soldiers shot to death a number of villagers who tried to farm their lands anyway, whether out of desperation for food, because the boundaries delimiting both the armistice lines and "closed zones" were not clearly demarcated, or both.[17] Those who managed to hold on to sizable plots were forced to sell their eggs, wheat, and other crops to a government-appointed firm at below-market prices.

In search of food security, physical safety, and in some cases a rise in local social status, many young men signed up to join the local police force or to serve as regime informants. Many leaders of large clans—who generally enjoyed more local power than their counterparts in the Galilee, where a combination of industrialization and decades of missionary education had loosened old patriarchal bonds—matched that cooperation. Far more than the British before them, Israel harnessed these forms of communal authority and nurtured these dynamics of dependence as a way to preoccupy the population with the immediate concerns of survival and to lower the costs of rule.[18]

These onerous and coercive conditions formed the backdrop to the stunning language of praise recorded in the first Independence Day celebrations that were held in the region. Each of the three celebrations assumed a slightly different form. In both Tayyibe and Jaljulya, neighboring villagers joined local residents to greet the governor, observe a formal military ceremony, raise the flag, and listen to speeches by teachers, school principals, mukhtars, and village council members. In Tayyibe, schoolgirls also sang the "song of the flag" (presumably "ha-Tikva," the Israeli national anthem), a boy from neighboring Qalansuwa "greeted the government in Hebrew," and a group of children performed athletic exercises. Officer Hanokh, the Jewish police officer who secretly recorded the proceedings, began his report by summarizing that the holiday was "gallantly celebrated" and that "the entire village was decorated in flags of the nation.... They danced the *dabka*, and the mood was uplifting." In Jaljulya, the Arab police chief devoted the bulk of his secret report to detailed transcriptions of the speeches presented. He did see fit, however, to inform his station supervisor in the nearby Jewish town of Kfar Saba that the party ordered by the *khawaja* (foreign) military governor lasted more than five hours, and that when the governor arrived halfway through the festivities, the people greeted him "with cheers and a magnificent welcome."[19]

In Kafr Qasim, villagers held a "twenty-four-hour popular celebration," which was coordinated by the school principal after the mukhtar "learned of the holiday" just two days before. Police officer Faraj Faraj's rich description of the event provides a blueprint of the model that many Palestinian celebrations would adopt, as well as the ways in which they would be narrated in the years to come:

> The [mukhtar and notables] informed [us] of their wish to obtain approval to hold this happy celebration in the village. Arrangements began under the direction of the school principal ... and the teachers. The first step was to clean the village, decorate the streets, and raise Israeli flags. ... Then the school was decorated in flags and victory arches, where the final assembly ... was held. As 8 P.M. neared ... even the rooftops of the village houses were lit up in bonfires. The celebrations were accompanied by cries and high-pitched trills, followed by popular songs that lasted late into the night. The police roamed among the revelers to maintain order.
>
> The next morning ... all the young men and notables ... assembled at the mosque to await the arrival of the principal and students. ... Afterward the gathering was over, the procession began from the mosque courtyard and passed by the police station. The young men sang anthems and the old men recited religious chants, invoking a blessing of peace and security for the state. Behind them were children holding flags and singing school anthems until the procession reached the schoolyard, where the young men broke out in the dance known as the *dabka*, the middle-aged men indulged in the joyful rhythms of the Bedouin *sahaja*, and the students played athletic games until 10 A.M. ... The party began with the hoisting of the flag on the roof of the school, an act received with good spirits by all. Then the speeches began ... interspersed with school songs.
>
> Before the end of the party, a message arrived from Jaljulya regarding the military governor's recommendation to go join the celebration there. Indeed

the cars began to make their way, and many people went by foot. There . . . all the speeches were repeated . . . and the party ended around 6 P.M. The youth and the schoolchildren of the village returned home singing folk songs until they arrived, where they began to celebrate all over again with the *dabka*, the *sahaja*, and . . . additional songs. They were joined by a group of Israeli Border Guard officers until midnight, when the people dispersed to their homes.

No troubling incidents took place throughout the celebrations.[20]

The coercion and surveillance that shadowed these events, as well as their animated retelling, reveal themselves through the details and omissions of the text. Although there is no explicit indication that the festivities in Kafr Qasim were ordered or arranged by the authorities, as they were in Tayyibe and Jaljulya, the police maintained a constantly visible presence. It makes sense that the orchestration of the ceremonies was carried out by the mukhtar, the school principal, and the teachers. It is likely that they constituted the only official links at the time between villagers and the Jewish authorities, and their privileged positions depended on their willingness to cooperate with the governor.[21] Also crucial is the role of Faraj, the Arab police officer who served as translator and cultural scribe for his European Jewish supervisor (note his description of the "dance known as the *dabka*"). His strikingly unconflicted account makes the villagers' jubilation seem natural, even unremarkable.

On the popular level, each of the socially legible groups in the community—women, young men, middle-aged men, the elderly, teachers, and schoolchildren—appeared to know and perform the normative role prescribed for them. No one remained standing on the sidelines, either confused about their role or even just to observe this largely unprecedented event.[22] On the level of the authorities, both the police presence and the "recommendation" of the Jaljulya military governor serve in this account merely to fulfill the genuine wishes of the people: whether to permit the celebration, to ensure that the villagers are safe, to foster their unspoken wish to continue the party elsewhere, or to join in the fun themselves.

It is not just the bonfires, flags, and prayers for state security that appear to blend seamlessly with the traditional Arab singing and dancing in the village. So too does the Border Guard, whose officers reportedly joined in the merriment on the second night. The irony cannot be exaggerated. In the late 1940s and early 1950s, both they and the civilian police officers stationed in the southern Triangle hailed primarily from Druze villages in the Galilee. Their reportedly cruel and degrading treatment of the local population during the War on Return earned them a lasting reputation in some of these villages that is equal to, if not worse than, that of their Jewish commanders, who often enjoyed the luxury of issuing the orders.[23] Intentional or not, Faraj's decision to label the dancing officers simply "Israeli" makes the presence of the military administration seem less imposed. The image of villagers dancing side by side with soldiers effectively blurs the distinction between occupiers and occupied while simultaneously obscuring the divisive politics of sectarian rule that made that moment—and perhaps the officer's own position—possible. This fact dispels any illusion that a spontaneous display of Arab-Jewish unity may have capped off the events of the day.

Despite the smoothness of Faraj's narration, it would be a mistake to read the almost carnivalesque atmosphere described in his report and the zeal of the speeches delivered in all three villages as a fully self-conscious and coherently staged performance. To be sure, many of the grandiloquent tributes to the state and its leaders, the heroism of the "soldiers of the intrepid Israeli army" who "fought without foreign aid," and allusions to the passion and "stirred emotions" that fueled the villagers to attend the celebrations on their own volition were presented to satisfy the seated rows of uniformed military officers and other distinguished government officials.

Yet a number of latent tensions emerge in these panegyrics. Although the speakers at all three ceremonies rejoiced over their liberation from the British and tacitly invoked the empire's Hashemite colluders, it would have been impossible to avoid the reality that Palestinians in the new state were being forced to shift their loyalty to yet another foreign master. Recall the Jaljulya police chief's reference to the military governor as a *khawaja*, a title of respect but also one that more generally denoted Westerners. In other words, whose republic was it? One speaker "congratulated *the Jewish people* in particular and the people of Israel in general . . . who waited two thousand years," while another thanked his guests for visiting his village, which "sought protection under the sanctuary of *your flag*."[24] While others spoke of the "compassion" and beneficence of "*our* Israeli state" and "*our* government," they did so while invoking Jewish biblical ties to the land. Notwithstanding the glaring instability of their claims on the new state, the speeches nonetheless served to obscure the historical reality that few, if any, of them had sought sanctuary under the Jewish flag during the war.[25]

The most lyrical presentation that afternoon was the recitation of a poem by Jaljulya schoolteacher Bakr 'Abd al-Malik Abu Kishk entitled "Our Leaders

Wadi 'Ara, May 20, 1949. Two villagers erect a makeshift Israeli flag just moments prior to the formal annexation of their village. Note the flag with the Star of David waving behind them. Photo by Beno Rothenberg, courtesy of the Israel State Archive (ISA).

and Our Holidays" (*Rijaluna wa 'Ayyaduna*). Beginning with tributes to Moses, King David, and King Solomon, he went on to mourn the loss of the Second Temple and the dispersion of the Jews in 70 C.E.:

> Their traces were dispersed, and they were scattered
>> Exposed to bombardment and other horrors
> Until Herzl emerged to bring us together
>> And led us like the true victorious leader
> Would that time had offered him
>> The chance to see the rising youths
> The thinker died, and the man who settled in his place
>> Is noble, distinguished, and strong
> Join me in saluting the president [Haim Weizmann], your king
>> This president, the bearer of good news
> Salute him in his loyalty and his courageous views
>> For he is the one who liberates ideas

Salute each and every worker
　In our field of endless fruits
Greet with me this noble man and his companions
　The way you'd greet the most noble of visitors
Sirs, we appreciate your efforts
　And we are pleased with your victories
Time is too limited to do justice to what you deserve
　But I place myself humbly in your hands
I have no mastery over the verse except that
　When I saw you this poem wrote itself.

The bombastic tenor of Abu Kishk's poem is more than a little suspect. Judging by its adherence to classical metrical form and its reliance on stock expressions, it was clearly the work of an artist skilled in the composition of *madih*, the genre of panegyric poetry that some Palestinians penned for British occupiers after 1918 before it began to vanish in the Arabic free-form revolution of the 1940s. Starting in the tenth century, the Abbasid caliph commissioned poets to compose and recite *madih* on his behalf. In its traditional form, the value of the panegyric hinged not only on the poet's talents as a maker of metaphor, but also on the credibility of his sincerity. This was critical because the most talented panegyrists often tread the line between genuine admiration and satire, *madih* and its invective counterpart, *hija'*.[26]

The potential for verbal subversion in the *madih* helps us to appreciate the rich ambiguity of "Our Leaders and Our Holidays" without reducing our analysis to the question of sincerity. Although it is implausible that Abu Kishk believed that Herzl's vision of a Jewish state included the Arabs of Palestine in anything but a diminished and subordinate capacity, he may have been playing to those Jaljulyans and refugees, including members of his extended family, who had actively collaborated with Zionist forces during the 1948 war.[27] The final line of his poem is particularly fraught. Read figuratively, it seems to say, "You are so wonderful that I could not help myself in composing this elegy." By contrast, a more literal reading would suggest the meaning, "I did not, and could never, write this tribute in your honor." Given the conditions of domination and fear that gave birth to the poem, it is possible to read it both ways. Because he simultaneously embraced and disavowed his artistic prowess, Abu Kishk both assumed and denied responsibility for the praise it contained. On the one hand, the unlikelihood that any of the schoolteacher's Jewish "guests" had the Arabic skills to register this ambiguity supports a more dissident interpretation of his performance. On the other hand, his act of writing Palestinians into a Zionist historical narrative helped to reconstitute the power of the regime at that moment.

The other performances that day lent themselves to equally indefinite interpretations. Several speakers paid homage to "our holiday" alongside references to the new classrooms that were opened during the year, and a reminder that the villagers' fate could have been worse. Referring to the day as "more awesome and pure than the holiday of tranquility," Kafr Qasim school principal Husni al-Salih, himself from the nearby village of Tira, directed his address not at the small number of Jewish military officials in attendance, but at village residents themselves. Referring explicitly to the 1948 war, he exhorted his "brothers" to recognize that they were celebrating not one holiday that day but two: the dawn of the new state, and the riddance of the Hashemite king. In Salih's view, they had both God and the Israeli president to thank for their good fortune:

> The dawn of our first holiday has dispersed the clouds of evil. Its very existence has served to rid us of the past toils, which . . . would have continued to plague us. . . . The earth would have been dusty, barren, and dull instead of blue. The meadows would have darkened, the birds would have left their nests for refuge and sustenance, and our fate would have been like theirs, the fleeting destiny of our noble ancestors. But His mercy and care have transformed the dawn of this day that we celebrate into a magnificent sight, culminating in the end of our barren days.
>
> No less important, and equally unique, is the second holiday, the celebration of independence, nay, freedom, which has been invoked since the dawn of history. This is the day on which our eternal democratic state, the state of Israel, was announced, ending the continual nightmare of degradation and colonialism. This is the day that long lasting tyranny was expelled, along with its woven webs and controlling ways. . . .
>
> Repeat with me and raise your hands to cry, long live Israel and its just founder, the honorable Shaykh Haim Weizmann, the president of the state and the man of our time. May colonialism be defeated and injustice extinguished!

There is no doubt that the awareness of military surveillance and the looming threat of further expulsions contributed to the ostentatious and obsequious tone of this and other speeches. Yet other factors were surely at play. Some of the speakers likely identified their interests with the state at that moment due to the relative economic security or local power it afforded them. It is also possible that Salih's expression of relief at not being homeless and his resentment toward King 'Abdallah for betraying and then abandoning them may have resonated with some villagers.[28]

This resentment was also directed at Israeli officials. In Tayyibe, resident Salim Khalil congratulated the leaders of the state but quickly went on to remind them of "the equality of rights for all citizens in the state such as family reunification, return of the lands . . . lifting the curfew, canceling the exit permits from the Triangle, freedom of movement, etc. . . . like [for] any other citizen of the state. . . . 'We were like a flock left alone by its shepherd,'" he exclaimed, "'and it was his fault that he left us. Why are we to blame?'" Again, it is impossible to know whether Khalil believed that the government would fulfill its pledge to abolish the emergency regulations as soon as the hostilities ended and implement the principles of equality enshrined in the Declaration of Independence. The fact that he chose to express his demands, as did another Tayyiban who asked the military governor for fertilizer for village farmers, suggests that at least some Palestinians perceived the ceremony as an opportunity to make small and large claims on the state. The fact that one month later Jewish police officers characterized the residents of the region as "insolent," not yet "reconciled" to the Israeli annexation, and generally in need of a heavier hand also testifies to his courage.[29]

The analysis of Isma'il 'Aqab Mahmud Budayr, a sixty-six-year-old man from Kafr Qasim with whom I spoke in August 2002, encapsulates why fixating on the sincerity of belief among Arab celebrants would miss the significance of their actions. Budayr himself had a complex relationship with the state since his childhood. In 1956 he was permanently disabled during a Border Guard massacre in the village, a subject to which I turn in the next chapter. At the same time, after the annexation, his father was part of a small group of *wujaha'*, or conservative men of influence, who met regularly with the governor and mediated with the population on his behalf. Like regime-appointed mukhtars, these figures occupied an ambivalent role in Palestinian village society in the early years of Israeli statehood. Despite their service to the regime by identifying unauthorized returnees as well as refugee-owned land, spying on government critics, and delivering votes to MAPAI's "Arab lists" during national elections, they also possessed the ability to help people—by vouching for them as legal residents, getting them released from detention, removing stains from their intelligence records, and securing them travel permits or shop licenses.[30] When I showed Budayr the declassified police report of what happened in his village on the second anniversary, he ripped the document out of my hands, began to stuff it through the copier in the office where we were sitting, and told me that everything in it was "exactly how it happened." After reading the address by Husni al-Salih, Budayr exclaimed that the school principal "should have said even more" because speeches like this "had to be delivered." He continued:

> It did not matter whether anyone believed in these things, because the fact was that the people were forced to say them. When the principal referred to our democratic state, it is clear that nothing was clear in the state at that time because it was still in the beginning [of Israeli rule]. Food was distributed then through the ration card system and people did not have bread or eggs.... We were living under military rule, and we were unable to express our real opinions. ... The most that could be said was to ask the state to help people.... The people were deprived of many things because they could not afford them. Many could not even buy milk for their children.[31]

Budayr declined to explain his eagerness for a copy of the report. It is possible that he sought written proof of the community's sycophantic enactments on Independence Day as a way to validate his father's cooperation with the regime during those early and uncertain years.

In his recollection, the celebrations at the time were the product of fear, coercion, and destitution, not a collective faith in Israel's liberal democratic pretensions. Either way, questions of faith and ideological affinity are beside the point. Budayr's insistence that these abstractions "did not matter" reinforces the problem with theories of hegemony that assume a binary distinction between coercion and persuasion as opposing techniques of rule.[32] To focus on the sincerity or dissimulation behind the celebrations would force us to adopt the categories of analysis of our historical protagonists. It would obscure how the inability of Israeli officials to assure themselves of the loyalty of their Palestinian co-citizens created expectations for repeat performances and lasting cultural and political effects in the process. To paraphrase social theorist Derek Sayer, it was not only that Palestinians lived in the lie of Israel's liberal democracy; the state itself also lived through their performances.[33]

MEASURING MOODS

Budayr was only partly correct that villagers were merely enacting the elaborate performances that were expected of them. In fact, Jewish policymakers and civil administrators were conflicted at first about their goals for Arab participation, the degree of involvement they sought, and the level of coercion they believed was appropriate. This ambivalence was symptomatic of a broader unease about how to govern Palestinians as occupied subjects, voting constituents, and (before 1952) potential citizens. For this reason, Independence Day celebrations began slowly and haltingly. On the first anniversary, in May 1949, this ambivalence was reflected in the limited number and modest scope of the celebrations they organized. Holiday events in the countryside were restricted to villages that resembled those in the southern Triangle, located relatively close to Jewish population centers and removed from the heart of the Arab Galilee. As in Abu Ghosh, outside Jerusalem, either these communities had also been spared the 1948 expulsions, or their residents had been allowed to return because of the specific contribution they made toward the war effort or the postwar settler economy.[34]

That year, celebrations in the urban sector were organized only in two "mixed" towns, where longstanding residents and recent refugees were crammed into a small quarter and surrounded by military checkpoints. In Jaffa, the formerly bustling port city and cultural capital of Palestine, the five thousand of the seventy-five thousand Arab residents who remained after the flight and expulsions of one year earlier were invited to join the events planned for their Jewish neighbors.[35] Only a slightly higher ratio of the original population had managed to hold on in the historic and more provincial fortress town of Acre.[36] Because there were still few settlers in the town, municipal authorities instead adapted well-worn scripts of late Ottoman imperial fealty, inviting carefully selected notables and clergy from area villages to present their blessings at the governor's reception and review the parade of troops and scouts who marched through the town.[37]

The apparently minimal deliberation that went into these events and the quaint character of their enactment looked different in their dramatic retelling in *al-Yawm*, MAPAI's—and thus the government's—Arabic-language mouthpiece.[38] The paper stressed the emotional authenticity of the celebrations: "Thousands [of villagers] flocked to [Acre]. . . . The streets swirled up in a series of dances from all the sects. Cheers were raised, and shots were fired in the air."[39] Yet for every article that emphasized the popular, genuinely affective character of Arab participation, there was at least one news story or op-ed that underscored the holiday's value as an object lesson in Jewish power. This tension was particularly stark on the first anniversary, when the conquest of specific Palestinian villages appeared on a list of the state's "most important" historical achievements, alongside an exhortation to Arab readers to appreciate that the celebration of the Jewish people's "miraculous return to its native homeland" was also "the holiday of your independence."[40] The same pages that conjured up images of spontaneous outbursts of Arab joy were also filled with didactic commentaries lecturing the public to dry its tears from the massacres of the recent war, accept its political defeat—the consequence of the people's "primitive mentality"—and show some gratitude for the "civilized living standards" the new state would offer them.[41]

The need for clarity began to emerge as Israel prepared for its third anniversary of statehood in early 1951. For the first time, military governors and the local "minorities officers" who worked under the district commissioner in the four mixed cities where military rule had since been lifted were asked to draw up holiday plans. Although none of them appeared to oppose Palestinian observance on principle, they sent word to the Interior Ministry's holiday committee that the Knesset's statutory parameters for the general (Jewish) public were inadequate as planning guides. The committee thus issued a series of memoranda designed to standardize government expectations. In February it announced that all Arab schools (like Jewish schools) would be closed, and that in all of the mixed cities, Jewish municipal officials should invite Arab clerical leaders, notables, and judges to the receptions and parades they were planning. Yet the government's vision for the holiday inside Nazareth and the roughly one hundred Palestinian villages left in the state was incoherent. One committee missive opened by stating that governors and their staff should "not in any way impose" flags, lights, and festive gatherings, but ended with a call for them to "use their influence and necessary tact to advise them" to do just that.[42]

The government's mission began to crystallize in the weeks leading up to the holiday. A new order clarified that the Arab village councils, all appointed by the Military Government, should "at a minimum" decorate their buildings, but they were also strongly encouraged to host formal gatherings.[43] To this end, villagers were granted special permission to enter Jewish cities to purchase flags and "victory arches" to erect in their local squares and along the main roads.[44] Al-Yawm, for its part, replaced its downbeat tone and stern lectures of the past with praise poems for the state[45] and florid essays on the holiday's "revelation."[46] Despite ongoing "challenges" in the pursuit of civic equality, the newspaper explained, "the Arabs of Israel have begun to realize that their lives and their fate are linked to this state, to which their loyalty increases and they prioritize their ties."[47] Perhaps to convince skeptical readers, the paper's Jewish editors announced special regional celebrations and athletic events in the Galilee and Little Triangle to which the population would "naturally" flock, as well

Beersheba, April 23, 1950. Bedouin camel riders join the holiday procession in regalia. This photo appeared in a 1955 promotional book called *The Arabs in Israel*, which was sent to libraries and embassies around the world. Courtesy of the Government Press Office (GPO), State of Israel.

as a "magnificent procession by Bedouin tribes" that would join the parade in Beersheba.[48]

Days before the anniversary, governors and municipal authorities received a request from Shimon Landman, director of the Interior Ministry's Minorities Affairs Division, for "full and detailed reports" on Arab holiday involvement around the country: the receptions, school events, and popular festivities they held; the decorations they displayed; and the "prevailing sentiments and atmosphere on and in relation to [the] day."[49] Landman did not explain the reason for his demand for these holiday surveillance digests, though it would have been obvious to his field staff. From the moment of occupation, Israeli officials had become fixated on the dubious loyalty of the population whose society they had deracinated to make room for their own. This concern was not parochial or "right-wing." Politicians on the left and liberal ends of the Zionist spectrum, who tended to oppose the demonization of the entire population as a fifth column in waiting, agreed that it was a problem that Palestinians had yet to internalize the truth-value of the state, to "adjust to [its] reality . . . and recognize [its] existence."[50]

Landman's field staff reported no complaints in the moods they measured among Arab celebrants in the handful of villages that had celebrated the year before. Paying close attention to differences of age and social status, his clerks dutifully catalogued the torches, candles, and bonfires lit; the number of flags raised; the songs and dances performed; the refreshments served; the speeches delivered; and the interest that villagers displayed in the military parades that either passed through their communities or which they were invited to come and see.[51] In the north, Minorities Officer Moshe Yetah seemed convinced of the authenticity of the celebrations he attended in the nearby Druze village of Daliyat al-Karmil, where the police and his staff were welcomed by men "dressed in holiday clothes and riding on decorated horses, in accordance with Arab custom at these kinds of parties."[52] In the two out of some thirty-four Palestinian villages that remained intact in the section of Jerusalem district that had fallen under Haganah control during the war, the "festive outfits," the "pleasant" school play performed in Bayt Safafa, and the signs placed throughout Abu Ghosh ("Growth and prosperity to the State of Israel," "Your holiday is our holiday—Independence Day 1951") sufficed to satisfy the district commissioner that a "festive atmosphere [had] prevailed."[53]

A more worrisome set of reports streamed into Jerusalem from the urban sector, where minorities officers reported that the "holiday was not felt" and that populations "did not participate enough."[54] Such was the case in Acre, where Yetah's follow-up investigation attributed the recorded apathy and low turnout on the anniversary of Palestinian dispossession to a series of administrative blunders. To start with, organizers had insulted local notables by failing to invite them to the municipal ceremony and reception after accidentally copying the guest list from the quasi-state United Jewish Appeal, which had "intentionally left off Arab names." The previous day, these same notables had delivered their holiday blessings to the city council, whose handful of Arab deputies accused the mayor of ignoring them in the holiday preparations and blamed him for the lack of activity in the Old City, where Palestinian residents were confined. Finally, the notables urged that the handful of notices that Yetah's assistants had tacked to the city's walls were of no use to the largely illiterate population of refugee farmers from nearby villages to which they were forbidden to return; the turnout would have been higher had they sent a special emissary to announce the holiday schedule in the streets. Yetah dutifully recorded these complaints. He agreed that the municipality's carelessness had been a major problem, but he also suspected that something else was at play. He insisted that were it not for the pressure that his embittered Arab interlocutors had imposed on local residents to keep their shops open and refuse to fly the flag of the Jewish star above their homes, Acre's four thousand Arab denizens would have embraced the celebrations of statehood naturally.[55]

Not all of Yetah's colleagues shared his faith in the inevitability of Palestinian enthusiasm. One of them was Minorities Officer Avraham Malul, the scion of a prominent Sephardic family in Palestine and a graduate of Hebrew University's Islamic history and civilization program.[56] The thirty-six-year-old clerk submitted a long and scathing memorandum to Jerusalem following the low turnout of celebrants in his hometown of Jaffa as well as Ramle and Lod (Lydd)—two other Arab cities that Jewish forces had all but eviscerated in the recent war.[57] Like his northern counterpart, Malul laid some blame on the negligence of the municipal authorities, who had mistakenly included on the guest list for the receptions and military parade several men who had died—obtaining "citizenship in paradise," as he put it—a year earlier. Unlike Yetah, however, Malul acknowledged that Palestinians in his jurisdiction had legitimate reasons to "brew . . . with feelings of displeasure and even hatred toward the state." First and foremost was the government's ban on refugee return, but there was also its delay in exchanging their temporary residency permits for civil identity cards, and the refusal of the celebrations' sponsors—the army and the municipality—to "recognize the population in practice."

Still, Malul's essentialist thinking made a structural diagnosis of the problem unthinkable. In his mind, the chief reason for the post-holiday bitterness was the flagrant disregard of "Oriental custom." In the invitations to the military parade, the authorities had failed to specify "who should be given priority and who should be honored in a more respectable seat." More important, they had denied Arab notables the chance "to stage shows of loyalty [and] . . . present their personal blessings" to local officials. Malul included himself on the list of guilty officials, but also the district police chief, who monitored the Palestinians' behavior; the Custodian of Absentee Property, who refused to return their property; and the "teachers, principals, and education inspectors" who taught their children to admire the achievements of Jewish colonization.[58]

Malul was typical among his colleagues, following the tradition of many of their British and Ottoman predecessors, in the paternalism that informed his insistence on empowering conservative communal elites to guide their flock.[59] But the second half of his memo—a detailed proposal for future anniversaries that prioritized outreach to the Arab public at large—stands out. The key objective of the holiday, he explained, should be to "sweep the population along in the stream of the celebrations" and instill among the people "true feelings of fondness." This goal was not something that could be achieved by continuing to manage the public through the intercession of their confessional leaders and local notables, he urged. Rather, the state would have to cultivate those feelings actively by establishing a direct line of communication (one that was unidirectional in form and propagandistic in content) with ordinary citizens. It would also require resources. Malul liked the idea of organizing joint events for Arab and Jewish schoolchildren, but he stressed the need for "separate and special" activities for the Arab population alone: film screenings, musical concerts, free admission to the amusement park, and more.

A number of subtle tensions ran through Malul's holiday memorandum despite its forceful language. The first part envisioned Independence Day as a critical opportunity to domesticate Arab elites, who would, in turn, keep their respective communities in line. The implication was that minimal effort would be required to make the most of the occasion: not only had these figures memorized the script of fealty expected of them, but they were humiliated when

"Nazareth notable " congratulates Israeli shaykh-cum-President Haim Weizmann in Rehovot in 1951. Photo by Fritz Cohen, courtesy of the GPO.

Tel Aviv, 1959. *From left to right*: Druze Shaykh Tarif and Catholic Archbishop Hakim sit in the front row at the holiday military parade. Courtesy of the GPO.

they were not permitted to perform it for their rulers. Although the second section of his memo did not vitiate the first, it did raise a question about the former's utility. Here Malul urged his supervisors to marshal considerable funds and effort into planning a range of entertainment activities that would remake Palestinians—especially their children—into grateful and thus loyal citizens. Did Malul want the Arab public to feel a genuine attachment to the racial-national order that excluded them, or simply to act "as if" they did?[60] Was it an inner patriotism he sought to produce, or bald submission disguised as a cultural ritual? Another question was the aspired target of the public's affection, or at least submission: was it the land's new overlords or an abstract, ostensibly independent entity—the state—with those overlords out of sight?[61]

THE LOYALTY CONUNDRUM

Malul's ambivalence indexed a broader predicament faced by Israeli officials: how to bind Palestinians to the Jewish state while denying them meaningful access to its resources. As with his discussion of Palestinian children, these problems were often expressed in emotional and even corporal terms. At a meeting of senior MAPAI leaders in February 1951, Labor Minister Golda Meir allegedly declared that the "sight of an Arab taking an oath of loyalty to the state three times a day" gave her the "'same bad feeling' . . . [that] rushes through her" when she sees an assimilated Jew in the Diaspora.[62] For Meir, the problem was not that Arabs were displaying enough loyalty, but rather too much. The possibility that Palestinian Arabs might one day feel as much a part of the Israeli state as many French, Egyptian, and other Jews felt rooted in their own countries could equally threaten Jewish nation-building by undercutting the security rationales used to justify inequality.[63] The Israeli army would confront this threat three years later. In June 1954, nearly all of the 4,520 Arabs it summoned to appear at the recruitment center, partly in response to MAKI's persistent demands that the authorities equalize the duties of all citizens, actually showed up. Stunned, suspicious of some volunteers' intentions, and apparently terrified by the prospect of having an Air Force pilot named Jihad, the commanders dismissed them at once.[64]

These contradictory concerns—over the lack of loyalty to the state and the potential surplus thereof—produced multiple visions of whether and how Jewish officials could cultivate an Israeli sensibility among Palestinian citizens without dismantling the racial hierarchies that dispossessed them. This question gave rise early on to a debate over whether it was "feasible [or] desirable" to integrate, or even "assimilate," the Arab population.[65] Proponents of this project failed to articulate what the success of any of these projects might look like, but support for reproductive fusion was never in the offing. In 1951, for instance, the army immediately shot down the prime minister's proposal to convert the population forcibly to Judaism en masse.[66]

As Malul's memo suggested, Arab children, who became subject to the Knesset's mandatory elementary education law in 1949, were identified as the best hope for removing the hostility that "persisted in the hearts" of the population.[67] Still, there were no obvious pedagogical models to follow. In the early 1950s, the Education Ministry's deputy director studied the history of European colonial education programs from the previous three centuries. To his dismay, none of their efforts to inculcate positive identifications among the Asian,

African, and Latin American populations they ruled seemed to offer a safe approach—one that would "help the Arabs get to know us better . . . learn the nicer aspects of our history, [and] become familiar with our contributions [toward] the advancement of human thought and science" without simultaneously encouraging their indigenous co-citizens to demand the same respect, recognition, and rights as they accorded themselves.[68]

In many ways, Israel's pursuit of a working balance between incorporation and exclusion resembled the challenge that all European empires confronted in the nineteenth and twentieth centuries.[69] At least two factors compounded this challenge, however. Most obvious was the fact that in 1948 the government had felt compelled to grant voting rights to the native Palestinians who remained, in exchange for international recognition. A subtler but equally challenging difference was that even if Israel's ruling elites *could* nurture Palestinian affinity to certain aspects of their national culture, they had yet to establish the parameters of that culture for themselves.[70] In the late 1940s and early 1950s, Prime Minister and Defense Minister Ben-Gurion worried openly about two problems that he believed confronted the young state. The first was the fact that the Jewish public, over half of whom had immigrated since 1948, had yet to develop the attributes of a nation. If the state did not act fast to "raise [the immigrants] to the level of the older [largely European] settlers," he warned in 1954, "the whole country [would] descend to a Levantine level."[71] His second concern was what he described as the public's "apathy" and "hedonism" in the face of the state's ongoing quest to colonize Palestine and make the Judaization of its land irreversible.[72] For the Old Man and those around him, the hardships of economic austerity, housing shortages, and postwar bereavement with which many families were coping during his period were trivial matters in the broad sweep of Jewish history.[73]

Many in the political and military establishment viewed these two problems—or at least their solutions—as related. To transform individual Jews, and especially the youth, into "Israelis," the state would have to provide more than language classes, land, and—if they were lucky—agricultural training. To "meld" the various cultures into a bona fide, Europeanized Hebrew nation and protect the state's wartime conquests required a complete resocialization through an extended conscription in a fighting force that would expand the frontier from within and combat the enemy from without. Once male veterans completed their service, they would return to duty for one month each year until they became middle-aged.[74]

May Day poster for the Histadrut, 1954. The caption reads: "With one hand on a weapon and one hand at work . . . (Nehemiah 4:11)." Designed by the Shamir Brothers, courtesy of the Palestine Poster Project Archives.

The key to "statist pioneering" (*mamlakhtiut*) was the production of stead-fast citizens who would sacrifice themselves for the nation out of love, not duty—a project that demanded a blurring of the lines between Jews in Israel and the apparatus that coerced them.[75] At government rallies, at military parades, and on the radio, Jewish citizens were thus urged to prepare for the "second round" and to think of themselves as "soldiers on eleven months' leave." It was not the Almighty that held the keys to their salvation, but the army.[76] A watershed in the veneration of the IDF occurred with the formation of Special Commando Unit 101 in the summer of 1953 to undertake cross-border raids in retaliation for individual acts of theft, sniping, sabotage, and occasional murder along Israel's armistice lines with Jordan and Egypt. Led by (future prime minister) Ariel Sharon, the unit spent most of its time undertaking murderous ambushes against Palestinian civilians in the West Bank and Gaza Strip.[77] The government often hid the consequences of these raids from the public, but Sharon and his officers quickly achieved cult status for their arrogant defiance of Israel's negotiated armistice lines and their willingness to flout the formalities of domestic and international law.[78] Moshe Dayan, who served as Sharon's mentor, called Unit 101 "the workshop for the creation of a new generation of [Hebrew] warriors"; he referred to its operations as "our elixir of life."[79]

It was hard to imagine how Palestinians could be included—much less recruited—into what some Jewish critics at the time condemned as "a psychosis of militarism" and "the glorification of martyrdom."[80] Although the government was anxious to stifle any expression of Arab dissent, the breakdown of the nation/state distinction entailed in Ben-Gurion's vision was predicated on their exclusion. The ties of affinity between the native minority and their compatriots now scattered across the other side of the armistice lines were rooted in language and culture, but also in family, social and commercial networks, schooling, professional associations, and a history of shared political struggle. These were the same people, after all, who owned and demanded the right to reclaim much of the land he was recruiting Jewish youth to settle and defend at all costs. They were also some of the same people targeted by Unit 101.

Partly for these reasons, but also because they were reconciled to the unpleasant business of occupation, Israel's leading Arabists disparaged any proposals to pacify Palestinians by turning them into Zionists-lite.[81] It was one thing to try to alienate the native minority from its local norms, its cultural identifications, and its past.[82] It was quite another to pursue Palestinian hearts—whether as a pragmatic strategy or, perhaps for the more liberal-minded policymakers such as the deputy education minister, to appease their consciences.[83] For Arab Affairs Advisor Joshua Palmon and his successors through the mid-1960s, the only way to deal with the population was to keep them internally divided, economically dependent, and frightened.[84]

But the contradictions of liberal settler rule, exacerbated by the fear that the slow pace of colonization could jeopardize the legitimacy of Jewish sovereignty, ensured that the loyalty conundrum would not go away.[85] In the summer of 1953, the government caved to popular pressure and the fear of foreign criticism and announced that the people of Nazareth—the only all-Palestinian city to survive the 1948 war intact—would be permitted to hold democratic municipal elections for the first time since 1946. Despite its vigorous efforts to manipulate the electoral outcome in April 1954, the local MAKI bloc won 40 percent of the final vote—ten times its strength in the Knesset—and became the council's largest single political bloc.[86]

The communist victory in newly renamed "Red Nazareth" was a vote of confidence for its leadership during the War on Return, the battle over the citizenship law, and the protests against the 1953 Land Acquisition Law. MAKI's triumph sent a chill through the halls of power in Jerusalem and Tel Aviv. Some hotheads in the ruling party openly proposed limits on the party's influence and lectured that "the Arabs of the Galilee should be advised that 'democracy' does not mean anything like this."[87] It was not that preventive measures had not already been taken. Eight months earlier, shortly after the government agreed to allow the elections to take place, the IDF settlement department, the Interior Ministry, and the Jewish Agency had begun to discuss plans to "Judaize" the Central Galilee, where Jews comprised just 7 percent of the population.[88] Immediately after the election, the army began to float the idea of creating a Jewish settlement inside the city itself. It would be "a colonizing act with difficulties," its planners acknowledged, but one that would "demonstrate state sovereignty to the Arab population more than any other settlement operation."[89]

For Palmon and others in the MAPAI political leadership, land confiscation was only part of the solution. Even before the Nazareth elections, a classified intelligence report revealed that the ill-coordination of the various state agencies operating in the "Arab sector" had lowered the "prestige" and "credibility" of Israeli officials among Arab citizens and thus the Shin Bet's ability to intimidate them, ostensibly a trend that had strengthened the influence of "MAKI and other nationalist groups." Since "the drastic operations" of 1948 were no longer possible, the report called on the government to do more to encourage voluntary emigration, disperse some of the population to the coasts (where Jews would surround them), and strengthen the power of communal leaders. It concluded by urging the authorities to attain the "effective blessing on the part of the Arabs" by extending them "full equality, in obligations as well as in rights," without compromising on "real security" needs.[90]

The failure to address precisely where "full equality" ended, "real security" began, and what the public's "blessing" would look like cast a shadow on a meeting of MAPAI leaders with Palmon's staff in May 1954 to discuss the implications of the Nazareth elections. On one side was Palmon's assistant, Shmuel Divon, who opposed trying to "incite a revolution in the hearts" of a population that was naturally hostile to the state. At best, he suggested without elaboration, the authorities could "minimize [the public's] hostility ... by [removing] some of the roots of its bitterness while remaining vigilant on security to the fullest extent of the law." On the other side was Foreign Minister Moshe Sharett, who insisted (also without explanation) that they could still "win the hearts of the Arab minority" and make them "truly loyal."[91]

Divon appears to have won that fight, and the discussion of equality was dropped in favor of keeping the population as divided, uneducated, and patriarchal as possible. In June Palmon's office, the police, the Shin Bet, and the Military Government established the top-secret Central Committee on Arab Affairs. Assigning itself to "strengthen the [military] regime and block the [political] crystallization of the Arab minority," the committee immediately secured the dismissal of three hundred of the eight hundred Arab teachers in the country—most of whom had eight to eleven years of experience—on political grounds.[92] It spent the next few years working to block university admission of Arab students, democratic local council elections, and the emergence of any Arab organizations that might unite the public.[93]

The Central Committee's sense of urgency only increased in the second half of 1954. Months earlier, Egyptian President Gamal Abdel Nasser, commander of the Revolutionary Command Council that had overthrown the British-imposed monarchy two years earlier, had tripled the airtime of Radio Cairo's thirty-minute program *Sawt al-'Arab* (Voice of the Arabs) and greatly increased the station's transmission capacities. The initial prompt for Nasser's outward orientation had been to galvanize popular sentiment throughout the region against the Baghdad Pact, the proposed Cold War security alliance with Britain, Pakistan, and Turkey that formed part of the anti-Soviet containment strategy. But the show soon became the most popular program in the Middle East, a fact that in November led the leaders of Algeria's National Liberation Front to choose it as the first venue in which to announce the start of their revolution against 150 years of French rule. *Sawt al-'Arab* eventually attained a station of its own, and its celebrated host, Ahmad Sa'id, spent much of his time calling for the liberation of Palestine and railing against Israel as an imperialist lackey.[94]

Israel was apparently unable to block these transmissions, but it was aware of their reportedly uplifting effect on the Palestinian public.[95] By 1955 the director of the Education Ministry's Arab Division felt confident enough to assert that the government's schools, where most children were educated, served as "points of psychological calm." Still, he admitted it was becoming harder to formulate a curriculum that would "teach the mother tongue, Arabic literature, without teaching Arabic [sic] nationality and without exciting the Arab child more than necessary or committing him to the Arabs outside the Israeli border."[96] It was around this time that Israeli school inspectors began to forbid the teaching of any Arabic language poem with the word *homeland* (*watan*) in it.[97] In the meantime, MAKI's relentless demands for racial equality, democratic local elections, the return of confiscated land, and the end of military rule had transformed it into the leading political force in the Arab community.[98]

It was not only MAPAI or the government that was alarmed by MAKI's victory in the Nazareth elections and the rise of Arab revolutionary politics in the region. In 1954, the left-Zionist MAPAM party launched the Arab Pioneer Movement to transmit "pioneering socialist values" to Palestinian youth. One of its main activities was to bring high school students to live for a year on a party-affiliated kibbutz and train them in agriculture, carpentry, metalsmithing, and other manual trades. Yet the movement's leaders also spoke openly about their ideological goals: on the one hand, "to teach [Arab youth] good citizenship, so they can learn about the liberation movement of the oppressed Jewish people, to look at us differently, to gain an appreciation for the achievements of the Jewish labor movement";[99] and on the other, "to distance ... [them] from their poisonous surroundings" and "save them from the teeth of the nationalist monster."[100]

It was against the backdrop of these unfolding concerns that a new, more forceful Independence Day agenda began to take shape, one that seemed to capture the spirit of Malul's vision to "sweep the population along in the stream of the celebrations." Already in 1952 the Interior Ministry had dropped its directive "not to impose" the celebrations.[101] That year the army also agreed to lift all curfews and travel restrictions for the entire twenty-four-hour period of the holiday.[102] The biggest shift occurred in the spring of 1955, in advance of Israel's seventh anniversary of statehood. Palmon formed a national committee to coordinate Independence Day celebrations "among the minorities," in cooperation with representatives from the Military Government and the Education and Interior Ministries.

In lieu of the makeshift, localized celebrations that had taken place until then, all military governors would now be required to host formal receptions in cooperation with the village councils (which they had helped to appoint) and carefully draft their guest lists.[103] Each school would also hold its own celebration, where the administration would distribute sweets to the younger pupils and arrange for buses to transport the older ones to the closest municipal parades. If the school had Jewish instructors, which most did until the end of the decade, they were to be tasked with "interesting [the residents] in *us* and in the meaning of this day."[104] Finally, the committee selected Nazareth and the large villages of Shafa 'Amr and Tayyibe as the sites for regional celebrations with athletic demonstrations, outdoor film screenings, and artistic performances to last into the night.[105]

The committee's protocols make no mention of attendance requirements at these events, but scrutiny of Palestinian "sentiments" on the holiday heightened alongside its expanded commemoration. Over time, the occasional reports of a handful of places where "special enthusiasm" had not been "felt" gave way increasingly to upbeat assessments of the "great impression" that the municipal and regional events made on its audiences and the "general and spontaneous joy" that overcame them.[106] It is clear that lifting movement restrictions helped to increase the turnout at these events to thousands of people.[107] Attendance continued to rise in 1956, when the government began offering free transport to the regional celebrations and added Acre and Beersheba to the roster.[108] Meanwhile, *al-Yawm*'s holiday supplements included large photo essays and elaborate narrative accounts of celebrations by Galilee locals known to be affiliated with the Arab satellite lists attached to the ruling party.[109]

In actuality, the insatiable desire for more definitive evidence of Palestinian "enthusiasm" on the holiday continued to dog government planners behind the scenes.[110] Part of the reason, of course, was that the decision to expand Palestinian celebrations had not followed a clarification of Israel's policy goals toward its Arab citizens. If anything, their growing demands for equality, democratic representation, and the restoration of their lands, coupled with the stirrings of revolutionary ferment outside, had made these goals even more uncertain. "What do we *want* our Israeli Arabs to become?" asked Edwin Samuel, an ardent Zionist, son of the first British high commissioner in Palestine, and former head of Israel's immigration office, in May 1955—as if it were all a matter of social engineering: "Do we want them to become good Israelis, speaking Hebrew and indistinguishable from their Jewish fellow citizens? Or do we want to keep them as a racial minority, speaking Arabic and wearing distinctive Arab dress?"[111]

Although no one had a long-term answer to this question, it was becoming clear that the state's leading Arabists wanted to cultivate *some* kind of "Israeli" sensibility among Palestinians in order to combat the growing challenge to their authority from within and without. But the project seemed to require opposing moves: on the one hand, to sever the identification of Palestinian citizens with their relatives, friends, and compatriots in exile, and to a great extent with each other; and on the other, to continue to enforce their segregation from the emerging "Israeli" nation.[112] The particular circumstances that shaped this dynamic put Palestinians in a position that was in some ways more impossible than that of other colonized minorities in the nineteenth and twentieth centuries. After American settlers closed the frontier, for example, Native Americans were invited to assimilate, so long as they discarded their "indigenous soul."[113] This was not the case for Israel's Arab citizens after 1948. Consider, for instance, the cover photo for the May 27, 1954 issue of *ba-Mahaneh* (At the Base), the army's weekly magazine sent free of charge to the homes of all personnel. Holding both a gun and a little boy in one hand, the soldier on leave could have looked like any other Jewish reservist. To underscore that he was, instead, a member of the "Minorities Unit," the editors chose a photo of him posing next

Making them Israeli but not Jewish. This picture of a Druze reservist on weekend leave adorned the May 27, 1954, cover of *ba-Mahaneh*. The headline reads, "The Minorities Unit demonstrates its power."

to a village elder—perhaps a relative—who wore traditional Druze garb. In the words of sociologist Khalil Nakhleh, whereas "their Jewishness [was] not sought after, their Palestinianness [was] denied."[114]

FONDNESS OR SERVILITY: THE CARROTS AND STICKS OF COERCION

The institutionalization of Independence Day celebrations in the mid-1950s created crises and opportunities for Israel's Palestinian citizens, the vast majority of whom lived in small villages severed from one another and the outside world. In 2001–2002, many of those old enough to remember this period cited fear, extreme poverty, and a desperate need to escape the confines of their community as the primary factors that led tens of thousands of people to decorate their homes and attend both local as well as regional holiday events.[115] Among the men and women I interviewed, there was no consensus on the correlation between the participation of any one person or community and the degree of their political consciousness. Some recalled the presence of themselves or their friends and neighbors at holiday events in terms of a shrewd cost-benefit analysis. Others emphasized the way military rule itself obstructed the awareness that might have persuaded people to stay home. In other words, older Palestinians today disagree over the extent to which Independence Day came to feel natural, part of the air they breathed, or what cultural theorist Stuart Hall calls the "horizon of the taken-for-granted."[116]

Fathiyya 'Awaysa was born in 1952 to parents from the depopulated town of Saffuriyya, near Nazareth. After several years of sleeping in tents and whatever other shelter they could find in nearby villages, they found a small apartment they could share with four other families—a "dream" compared to their prior years of wandering. Like many internal refugees who were barred from returning to their homes after the war, 'Awaysa usually avoided the celebrations.[117] Today a seasoned feminist activist in Nazareth, what stands out in her memory is the ease with which regime informants and mukhtars were able to elicit compliance from a community driven first and foremost by fear:

> In Mashhad they used to hold the celebrations on the fields of the threshing floor. They raised Israeli flags and decorated the place with balloons and roses. At the end, one of the ministers or someone from the government would come. I remember [in the mid-1950s] when Golda Meir came for the occasion. All the girls and women were gathered, even the old ones. Many were [so poor they were] barefoot, without shoes or slippers, but they were forced by those

working for the government who organized the celebrations to dance the *dabka* in honor of [her] arrival. They convinced the others to participate by saying, "Our situation is bad; who knows what will happen if we do not welcome her? Maybe they'll cart us off to jail." I'll never forget how a group of them came barefoot and danced [for her]. At the time there was no political consciousness, but people were also afraid. The military regime was still there, and no one dared speak out. I remember as a girl how we were told never to take down the Israeli flag or we would be arrested and taken to prison. The mukhtars said that we had to carry out the government's orders.[118]

For some people, fear may have played less of a role than the yearning for a taste of freedom. Like 'Awaysa, Najla Abu Ra's, born in 1936, was kept at home on the anniversary by her early politicization. In 1949, shortly after Israel annexed her village of Tayyibe, the Border Guard shot her father dead as he farmed his fields.[119] When she got older, she would wait by the railroad station for an activist on the train to throw out copies of *al-Ittihad*, and then smuggle them under the basket of vegetables on her head. Although she did not participate in the holiday herself, Abu Ra's recalls vividly how most people jumped at the chance to escape the ghetto that their village had come to feel like during the rest of the year:

> The authorities forced the people to celebrate, enlisted them to sing, tried to mold (*yishakkilu*) them to have fun. Everyone knew that the school principal had to go along with the state program. [Then] people went in cars brought by the authorities . . . to watch the dance performances and military parades in Haifa and Tel Aviv. It was just an excuse to get out. The important thing was that people were imprisoned, and they wanted to leave. . . . To get out, to work, to live. It was just something to do (*mashru', ya'ni*). This began to stop after military rule, when people began to realize what was going on.[120]

Holiday involvement fell along a spectrum. Some young men were willing to attend the annual reception hosted by their military governor in the hopes of sheltering their families from regime harassment and possibly securing a work permit the next day. However, even those who were unwilling to pay this "symbolic tax" took advantage of the fleeting freedoms occasioned by the anniversary.[121] Abu Ra's's husband, Muhammad, born in 1932, and his older brother, 'Abd al-Karim were counted among a handful of active communists and thus consistently denied permits to look for work outside of Tayyibe.[122]

Jerusalem, May 2, 1960. Dancing in the Independence Day Parade. Courtesy of the GPO.

Every Independence Day morning the young brothers would distribute political fliers against military rule, which had facilitated the expropriation of the village's vast farmlands after the war. Sometimes, after they had finished with their political work, they would hitch a ride to the nearby celebrations in Netanya and Tel Aviv. According to Muhammad, they did this not only to pick up a few days of construction work with a Jewish boss they knew who would allow them to sleep on the site illegally, but also just to watch.[123]

Today 'Abd al-Karim points to the ubiquitous presence of the regime's informant network, the limited dissemination of critical news, and the temptation to transgress cultural norms to explain why the young men of the village went to dance the song of King David with Jewish girls in the city: "They danced," he explained in a metaphor I heard repeatedly, "but their dancing was similar to a rooster who does not realize it has been slaughtered. They danced even though some of their brothers were in jail or their neighbors were suffering, which they did not know."[124]

Older Palestinians in Israel today continue to dispute the authorities' aim in encouraging these performances, and the extent to which they achieved it. This makes sense in light of the ambivalence of Israeli officials themselves. Was the government interested solely in the outward compliance of Arab celebrants, or was it after their inner affection?[125] If, as 'Awaysa recalls, the people of Mash-had simply enacted the performances they thought Jewish authorities wanted to see, others emphasized the coercion that state officials applied on the holiday as more direct, calculated, and insidious. Journalist Ghazi al-Sa'di, for example, was thirteen years old when he and his family were expelled from their home and their 125 acres of land in Miske, near Netanya. They were among the lucky ones. A distant tie that the family had had with the son-in-law of Israel's chief of staff enabled them to become one of the few Miske families allowed to resettle in Tira, just a few kilometers away. Al-Sa'di's clearest memory of Independence Day is of the annual pilgrimage by state journalists who came "to photograph people as though they were dancing." Instead of allowing the villagers to pass the day quietly (*yawm samt*), the authorities treated it as a "training day in servility" (*yawm tadrib 'ala al-khunu'*).[126]

Others echo al-Sa'di's training metaphor and take it a step further. In the Upper Galilee village of Mi'ilya, only a few kilometers from the Lebanon border, geographer and former high school teacher Shukri 'Arraf argues that the authorities used Independence Day as part of a broader tactic to discipline the population in order to habituate them into thinking their dispossession was normal.

> What the Military Government did was to tame the Arabs, to force them *to feel Israeli* . . . , to make people stop thinking. The authorities did not really believe the Arabs were happy, but it was their tactic, due to a lack of strategy. In Arabic we call that putting out the fire. This year, they do something small, the next year the same, and so on. It's like taking drugs, where one starts, little by little. . . . We used to stand up and sing for Independence Day. Sometimes we sang throughout the year, whenever there was a guest.[127]

Nowhere did Palestinians sense that state officials sought to "mold" their feelings more acutely than in the schools. At least until the mid-1980s, Arab schoolchildren in Israel were taught to memorize a special holiday anthem that saluted the "joy [that] filled the land" and the people as they celebrated "the birth of Israel . . . my eternal country."[128] "They used to give us flags and we would go out to sing, this is my country's independence and I am happy," explains Muhammad 'Abd al-Raziq 'Adawi, who came of age under military rule in the Nazareth-area village of Tur'an. "A six- or seven-year-old might be happy to sing, but he does not know why."[129]

Umm al-Fahm, April 29, 1958. Young teacher leads his pupils in a performance for the local celebration. This photo appeared in *al-Yawm* on May 5, 1958. Photo by Moshe Pridan, courtesy of the GPO.

The school celebrations orchestrated on Independence Day would not have been possible without the active recruitment of Palestinian teachers, who owed their positions to a political clearance that could be withdrawn at any time. In collaboration with military and intelligence officials, the Education Ministry carried out regular "sweeps" for instructors known to have a "nationalist past" or for being "active or inactive Communists."[130] As one former grade school teacher from Mashhad explains in her son's 1994 documentary film, *Istiqlal* (Independence), she and her colleagues were forced to swallow their pride as they decorated their classrooms with flags, hung pictures of state leaders, rehearsed student performances, and explained to the children that "the state was our state."[131] (Throughout the year they were also forced to abdicate part of their salary to mandated subscriptions to *al-Yawm*.[132]) It was not only their supervisors that teachers had to worry about; their colleagues, and even their pupils, were monitoring them as well.[133] In an era when teaching was virtually the only career option open to Arab high school graduates, and the combination of land confiscation, labor exclusion, and military rule rendered most villagers dependent on the state for their survival, the imperative to put food on the table often trumped their principles.[134]

Born and raised in the Galilee village of Fasuta, on the Lebanese border, novelist, playwright, and essayist Anton Shammas insists that neither the students nor the teachers at his school grasped the emptiness of the regular spectacles they performed for state inspectors. For years, he explains, the Catholic peasants were unaware that the state sought not to capture their hearts but to "sear" them with a stamp of ownership:

> Even according to the Arabic translation of the Declaration [of Independence], the state was defined as a Jewish state, but nobody seemed to pay any attention to that trivial fact. You see, we had the flags in our hands, so declarations did not matter, nor did the fact . . . we discovered later—that there was an utter rift between the signified and the signifier; those flags did not signify a single thing. They were meant by the state to be utterly void of any symbolic meaning and were cynically used as mere decorative objects, completely detached from their statism. And we were hung there at half-mast, like a mourning flag: too high to touch the receding Palestinian ground, but still not high enough to have a sense of the Israeli skies.[135]

From the "Palestinian ground . . . [to] the Israeli skies." Tira, May 7, 1950. Soldiers guard as Arab schoolchildren march to commemorate the first anniversary of Israel's annexation of the Little Triangle. *Al-Yawm* printed this photo in its April 23, 1958 holiday supplement as though it had been taken at a previous Independence Day celebration. Photo by Fritz Cohen, courtesy of the GPO.

THE MAKING OF THE "ISRAELI-ARAB"

In Shammas's eloquent account, nothing could be farther from reality than the goal to create "true feelings of fondness" as proposed by Minorities Officer Avraham Malul in 1951. As we have seen, the exclusion of Palestinians from the government's project to forge a nation was necessitated by its decision to mobilize the Jewish majority around a common enemy rather than a common set of values. Whereas Jews were taught to view the state as the highest fulfillment of their national identity, Arabs were called upon to revere it as an omniscient apparatus that stood above and apart from them. Yet it is critical that the Israeli state was not content to leave "its" Arabs to themselves on the holiday, or any other day for that matter. Although the songs that Shammas and his classmates sang and the flags they raised did not carry the same meaning as that intended at celebrations for Jewish schoolchildren, the very enactment of these gestures left a lasting mark that reached far beyond the experiences of individual Arab celebrants and the Jewish officials and guests who hosted, monitored, or attended them.

By the middle of the decade, visual and narrative depictions of Arab citizens smiling, clapping, and dancing on Independence Day circulated with increasing frequency in the Hebrew-language press, government newsreels, and public relations bulletins sent abroad. They often shared space with stories and photographs designed to illustrate the state's ostensible magnanimity in ushering the population into health, wealth, and modernity: a camel making way for a combine, a veiled woman at the polling booth, or a group of Druze soldiers paving a new road to their village.[136] The representation of the Palestinian minority as the state's beneficiaries, rather than as the nation's pioneers, reinforced the fiction of an ontological distinction between Arabs and Jews as the base on which racial privilege rested. Simultaneously, it served to disavow the violent history and continuation of Palestinian dispossession.[137] The photo of a young mother receiving postnatal care for her infant at a new rural clinic in the August 27, 1957 issue of ba-Mahaneh illustrates this disavowal. In addition to praising the benefits of the "modern care" provided by the new clinic, the caption boasts of the new electric cables and water pipes installed in the southern Triangle village of Tira as "part of the effort to raise the living standard in the minorities' villages." The backdrop to these new services—the government's effort to convince Palestinians to "forget" the recent massacre of forty-eight citizens in nearby Kafr Qasim—goes unmentioned.

Beyond a handful of Border Guard units and the two hundred permanent officials of the Military Government itself, the vast majority of Jewish citizens

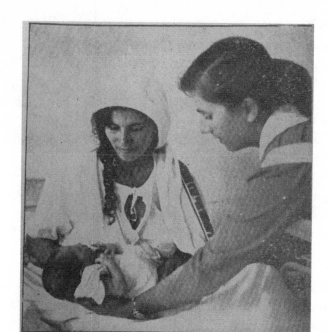

Touting the health clinic, electricity lines, and water pipes in Tira, in the southern Triangle. Accord-ing to this photo essay, published in the August 27, 1957 issue of the IDF weekly, *ba-Mahaneh*, all of these services were "added recently as part of the effort to raise the living standard in the minorities villages."

had the luxury of averting their gaze from the reality of deprivation behind these portraits of humanitarian uplift.[138] The state's expropriation of nearly half of all Arab-owned land between 1953 and 1954 alone—part of a deliberate policy to "strike at [the Palestinians'] tottering land base"—spared few villages or land-owning town dwellers.[139] Those families who retained sizable parcels of farmland found it increasingly difficult to live off it because they were forced to sell their crops at one-third the price of crops grown on Jewish farms. With the exception of a handful of informants, particularly cooperative mukhtars, the government also denied Arab landowners agricultural loans to mechanize and raise their output per dunam.[140] In the spring of 1955, just as these policies were forcing growing numbers of Arab villagers to seek outside work, the authorities tightened the noose around them by formally banning all Arabs from entering Jewish colonies in the Galilee.[141]

The socioeconomic strangulation of Palestinians transcended the family unit. In contrast to all 891 Jewish settlements, only a handful of more than one hundred Arab locales enjoyed electricity, running water, or functioning sewage systems. Medical care was another problem. Until 1959, most Palestinians were denied full membership in the Histadrut, the country's primary medical provider. For this reason, most had to travel kilometers from their home to see a doctor, a trip requiring both a military permit and bus fare that, because of the high unemployment rate, was prohibitively expensive. To fill this vacuum, the Military Government and the Health Ministry provided separate and sparse services to the Palestinian population. Until 1954, the state did not assign a single state doctor to the villages of the Western Galilee.[142] In 1955–1956, a spate of preventable child and elderly deaths caused by the refusal of the authorities to issue permits to transport them to the hospital captured enough media attention that the government established several clinics in large villages. According to a Central Bureau of Statistics report in December 1955, the mortality rate for Arab children was twice that of their Jewish counterparts.[143]

One of the chief obstacles to securing basic public services, new roads, and the ability to expand their local economies was the government's refusal to allow Palestinians to establish local and municipal councils.[144] Within these communities, internal refugees were consistently the worst off. The United Nations Relief and Works Agency cut off its international aid to them in 1952, yet Israel provided almost no public welfare assistance to compensate them for the loss. Through much of the decade, they continued to live in tin shacks on the edges of the villages and towns that housed them.[145]

Even without an awareness of the fabrication contained in the photographs of Palestinian joy and appreciation at state celebrations, at least some of the Jewish public may have found these images confusing. This was because they joined, rather than replaced, the generalized representations of Palestinians as revenge-seeking infiltrators, kuffiyya-masked marauders, and trespassing squatters.[146] This coexistence—of the loyal, grateful, and progressive Arab alongside the hostile, menacing, and intransigent one—came to embody the construct of the "Israeli-Arab." If one part of him was tied to the state and its future, the other was a reminder of his potential to slip back into his true essence—a rationale for why he would always be kept at arm's length.[147]

The tension between these two poles would become more pronounced over time, as Palestinians became more assertive and began to make growing claims on the state. This claim-making would, in turn, lead to reconfigurations in the dualism that inhered in the figure of the "Israeli Arab." At times the authorities and the dominant media would pit the "good" Arabs (passive, quiet, cooperative) against the "bad" ones (defined as anyone who challenged the legitimacy of settler entitlements). At other moments, the entire population would be vilified as a "grave security threat."[148]

. . .

As Israel's founders insisted on keeping Palestinians apart, they became fixated on the question of whether the population was really "with" them. Since feelings were difficult to measure, the demand for reassurance that Palestinians had "recognized" them came to revolve around things that could be heard, seen, and touched. Songs, clothing, decorations, and mere gestures of joy all testified to the reality of a state in which the vanquished citizens had a special, albeit unequal, part to play. Like the casing of equality that Israel extended to the Arabs of Palestine who remained after 1948, it was ultimately just the shell of their loyalty that, by the mid-1950s, most Jewish officials demanded, not its substance. Most became citizens, but they remained strangers nonetheless—denied the fruit of the state's advances in construction, industry, and agriculture whose details they were nonetheless urged to imbibe in *al-Yawm*'s annual holiday supplements.

During the first decade of statehood, most Palestinians who opposed the holiday on political grounds found it safer to avoid or go along with the performances requested of them rather than risk the denial of a travel permit or a summons to the governor's office. The lack of open resistance on Independence Day did not make the celebrations less fraught for Israeli officials. It did, however, create a space in which to propagate an image of happy and grateful minorities, a community as unperturbed by the military occupation of their villages and towns inside Israel's de facto borders as it was immune to the forces of decolonization and Arab nationalism outside them. Nonethless, the contradictions between the inexorable logic of colonization inside and the growing demands for decolonization outside ensured that this image would burst sooner rather than later.

5 BOTH CITIZENS AND STRANGERS

IN LATE NOVEMBER 1957, the Hebrew and state-sponsored Arabic press in Israel printed a series of articles describing an extravagant "ceremony of reconciliation" held in the small and impoverished border village of Kafr Qasim. More than four hundred distinguished guests attended the event, including cabinet ministers, Knesset members from the ruling MAPAI party, Military Government officials, national trade union leaders, and government-recognized village notables from the Little Triangle. The idea behind the *sulha*—so named after the Bedouin custom in which two tribes make peace over bread and salt—was to heal the remaining wounds from the October 29, 1956 Israeli Border Guard massacre of forty-eight Palestinian Arab citizens, all but four of whom were residents of Kafr Qasim.[1] The day of the ceremony, November 20, marked exactly one year and three weeks since the first day of the Sinai War and the fateful evening when day laborers returning home were lined up and executed for unknowingly violating a curfew that had been announced only thirty minutes before.

A heavy cloud of intimidation, grief, and anger lurked behind the fanfare of the ceremony, comprising speeches calling for villagers to move beyond the tragedy for the sake of coexistence, promises of generous reparations to the wounded and the families of the slain, and a sumptuous full-course meal. In contrast to the mainstream media, editors of *al-Ittihad* and MAPAM's Arabic-language organ, *al-Mirsad*, denounced the so-called truce as a fraud. The government, they charged, was deploying pomp and circumstance to conceal the pressure it had exerted to force representatives of the injured families to accept the paltry compensation it was offering them and to cancel the ongoing trial of the eleven

Kafr Qasim, November 20, 1957. Dignitaries arrive for the "ceremony of reconciliation." Courtesy of the IDFA.

border guards accused of perpetrating the crime.[2] Like the annual celebrations on Independence Day, the *sulha* was orchestrated to normalize the subordination of Palestinian citizens for the sake of Jewish privilege, an attempt to rewrite the practices of Israeli violence and dispossession as a narrative of appeasement and multiculturalism. More than ever before, however, state officials imposed this particular spectacle of sovereignty on the defensive.

This chapter traces the fierce discursive and physical clashes that erupted over the government's heavy-handed response to the massacre in Kafr Qasim, and the grassroots Palestinian movement to commemorate its victims. For many years, Qasimis remained isolated and traumatized by the crime. Under the pressure of conservative elders who relied heavily on the Military Government for their positions, the annual remembrances were largely quiet and personal. Elsewhere in the country, however, commemorations quickly assumed a political overtone, and the repressive measures that the authorities deployed to quash them seemed only to deepen the defiance of their participants.

The timing of the massacre played a crucial role in the way these memorial confrontations unfolded. Leading activists and intellectuals were watching with cautious optimism as both European empires and the authoritarian regimes they had helped put in place in the Middle East teetered, and some sought to galvanize the Arab public and attract international attention to their plight by riding its wave. The identification of Israel's Palestinian citizens with national liberation movements in Africa and Asia was, however, a fraught and risky endeavor. For Palestinian intellectuals—communist and otherwise—the growing representation of their people as a colonized nation akin to Algeria—one seeking the total withdrawal of the settler community—stood in tension with the party's official position since 1948 that the borders of historic Palestine contained two legitimate national movements, not just one. The efforts of figures such as Tawfiq Tubi, Emile Habibi, and Hanna Naqara to resolve this tension by consistently drawing the borders of their future liberation at the UN partition lines of 1947 would appease few of their Jewish co-citizens. Not only had the partition map long since disappeared from acceptable public discourse, but the repatriation of Palestinian refugees and the end of settler privilege even *within* the lines of Resolution 181 would spell the end of the Zionist dream. As preparations to host record-breaking numbers of tourists for Israel's tenth-anniversary celebrations got under way in the fall of 1957, the government was eager to nip in the bud any untoward attention to the Jewish state—particularly in the context of colonialism. What followed was a ferocious clash over the relationship between the Jewish state and its Palestinian Arab citizenry, with political losses incurred on all sides. The stakes had never been higher.

. . .

As we have seen, the massacre in Kafr Qasim was by no means the first act of physical or deadly violence committed against Palestinian citizens by uniformed officers (or civilian settlers) in Israel. For the previous seven years, the government had enjoyed widespread support for the sweeping emergency powers it deployed against the Arab minority. The "ruffian despotism"[3] with which the military had ruled in the name of combating refugee return, guarding settlements, and colonizing Palestinian land had produced patterns of police brutality, lethal medical neglect, and murder that regularly went unpunished.[4] In the meantime, the prevalent cultural sentiment among Israeli Jews was that Arab citizens—like Arabs everywhere—were backward, parasitic, and responsive only to the language of force.[5] These sentiments bore witness to the legacy of the pre-state settlement movement, but the Yishuv's wartime ethnic cleansing of Palestine had exacerbated them.[6]

Additional factors nourished Jewish chauvinism against Palestinians during the first decade of statehood as well. State officials and labor leaders, for instance, often explained the denial of civil rule and full Histadrut membership to the Arab minority on the grounds that it would take time to "build [their] consciousness."[7] It is difficult to delineate where this paternalism ended and the broader xenophobia began. The conflation of Arab movement, and Arabs generally, with trespassing and danger; the growing sight of Palestinian workers sleeping in bus depots, stables, construction sites, restaurant kitchens, and the ruins of former Palestinian homes on the outskirts of Jewish cities because they were forbidden to stay there overnight; and the Manichean appearance of Arabs in pulp fiction and school textbooks as lazy fools or murderous anti-Semites, all created the ideal conditions for popular "permissions to hate."[8] By the mid-1950s, these phenomena had given rise to de facto segregation on public transportation, genocidal sentiments among Jewish youth, and attempts by Palestinian workers to "pass" as Jews in order to avoid verbal and physical harassment.[9]

Still, most of the Jewish public knew little about the brutality of the military regime or the devastating economic strangulation of Palestinian communities resulting from the confiscation of their lands, the effective color bar it imposed on their wages, their crop prices, and their access to the labor market and higher education.[10] These blinders extended to sections of Tel Aviv's bohemian intellectual circles, just a few kilometers from the Little Triangle, who knew nothing about the nightly curfew imposed there.[11] In September 1955, the *Jerusalem Post* reported that Israeli Jews knew more about Saigon and Rangoon than Nazareth, the only all-Arab city that remained after 1948.[12] The authorities created the ideal conditions for this ignorance by physically sealing off Arab villages from neighboring Jewish towns and colonies. In addition to granting wide license to the military censor, the government routinely denied charges of racial discrimination and invoked the state of emergency to strike unwanted comments from the Knesset record.[13] The High Court also deferred to "security experts" on all matters pertaining to Palestinian rights and civil equality, reproducing the regime's self-depiction as an agent of modernization and peace between warring clans.[14]

The slaughter of forty-eight Arab citizens on the eve of the 1956 war opened a brief crack in this thick wall of silence, for its scale and brutality were too large to hide completely from view. A considerable section of the Jewish public was outraged that the authorities would prosecute rank-and-file troops for merely following their orders. Others, however, viewed the massacre as a gruesome negation of their humanist self-image and supported the trial of the accused as an affirmation of Israeli democracy.[15] The legal proceedings were critical for international reasons as well.[16] By 1956, Israel had just seven international embassies, all in Europe and North America.[17] Over the previous three years the state's global standing had been bruised. A string of UN censures had followed Israel's reprisal raids in the West Bank and Gaza Strip, which killed an estimated four times as many Palestinian and other Arab civilians as the number of Jewish soldiers and settlers whose deaths the operations were avenging.[18] In the meantime, both the Soviet Union and the United States had begun to distance themselves from the Jewish state.[19]

Another blow had come with Israel's exclusion from the Asian-African Conference in Bandung, Indonesia, in 1955. That April, in response to the slow pace of decolonization and the failure of the United Nations to admit new members since 1950, delegates from twenty-nine countries in Asia, Africa, and the Middle East convened in Indonesia to demand "respect for the[ir] sovereignty" in the face of mounting US aspirations to global hegemony. Among other objectives, they pressed for the end of "racialism" and "colonialism in all its manifestations."[20] In the early 1950s, especially after the 1952 Free Officers coup that brought Gamal Abdel Nasser to power in Egypt, Israel had worked hard—and largely in vain—to establish formal diplomatic ties with India and other emerging states in Southeast Asia.[21] To compensate for the embargo of the Arab League, the Jewish state sought to build international commercial networks and to combat its image as a foreign implant and "seedbed of imperialism." Of great concern was the prospect that the leaders of the new Asian states, inhabited by the largest Muslim communities in the world, would seek common cause with the Arab world in its support for Palestinian self-determination.[22]

In the months leading up to Bandung, Israeli diplomats had tried desperately to secure an invitation to the conference. Behind the scenes, they worked with the Burmese and other delegates with whom they enjoyed informal ties to prevent the subject of Palestine from being raised, much less inserted into a discussion about imperialism or racial discrimination.[23] But the participation of the Jewish state was a nonstarter. The organizing Columbo powers of South Asia sought Arab support in opposing American and British intervention in Korea and Taiwan, respectively, and Nasser made clear that Arab states would boycott the conference if Israel attended.[24]

The diplomatic frenzy preceding Bandung notwithstanding, pressure from the Burmese and Indian delegations forced the attending Arab member states to make a meaningful concession in the conference's final communiqué.[25] Along with disputes over Yemen and West Irian (also known as Papua), the resolution on Palestine appeared in a section entitled "Other Problems," detached from the sections on "Human Rights and Self-Determination" and "Problems of Dependent Peoples," which raised the cases of northern and southern Africa. Without mentioning the words *colonialism*, *racialism*, or *self-determination*, the resolution merely expressed the conference's "support of the rights of the Arab people of Palestine and called for the implementation of the United Nations resolutions on Palestine and the achievement of a peaceful settlement of the Palestine question."[26]

Bandung put Israeli leaders in an uncomfortable position. For domestic reasons, Nasser had insisted on keeping the resolution oblique. It was, however, undeniable that the Egyptian president was offering to sign a peace treaty if Israel would agree to repatriate a substantial number of Palestinian refugees and relinquish its territorial conquests beyond the 1947 partition borders.[27] Given Jerusalem's maximalist stance on these questions over the previous seven years, it came as no surprise that it received the Palestine resolution as a negation of "the rights of the Jewish people."[28] Israel's insistence on its territorial integrity and its right, as a UN member, to refuse outside interference hardly turned it into a pariah state. Nonetheless, the Bandung resolution was important because it marked the first time that Israel had to reject publicly a peace offer from the most powerful leader in the Arab world on terms previously endorsed by the international community and the Yishuv itself.[29]

The peak of Israel's outsider status in the international community followed its surprise attack on Egypt in October 1956. The immediate goal of the invasion had been to regain control of the French- and British-owned Suez Canal Company, which President Nasser had nationalized that July after the World Bank withdrew its loan offer to finance the construction of the Aswan Dam. Nasser's defiance of the world's largest imperial powers had electrified the Middle East and much of the Third World, but this was not the main reason why

Israel joined the attack. For more than a year Ben-Gurion had wanted to launch a war on Egypt: to undermine its president's regional popularity, and to prevent him from lending diplomatic and military support to Palestinian refugees.[30]

It was not only Egypt and the Arab states that would condemn Israel's role in the Suez invasion three months later. So would Nikita Khrushchev, who in December 1955 had already announced Moscow's reevaluation of its prior support for partition and declared that Israel had been an aggressor state since its birth, partly as a way to expand its influence in the Middle East.[31] Then there was US President Dwight Eisenhower, who had spent the previous two years quietly trying to mediate a peaceful settlement between Israel and Egypt. Concerned about escalating tensions with the Soviets and wanting not to alienate the Arab world, particularly America's oil suppliers in the Persian Gulf, Eisenhower excoriated Ben-Gurion for ignoring his warning not to join the invasion. Together with Khrushchev, he helped to push through an immediate UN condemnation and subsequently threatened sanctions until Israel agreed to withdraw from the Gaza Strip and the Sinai Peninsula by March 1957.[32] This diplomatic debacle only heightened the Israeli government's concern that its collusion with Britain and France would bolster Arab claims that the state was an expansionist proxy of European imperial powers and thus further alienate it from the emerging "Afro-Asian bloc" at the UN.[33]

For Israel's public at home and its allies and friends abroad, then, Jerusalem needed to demonstrate its commitment to the rule of law by punishing the "cruel and methodical murder" of its own, ostensibly equal, citizens.[34] Still, the limits of Israeli liberalism were firmly in place, and the "festival of triumphalis[m]" and Jewish "national swaggering" that erupted after the 1956 war hardly created the conditions to push against them.[35] It was one thing for the public to condemn the barbarity of a few low-ranking soldiers whose personal histories might explain how they had "lost their minds," as Prime Minister Ben-Gurion suggested early on.[36] It was quite another to denounce the atrocity as a logical, if extreme, outcome of military rule and the structures of settler privilege.[37] This was precisely the conclusion that many Palestinians and a small number of Jews drew from the crime. News of the massacre revived old fears of the kind of mass expulsions that Israel carried out in 1948 and 1949. It also sparked new fears about the absence of political, legal, and cultural safeguards to prevent the repetition of a similar assault.[38]

By the middle of the 1950s, and especially after the Sinai campaign, a growing number of Israeli officials were beginning to come to terms with the presence of the sizable Arab population in the country. They made this mental accommodation less because they found no evidence of the population's attempt to undertake sedition against the state than because the opportunity to carry out mass expulsions appeared to have ended after the fog of the 1948–1949 war had cleared.[39] Yet Israel's gradual reconciliation with the fact of a sizable and unwanted indigenous minority, still 10 percent of the population despite the doubling of the Jewish population by 1951, did not translate into a view of their co-citizens as co-nationals, or bona fide members of the body politic with equal (if any) entitlement to the state. Thus, when Palestinians began to articulate their own analysis of the massacre; to openly contest its official narrative as an aberration from the state's otherwise fair (if not righteous) treatment of them; and to make unprecedented demands to end the conditions that had produced the crime, Israeli officials fought back with a vengeance. Never had the contradictions of the liberal settler state—between those who lived in the state and those who were entitled to it—been so pronounced.

"MOW THEM DOWN!"

The massacre in Kafr Qasim occurred just as Israel was preparing to attack Egypt's Sinai Peninsula. On the morning of the attack, IDF Brigadier Yissachar Shadmi, who commanded a battalion in Israel's Central District, was ordered to take all precautionary measures to maintain quiet along the Jordanian armistice line.[40] To this end, he received permission to move up the start of the evening curfew from 10 P.M. to 5 P.M. in the seven southern Triangle villages under his jurisdiction, including Kafr Qasim. Shadmi then summoned Major Shmuel Malinki, commander of the Border Guard battalion placed under his authority, and orally instructed him to "shoot to kill" everyone found outside his or her home after the curfew, "without sentiments." He emphasized that killing the curfew "breakers" would entail "fewer complications" than making arrests. When Malinki asked about those day laborers who would return home after 5 P.M., unaware of the curfew, Shadmi replied with the Arabic phrase for the deceased, *Allah yirhamu*, "May God have mercy on him." Soon after, Malinki passed on Shadmi's orders to his platoon and company commanders, adding that it would be desirable to kill a few people in each village as a deterrent against any trouble during the war.[41]

Six of the seven villages under Shadmi's control were spared bloodshed because local commanders chose to quietly evade or change Malinki's order.[42] Not so in Kafr Qasim, headed by Commander Gabriel Dahan. That afternoon at 4:30, a young sergeant visited the home of the seventy-four-year-old mukhtar to inform him of the curfew change. Wadi' Muhammad Sarsur pleaded that there was not enough time to spread the word to the four hundred day laborers in the quarries, olive groves, and fields located as far away as Lydd, Jaffa, and Ramat Gan. When these entreaties proved fruitless, the mukhtar and several of his relatives left to spread the word. By 4:55 P.M., everyone inside the village was in their homes. Soon thereafter Sarsur began to hear shooting, which continued, according to the watch of his grandson, until 7 P.M.[43]

The majority of the murders took place at the entrance to the only road leading to the village, on its western edge.[44] Dahan's unit used rifles and machine guns to carry out nine waves of killings, ranging from small attacks on a few men returning on bike, foot, or donkey, to larger assaults on groups of up to twenty men and women arriving in trucks. The unit took the "shoot to kill" order quite seriously, firing repeatedly at anyone wounded who appeared to be alive. Other survivors would repeat many elements of the testimony of 'Abd Allah Samir Budayr, who arrived with the first group of workers:

> Roughly five minutes before 5 P.M., I arrived at the entrance of the village . . . along with three other workers—on bikes. We came across a unit of border guards in a car—about twelve with an officer at their head. The workers said, "Shalom, officer." The officer asked them [in Hebrew], "Are you happy?" They answered, "Yes." The guards got out of the car and ordered the workers to stand. The officer ordered, "Mow them down! [*Tiktsor otam!*]" When the guards began to shoot, I lay on the ground and rolled over onto the road, at which point I screamed, even though I wasn't injured. I stopped screaming and pretended to be dead. The guards continued to shoot the other workers who had fallen. Then the officer said, "Enough! They're dead already. It's a shame to waste the bullets."[45]

In the course of two hours, Israeli border guards murdered nineteen men, six women, ten teenage boys (ages fourteen to seventeen), six girls (ages twelve to fifteen), and seven young boys (ages eight to thirteen). In almost every killing wave at least one person survived with injuries and a small number escaped unharmed.[46] Late that night, while the curfew was still in effect, the army drove some thirty-five men from the nearby village of Jaljulya, provided them with hoes, and ordered them to dig as deep and as quickly as possible. Although they did not yet know it, these men were standing in the middle of the village cemetery and digging the graves of the slain.[47]

UNVEILING THE "CONSPIRACY OF SILENCE"

News of the atrocity in Kafr Qasim leaked out almost immediately, but it would take nearly two months and a sustained public campaign by MAKI deputies and a handful of leading writers and artists before the public learned the full gravity of the crime.[48] Although Prime Minister David Ben-Gurion claimed to be horrified when he first received word of the massacre and immediately appointed a closed commission to investigate it, his primary concern was to clear the name of the army, which had just pulled off what the majority of the Jewish public celebrated as a stunning victory against Egypt. As far as he was publicly concerned, the massacre was a tragic mishap—the outcome of ambiguous orders, poor coordination, and a group of savage and mentally disturbed border guards.[49]

Five days after learning of the incident, the premier's three-member commission buttressed this account by accepting at face value Brigadier Shadmi's denial that he had issued the oral execution orders that Major Malinki, the Border Guard commander, continued to attribute to him.[50] Because the Zohar Commission's protocols remain classified, the role that Ben-Gurion played in its meetings is unknown. The civilians who staffed the commission, including District Court Judge Benjamin Zohar, likely knew nothing of the plan that the army had shelved days earlier to relocate all Palestinians of the Little Triangle in temporary detention camps, or possibly to expel them permanently eastward, as part of a faked invasion of Jordan to throw Nasser off guard.[51] Yet their decision to believe Shadmi's word over Malinki's was crucial for Ben-Gurion: within the Israeli military hierarchy, the brigadier was only two steps removed from Moshe Dayan, the nationally beloved chief of staff, and only one more step removed from the Old Man himself.

Upon learning that the commission had absolved the army brass of any responsibility for the crime, the prime minister immediately issued an obscure public announcement regarding the "injury" of a number of villagers who were "innocently returning to their homes after [a] curfew" that the army had imposed to "protect" them in the face of increased Palestinian guerilla activities along the border.[52] The government would adopt the commission's recommendation to try the suspected border guards for "obeying an illegal order," he explained, and offer a modest payment to the victims' families before determining the total amount of damages to award them. This brief declaration was all the general public would know for the next five weeks, thanks to the gag order the premier imposed on the media, the physical cordon he ordered around Kafr

Qasim itself, and the isolation of the wounded survivors in the military hospital ward.[53] Even after a young MAPAM secretary and two MAKI deputies stealthily bypassed these barriers and circulated the testimonies they recorded from survivors to news agencies, diplomats, and private citizens, attempts to raise the issue in the Knesset were vilified and permanently struck from the record.[54]

Yet it was easier for the government to dismiss a handful of leftist—much less communist or noncommunist Palestinian—parliamentarians than a group of leading Zionist intellectuals who rarely questioned the regime on civil liberties or military affairs.[55] The limited news of the massacre that had trickled out from activists over the previous weeks struck a nerve with some members of the Jewish cultural elite, who viewed the state's duty to protect the life of all citizens as a cornerstone of their liberal value system and a symbol of their unequivocal repudiation of Nazi crimes.[56] The authorities' bulwark against grassroots pressure for more information thus began to crumble in early December, when seven leading journalists, poets, and playwrights—many of whom had earned their nationalist credentials lionizing or fighting with Zionist paramilitary groups before 1948—edited, printed, and hand-delivered thousands of copies of a one-time magazine entitled *Everything on Kfar Qasim*.[57] The media floodgates opened one week later, after MAPAI's *Davar* published a poem denouncing the cover-up. Its author was Natan Alterman, a party loyalist and close associate of the premier.[58]

Recognizing the futility of the media blackout, Ben-Gurion called a special session of the Knesset on December 12. Omitting most details of the crime and any reference to the army or his attempted cover-up, he announced the government's response to the "shocking deed" that the Border Guard had perpetrated in "certain villages on the eastern border."[59] He further assured his audience that the families of the slain and "Arab notables" around the country had already thanked the authorities for their decision to bring the suspects to trial. "There is no people in the world which holds life dearer than the Jewish people," he declared:

> Not only is there to be one law for the stranger and the citizen, but the stranger living among us is to be treated with love. The Arabs of Israel are not strangers, but citizens with fundamentally equal rights. In regard to human life, however, the civil status of any man makes no difference. The lives of all men are sacred.[60]

It might have been tempting for Knesset deputies, ordinary citizens, and the international community to read the words of the premier as a clear commitment to uphold the sanctity of human life and the equality to which the Declaration of Independence had pledged. The biblical injunction he invoked enjoyed iconic status among Diaspora Jews because of their own historic persecution as "strangers." From the 1880s until the day Israel was admitted to the United Nations in May 1949, Zionist leaders had argued that the only way for the Jewish people to become "normal" and eliminate the blight of anti-Semitism was for them to be sovereign, "a nation like all others."[61] At the same time, in recognition of the historic vulnerabilities of liberal nationalism and their own experience as an oppressed minority, they had vowed that their devotion to democracy and equality would render their state "a light unto other nations."[62]

Seven years later, the equivocation in Ben-Gurion's own words testified to the hollowness of that oath. Referring to the "strangers living among us" even as he insisted that "the Arabs of Israel are not strangers," the prime minister betrayed the existential conflict that characterized the relationship of the Jewish state to the small minority of Palestinians who had managed to stay or return to the country after the Yishuv's ethnic cleansing operations of 1948. The lip service he paid to Arab equality likely appeased some in the room, but his exhortation reinforced the extent to which the "us" of the Jewish public, a group composed largely of immigrants, continued to view native-born Arab citizens as strangers—fundamentally no more "at home" than noncitizen Palestinian refugees outside Israel's de facto borders. (One border guard who was posted regularly in Kafr Qasim later resigned in protest over the conviction of his friends on the grounds that they had never been trained to make such distinctions.[63])

By having to appeal to natural law to convince the public of the sacredness of Arab life, the prime minister acknowledged the superficiality of the shared legal status of Arab and Jewish citizens. Given the army's systematic disdain for human life over the border (a reality that made a mockery of the values he espoused in Israel's name), it is difficult not to see Kafr Qasim as a particularly brutal outcome of the salience of race over civic status in Israel.[64] It also helps to explain why Major Malinki testified during his trial that he had found Shadmi's instructions to kill curfew-breaking citizens to be "extreme . . . [but] not incommensurate with the spirit of the times."[65] As one of his fellow commanders put it, the suspected guards could not understand why one day they were "killing infiltrators and getting prizes," and the next day they were on trial for murder.[66]

THE INITIAL AFTERMATH

The weeks and months following the massacre produced an array of reactions among Palestinians in Israel. For the mourning residents of Kafr Qasim, virtually the only thing that mattered was figuring out how to move on. Inside the village, residents lived for months in a state of grief, terror, rage, and (for some) hunger. In a small community of only two thousand people, most of whom belonged to one of six extended families, almost every Qasimi had lost a relative to the slaughter. Tens of others survived physically unscathed but witnessed the carnage on the road as the drivers of the lorries bringing them home disobeyed the soldier's orders to stop at the entrance and sped inside. As a result of the collective trauma, schools were closed for more than a month and workers reportedly stayed home for fear of returning after the curfew.[67] Meanwhile, the army extended its cordon around the village, denying entrance to journalists, friends, and other members of the public who came to pay their condolences.[68]

Palestinians outside Kafr Qasim also received the news of the massacre with a mixture of horror and fear, but their ability to take action was shaped by their distance from it.[69] At the formal political level, MAKI presented the most radical analysis of the crime, accusing the government of pathologizing the shooters in order to conceal what had been a premeditated murder ordered by the highest ranks of the state.[70] Not everyone was prepared to level this accusation—not openly, at least. Nonetheless, a broad consensus appeared in the deluge of letters from Palestinian students, community leaders, lawyers, and others that the massacre was the inevitable outcome of the regime's "policies of national oppression" against them over the previous eight years.[71]

In late 1956, neither these policies nor the crises they had produced were on the public agenda. The run-up to the July 1955 parliamentary elections had witnessed widespread charges that MAPAI had reduced the Military Government to a political machine that secured Arab votes during election seasons. Warnings had also spiked that the regime's rumored excesses would further push the population into the hands of Nasser and the emerging Arab nationalist currents over the border.[72] These charges cost MAPAI several Knesset seats, while MAKI's political strength peaked; but MAPAM also gained seats, and it agreed to join the ruling coalition and vote against future MAKI motions to end military rule on the condition that it be appointed to head a commission to investigate the regime's future.[73] Seven months later, in February 1956, the commission affirmed MAPAI's claim that emergency rule remained vital for security.

Palestinian and Jewish activists denounced the findings of the Ratner Commission, named after the MAPAM-affiliated general who headed it.[74] The lackluster recommendation in its final report to reduce the suffering of the population was only one reason for their alarm. More insidious was the report's conclusion that the regime, and particularly the system of evening curfews, closures, and movement permits it enforced, was necessary in order to bar Arab citizens from inhabiting land that the state had confiscated or coveted for Jewish settlement. By embracing the commission's finding that the entire Arab population posed a threat to Jewish colonization, the government implicitly confirmed its definition of national security in racial rather than military terms.[75]

The Ratner Commission elicited countervailing reactions among Palestinians. The legitimacy that it extended to the status quo and the broad hope for change that it dashed may have contributed that July to the flight to Jordan of more than sixty-five youth who claimed they could no longer tolerate government persecution.[76] But the release of its final report in early 1956 appears to

Nazareth, early 1956. City Councillor Fu'ad Khuri speaks at a nighttime MAKI protest in Nazareth. Attorney Hanna Naqara sits at the end of the table. Courtesy of the Emile Touma Institute for Palestinian and Israeli Studies.

have pushed others toward greater militancy. Part of this shift was a function of timing. The commission began its work just three months after Khrushchev's stinging speech against Israel. Feeling betrayed, many Jewish members began to leave MAKI in the months that followed, and the party began to undergo an "Arab tilt."[77]

One expression of this shift was the wide participation of noncommunist Palestinians in party-led protests against Ratner and military rule. MAKI's Palestinian orientation became much more visible after Nasser's July nationalization of the Suez Canal. In September 1956, when MAKI leaders met to formulate their platform in advance of the party's upcoming Thirteenth Congress, the Palestinian members of the Central Committee had insisted that the party take a more explicit stand on Palestinian national rights by linking their realization to a specific territory.[78] MAKI's congress was postponed due to the outbreak of the war on Egypt, but the massacre in Kafr Qasim, followed by the media blackout and the government's refusal to hold a public trial or undertake a parliamentary inquiry, became for many Palestinians the straw that broke the camel's back. It was in this context that record numbers of citizens would begin to speak out against the conditions of their subordination and to demand the realization of their equality as promised in the Declaration of Independence.[79]

Roughly two weeks after Ben-Gurion's Knesset address, more than thirty Galilee merchants, clergy members, landowners, teachers, attorneys, and peasants from a range of faith communities and political affiliations convened in Haifa at the home of Elias Kusa, a prominent nationalist attorney who was debarred under the Defense Emergency Regulations after 1948, to plan a national response to the crime.[80] Building on the historic Palestinian tradition of civic boycotts and the citizenship law strike in July 1952, the group decided to organize a general strike on the morning of January 6, the date scheduled for the opening of the military trial.[81] In the days that followed, planning meetings were held in Nazareth, Haifa, and the villages of the Galilee and Little Triangle, accompanied by growing reports of police subterfuge and harassment, the tightening of travel restrictions, and the ongoing military closure of Kafr Qasim.[82] Further momentum gathered with celebratory calls to action in *al-Ittihad*, which promised "a memorable day in the history of struggle against the policies of national oppression that led to the Kafr Qasim slaughter." The day would succeed, the editors declared, despite the authorities' campaign to sabotage it.[83]

The general strike transformed town and village streets of the Galilee and Little Triangle into virtual battlegrounds between Israeli police and Palestinian workers, peasants, merchants, and students. Despite the modest itinerary for the day—a two-hour work stoppage, mourning prayers, and public meetings— the authorities did everything they could to undermine the memorial activities. As armed police bands roamed the streets to intimidate the population and hunt down local organizers, other units, intelligence agents, and Arab inform- ers paid "home visits" and pressured inhabitants to break the strike. In several cases, authorities entered shops and cafes, threatening to revoke the owners' li- censes if they participated; in others, police ordered already striking merchants to reopen their stores. In the MAKI stronghold of Tayyibe, a group of military officers reportedly slept at the homes of MAPAI supporters on the local council in order to crush the strike before it began. In Nazareth, surrounded on all sides by police reinforcements to prevent anyone from coming in or out, residents had to push past a police unit blocking the streets in order to enter the mosque and recite the mourning prayers.[84]

The fiercest clash took place in Acre, where a dramatic three-day dispute between strike organizers and the MAPAI-backed Islamic Committee culmi- nated in the closing of the Jazzar mosque and the seizure of the city by hun- dreds of security forces aiming to block outside delegations from attending prayers and the scheduled public gathering. In the early morning hours, three signatories of the December petition walked through the Old City bazaar and convinced proprietors to close their shops, only to be followed by known MAPAI supporters who pressured the same storeowners to reopen for busi- ness. Meanwhile, the police dispersed themselves throughout the city, with one ring heavily guarding the mosque to prevent the open meeting from tak- ing place, and others roaming the narrow alleys of the Old City to escort hesi- tant laborers to work. Despite these efforts, at least forty men managed to pass through a thick police barricade to enter the Dallalin Café, which organizers had selected as an alternate meeting site. Following the recitation of the *fatiha*, the Qur'an's opening chapter, over the souls of the victims, the men spoke in turn about the details of the massacre, as well as about the problems faced by Arab citizens in employment, land, and civil rights.[85] According to an intel- ligence report, Kusa emphasized that "he was not a communist, that he [had come] to explain to the people at the meeting that the order to kill the people of Kafr Qasim came from above, and that the incident [had not been] a mis- take of lower-rank officials."[86]

The confrontations in Acre illustrate that the strike was not confined to party politics. Although MAKI activists participated widely in the event, they did so alongside a small and growing grassroots force, which—thanks to the aggressive intimidation tactics of the authorities—was quickly beginning to appreciate the political potential of memorial work.[87] At the end of the day, strike organizers were able to note some impressive successes, including the scores of protest letters cabled to Jerusalem from Palestinians around the country, and the mobilization of hundreds of citizens around the memorial events. These numbers were significant given the near-total reliance of the population on the Military Government and other MAPAI-dominated institutions for employment, health care, and other basic social services during this time.[88] It is impossible to measure the extent of hyperbole in al-Ittihad's claim that the strike was "followed by all."[89] More important is its legacy. On successive anniversaries, editors would continue to remind their readers of the day as a historic moment in the Palestinian struggle for equality, further inscribing it as part of the community's—and the massacre's—collective memory.[90]

The only serious fallout from the January strike was the one-month banishment order issued to nine residents of the Little Triangle, one of several emergency measures that the authorities used against Palestinians without having to charge them with a specific crime.[91] Ben-Gurion took the unusual step of announcing the orders as punishment for the nine Palestinians' attempt "to exploit the tragic incident for the purpose of racial incitement."[92] In a furious speech to the Knesset, deputy Tawfiq Tubi connected the illegality of the banishment orders to the broader clampdown by the authorities: "Is it not a natural thing that the entire Arab population felt itself . . . wounded by this abominable massacre?"

Ben-Gurion denied receiving any letters from the Arab public, just as his party's newspaper had depicted the strike as "wild disturbances" bearing no relationship to the slain.[93] The country had already denounced the incident, declared the premier, adding that Tubi had no right to speak for the Arab community because there were "other parties" representing it.[94] It is unlikely that Ben-Gurion was unaware of the cabled letters. By denying them, he was effectively able to deny the existence of the people who had sent them. Here was a moment—like many others that preceded and followed it—where the partial failure of force to silence independent Palestinian expression led to an unbalanced war of words and concluded with the official suppression of an alternative historical memory.

What happened in Kafr Qasim itself during the celebrated January strike? Apart from a one-line note in *al-Ittihad*'s otherwise detailed report stating that residents had struck "completely," we have no written record of their experience.[95] As Palestinians outside the village continued throughout the winter and spring to press their demands for an open trial, the families of the wounded and killed were relying on charity to make ends meet. By late January, the government had failed to distribute any damages, including the advance payment promised by the premier.[96] For the rest of the year, the village remained effectively under siege and would be all but cut off from the stepped-up opposition campaign waged by sections of the Palestinian community outside.[97]

COMPENSATION, COMMEMORATION . . . "CELEBRATION"

On the surface, the sulha and the commemoration of the massacre's first anniversary in October 1957 appear as though they were independent events. It makes more sense, however, to view them together as the culmination of a protracted legal battle that began soon after the early crisis over damages and ended with the government's attempt to end the affair on its own terms. Both events were the product of its desire to pay as small a financial and political price as possible for the crime.

The compensation crisis began in June 1957, when the damages that Ben-Gurion had promised to distribute to the wounded and the bereaved families had still not appeared. Still unable to return to work and distrusting the Zohar Commission's intention to act in their best interests, eight of the thirteen wounded survivors began to work with Jewish attorneys to press for the establishment of an interministerial committee to determine the proper compensation they were owed.[98] At stake was the classification of the cause of their injuries: the families were demanding the same damages granted to soldiers wounded in war, but the government was hoping to offer them the much lower social security payment, which covered "work accidents."[99] Meanwhile, unbeknownst to the lawyers, a group of five local "mediators" led by Pinhas Rashish, mayor of the nearby Jewish town of Petah Tikva and an employer of many village residents, paid a series of visits to the injured and bereaved families.[100] Accompanied by Military Government officials who threatened to deny travel permits to anyone who did not cooperate, the so-called Public Committee coerced the villagers into accepting private settlements on the condition that they cancel their claims against the state.[101] By the time the attorneys discovered what had happened, the committee had already obtained the families' signatures and the prime minister's endorsement.[102]

It was in the shadow of this undercover legal maneuvering that the people of Kafr Qasim marked the massacre's first anniversary. Although the bereaved had wanted to hold their memorial service in private, the military authorities had other plans. Due to the public attention to the trial and the government's desire for a speedy resolution of the damages settlement, they sought to strike the right balance between appearing sensitive to public opinion and ensuring a quiet and controlled ceremony. To this end they waged a quiet pro-government, anti-MAKI media campaign and worked with the MAPAI affiliate branch in the village to arrange a suitable guest list.[103]

On the morning of October 29, 1957, Arab and Jewish well-wishers who came to pay their respects had to obtain clearance at three police barricades in order to enter the village. Only strict party loyalists, representatives from the army and Border Guard, non-MAKI journalists, and select delegations from nearby Arab villages were permitted entry. Guests found Kafr Qasim shrouded in two layers: civil and military police surrounded its entrances, while black ribbons covered the rest—schools, shops, and the entire road from the western entrance to the central site of the crime.[104]

For the most part, the carefully prepared list of speakers and the very presence of Military Government officials enabled organizers to maintain tight control over the tone and content of the ceremony.[105] On a few occasions, however, mourners disrupted the organizers' attempt to frame the event as a demonstration of the state's goodwill. In the courtyard of the mosque, Husni Wadi' Sarsur, local MAPAI leader and son of the mukhtar, called for a moment of silence before giving the first in a series of speeches, each of which expressed condolences and praised the authorities' response to the incident.[106] One participant later told *al-Ittihad* that

> when . . . Sarsur stood and called for people to forget the massacre and announced that the government promised to pave the road to the village and connect us to the water grid as compensation for the blood that was spilt, loud grumbling began to occur among the villagers. . . . They began to cut him off, taking these words as an insult to the memory of their slain.[107]

The remarks of Eliyahu Agassi, head of the Histadrut's Arab Affairs Department, met a similar response from mourners when he referred to the massacre as a "casualty of misunderstanding" between Jews and Arabs and moralized that the villagers should be grateful for the strength of Israel's democracy, as evidenced by the trial and the right of citizens to express their outrage.[108] The same participant testified that after the mourners made their way to the cemetery,

> the entire village gathered by the side of the graves, crying and weeping. When Agassi arrived . . . where the mourning prayers were being held, the worshippers screamed in his face, demanding that he leave the area and saying, "Leave us, Agassi. [How dare] you kill a man and show up at his funeral!"[109]

Whether the Jewish journalists in attendance did not understand Arabic or chose, along with the reporters for the Arabic organs of MAPAI (*al-Yawm*) and MAPAM (*al-Mirsad*), not to record these uncomfortable exchanges, the dissent remained buried in the pages of a single newspaper that the majority of Israeli citizens would never read.

Just one week after the crowd of unwelcome visitors left residents of the besieged village to themselves, news of the Public Committee and its final recommendations was leaked to the media, and Kafr Qasim again returned to the media spotlight and heightened regime surveillance. To conclude the affair "in a celebratory manner,"[110] the committee announced its plan to hold a special ceremony along the model of the sulha, paid for by the government.[111] The decision to appropriate this traditional Bedouin ceremony—an arbitration mechanism used to resolve internal disputes without the heavy hand of state intervention—was deliberate. In contrast to the ongoing trial, the sulha could gloss over the gross imbalance of power between the state and the subjects of its military regime while reinforcing the popular image of Palestinians as backward tribesmen who either rejected or did not understand modern judicial procedures.[112]

The "truce" imposed on the people of Kafr Qasim was the product of Ben-Gurion's desire to wash the hands of the Military Government, MAPAI, and the Border Guard all at once. First, applying the regulations of social security enabled the state to rob the villagers financially and evaded its responsibility for the crime.[113] Second, presenting the sulha as a reconciliation arbitrated by a neutral bystander on behalf of two warring parties allowed the government to situate the massacre within a contrived history of symmetrical violence between Arabs and Jews.[114] It is difficult, moreover, not to draw connections between the sulha and the ongoing military trial, a link that the Public Committee denied. The government's attempt to bring the accused murderers themselves to the ceremony—the only aspect of the entire affair that villagers successfully opposed—lends support to the argument advanced by many Qasimis today, that

the sulha was designed to lighten the weight of the court verdict and, if necessary, to clear the path for the soldiers' early release.[115] If the victims could pardon the perpetrators, the council asserted, it would be that much easier for the
judges and the government to do the same.[116]

The actual sulha was carried out with the same staging and control as the
first anniversary ceremony, only it required more preparation, a greater enforcement of discipline, and a more elaborately choreographed performance.
Even more than the usual planning for Independence Day, nothing was left to
chance. From the elegant invitations and seating arrangements, to the recruitment of some of the country's finest chefs to oversee the preparation of the
meal, to the opening of three new water taps in the village, the event was carefully designed for the consumption of the general, if not especially the Jewish
and international, public.[117] The following excerpt from the *Jerusalem Post* captures the way the dominant press uncritically accepted the authenticity of the
ceremony and the peace and closure it had supposedly achieved:

> The men sat down to eat, and the youth and children of the village gathered
> around the guests, laughing and joking and stopping every now and then to drink

Military and police commanders take a break from their meal to listen to speeches at the sulha.
Courtesy of the IDFA.

from the newly installed water taps, which are more prominent in everyone's mind by now than last year's tragedy. . . .

[Although] the sulha seems cruel, with its roasted meats and dishes of fruit set before the relatives of the dead . . . it is a necessity [for] the healing process . . . just as a festering ulcer must be cut out to save a limb.[118]

Sulha organizers required representatives of each family scheduled to receive compensation to attend the ceremony. There they were seated next to members of the civil and military administration and forced to listen to speakers' appeals for the restoration of good feeling, as well as to assurances that no pressure of any kind had been exercised to bring the villagers to the table.[119] The speakers included Public Committee member Hasan 'Abd Allah Mansur, a reportedly wealthy landowner from the nearby Arab village of Tira, whose

Hasan 'Abd Allah Mansur reads from prepared remarks at the sulha. Courtesy of the IDFA.

perceived need to clarify that he was not a government agent seemed to have the opposite effect:

> I have never been in the pay of anyone, and I have never sold my conscience. We served on the committee for compassionate reasons, so that widows and orphans might receive help. We did so also because otherwise their claims would have been taken over by persons with questionable motives, who would have tried to serve their interests more than those of the unfortunate victims.[120]

Perhaps their success in preventing the disruption of the dissenters was one of the reasons organizers were so proud of this event. Indeed, Avraham Shapira, the emcee of the ceremony, could not refrain from declaring in his opening remarks that "although it is difficult to say this, today is a great day."[121]

The families of Kafr Qasim participated in the charade of the sulha out of fear and in the absence of a viable alternative.[122] Their practical decision notwithstanding, for them and for most Palestinians in Israel who personally remember the event or learned about it from others, it remains an indelible stain on the historical record, an assault on the dignity of the victims and the Arab community as a whole. Although the state, with the help of the dominant media, may have succeeded that day in dramatizing its hegemony and imposing its own memory of the massacre, it did so only through the threat of force and the imagery of exoticism—a fact that few villagers or activists have forgotten. "We considered [it] . . . a moral massacre even more savage than the Kafr Qasim massacre [itself]," Knesset deputy Emile Habibi would later recall.[123]

The fortieth anniversary memorial book published by the Kafr Qasim Local Council in 1996 echoed this assessment, describing the sulha as no less than a second massacre of the victims and "an expression of the complete disdain for the feelings of the residents of Kafr Qasim and of the Arab people as a whole."[124] "The Hebrew press," it charged, "endeavored to give the impression that the people of Kafr Qasim, like the rest of the Arabs, were simple people who could easily forget what had happened, and that in exchange for fifteen lambs [slaughtered for the meal] they were prepared to pardon the state for its crime."[125]

POLICING MEMORIES, REMEMBERING POLICE—
THE FIRST NATIONAL ANNIVERSARY STRIKE

Although the Military Government succeeded, overall, in policing the people of Kafr Qasim during the massacre's first anniversary and the fabricated truce ceremony, the authorities would encounter bolder opposition from the Palestinian public at large. Far surpassing the turnout in January 1957, several thousand citizens joined the memorial processions, strikes, and meetings held that October.[126] Participants came not only from the urban centers of the north and the Galilee villages, where MAKI had a well-established presence, but also from the villages of the southern Triangle, which had no party chapters and enjoyed a relatively small base of supporters.

The size of these events testifies to the attenuated isolation and rising confidence that many Palestinians—including those unaffiliated with the party—had felt since the Sinai war.[127] To the government's consternation, growing numbers of citizens were gathering in cafes to hear Ahmad Sa'id, host of Cairo's "Voice of the Arabs," inveigh against the Jewish state—not only for serving as a foothold of Western imperialism but also for oppressing them as a national minority.[128] The organization and wide attendance of a three-hour poetry festival in the Acre-area activist village of Kafr Yasif in July 1957 also reflected the guarded optimism that was rising alongside the popular revolutionary ferment against the antidemocratic regimes of entrenched Western allies in Lebanon, Iraq, and Jordan.[129] According to intelligence reports, this sentiment had spread to Palestinian teachers. Just two years earlier the Education Ministry had concluded reassuringly that they did "not dare to disrespect state authority."[130] It now warned that teachers were in urgent need of more "'Israeli ingredients' that would attach [them] to the state both in knowledge and emotion," a vague prescription at best.[131]

Of course, the Arab East was only one place where Western powers were being pushed onto the moral and political defensive.[132] The editors of al-Ittihad, like their ideological comrades around the world, made much of this point, devoting considerable print space to Morocco's and Tunisia's newfound independence and to the intensifying struggles for racial equality in the current and former British settler colonies of Kenya, South Africa, and the United States.[133] In their coverage of the Algerian revolution, Palestinian communists used every opportunity to highlight Israel's increasingly solitary support for the French in the United Nations as evidence of Jerusalem's failure to appreciate that it was on the wrong side of history.[134]

As confident as al-Ittihad's solidarity reportage was, Israel had little reason to worry about the future of its sovereignty—or its ability to uphold the structures of Jewish privilege—inside the 1949 armistice lines. The determination of UN member-states to block foreign meddling in the racial, ethnic, and religious cleavages within their own borders continued to stymie the organization's already feeble commitment to "minority protection."[135] In early 1957, it was also far from foretold that France would withdraw from Algeria, much less that the UN General Assembly would pledge to "bring . . . to a speedy and unconditional end colonialism in all its forms and manifestations," as it would do nearly four years later.[136] Even South Africa's notorious system of white minority rule had yet to confront international opprobrium.[137]

Within this laisser-faire global climate, it is telling that Israeli officials felt compelled to counter regional charges of the state's expansionist aspirations abroad and its oppression of the '48 Arabs (as Palestinian citizens were often called) at home. To combat their radio rivals in Cairo, Damascus, and Ramallah, Foreign Ministry officials poured considerable funds into swelling both the airtime and staff of its Arabic radio program, *Sawt Isra'il* (Voice of Israel).[138] Fearful that Egypt might lure newly independent and future sub-Saharan African states into its anticolonial bloc at the United Nations, the government also teamed up with the Histadrut to undertake joint commercial and industrial ventures on the subcontinent.[139]

The authorities also found itself contending with unexpected challenges from within. In April 1956, the Knesset had passed a law making Druze military enlistment compulsory, the culmination of a multiyear project to further institutionalize their separation from other Arab citizens. Defying the handful of communal patriarchs who had supported the enlistment law, protests of young Druze men began to spread that spring and summer. In January 1957—in the aftermath of Suez—fifteen hundred students and teachers signed a petition demanding the same treatment as other Palestinians in Israel.[140] This kind of unity terrified Israeli authorities for what it could portend in the future. After quashing the opposition with an assortment of carrots and sticks, the military exempted all Druze soldiers from movement restrictions.[141] Soon thereafter, the Interior Ministry announced its recognition of the community as its own "nationality," paving the way toward replacing the word *Arab* with *Druze* on their identity cards.[142]

This was only a taste of things to come. A combination of rising expectations outside and the deterioration of conditions inside was emboldening Palestinian communist and noncommunist citizens to speak out more assertively. Not only had the public debate over ending military rule, or even reducing its scope, been dead since May 1956, but the state's march to colonize Arab land in the Galilee was proceeding apace. The push to expand was particularly vigorous in the north, where Jews still comprised only 7 percent of the population.[143]

Nowhere was the racism of the Jewish settler project more pronounced than in Nazareth. Like all Palestinian villages and towns in Israel, Nazareth was the victim of severe infrastructural neglect despite the efforts of local residents to improve public services.[144] Less than two months after the massacre in Kafr Qasim, the first Jewish residents moved into a new colony established on land expropriated from local families. Upper Nazareth, as it would later be named, was designed explicitly to "swallow up" the Palestinian city and "safeguard the Jewish character of the Galilee as a whole."[145] Behind the relative safety of anonymous reports, local activists denounced the "racial supremacy" that underlay the segregated housing, separate municipal services, and free movement of Jewish residents in the town, warning that they would not allow the government's "European neighborhood" to turn their city into "a new Johannesburg."[146] On top of the massacre and the new colony in Nazareth, Arab fears of being killed or pushed out to make room for Jewish settlers was compounded when the authorities failed to investigate a series of land mine explosions and military shooting exercises in the Galilee that resulted in the deaths of twenty-two Palestinian children and the injury of eight others.[147]

The simultaneous outrage and desperation caused by these developments translated into a marked shift in the language and tone of Palestinian activists. At MAKI's Thirteenth Congress in May 1957, members of the party's executive committee managed for the first time since the National Liberation League's reunification with Jewish communists in 1948 to reinsert a reference to UN Resolution 181 and the right of Palestinians—including those who were citizens of Israel—to establish a state within the 1947 partition lines. The final wording of the congress's resolution on the national conflict directly invoked the elephant in the room: "Israeli-Arab peace demands the recognition by Israel of the right to self-determination, *up to secession*, of the Palestinian Arab people, *including its part living in Israel.*"[148]

Publicly, MAKI suffered further isolation and lost more of its Jewish base as a result of its revised position. The fact that Palestinian Communist leaders had raised secession as a political possibility rather than as a military demand was cold comfort to the majority of the party's rank and file, for whom the struggle of the Jewish working class had always trumped the question of Palestinian national rights. Behind the flurry of internal criticism, however, senior Arabists in Jerusalem began quietly to reevaluate Israel's strategy of absolute domination and deprivation.[149] Already in April, the MAPAI secretariat had established a new policy committee to compensate for the previous nine years of "neglect[ing] the Arabs." Six weeks after MAKI's congress, Ben-Gurion's closest security advisor presented a "serious and worrying report" forecasting an irredentist "civil rebellion" led by young intellectuals.[150]

The military and political establishments—both headed by Ben-Gurion— wasted little time in responding to this danger. In July, Galilee residents were told they would no longer be required to carry a permit in order to enter Acre, Nazareth, and the nearby Jewish-only town of Afula. The Military Government also promised to distribute a certain number of permits to village mukhtars for medical emergencies. Free access to these towns located far from the engines of the Israeli economy would do little for the overwhelmingly unemployed Galilee workforce.[151] Still, the new provision would make it easier to visit two of Palestine's surviving urban centers than it had been in nearly a decade. The Old Man also promised to expand road construction, provide drinking water, and grant agricultural loans after holding his first meeting ever with the seven deputies from his own party's "Arab lists."[152]

The fear of a "civil rebellion" led by educated Palestinian youth concerned other Labor Zionist circles as well. In May 1957, the MAPAM-affiliated general who had headed the Ratner Commission over a year earlier, urged the public to recognize that although the military regime was "regrettably" still necessary, it did "harm the daily lives of the residents" and "squash ... the [Arab] individual and public." It is true, the general conceded to his detractors, that "the minority has received from the State of Israel ... personal benefits ... in its economic medical and cultural development." Nevertheless, he admonished, Israeli Jews needed to renounce the fantasies of previous colonizers who convinced themselves of the humanitarian nature of their mission:

> Let's not dishonor ourselves by rehearsing the arguments of colonial apologists regarding their treatment of "natives". . . . [We must] prevent the rise of a style of a contempt that we saw in the "good old days" of colonial rule.[153]

Activists were not swayed by these material concessions or high-minded appeals. With their sights set on ending military rule altogether, it was crucial to sustain the momentum of grassroots protest that they had started in January and that was continuing to show signs of persistence.[154] The timing of the much-touted "alleviations" was also suspect. Plans for an extensive calendar of events to inaugurate the upcoming tenth anniversary of Israeli statehood were already under way, and it soon became clear that Palestinian citizens would be expected to participate on a scale grander than ever before. In September 1957, municipal leaders from Nazareth and Shafa 'Amr and local village leaders from around the Galilee were asked to cooperate with the national planning committee to organize "minority" celebrations. The idea, they were told, was to welcome foreign and local tourists "with joy and honor,"[155] and to "show the world how different races could live together."[156]

The lavish "minority" parties and events that Jerusalem's holiday planners had in mind would impose unprecedented burdens of time and resources on the Arab public.[157] The government was prepared to cover some of the costs to pay for bands, loudspeakers, fireworks, acting coaches, choral leaders, and school exhibitions. It would also supply the generators to light up performance stages, mosques, and churches—an unavoidable necessity because it had refused to connect more than a handful of the 104 Arab villages and towns to the national electric grid up to that point.[158] However, Arab village councils—largely unelected and systematically underfunded relative to their Jewish counterparts—would also be expected to shoulder a significant portion of the holiday expenses.[159]

For communists and independent activists, the demand that Palestinians fete Israel's first decade of sovereignty with "surplus glory" was not only insulting but a dangerous development, threatening to bury the very seeds of local and foreign attention to the institutionalized maltreatment that the massacre in Kafr Qasim had helped to plant.[160] In previous years, disruptions to Independence Day celebrations had been rare and inchoate, expressed mostly through gestures of indifference or polite, scripted calls for an end to movement restrictions. Even Palestinian MAKI leaders, bound as they were by the party's endorsement of the Jewish right to self-determination, had refrained from publicly opposing the holiday.

Yet the stakes of representation had grown deeper since the massacre. The need to counter the impression that Arab citizens would simply forget about the slaughter and the government's efforts to cover it up—the idea that they would "ignore their differences [with the state] and celebrate in good spirit" like any "family" does, as the mayor of Haifa urged municipal leaders in September—was simply too great.[161] These circumstances, coupled with MAPAM's vote in July against MAKI's Knesset bill to cancel military rule, informed the planning of a much larger memorial strike, as well as MAKI's decision to expand the number of gatherings planned for the first anniversary of the crime.[162]

Cognizant of the regime's ability to instill fear in the general public, *al-Ittihad*'s pre-anniversary announcements combined strident denunciations of the authorities' renewed intimidation campaign with rallying cries to defy it. Four days before the event, the paper's cover banner proclaimed, "For the right of Kafr Qasim and the innocent blood, we will challenge the oppressors and confirm our wishes for life in a strike next Tuesday!" Editors reminded the public of its inalienable "national and civil rights" and urged readers to "defend the struggle for a free, secure, and honorable life."[163] In a rhetorical shift, they also modified the familiar call to oppose the "policies of national oppression," instead announcing the intention of "the Arab people [to] express their vengeance against the ongoing policies of Kafr Qasim."[164] On the eve of the strike, the party's representative on the Nazareth City Council, Fu'ad Khuri, used unusually charged language in his op-ed on Jewish settlement when he replaced the politically neutral terms *village* and *town* with the unmistakably Arabic word for *colony*—*musta'amara*—to denounce the racial lines of development and stagnation in the Galilee: "The government supplies every new Jewish colony with roads, electricity, and water before anyone moves in. Why would electricity poles and water pipes pass Arab villages but leave them dark and dry?"[165]

Both strikers and the authorities were more determined and better prepared to face down their opponents than they had been in January. Despite the reported threats of mobile police squads from the early morning hours, workers, students, peasants, and merchants joined strikes and memorial meetings in all Arab urban centers as well as scores of villages.[166] Not surprisingly, the dominant Hebrew press disputed the level of compliance reported by *al-Ittihad*, downplaying the numbers of adults and schoolchildren who upheld the strike, affirming that "total quiet prevailed" in "all minority centers" of the Western Galilee, and assuring readers that "order was restored" in those sites where demonstrations had taken place.[167] In some cases, the police fulfilled this mission by arresting strike organizers and demonstrators. In others, their tactics betrayed a new level of desperation to prevent the visible and vocal protest of Arab citizens—conducting early morning home raids to confiscate microphones, circulating rumors of travel bans to Jerusalem on Christmas, and forcing villagers to erase memorial slogans on the walls outside their homes. Nazareth witnessed the most violent clashes with police, who forcibly dispersed the crowds of strikers who had gathered to hear a speech by Knesset Member Emile Habibi and arrested city councilor Fu'ad Khuri, along with nine others, as he was gathering signatures for a petition to the Knesset.[168]

BOYCOTT

Three weeks after the historic October commemoration of the massacre in Kafr Qasim, narrative and pictorial depictions of the sulha served to deepen the public impression that the affair would soon be behind them. The fact that the trial of the Border Guard officers was ongoing was not the only reason that Israeli officials knew better. If anything, Palestinian activists outside Kafr Qasim showed signs that their struggle was just getting started. On January 2, 1958, more than four hundred people attended the first ever Conference of Arab Poets and Intellectuals, held in Nazareth; half of them were high school students.[169] Weeks later, what began as a routine military tribunal of two Nazareth residents arrested in the northern town of Safad for entering a "closed zone" without a permit ended with an unprecedented blow to the army's claim that it drew these zones along territorial (rather than racial) lines.[170] When the defendants' seasoned attorney, Hanna Naqara, demanded proof of Safad's "closed" status given that Jews and tourists entered and exited it freely, the local police chief got flustered and admitted that they had been using a less visible system of racial profiling to deny Palestinians access to the town.[171]

The spirits of some activists were high for a third reason as well. One month earlier, Cairo had hosted the first meeting of the Afro-Asian People's Solidarity Organisation, a group that had formed out of the Bandung conference in 1955. In contrast to Bandung's final resolution on Middle Eastern peace, which had called for the implementation of UN Resolution 181, AAPSO's resolution supporting "Arab rights in Palestine" questioned the legitimacy of the Jewish state altogether.[172] Most Jewish leaders of MAKI denounced this language—not for criticizing Israel's current rulers as puppets of Western imperial powers, but for suggesting that the problem was with the state itself.[173] But senior Palestinian communists and unaffiliated nationalists treated AAPSO as a diplomatic breakthrough. Although the resolution's three-point declaration made no mention of the Arab minority by name, they latched onto the text as a sign that the inexorable tide of national liberation would soon reach them. More than ever before, the pages of *al-Ittihad* began to assert the national rights of Arab citizens, both as *Palestinians* and as part of "the people of Asia and Africa."[174]

Just six months earlier, MAKI's revised formulation on Arab-Israeli peace had led Jerusalem to conclude that the obedience of the native minority required the provision of some positive, material inducements. Now, the unfolding developments prompted senior Arabists to remove their kid gloves once again. As the question of how to "deepen [Arab] affinity to the state" returned to the center of policy discussions, new proposals congealed around the need to establish a "counterforce" to combat MAKI's political influence and—if necessary—to issue "the threat of annihilation."[175] Tensions peaked on February 2, 1958, when Egypt and Syria announced that they had formed the United Arab Republic (UAR). Days later, the Shin Bet invited correspondents from all but the communist press to plant an unsubstantiated rumor that MAKI's Palestinian leaders were conspiring to undertake "a rebellion on the Algerian model."[176]

None of the correspondents who attended the meeting seemed to notice the irony of this accusation. The internal security service's projection of the Jewish public as vulnerable to a threat similar to that faced by French settlers in North Africa testified to the fragility of Israel's disavowal of its colonial relationship with native Palestinians. Still, the timing of the Algeria charge could not have been more explosive. The next morning, even before the press had the chance to publish the "leak," Fu'ad Khuri announced that he would be boycotting the tenth anniversary celebrations. "Beware of treason!" he declared, warning his fellow Nazareth city councilors and their counterparts around the country to do the same:

> Every year the military governors use noise and shouts in the celebrations of Independence Day in order to disguise their hostile policies and indecent acts. This year . . . they are not content with the usual routine but rather intend to beat the drums and insert distortion and confusion in every mouthpiece. Over the past ten years they have tried to humiliate the Arab people and now. . . . they wish to bring everyone to the slave market and an exhibition that is a cover-up for deceived tourists and foreigners. . . .
>
> But the accumulation of savage injustice over the past ten years . . . has created a new situation in the souls of our people. This time . . . [we] will not permit any sycophant who has lost his conscience to appear before public opinion and the tourists to demonstrate that the Arab people dance on their graves.
>
> We have the right to full equality, to determine our future, and to unite with other Arabs. We respect the right of the Israeli people to independence, but we won't give up our own."[177]

The assertion of Palestinian national rights to sovereignty within the 1947 partition borders was, in and of itself, not new. What was radical, indeed unimaginable at that time, was the call to public action on the basis of this claim: an appeal to Israel's Arab minority to openly refuse to join Jewish citizens in honoring their national rights until that honor was reciprocated.[178] Even more daring was

Khuri's insistence that Palestinian self-determination for those citizens living in areas outside the partition lines included, by definition, the right to consider unification with the UAR—Israel's newest and most formidable foe. For political pundits, these assertions would only fuel the media firestorm that followed the "revelations" of an imminent armed anticolonial uprising on Israeli soil.[179]

Both Jewish and Arab MAKI leaders cried foul in response to the news scandal, decrying the regime's efforts to divide them and to incite the Jewish majority against the Arab public at large.[180] Rather than back down, however, Palestinian activists began to identify themselves more openly with Algeria's liberation movement. Some caution continued, to be sure, particularly among Arab Knesset deputies. When, in a column on Upper Nazareth, Emile Habibi warned "the colonizers [musta'amirun] . . . [to stop] deluding themselves into thinking that their 'democracy of expulsion' could 'cleanse' the country of its Arab people," he used his regular pseudonym, Juhayna.[181] Nonetheless, throughout February and March, Palestinian communists and their sympathizers held large, unauthorized solidarity gatherings in communities in and outside the Galilee to coincide with global meetings in support of Algerian independence.[182] There, speakers anchored their demands for equality and self-determination in the moral authority of the Algerian struggle and tied Ben-Gurion's support for France's *pied noirs* to his hostility to Palestinians.[183] Assuring their audiences that the forces of decolonization had finally recognized the plight of Israel's Palestinian citizens, Tubi, Habibi, Naqara, and others urged them to join the boycott of the upcoming celebrations in order to obstruct the government's wish for "false testimony."[184] These events did not go unnoticed. Ben-Gurion quickly formed a second commission to investigate the future of military rule, and he soon found himself dodging questions from foreign journalists about when he would abolish it.[185]

Popular support for the boycott of Israel's tenth anniversary trickled in slowly in March, a sign that organizers attributed to a generalized fear, lack of political awareness, and demoralization that continued to prevail in the Arab public at large.[186] But the floodgates of opposition opened in April, following the announcement of several endorsements from independent (non-MAKI) activists, and as the grandiosity of the desired celebrations became clearer.[187] "The time has come for us to wake up," beseeched one resident from 'Arrabe to his neighbors in the pages of *al-Ittihad*. The unnamed man described a rivalry that had developed between local thugs (*zulam*) after the Histadrut and Military Government reportedly offered 400 Israeli lira to the first group who would agree to organize the celebrations in their Eastern Galilee village. "We have had enough of past . . . incidents like this dissemblance . . . " he continued:

> Do you remember the incidents of land confiscation and the seizure of threatened property and blood. . . . Do you want to watch the fabrication before the one thousand journalists expected to visit the country . . . or . . . ignore the expulsion of your people . . . ?[188]

Given the centrality of the Arab school system on prior Independence Days, it is not surprising that young people—who lacked monthly salaries they could lose—played a leading role in the consciousness-raising campaign. The Nazareth Scouts was the first group to join the call. The newly formed Movement of Free Students soon followed suit, urging their peers to "arise, unite ranks, and sabotage the conspiracies that aim to separate the students from their people" by erasing the history of their national dispossession and teaching them that their villages had been "civilized [irtaqat] . . . thanks to the government of Israel."[189] This included the exhibitions highlighting the state's "achievements" in the Arab sector that every school was asked, "under veiled threats,"[190] to build, as well as the sponsorship of competitions for the best essays on Israel's peace offerings toward its neighbors and the "development of the Arab village" since 1948.[191] In subsequent weeks, news dispatches and open letters announcing more groups who planned to uphold the boycott appeared in the press. Many were composed of schoolchildren, who in one case struck over the principal's "theft" of the school savings fund to cover the cost of the celebrations and the cancellation of days of instruction to prepare for them.[192]

Local councils, especially those staffed with men accused of enjoying particularly close ties to the military regime, were the other primary targets of condemnation. In some communities, citizens sent in anonymous letters condemning their council for squandering precious municipal funds to put on what everyone knew was a charade of joy, or for agreeing to time the inauguration of new public works projects to the holiday so as to obscure the "terrible ghetto system" under which they continued to suffer.[193] Activists took a different tack in Shafa 'Amr, calling on their town council to act like a truly representative body and hold an open meeting to discuss the celebrations, the need to repair the main road, and the newly appointed commission to investigate military rule.[194] Still other communities kept their focus on Jerusalem. This included a group of internal refugees from al-Mjaydal, outside Nazareth, who told al-Ittihad's readers that although they had never celebrated Independence

Day, this year the government had "gifted us . . . with a court summons on the charge of building without a permit."[195]

The campaign to boycott the celebrations did not go uncontested, particularly in the final weeks leading up to the official holiday on May 1, which was timed to the Jewish calendar. Pro-boycott leaflets circulating throughout the country met with the midnight distribution of counter-leaflets by new groups who accused their adversaries of only making things worse.[196] The extent of the military regime's involvement in the leaflets signed by the "Sons of the Galilee" and the "Arab Voice in Israel" is unknown, but personal memoirs reveal the tremendous pressure its staff put on Palestinians to participate in the holiday during the last two weeks of April 1958.[197] The authorities would later claim that eight thousand people attended festivities in Nazareth on April 26.[198] Yet forces eventually came to a head. The night before May Day, the police arrested twenty-six activists after they tried to destroy Nazareth's performance stage and then reportedly stoned riot and military police for trying to stop their truck from driving through city streets to publicize their upcoming demonstration.[199]

The drama of these events would pale in comparison to the next day, when local and auxiliary police clashed violently with hundreds of boycotters from Nazareth and the surrounding villages after MAKI refused the Military Government's demand to delay its scheduled May Day demonstration for the sake of MAPAI's holiday gathering. The following day, May 2, a similar clash erupted in Umm al-Fahm, the Triangle's largest village. All told, tens of citizens and police officers were injured, and hundreds of men, women, and children were arrested.[200]

As with the Kafr Qasim memorial strikes, the government and its media organs dismissed the May Day clashes as the lone acts of a few communist rabble rousers whose "poisonous propaganda" had failed to spread to the rest of the country.[201] Indeed, most Palestinian villages and towns held their celebrations as scheduled, joined by as many as ten thousand local and international tourists who flocked to watch them.[202] This included Kafr Qasim, whose school principal would later be pressed by a *Ma'ariv* reporter about whether the villagers were really as "loyal" and "happy" as the local school exhibition and celebrations had made them seem.[203]

The five months of verbal and physical confrontations that climaxed on Israel's tenth anniversary further polarized its citizens along racial and national lines. Incidents of police violence, popular harassment of Arab citizens in public spaces, and the refusal by Jewish barbers and other merchants to serve Arab clientele, all appear to have increased.[204] Similar trends were documented on the

نشاط الاول من ١٩٥٠ - اول ايار

May 1, 1958. Palestinians march in Nazareth on May Day in boycott of the celebrations of Israel's tenth anniversary and in solidarity with the Algerian revolution. Courtesy of Na'ila Naqara.

Egged bus system, the Histadrut subsidiary that enjoyed a virtual monopoly in the Galilee but consistently refused to provide enough vehicles and direct lines to transport Arab day laborers from their villages to the country's urban centers. The fact that Egged forced its Palestinian passengers to stand for hours at a time—either to save money by operating fewer buses or because of the practice of some drivers to give Jewish passengers priority of seating—was not new. What was new was the growing confidence of passengers to complain about these conditions, challenges that met increasingly with insults, physical assaults, and police arrests.[205]

These tensions also found expression in the judicial sphere. By the second anniversary of the massacre in October 1958, more than three hundred May Day detainees remained behind bars.[206] That month, a district court convicted eight of the eleven border guards on trial and sentenced them to a range of seven to seventeen years in prison for obeying "a manifestly illegal order"—in this case, shooting innocent citizens.[207] Much of the Jewish public found the sentences unduly harsh and lent their support to an amnesty campaign for the convicted killers.[208] Many activists, for their part, criticized the sentences for failing to correspond to the gravity of the crime, and they continued to press for a parliamentary investigation higher up the chain of military command.[209] Still, their widespread circulation of the ruling, with its unequivocal denunciation of the "cruel and systematic murder of helpless people," suggests the belief of some people that at least some justice had been served.[210]

This morsel of trust in Israel's effective separation of powers would be crushed over the next fourteen months—first as Brigadier Shadmi was convicted of an administrative error and fined a symbolic *grush* (a piaster, the equivalent of one hundredth of a lira) for issuing the original curfew order without the authorization of the military governor,[211] and then when Prime Minister Ben-Gurion amnestied all the convicted murderers in late 1959 and appointed several of them to top government posts.[212] "We shall not forget," poet-activist Tawfiq Zayyad vowed shortly after the release of Shmuel Malinki, when the army major whom Palestinians reviled widely as "Murderer Number One" expressed his hope that the Israeli public would quickly put the affair out of their mind.[213]

Zayyad's prophecy would come true. The government's derision of the judicial process, which compounded the affront of the sulha two years earlier, would help to keep the massacre at the forefront of Palestinian political consciousness and served to deepen its symbolic charge.[214] Nowhere was this more pronounced than inside Kafr Qasim itself. In October 1960, the first anniversary following the release of the convicted border guards from prison, a handful of young villagers defied the threats of a military governor and the warnings of local elders to organize a community-wide procession in the village.[215]

THE BEGINNING OF THE END

Few Israeli Jews knew about this or subsequent struggles to commemorate the massacre inside Kafr Qasim. Just as Malinki had hoped, the dominant Hebrew press lost interest in the crime following the general amnesty. The subject of military rule was a different matter, however. The popular mobilization of Palestinians prompted by the massacre and the government's effort to cover it up, the growing international access to information about the oppression of Israel's Arab citizens, and the brutality of the police response to the May Day/Independence Day protests had all prompted prominent intellectuals and a rising generation of military and political elites to initiate a public conversation about the wisdom of maintaining the regime.[216]

The first seeds of this shift appeared in the summer of 1958, when hundreds of Jewish academics, artists, and even some settlement leaders petitioned the government to end the "ten years of discrimination" and the manifest despotism with which the military regime had ruled. These petitions were followed by two damaging exposes (first in MAPAI's daily, *Davar*, then in a state comptroller report) that confirmed longstanding Palestinian charges about the regime's mockery of the rule of law and its insidious interference in every aspect of their lives.[217]

Scholars have yet to provide a full account of how and in what way Jewish public opinion shifted in favor of ending the regime. Nor have they studied the extent to which there was a strategic decision on the part of veteran Palestinian activists and their small cohort of Jewish allies to narrow the scope of their broad demands for equality—to repeal all emergency regulations and to amend all legislation that curtailed Palestinian access to immigration, citizenship, and land—and focus on a more limited campaign to end the most visible expressions of segregation in order to enlist the support of Jewish liberals. Although all of these early petitions and reports touched in some way on the ethical problem of imposing martial law on a law-abiding racial or national

Tel Aviv, August 1958. Bearing Hebrew-language placards, Palestinian and Jewish activists march to demand the release of the 1958 May Day detainees from Nazareth, the "elimination of the ghettos of the military regime," and an end to "the oppression of the Arabs of Israel." Protestors also remind the public that "an attack on the Arab worker also attacks the Jewish worker," and they admonish Jewish citizens for forgetting their own history of persecution. Courtesy of the Communist Party Archives at Yad Tabenkin.

minority, the main question they raised was whether the regime was good or bad for security. For the overwhelming majority of Jewish citizens, "security" was shorthand for Jewish dominance—the ability to maintain the status quo that ensured Jewish privilege in land, resources, and political power. To the profound detriment of Palestinian citizens, this focus on preserving settler security rather than on ending settler privilege would remain at the heart of the public and parliamentary movement to end military rule.

In July 1959, the commission that Ben-Gurion had appointed the previous year recommended the temporary suspension of military rule. According to its report, there was no precedent in the democratic world for the permanent imposition of martial law over equal citizens that have shown no plan for mass action against the state, and the military regime was not the reason for the lack of this subversion. Instead, national security would be better served by creating more Jewish settlements in the parts of the country where Arabs continued to constitute a majority. The premier promptly rejected these findings, insisting that the high security alert the regime helped to maintain along Israel's armistice lines continued to deter Arab states from attacking the country.[218]

The release of the Rosen Report, named after its esteemed chair, Justice Minister Pinhas Rosen, had little immediate impact in the political sphere. Five parliamentary blocs submitted bills to cancel parts or all of the regime, all of which failed. From the perspective of activists, it would take four long years and an energetic civil protest movement with substantial Jewish participation before the government agreed to start dismantling the military regime in November 1966. In hindsight, however, the political and economic conditions that paved the way for that decision were already taking root by the dawn of Israel's second decade of sovereignty.[219]

The convergence of the Rosen Report with the end of Israel's recession was one key to this process. For the first time in nearly a decade, the construction and manufacturing sectors had begun to boom, and Jewish unemployment was falling. Ben-Gurion himself conceded the fact that the exclusion of Arab labor no longer made sense. In August 1959, just one month after repudiating the Rosen Report, the prime minister announced the lifting of daytime movement restrictions on Arab residents of the Galilee and the Little Triangle into Jewish cities where work was available. Shortly thereafter, the Histadrut voted to allow Palestinians to join the trade union federation as full members.[220] A second factor behind Israel's ultimate decision to abolish the regime was the challenge it posed to Israel's self-portrayal as a postcolonial democracy. Unlike the

era which had given birth to the Jewish state, by the early 1960s European imperialists and settlers in Africa, and advocates of racial segregation in the United
States and the former British settler states, were all on official notice.[221] Ben-
Gurion's closest advisors and party allies were slow to catch onto this shift in
the global political climate.[222] For three years following the Tenth Anniversary
boycott in May 1958, they continued to vilify Palestinian activists as would-be
Algerian rebels; to stand more openly in solidarity with French settlers; and to
justify the preservation of military rule as the only thing preventing an armed
national liberation struggle within Israel's borders.[223] The damage caused by
these statements were compounded by the government's early equivocation on
the apartheid regime, including the defamation of black South Africans as "violators of law and order" on its Arabic-language radio station, and its refusal to
condemn the Sharpeville massacre in March 1960.[224]

The growing success of Palestinian citizens in bringing international attention to their plight also forced Israel to defend itself at the United Nations
against the charges of both colonialism and apartheid.[225] Between 1960 and
1961, UN delegates from Arab states distributed detailed petitions from Palestinian intellectuals imploring the organization to intervene on their behalf.[226]
Jerusalem's initial efforts to counter their charges by distancing itself from Pretoria did not always go smoothly. In November 1961, Israel joined the General
Assembly's call for sanctions against South Africa. President Verwoerd immediately cried foul, noting that his country had always "believed in Israel" since
it, too, "followed a policy of separate development."[227] The apartheid charge
would continue to haunt Israeli diplomats and participants in international
conferences through the end of 1966.[228]

The third, and perhaps most important, reason why military rule was abol-
ished in 1966 was that a growing number of officials in the political-military
establishment became convinced that it was no longer necessary to carry out
Jewish colonization. In 1960, the Knesset passed a new Basic Law that barred
Palestenian citizens from owning, leasing, or working on 97 percent of state-
held land. By 1964, they had lost over three-quarters of the land they had held
before the establishment of the state.[229] One year before, leading intelligence officials concluded that they "had the Arabs well 'covered,'" and that it would be
more effective politically to impose restrictions on individual activists rather
than punish the population as a whole.[230]

By the summer of 1963, there was little need for debate when MAPAI's Levy
Eshkol declared the government's intention to cancel the military regime within

Haifa, early 1960s. Behind the Israeli flag, Palestinians and Jews march in the Hadar neighborhood during the groundswell of parliamentary opposition to military rule. In Hebrew and Arabic, all of the signs read "End Military Rule," with the iconic "X" that became the symbol of the protest movement. Courtesy of the Communist Party Archives at Yad Tabenkin.

three years' time. Eshkol had replaced Ben-Gurion as prime minister following the Old Man's resignation, and his announcement appeared to affirm the wave of large anti-regime demonstrations in Israel's urban centers. A consensus had emerged that Israel could safely remove the *appearance* of discrimination and thus the stain on its global image while maintaining the emergency regulations; transferring the powers of the regime to the civilian police; and inaugurating a new push to settle the Galilee with more Jews.[231] As Labor Minister Yigal Allon

told Ben-Gurion shortly before he left office, dismantling the physical apparatus of the regime would be "one of the smallest risks we have undertaken in the
eighty years of Jewish settlement in the Land of Israel."[232]

These tactical shifts, rather than a broad, civic movement for democracy
or a fundamentally new attitude towards the country's Arab minority, explain
why Israel's military regime was dismantled eighteen years after it was established. Instead of a move toward the abolition of Jewish privilege, or a decision
not to pursue the colonization of the sliver of land that remained in Palestinian
hands, the end of military rule inaugurated a new theory of population control—to see but not be seen. This theory would carry the day six months later,
when Israel occupied the West Bank and the Gaza Strip. In the summer of 1967,
the military leaders who took over the administration of the one million new
Palestinians under their rule vowed never to repeat the mistakes of the previous regime.[233]

If public opinion polls in the late 1960s are any indication, the end of military rule did not signal the willingness of Israeli Jews to question the privileged access to land, jobs, education, and social services that they had come to
enjoy over the previous two decades. This dynamic might be seen as evidence
that Palestinians and their committed Jewish allies won the battle but lost the
war. Indeed, the very success of their struggle for civil equality—a victory that
forced the government to remove some of the most visible expressions of Palestinians' collective subordination—would make it more difficult for them to
address the deeper structural questions of land, sovereignty, and the refugees.

CONCLUSION

IN NOVEMBER 2006, former president Jimmy Carter earned wide popular and congressional censure in the United States for his book *Palestine: Peace, Not Apartheid*, a journey through four decades of Israel's colonization of the West Bank and Gaza Strip and its violent occupation of an area inhabited by 3.5 million Palestinian Arabs. Much of the alarm surrounding the book stemmed not from its uncontroversial factual content, but from its provocative yet unexplained title. Questioned by the media, the Nobel Peace Prize winner refused to back down from the analogy between the South African racial regime that ended in 1994 and Israel's treatment of Palestinians in the Occupied Territories. He also stressed repeatedly, however, that his critique stopped at the Green Line. Inside Israel's pre-1967 armistice lines, he assured the American people, the state was "a wonderful democracy with equal treatment of all citizens, whether Arab or Jew...."[1]

The timing of Carter's insistence on the strength of Israel's democracy within its post-1949 armistice lines could not have been more ironic. That same week, a team of leading Palestinian "intellectuals and community figures in Israel issued two unprecedented policy papers calling for a national dialogue about the need to transform Israel into a "democratic, bilingual, multicultural state." In addition to calling for the end of Israel's then forty-year occupation of the West Bank and Gaza Strip, the authors' "Future Vision" imagined both a public reckoning with the state's settler-colonial origins and a radical redistribution of power and resources within it. This vision, as they outlined, would entail the dismantlement of all institutions and the cancellation of laws that have ensured Jewish privilege in land access, immigration rights, political power, education, language, and culture since Israel's establishment in 1948.[2]

For most of the Jewish public, including many liberal elites who were known for their support of civil equality for "Israeli Arabs" as individuals, the idea of a "joint homeland" with the Arabs of Palestine whose parents and grandparents had managed to remain in or return to the new state after 1948 was unfathomable.[3] Their reactions were emotional, with expressions ranging from "dismay" to "severe anguish" at the betrayal.[4] Some public figures read the Palestinian call for a national discussion on the nature of the Israeli state as nothing less than a "declaration of war."[5] The government, for its part, threatened to "thwart the activity of any group or individual seeking to harm the Jewish and democratic character of the State of Israel, even if such activity is sanctioned by the law."[6] Summing up this backlash, the editor of one Palestinian newspaper in Israel concluded that little had changed since December 1966, the month when the government formally dismantled the military regime inside Israel's 1949 armistice lines.[7] Indeed, the events of that month seemed only to confirm the observation of anthropologist Patrick Wolfe that settler colonialism is "a structure, not an event."[8]

It is unknown precisely what former Knesset Member Tawfiq Tubi—by then eighty-three years old and just slightly more senior than Old Man Ben-Gurion had been during their anti-climactic meeting forty years earlier—thought about the Future Vision documents and the public Jewish outcry they elicited. In the years after the June 1967 war and Israel's sudden occupation of one million more Palestinians in the West Bank and Gaza Strip, Tubi and his colleagues in Israel would continue to work in vain to alert the public that the ostensible abolition of military rule in December 1966 was a scam: the emergency regulations and the security zones remained in place, and the authorities had merely replaced the regime's collective movement restrictions with targeted blacklists of government critics like themselves.[9]

Countervailing trends emerged over the two decades that followed. Most Palestinian citizens gained the freedom to travel within the country and the right to be tried in the same courts as Jews. While overall economic disparities remained, Palestinians also began to participate somewhat more meaningfully in the country's social and economic life. However, the opening of public life to the entirety of Israel's citizens met a backlash. The growing confidence of Palestinians to organize themselves politically, to oppose the ongoing confiscation of their land, and to use their expanding education to fight the structural discrimination against them in the academy, the courts, and the Knesset, all fueled the rise of political parties that espoused openly racist platforms and called for their unilateral expulsion. In 1985, the Knesset banned the electoral participation of any political party that "negated the existence of the State of Israel as the state of the Jewish people."[10]

The 1990s witnessed similarly bipolar tendencies. The initial optimism that prevailed among many Israeli citizens following the signing of the Declaration of Principles by Israel and the PLO contributed to the government's first serious effort to narrow the gaps in budget allocations to Palestinian and Jewish municipalities. Several High Court rulings also seemed to indicate the judiciary's growing acknowledgement of the incompatibility of the Zionist mission with democratic equality for all citizens.[11] Alongside the liberal fanfare about the move toward meaningful coexistence, however, was a very different trend. The growing acceptance that regional peace and Israel's imagined neo-liberal re-alignment required "separation" from the Palestinians in the Occupied Territories simultaneously reignited popular concerns about the "threat" posed by the presence of Palestinian citizens to Israel's future Jewish identity.[12] One manifestation of this anxiety was in the continued hunt by police, intelligence authorities, pollsters, and journalists for evidence of Palestinian "sentiments" on Independence Day. Although holiday celebrations were no longer imposed as they had been under military rule, the Jewish public's demand for reassurance that Palestinians continued to accept the historical legitimacy of their national dispossession remained fully in place.[13]

The tension between these two trends exploded in the fall of 2000, as Palestinian citizens demonstrated en masse to support the eruption of a second uprising in the Occupied Territories and to protest the ongoing discrimination they faced within Israel's 1949 armistice boundaries. The popular and official rage that followed what was quickly dubbed the October Events is well known: Israeli police shot and killed thirteen of the protesters, and the army's brutal response to the second Intifada, which helped to fuel suicide bombings, redounded against Arab citizens inside the Green Line.[14] The last twelve years have witnessed legislative assaults on Palestinian Knesset members; the rise of hate crimes against Arab citizens; skyrocketing Jewish support for their disenfranchisement and expulsion; and the growth of openly racist calls to deny them housing and employment in Jewish cities.[15] This national chauvinism has assumed a gendered dimension more recently. Since 2010, local governments and parent vigilante committees have enjoyed government and military support in their programs to "rescue" Jewish girls from "abduction" by their "minority" boyfriends and husbands.[16]

Recent rulings by Israel's High Court are also foreboding. In January 2012 the Court struck down a petition from local civil rights groups to rule on the unconstitutionality of a temporary amendment to the 1952 citizenship law that would make it impossible for Palestinians from the West Bank and Gaza Strip to live inside the Green Line with their citizen spouses. Although, as we have seen, the Knesset deliberately buried the constitutional process in early 1949, the petitioners hoped the Court would agree that the amendment violated the spirit of racial equality inscribed into the Declaration of Independence, because in practice it affected Arab citizens alone. The government had first introduced the amendment in July 2003 after accusing several Palestinian citizens and applicants for the historic Family Reunification program of involvement in terrorist attacks in Israel.[17] It has since split up tens of thousands of families and affected an estimated 130,000 Palestinians on both sides of the 1967 lines, reviving many elements of the Temporary Residency Permit system. For example, even Palestinian spouses who meet the age- and gender-based criteria for residency are denied work permits, social benefits, and the chance for permanent residence. The state also disqualified any applicants with relatives deemed a potential threat to national security.[18] In 2005, Prime Minister Ariel Sharon told his cabinet there was "no need to hide behind security arguments," because the law's real purpose was "to ensure a solid Jewish majority for years to come."[19]

A second blow to democracy activists in Israel came in January 2012, when the Supreme Court refused to rule on the constitutionality of a Knesset statute passed in March 2011 that legislated the withdrawal of state funding from any organization or institution that commemorates the Palestinian nakba, or catastrophe, of 1948. Among other things, it is clear that this law was a response to the growing number of memorial marches by internal refugees and other Palestinian citizens to the sites of former villages on Israel's Independence Day. This movement began in earnest in 1998, on Israel's fiftieth anniversary, but its seeds were planted on a more localized basis in the mid-1960s, as travel restrictions on Palestinian communities began to be lifted.[20]

. . .

Liberal pundits in and outside Israel have begun to notice these developments, and some have warned that Israel is facing a crisis of democracy within its borders. This book has argued for a different interpretation of these trends. In contrast to this view, it has demonstrated that the crisis facing democracy in the

Jewish state is as old as the state itself. Israel's development as a liberal settler state was the outcome of the imperative to establish a colonial rule of difference within a liberal order imposed largely from the outside—to find a legal way to partition the population, and thus facilitate colonization for exclusive Jewish use. The composite shape of the state was a product of its time, a crossroads in international approaches to problems posed by heterogeneous polities in a post-Nazi and ostensibly decolonizing world. Liberal settler rule relied on a combination of legislated privilege, practices of informal discrimination, and the creation of territorial zones where the standard rules of governance did not apply.

For more than sixty years, Israel's essential paradox has pivoted around its attempt to pursue the Jewish conquest of land and labor while extending individual political rights to the Arabs of Palestine who remained after 1948—to bind voting Palestinians to the state while simultaneously denying them access to its management. At first this endeavor turned out to be Israel's greatest source of diplomatic strength, because its ruling elites figured out how to render that citizenship and suffrage all but meaningless (combining statutory law, emergency law, and dual sovereignty in the name of security and territory rather than racial science). This enabled state officials to pursue the entrenchment of settler privilege with fewer public relations problems than traditional colonial regimes in north and sub-Saharan Africa. Meanwhile, the Arabs of Palestine fell on the wrong side of decolonization. First, their dispossession in 1948 took place before popular international opinion had shifted in earnest toward support for the self-determination of colonized peoples.[21] By the time that shift took place in the mid-1960s, their dispersal in multiple countries had disqualified them from eligibility for national self-government according to the UN's 1960 definition of colonialism, which focused on overseas, racial majorities inside a delimited territory.[22]

In the late 1950s, the relative stability that liberal settler rule had offered Israeli leaders began to crumble. Thereafter, the state's internal contradictions became a source of profound instability, not least as Palestinians increasingly deployed the limited political rights extended to them to demand a more meaningful democracy. Today, the instability of the liberal settler state is greater than ever, a problem that will not simply disappear with the establishment of two states.

REFERENCE MATTER

NOTES

ABBREVIATIONS

AHC	Arab Higher Committee
ALA	Arab Liberation Army
CSM	Coordination Subcommittee meeting
DC	District Commissioner
DERs	Defense Emergency Regulations
EG	Eastern Galilee
IDF	Israel Defense Forces
KQLC	Kafr Qasim Local Council
MAKI	Communist Party of Israel
MAPAI	Workers' Party of the Land of Israel
MAPAM	United Workers' Party
MFA	Ministry of Foreign Affairs
MG	Military Government
MGC	Military Government Command (Commander)
MK	Member of Knesset
MoD	Ministry (Minister) of Defense
MoH	Ministry (Minister) of Health
MoI	Ministry (Minister) of Interior
MoI/Mins	Ministry (Minister) of Interior, Minorities Division
MoJ	Ministry of Justice
MoM	Ministry of Minorities
MoP	Ministry (Minister) of Police
MoR	Ministry of Religions
NLL	National Liberation League
PCP	Palestine Communist Party

PM   Prime Minister

PMB   Prime Minister's Bureau

TRP   Temporary Residency Permit

UNGA   United Nations General Assembly

UNSC   United Nations Security Council

UNSCOP United Nations Special Committee on Palestine

INTRODUCTION

1. Weather report, *Ma'ariv*, October 27, 1966.

2. Khalidi, *All That Remains*; Benvenisti, *Sacred Landscape*; Pappe, *Ethnic Cleansing*.

3. This story is adapted faithfully from a transcript of the meeting that was annotated and translated into English in Shalom, "Finally Meet." I thank Zaki Shalom for sending me the original Hebrew transcript, from which I have reproduced Tubi's final charge verbatim. Although the most literal translation of the word *yelidim* would be "native-born," I agree with Shalom that the pejorative-sounding "natives" conveys the precise spirit of Tubi's assertion.

4. See, for example, R. Khalidi, *Iron Cage*; Nadan, *Peasant Economy*; Robson, *Colonialism and Christianity*.

5. Said, *Question of Palestine*; R. Khalidi, *Palestinian Identity*.

6. Beinin, "Forgetfulness"; Ben-Ze'ev and Lomsky-Feder, "Canonical Generation." One of the first documented Palestinian accounts that this literature corroborated was Walid Khalidi's 1959, "Why Did the Palestinians Leave?"

7. Morris, *Birth*; Pappe, *Britain*; Shlaim, "Debate About 1948." See also Masalha, *Expulsion*.

8. The question of how Arabs and Jews in Palestine have "made each other" since the 1880s may not suit all contexts, and scholars must be careful not to downplay Palestinian voices outside the prism of Zionism. Feldman, *Governing Gaza*; Abu Lughod, "Pitfalls."

9. Classics include Kimmerling, *Zionism and Territory*; Shafir, *Origins*; Lockman, *Comrades and Enemies*; Beinin, *Red Flag*; Piterberg, "Domestic Orientalism"; Bernstein and Swirsky, "Rapid Economic Development"; Y. Shenhav, "Jews of Iraq"; Khazzoom, "Great Chain"; LeVine, *Overthrowing Geography*; Campos, *Ottoman Brothers*.

10. In anthropology, see Swedenburg, *Memories of Revolt*; Abu El-Haj, *Facts on the Ground*; Kanaaneh, *Birthing the Nation*; and Feldman, *Governing Gaza*. Said's *Question of Palestine* and *Orientalism* greatly influenced this work.

11. Some who accept the legitimacy of the framework reject the moral taint it tends to carry. According to historian Anita Shapira ("Politics," 29–30), scholars must not study this model "from positions of *a priori* reject or blame, [since] not every colonization movement is to be dismissed out of hand." Prominent holdouts to this framework

reject the analogy through assertion and specious logic without engaging seriously with the existing literature and evidence. See also Aaronsohn, "Settlement in Eretz Israel"; Shapira "Politics," 29–30; Ben-Ami, *Scars*, 3.

12. Shafir, *Origins* and "Settler-Citizenship"; Lockman, *Comrades and Enemies*; Shamir, *Colonies of Law*; Piterberg, *Returns*; Kimmerling, *Clash*, 181. Kayyali's *Zionism, Imperialism and Racism* offered an earlier iteration.

13. Beinin's *Red Flag* is the most notable exception to this rule. Abu El-Haj's *Facts on the Ground* and Slyomovics' *Object of Memory* point to colonial continuities in Zionist material culture after 1948 but do not explore military rule per se.

14. See especially Forman and Kedar, "From Arab Land"; and Forman, "Historical Geography."

15. Examples include Salamanca et al., *Past Is Present*; Scholch, *Green Line*; Abdo and Yuval-Davis, "Zionist Settler Project"; Greenstein, *Genealogies*; and Ehrlich, "Conflict."

16. Scattered challenges to the depiction of the 1967 occupation as total rupture have begun to appear. For a start, see Nakhleh, "Two Galilees"; Forman, "Tale of Two Regions"; Weizman, *Hollow Land*, 63–64; Segev, *1967*, 494; Eldar and Zertal, *Adone ha-Arets*, 449; and Stein, "Traveling Zion."

17. Dowty, "Civic State," 36. See also Medding, *Founding*, 233.

18. Quoting Eldar and Zertal, *Lords of the Land*, x. See also Jeffrey Goldberg, "Unforgiven," *Atlantic Monthly*, May 2008; Ben-Ami, *Scars*, xii; Gorenberg, *Unmaking of Israel*, 54; Beinart, *Crisis of Zionism*, 16–18; Lahav, "Tsedek ve-kibush," 562; Editorial, "Israel's Existence Is Not a Question," *Haaretz*, March 13, 2007; Akiva Eldar, "The Jewish Lobby Israel Needs," *Forward*, November 7, 2007; and Ze'ev Sternhell, "Colonial Zionism," *Haaretz*, October 17, 2008. In October 1967, Israel's now celebrated dove, Amos Oz, declared that there is "a vast moral difference . . . between making Jaffa and Nazareth Jewish, and making Ramallah and Nablus Jewish." Oz, *Blazing Light*, 83. For another early formulation, see Amitai Etzioni, "Israel's Colonial Temptations," *New Outlook*, July–August 1968, 32–37.

19. For similar critiques see Robinson, "My Hairdresser"; Kimmerling, *Clash*, 185–186, and "Sociology," 452; Peleg, "Constitutional Order"; Stein, "Shmaltz"; Bernard Avishai, "Saving Israel from Itself," *Harper's Magazine*, January 2005, 37; and Meron Benvenisti "Poetic License," *Haaretz*, November 16, 2006.

20. Zureik's *Internal Colonialism*, published in 1979, drew almost exclusively on secondary sources and government surveys to examine the proletarianization of Arab farmers after 1963, when the state was already beginning to dismantle the military regime. Because his analysis borrowed heavily from theories of US race relations, it also offered a less robust conceptual intervention than his title promised. Shafir and Peled's recent *Being Israeli* offers an original exploration of continuity and change in the Zionist settler project since the 1880s, but their coverage of military rule is limited to a few paragraphs that summarize the existing literature.

21. In 1980, Lustick's *National Minority* used the prism of majority-minority relations to offer the most holistic analysis of Israeli policy since the publication of Jiryis's pioneering *Arabs in Israel* ten years earlier. Lustick drew somewhat on the Hebrew- and English-language press, but relied heavily on published government sources. In Hebrew, Ozacky-Lazar's "Hitgabshut" and Bäuml's *Tsel kahol lavan* offer the most detailed, archive-based institutional surveys to date of the military regime during its first and second decades, respectively. Other critical works that examine or touch on pre-1967 policy toward Arab citizens include Peretz, *Israel and the Palestine Arabs*; Qahwaji, *Dhill al-ihtilal*; Falah, "Judaization"; Haidar, *On the Margins*; Benziman and Mansour, *Dayare mishneh* (hereafter, Benziman and Mansour, *Subtenants*); Al-Haj, *Education*; Masalha, *Land Without a People*; Yiftachel, "Ethnocracy."

22. Works that have drawn on the archives and/or the press with particular creativity and insight include Copty, "Knowledge and Power"; Korn, "Political Control"; Kemp, "Dangerous Populations"; Sorek, *Arab Soccer*; Cohen, *Good Arabs*; Nassar, "Affirmation and Resistance"; and Dallasheh, "Nazarenes."

23. Pitts, "Empire and Democracy"; Young, "Polity"; Taylor, "Democratic Exclusion," 146.

24. Cooper and Stoler, *Tensions of Empire*; Brown, *Regulating Aversion*, 21–23, 70, 77; Conklin, "Colonialism and Human Rights"; Pitts, "Empire and Democracy," 297, 302–304; Schreier, "Napoléon's Long Shadow," 96–97, 102–103; Cooper, *Colonialism in Question*, 28.

25. Space does not allow for a thorough list. In addition to the sources listed in note 26 of this chapter, see, for example, Veracini, *Settler Colonialism*. Kennedy's *Islands of White* was a key precusor to this work.

26. Critiques include Wolfe, "History and Imperialism," and "Elimination of the Native," 397; Elkins and Pedersen, *Settler Colonialism*, 3–4; Schaller and Zimmerer, "Settlers, Imperialism, Genocide"; Kramer, "Power and Connection," 1362; and Lake and Reynolds, *Global Colour Line*.

27. "We are less skilled at identifying the scope of empire when the contracts are not in written form, when policies are not signaled as classified, nor spelled out as confidential, secreted matters of state" (Stoler, "Degrees," 142). See also Stoler, "Opacities of Rule," 57; Kramer, "Power and Connection," 1359, 1382–1383; and Brower, *Desert Named Peace*.

28. Meouchi and Sluglett, *Mandates*; Anghie, "International Institutions."

29. Kramer, "Empires, Exceptions"; Go, "Provinciality"; Olund, "Savage Space."

30. Stoler, "Degrees," 139.

31. They did so even as they invoked the noninterference clauses that permeate the Charter. Kuntz, "Chapter XI"; Wright, "Recognition"; Thornberry, "Self-Determination"; Österud, "Narrow Gate"; Ka Pakaukau, "Reinscription"; Shepard, "Algeria"; Penvenne, "Against the Tide," 87.

32. Anaya, *Indigenous Peoples*, 76; Kauanui, "Colonialism in Equality," 647.

33. Elkins and Pedersen, *Settler Colonialism*, 3.

34. Zureik, *Internal Colonialism*; Lustick, *National Minority*; Yiftachel, "Ethnocracy"; Shafir and Peled, *Being Israeli*.

35. On the emergence of race as a by-product of French colonialism in Algeria, see Saada, "Race and Sociological Reason," 363–366. On the way that race came to shape Turkishness as a vehicle of cooptation and inclusion, see Cagaptay, "Race, Assimilation and Kemalism."

36. Saada, "Race and Sociological Reason," 379.

37. Wolfe, "Elimination of the Native," 397.

38. Stoler, "Degrees," 139.

CHAPTER 1

1. Lockman, *Comrades and Enemies*, 23–26.

2. R. Khalidi, *Palestinian Identity*.

3. Doumani, *Rediscovering Palestine*.

4. Robson, *Colonialism and Christianity*, 2.

5. This paragraph and the next draw from Shafir, *Origins*.

6. Segev, *One Palestine*, 115–116; Ben-Ami, *Scars*, 12–14; LeVine, "Nation from the Sands," 19; Ben-Eliezer, *Israeli Militarism*; Shapira, *Land and Power*, 275–281; Sa'di, "Afterword," 307; Shalom, "Finally Meet," 56; Silberman, *Prophet*, 84–87.

7. R. Khalidi, *Palestinian Identity*, 35–117, 120–144; Campos, *Ottoman Brothers*.

8. Lockman, *Comrades and Enemies*; Shapira, *Land and Power*; Saposnik, "Europe and Its Orients."

9. In 1921, Chaim Weizmann reminded the World Zionist Congress of "the inevitable percentage of failures which occurs in all colonizing work" and encouraged its members to consider the Yishuv's impressive achievements in comparison to those "of the British dominions" (*Trial and Error*, 277). See also Kornberg, "Theodore Herzl"; Piterberg, *Returns*, 36–42; Agassi, *Liberal Nationalism*, 102–103; Sternhell, *Founding Myths*, 70.

10. Ber Borochov (1906) and Theodor Herzl (1898), cited in Lockman, *Comrades and Enemies*, 32 and 41; Haim Weizmann to the Zionist Commission 1918, cited in Segev, *One Palestine*, 109–110.

11. Ben-Gurion, *Rebirth*, 5–6, 9; Trakhtenberg, "ha-Mizrah," 33–34; Zalmona, "Mizrahah!" 47–93.

12. In 1901, Theodor Herzl, the Viennese Jewish journalist who spearheaded the diplomatic effort to attain a Jewish state, tried briefly and failed to secure Ottoman support for the Jewish settlement project. On his subsequent meetings with British Colonial Secretary Joseph Chamberlain in 1899, see Herzl's *Complete Diaries*, 1361–1363.

13. Quoted in Said, *Question of Palestine*, 16.

14. Manela, *Wilsonian Moment*; Weitz, "From the Vienna to the Paris System," 1326.

15. Robinson, "Problem of Privilege."

16. R. Khalidi, *Iron Cage*; Makdisi, *Faith Misplaced*.

17. Pedersen, "League of Nations"; Anghie, "International Institutions."

18. Thompson, *Justice Interrupted*, chap. 5.

19. Makdisi, *Faith Misplaced*, 134–146.

20. This included Palestine's native Eastern Jews. See Trakhtenberg, "ha-Mizrah," 33–45; Berkowitz, *Western Jewry*; Lockman, "We Opened Up the Arabs' Minds"; and Buber's critique of the movement's "imperialism masquerading as humanitarianism" in "Toward the Decision," in Mendes-Flohr, *Land of Two Peoples*, 41.

21. By this point, some ten thousand Jews lived in nearly four dozen agricultural colonies. Campos, *Ottoman Brothers*, 12–14.

22. Ben-Gurion, quoted in Segev, *One Palestine*, 119.

23. Bashkin, *Other Iraq*; Thompson, *Colonial Citizens*.

24. Pedersen, "League of Nations," 113–114.

25. R. Khalidi, *Iron Cage*.

26. Seikaly, "Meatless Days."

27. Quoted in Greenberg, *Race and State*, 379.

28. The other state was Iraq. The law also shortened the normal waiting period to two years and demanded only adequate knowledge of one of the three official languages, including English. See Art. 1.3 of Government of Palestine, *1925 Order in Council*; Qafisheh, "International Foundations," 78, 97; and Bentwich, "Nationality," 97–109.

29. Weitz, "From the Vienna"; Mazower, "International Civilization"; Saada, "Race and Sociological Reason." The conflation of "race" with nationality appeared both in the 1923 Lausanne peace treaty and in the nationality law of every post-Ottoman mandate.

30. Yuval-Davis, "Nationalism and Racism"; Pitts, "Empire and Democracy," 297, 302–304; Stoler, *Carnal Knowledge*, 112–139; Wolfe, "Race and Racialisation." See Lake and Reynolds, *Global Colour Line*, on the ascendance of "whiteness" in the United States and Britain's setler dominions in the early twentieth century.

31. Brown, *Regulating Aversion*.

32. Makdisi, *Culture of Sectarianism*.

33. Campos, *Ottoman Brothers*; Rodrigue, "Difference and Tolerance"; Krämer, "Moving Out of Place."

34. Weitz, "From the Vienna to the Paris System." On the fear of difference nurtured by liberal nationalism's homogenizing impulse, see Asad, *Genealogies of Religion*, 257; Appadurai, *Fear of Small Numbers*; and Jabareen, "Likrat gishot bikortiot."

35. Arendt, *Origins of Totalitarianism*, 267–302; Baer, *Dönme*, 239, 254.

36. The League did eventually call on all mandates to guarantee the "effective protection of racial, linguistic, and religious minorities" as well as "the privileges and immunities of foreigners." In Palestine, the only intended beneficiaries were Jewish immigrants rather than Christians, Druze, or other religious minorities (Mazzawi, *Palestine and the*

Law, 83–85). Outside Palestine, see White, *Emergence of Minorities*; Watenpaugh, "Cleansing"; and Beinin, *Dispersion*.

37. Robson, *Colonialism and Christianity*, 55–58.

38. Ibid., 19, 51–54, 101–108, 120. This was a direct reversal of the trend that the Ottomans had started in the 1860s. In response, Arab Christian activists argued that Britain's "racial" representation of the Palestinian population was backward and primitive.

39. Ibid., 107–108.

40. Quoted in Qafisheh, "International Foundations," 255.

41. 1937, quoted in Greenberg, *Race and State*, 358. American Zionists continued to echo these arguments after World War II. See Levinthal, "Case," 94. See also Piterberg, *Returns*, 69–78.

42. Quoted in Pedersen, "League of Nations," 128.

43. Ibid., 116.

44. Figures cited in Hope Simpson, *Palestine*.

45. Pedersen, "League of Nations," 124–129.

46. Simon, "Costs," 259.

47. Some have attributed this failure of imagination to the persecution of newly emancipated Jews in the Austro-Hungarian Empire, post-1905 Russia, and post-partition Poland. Avineri, "Herzl's Diaries," 10; Weiss, "Golem," 98.

48. Their success in segregating themselves from Palestinian Arabs began to bear fruit especially in the 1930s, but there was significant regional variation, and it was never entrenched. LeVine, *Overthrowing Geography*, 84–120.

49. Cohen, *Army of Shadows*.

50. Parsons, "Palestinian Druze," 74.

51. Ibid.

52. Cohen, *Army of Shadows*; Swedenburg, *Memories of Revolt*; R. Khalidi, *Iron Cage*, 105–124.

53. Forman, "Historical Geography," 800; Kedar, "First Step," 150.

54. See the protocols leading up to the formation of UNSCOP and the debate over its "terms of reference" in the UN Department of Public Information, *Yearbook*.

55. UNSCOP, *Nineteenth Meeting*.

56. UNSCOP, *Eighth* and *Thirty-Fifth Meetings*, respectively.

57. See, respectively, the testimonies of the Ihud ("Unity" in Hebrew) Association, the League for Jewish-Arab Rapprochement, and the Palestine Communist Union (not to be confused with the Palestine Communist Party) in UNSCOP, *Thirtieth*, *Thirty-Second*, and *Thirty-Fifth Meetings*, respectively.

58. Qafisheh, "International Foundations," 253–255. UNSCOP's Minority Proposal (representing India, Iran, and Yugoslavia) concluded that "a single state with Jewish minority rights" was the only option because the "bi-national solution with parity" violated the right of democratic representation, and because the "cantonal so-

lution" (the Majority Proposal) was "impossible" (UNGA, "Special Note by Sir Abdur Rahman").

59. UNGA, *207th Plenary Meeting*. The tally was 37 to 12, with nine abstentions.

60. During the 1947 UN debate, Jewish Agency officials spoke of Jews as immigrants and Arabs as natives. J. Robinson, *Palestine at the United Nations*, 175.

61. Kumar, "Troubled History."

62. R. Khalidi, *Iron Cage*, 127–129; Ginat, "India."

63. UNSCOP's projected figures for the Jewish state were 498,000 Jews and 497,000 Arabs, though the latter figure was broken down into "Arabs" (407,000) and "Bedouin" (90,000)—a distinction that Israel would embrace. Just 10,000 of the 735,000 people who lived in the territory allotted to the Arab state were Jews. Qafisheh, "International Foundations," 262.

64. British officials echoed this point when they reminded UNSCOP that the League of Nations had deemed the 1938 partition proposal unviable for the same reason. UNGA Ad Hoc Committee on the Palestinian Question, *Memorandum*.

65. Claude, *National Minorities*, 208.

66. Mazower, "International Civilization," 562–565.

67. Mazower, "Strange Triumph," 387; Claude, *National Minorities*, 1, 203–206. On the iteration of this idea in post-partition India, see Pandey, "Can a Muslim Be an Indian?"

68. On US President Eisenhower's desire to keep racism off the UN agenda, see Lauren, "Seen from the Outside," 29–32; and Mazower, "Strange Triumph," 379–398.

69. Claude, *National Minorities*, 144–175.

70. Mazower, "Strange Triumph," 389.

71. UN Department of Public Information, *Yearbook*.

72. Kuntz, "Chapter XI," 103–105.

73. Cited in Ginat, "India," 200–201. Delhi was horrified and issued an immediate retraction.

74. R. Khalidi, *Iron Cage*; Cohen, *Army of Shadows*, 230; Pappe, *Ethnic Cleansing*, 46–52.

75. R. Khalidi, *Iron Cage*, 131; Ben-Ami, *Scars*, 15, 34–37; Pappe, *Ethnic Cleansing*, 28; Ben-Eliezer, *Israeli Militarism*, 25.

76. Landis, "Syria."

77. Naor, "Israel's 1948 War"; Ben-Ami, *Scars*, 39.

78. Doron, "Judges," 593.

79. Some hoped that the process would "direct the transition period from abnormal Jewish existence to a normal, democratic national existence in its country" (Agassi, *Liberal Nationalism*, 22). See also Rozin, "Forming a Collective Identity."

80. Quoted in Elam, *Memal'ei ha-pkudot*, 62 (hereafter, *Executors*).

81. Masalha, *Expulsion*; Morris, *Refugee Problem Revisited*, 39–64; Shlaim, *Iron Wall*, 18–22; Ben-Gurion, "Letter;" Reichman, "Partition and Transfer," 321.

82. This preparation included the collection of detailed intelligence about Palestinian villages so as to be able to exploit their resources, social fissures, and strategic vulnerabilities. Pappe, *Ethnic Cleansing*, 17–22; Eyal, *Disenchantment*, 62–93.

83. Pappe, *Ethnic Cleansing*, 68; Morris, *Birth*, 52–54.

84. See especially Morris, *Refugee Problem Revisited*, xiv–xviii; Esber, *Cover of War*, 386–392; and Pappe, *Ethnic Cleansing*, 59 and 75–76.

85. Quoted in Morris, *Refugee Problem Revisited*, 164. See also W. Khalidi, "Plan Dalet."

86. Kidron, "Truth Whereby Nations Live;" Esber, *Cover of War*, 179–181; Morris, *Refugee Problem Revisited*, 164–165. According to Pappe, this term began to appear more frequently in written orders from the Haganah Command from April 1948 onward. See *Ethnic Cleansing*, 131.

87. Esber, *Cover of War*, 387–392; and Pappe, *Ethnic Cleansing*, 82–104.

88. Naor, "Israel's 1948 War," 250–254.

89. The exception was in the southern desert, territory allotted to the Jewish state that Egyptian troops managed to hold until December 1948. Shlaim calls the Arab coalition "one of the most divided, disorganized, and ramshackle coalitions in the entire history of warfare" ("Israel and the Arab Coalition," 81–82); see also Landis, "Syria."

90. See Pappe, *Ethnic Cleansing*, 126, on the role of Britain and the UN. On September 26, Ben-Gurion promised his cabinet that the Galilee pocket would be *naki*, or "clean," of Arabs. Zilber, "'Naki me-'aravim!'"

91. Khalidi, *All That Remains*. Morris (*Refugee Problem Revisited*, 1) offers a 600,000–760,000 range, but this count includes figures from up to October 1950.

92. Estimates range between 380 and 470. W. Khalidi, *All That Remains*, 585–586; Morris, *Refugee Problem Revisited*, xiv–xviii; Falah, "War and Its Aftermath."

93. The draft identified Hebrew as the official language, with "suitable possibility" for "Arabic speakers" to use their language in contact with state bodies. Kohn, *Hukah le-yisra'el* and "Constitution of Israel"; Radzyner, "Constitution for Israel."

94. Shahar, "Yisra'el ke-medinah du-horit," 44–45; Moshe Gorali, "How God and Democracy Were Left Out," *Haaretz*, May 7, 2003. On Ben-Gurion's triumph over the insistence of Justice Minister Pinhas Rosen that the declaration delimit Israel's borders, see also Weiss, "Golem," 89–93.

CHAPTER 2

1. Rashid Husayn, *al-Mirsad*, April 14, 1960, translated in Marmorstein, "Rashid Husain [sic]," 9.

2. I borrow this term from Wolfe, "Elimination of the Native," 397.

3. Segev, *1949*, 95.

4. Jiryis, *Arabs in Israel*, 289.

5. Kamen, "After the Catastrophe I," 460–463. The overall ratio of town dwellers within the Palestinian population dropped from 36 percent to 26 percent.

6. Piterberg, "Erasures."

7. "Armistice Agreements with the Arab Countries," April 4, 1949, in Lorch, *Major Knesset Debates*, 514–515.

8. Ibid. The Haganah denied any involvement in Dayr Yasin and placed responsibility with the Irgun—the paramilitary unit that had broken away from the Haganah in 1931 over its "defeatist" stance toward the Palestinians and the British—and the Stern Gang (LEHI, for Lohame Herut Yisra'el, Fighters for the Freedom of Israel), an even more activist group that split from the Irgun in 1940. Yet the Haganah had offered its "reluctant, qualified consent" for the attack on the village, whose residents had repeatedly demonstrated their desire to stay out of the fighting. Morris, *Refugee Problem Revisited*, 237–240. See also Pappe, *Ethnic Cleansing*, 91.

9. This includes families from seventeen of the twenty-five destroyed villages in the Acre and Nazareth districts; it excludes the large number of refugees among the Bedouin in the south. Numbers fluctuated significantly until late 1949. One exception to the ban on return was eventually granted to the Nazareth-based refugees from Haifa, probably as a way to reduce the swollen refugee community in the all-Arab town. Falah, "Judaization"; Lustick, "Zionism and the State," 132–133; Kamen, "After the Catastrophe I," 471; Masalha, *Catastrophe Remembered*, 11; Abu Sa'ad, "Forced Sedentarization," in Masalha, *Catastrophe Remembered*, 117; Hoffman, *My Happiness*, 197.

10. Hoffman, *My Happiness*, 197. Between 1949 and 1951, further expulsions, along with the army's decision to allow refugees to return to Haifa and some villages that remained fully intact, reduced that figure to 25 percent. On Acre, see Lehrman, "Arabs of Israel," 526–527.

11. Hoffman, *My Happiness*, 197. The curfew was later pushed back to 7 P.M. By March 1949, the curfew imposed on Jaffa's Arab population had been eased from 7 P.M. to 10 P.M. See the third issue of the MoM's internal bulletin, 'Al ha-Na'aseh be-Kerev ha-Mi'utim [Happenings Among the Minorities], March 13, 1949, ISA 49/G304/57. By this time the curfew in Acre had been eased from 10 P.M. to midnight. See Governor of the Western Galilee and Haifa area villages to MG Headquarters, March 27, 1949, in ibid.

12. See the complaint from the Arab Emergency Committee in Jaffa on December 16, 1948, MoM, 'Al ha-Na'aseh, February 10, 1949, ISA 49/G304/57.

13. Wolfe, "Elimination of the Native," 388.

14. Forman and Kedar, "From Arab Land."

15. Ben-Gurion, "Civil Defense," speech to the Knesset on the Civil Defense Bill, January 2, 1951; and "Call of the Spirit in Israel," *Government Yearbook*, October 1951, in *Rebirth*, 388, 400–401.

16. Wolfe, "Elimination of the Native," 388.

17. Ozacky-Lazar and Bäuml, "Tahat shilton," 55–56.

18. Sussman, "Law and Judicial Practice," 29–31. Another decree legalized the status of all Jews in the country.

19. Hussain, "Jurisprudence of Emergency."

20. Kostal, "Jurisprudence of Power," and *Jurisprudence of Power*, especially 461–487.

21. Quoting the Duke of Wellington in, respectively, Kostal, "Jurisprudence of Power," 25–26; and Hussain, "Jurisprudence of Emergency," 97–98.

22. Townshend, "Martial Law."

23. Duke of Wellington in Hussain, "Jurisprudence of Emergency," 98.

24. Ibid., 111–114.

25. Simpson, *Human Rights*, 80–88. On British violence, see Swedenburg, *Memories of Revolt*; and R. Khalidi, *Iron Cage*, 105–124.

26. Simpson, *Human Rights*, 830–832.

27. Bernard Joseph in early 1946, quoted in Jiryis, *Arabs in Israel*, 11–12.

28. Sussman, "Law and Judicial Practice."

29. Kohn, "Constitution."

30. Lustick, "Zionism and the State," 135.

31. Pappe, *Ethnic Cleansing*, 28.

32. Forman and Kedar, "From Arab Land." See also Abu Sitta, *Financing Racism;* and *Dividing War Spoils*.

33. Quigley, "Displaced Palestinians," 182, 201.

34. Mazzawi, *Palestine and the Law*, 83–84; Liang, "Conditions of Admission." Another problem was the future status of Jerusalem, which the Partition Plan had proposed to internationalize.

35. Claude, *National Minorities*, 180–182; UNSC, *385th Meeting*.

36. Ben-Gurion, *Yoman ha-milhamah* (hereafter, *War Diary*), December 18, 1948, 882–884. The MoM's Bechor Shitrit, widely remembered as a "moderate," argued that granting suffrage to Palestinians living in areas allocated to the Arab state by Resolution 181 would be "absurd in terms of international law" and "even more absurd in terms of Jewish interests" (Shenhav, "Worthless Flock," 261–263).

37. Liang, "Conditions of Admission," 299–301. Out of eleven council members, Egypt voted against the bid and Britain abstained.

38. UNGA, *Application of Israel*. The tally of the final vote was 37 to 21.

39. Ibid.

40. Claude, *National Minorities*, 179–183.

41. Some members of MAPAI believed that the opportunity for mass expulsions had ended as early as July 1948, before the conquest of the Galilee pocket and the Naqab/Negev. "It is clear that we do not have enough strength to take the Palestinians residing in the country and remove them," said Shlomo Lavi at a meeting of the party's Central Committee. "But we do have enough strength not to let those who have already left return" (Kemp, "Dangerous Populations," 78). See also Benziman and Mansour, *Subtenants*, 56–57.

42. Although Israel was more determined to expel Palestinians in the summer and fall of 1948, Palestinians also became more determined to stay put as a result of the

reports they heard about the plight of the refugees in Lebanon and Jordan. Morris, *Birth*; Shoufani, "Fall of a Village."

43. Of the 735,000 people projected to live in the Arab state of Palestine, only 10,000 were Jews. In December 1948, Jews comprised less than 1 percent of the 33,574 living in the Nazareth region. Jewish residents in the other administrative districts comprised 4 percent (Acre), 7.5 percent (Beersheba), 24 percent (Ramle, including Jerusalem), 47 percent (Haifa), and 72 percent (Lydd, including Tel Aviv, Jaffa, and Petah Tikva) of their populations. Qafisheh, "International Foundations," 262; Y. Shimoni, MFA/Middle East Division, to MoI, December 29, 1948; MFA, "The Minorities in Israel," November 9, 1948, both in ISA 130.15(2)/HZ2564/22; Pappe, *Ethnic Cleansing*, 35.

44. Lustick, "Zionism and the State," 141–142.

45. "It would be folly," noted one government pamphlet in 1950, "to resurrect artificially a minority problem which has been almost eliminated by the war" (Moleah, "Violations," 28l). In late 1952, Ben-Gurion recalled that in May 1948 there were only "a few [villages] which were not Jewish" (*Rebirth*, 466).

46. Lehrman, "Arabs of Israel," 531. This comment was made by a Foreign Ministry official, who added, "The modern trend is to transfer minorities, not re-establish them, particularly when a minority has decamped of its own accord."

47. Ibid. This included "the forced deportation of German-Hungarian minorities from Czechoslovakia, wartime Britain's shipment of enemy aliens to Canada, and even America's concentration of her Japanese in Colorado and Arizona."

48. Ibid., 525. Quakers distributed flour, lentils, and olive oil on behalf of the UN in 1949. In Nazareth, the Belgian Church Mission provided one portion of bread and soup to six thousand people every two days. The Red Cross, UNICEF, and local hospitals and churches "also scrambled to help" (Hoffman, *My Happiness*, 194–195). The Red Cross ceased operations in September 1951. ISA 102/GL17116/20. See also Gallagher, *Quakers*.

49. Israeli delegates underscored that the derogation clauses in the Charter and the Declaration of Human Rights nullified any obligations on member states, and they opposed the rights of individuals and NGOs to petition the UN. Carnegie Endowment, *Israel and the United Nations*, 256–258; Bruegel, "Right to Petition," 560, 76n.

50. Jiryis, "Domination by the Law."

51. Falah, "War and Its Aftermath," 276; H. Baruch, "Facing the 180,000: How Does the Military Government Work?" *Davar*, August 1, 1958.

52. E. Mor to MG North, May 22, 1951, ISA 102/GL17118/15; Schwarz, *Arabs in Israel*, 65, 85. Israel's Central Bureau of Statistics continues to define "mixed cities" as "localities in which the decisive majority of the population is Jewish but which have a sizeable minority of Arab residents." See Inter-Agency Task Force on Israeli Arab Issues, "Mixed Cities in Israel Fact Sheet," http://www.iataskforce.org/mixed-cities-israel.

53. Lustick, *Arabs in the Jewish State*, 84–85; Rosenfeld, "Class Situation," 391.

54. Bäuml, "Military Government"; Ben-Porath, *Arab Labor Force*, 51–54.

55. Dror, "Emergency Regulations," 140–141.

56. Tarazi, "Planning Apartheid."

57. Marx, *Bedouin of the Negev*, 35. Many of these communities managed to remain because they had cooperated with Jewish forces during the war. After 1948, tribal recognition came only to those who cooperated with the military regime.

58. Falah, "How Israel Controls the Bedouin," 36–40.

59. Marx, *Bedouin of the Negev*, 40.

60. Ibid., 46–49; Schwarz, *Arabs in Israel*, 159.

61. Korn, "Crime and Legal Control," 586.

62. In 1951, hundreds of people in Umm al-Fahm, in the Triangle, cabled the prime minister demanding travel permits; the distribution of the same amount of food and clothing rations as those given to Jews; an end to the "beatings, insults, and torture" by the governor and his staff; the ability to take their cases to court; and free legal counsel. The governor reportedly told them that anyone unhappy with the situation should move to Jordan: "'We'd rather meet in the darkness of prison than remain in this situation,'" *Al-Ittihad*, February 17, 1951. Years later, an activist from Tayyibe recalled how one permit officer "used to humiliate and frighten people by bringing his dog with him and setting it on anyone he wanted to scare." In Nazareth, officer Ya'qub Ya'qubi was also known for his cruelty: "If anyone got slightly out of line by mistake, [the officer] would . . . order him to kneel down with his head on the floor near an old harvesting machine he kept in his room, and make them stay like that for a very long time" (Baransi, "Story of a Palestinian," 16). See also *al-Ittihad*, July 13, 1956, for an account of two hundred workers who were forced to wait outside the governor's office in 'Ara (also in the Triangle). When the governor arrived at 3 P.M., he slapped one of the workers and angrily ordered everyone to return in three days. Clipped in ISA 56/G2220/31–33.

63. It could take months, for instance, for a woman in Haifa to get a permit to visit her mother in the Galilee. Korn, "Kavanot tovot" (hereafter, "Good intentions"); Rosenfeld, *Hem hayu falahim*, 391; Ozacky-Lazar and Bäuml, "Tahat shilton," 58.

64. Meir joined the Histadrut's Executive Committee in 1928. *The Observer*, January 24, 1971, cited in Davis, *Utopia*, 142.

65. These figures cover the 1949 to 1952 period. The smallest gap was among skilled workers. Until at least 1963, the annual income of Arab citizens was just 55 percent of that of Jewish citizens who did the same work. Ben-Porath, *Arab Labor Force*, 60–64; Shalev, "Jewish Organized Labor."

66. Lehrman, "Arabs of Israel," 526–527. This was the assessment of the local governor. Among other places, Palestinians had worked in factories, the oil refinery, the railways, the port, and the postal and telegraph service. Most clerks who had worked in the Mandate's civil service or with global firms that pulled out of Palestine during the war also lost their jobs. Ben-Porath, *Arab Labor Force*, 78–79.

67. Lustick, *Arabs in the Jewish State*, 299, 96n, citing the *Jerusalem Post*, April 4, 1956.

68. Yossi Melman, "I am not your husband Ahmad, I am Yossi from the Shin Bet," *ha-Arets*, September 29, 1998.

69. Lustick, "Zionism and the State," 135.

70. Meeting of the Committee alongside the Military Government, September 14, 1948, ISA 130.15(2)/HZ2564/11.

71. Ben-Gurion, *War Diary*, November 1948, 807–809; Yetah, MoM/Haifa to Shitrit, n.d. (probably Spring 1949), ISA 102/GL17118/40.

72. Pappe, "Uneasy Coexistence," 639–640; Korn, "Good intentions."

73. Masalha, *Land Without a People*, xii–xiii. He translates the Hebrew as "evacuate the population."

74. Saltman, "Mandatory Emergency Laws," 387, 392–393; Shamir, *Colonies of Law*, 11; Sebba, "Sanctioning Policy," 266–267; Dowty, "Emergency Powers," 36–37.

75. "Are you Arab or Jewish? This is what they asked us during the Mandate, and now as well!" *al-Ittihad*, January 29, 1950; Ramzi Khuri, "Military rule and the permits are the most prominent expressions of racial discrimination against the Arabs: A day in Acre," *al-Ittihad*, May 1, 1950; Korn, "Political Control," 165.

76. See Watad, "Coexistence," and the complaint of racial profiling by a resident of Tira, in the Triangle, published in *al-Mirsad* on July 19, 1956, clipped in ISA 56/G2220/31–33.

77. Korn, "Political Control," 167–170.

78. "Arab Workers Congress Executive Committee presents powerful memo to Knesset's Arab Affairs Committee explaining woes of the Arab masses," *al-Ittihad*, August 6, 1950. Jiryis, *Arabs in Israel*, 33. Appeals became possible only in July 1963, but few succeeded and in any event were not enforced. Schiff, "Pros and Cons"; Schmidt, *Foundations*, 321–326; Kimmerling, *Clash*, 193; Schwarz, *Arabs in Israel*, 61; Ozacky-Lazar and Bäuml, "Tahat shilton," 55–56. The first tribunal was held in Nazareth on February 28, 1950, when five Arab communists were tried on the charge of "thwarting people occupied with vital tasks" for blocking one of the doors to the governor's office during a demonstration for work, food, and an end to military rule. Each was sentenced to one week in detention. ISA 102/GL17109/44.

79. Jiryis, *Arabs in Israel*, 31 and 246, 45n. This figure, out of a total of 30,500 cases, is inclusive of the years 1953 to 1967. Sometimes hundreds were convicted monthly. Of the other 2 percent, 17 were expelled without trial, 35 cases were dropped, and 2 were sent to the High Court.

80. Shoufani, *Rihla fi al-rahil*, chap. 4; Schwarz, *Israel's Arabs in Israel*, 159; Khuri, "Military rule." See also "On the conditional permits: We won't arrive at the system of the Untouchables and the Brahmins," *al-Ittihad*, March 8, 1955.

81. In September 1951, the Shin Bet reported that there was no evidence of any serious effort to sabotage state security and no signs of an Arab underground. The Arab public remained terrified of expulsions and despaired over the idea of a second war. Benziman and Mansour, *Subtenants*, 104–105.

82. To the extent that Arabs were convicted on criminal charges, such as physical assault, it was almost always for actions perpetrated against other Arabs. Between 1948 and 1967, DER violations comprised 40 percent of all Arab convictions and 86 percent of all political status convictions. Of the remaining 14 percent, less than 0.5 percent was for charges of sedition, weapons possession, or divulging sensitive information. The rest were for violations of Israel's own emergency regulations, such as the 1949 Security Zones Law (4 percent), for disturbing public order or violating an order that restricted the defendant's personal movement (6 percent), and for breaking the 1954 Prevention of Infiltration Law (8 percent), which I discuss in the next chapter. Korn, "Political Control," 171–173; "Crime and Legal Control," 583–588; and "Pshi'a," 197.

83. Korn, "Pshi'a," 181–184. Most detentions did not last longer than one month.

84. "Looking for work is a crime in the ghettos of the military rule," al-Ittihad, October 23, 1953. In the summer of 1954 a seventy-five-year-old man in Bi'na, near Acre, was sentenced to two months in prison for not turning in his "infiltrator" son even though the authorities had known he was there for years. His son's wife, who was six months pregnant, was sentenced to three months. A. Goldstein, "Anti-Arab terror continues," Kol ha-'Am, August 19, 1954. See al-Ittihad, March 18, 1958; and Hadawi, Israel and the Arab Minority, 10–11, on the reported conviction of forty-seven citizens at a military tribunal in 'Ara that lasted just thirty minutes. One of those fined was a twelve-year-old boy caught working with his ninety-year-old father without a permit in the settlement of Zikhron Ya'akov. The sentencing of children and the elderly, and the serving of time on their behalf by family members, also appears in fiction from and about this period. See "Mahkamat shaykh" [The shaykh's trial] and "Ba'i'a al-falafil" [The falafil seller] in Mu'ammar, al-Mutasalilun, 16–26 and 35–49.

85. Khuri, "Military government;" Jiryis, Arabs in Israel, 246, 45n. Between March and December 1951, the military collected 13,606 Italian lira (IL) in fines. The average was IL 6.7, then worth at least a week of wages for those who had work outside their villages; for those who worked inside them or in local quarries (more common since it became nearly impossible to obtain a work permit), the fine amounted to at least two weeks' worth of wages. Ben-Porath, Arab Labor Force, 60–64. Within two years, fines had skyrocketed to a range of IL 25–50. Al-Ittihad, October 23, 1953.

86. Korn, "Rates of Incarceration," 36–40.

87. Interview with Zvi Elpeleg, former Triangle governor; Bäuml, "Military Government," 48–49; Cohen, Good Arabs, 159–164.

88. Bäuml, "Military Government," 46–49; Lustick, Arabs in the Jewish State, 123–124; Kanaana, "Survival Strategies."

89. Cohen, Good Arabs, 62–63.

90. Shmuel Divon, quoted in Schwarz, Arabs in Israel, 119 and 141 (emphasis in original).

91. Saban, "Le'ahar ha-barbariot," 66–71; Kimmerling, Clash, 149.

92. In 1951, for example, the army censored part of an atypically critical poem in *Davar* that denounced the fatal shooting of a boy in Umm al-Fahm (*al-Ittihad*, September 15, 1951). See, conversely, *Davar*'s mockery on November 9, 1953, of allegations by Tayyibe residents of Border Guard abuse and its dismissal of them as "smugglers and their friends." The dominant media were reportedly silent in 1953 after military police armed with submachine guns invaded a Jewish colony to search for Arab youth who were working without permits. Daniel Ben Nahum, "Uproot the disease!" [Ya'ker ha-neg'a!], *'Al ha-Mishmar*, April 26, 1953, clipped in "Arab Complaints Against Army Treatment, 1949–1954," ISA 102/GL17118/40.

93. "PM Sharett rejects complaints of discrimination against the Arab minority," *Davar*, May 13, 1954. See also Chapter Three of this book.

94. Lahav, "Supreme Court," 45–48.

95. On March 23, 1949, three refugees from Ma'lul appealed to the premier for the return of their goats, which they claimed three guards from the Nahalal colony (*koloniya*) had stolen from them. Two months later the government secretary replied and advised them to turn to the courts. ISA 102/GL17118/40. Around 1954 MAKI activist Tawfiq Zayyad, later elected as Nazareth's mayor in 1975, won a case against two police officers for attacking him after a demonstration there (*al-Sira al-dhatia*). See also "Judge silent while Arab cursed in court!" *Al-Ittihad*, 9 April 1965.

96. Schmidt, *Foundations*, 123–125; 317; 326; Bracha, "Safek miskenim, safek mesukanim," 379–393 (hereafter, "Unfortunate or perilous"); Kimmerling, *Clash*, 193; Saban, "Hashpa'at bet ha-mishpat," 541, 554; Saltman, "Mandatory Emergency Laws," 390; Dowty, "Emergency Powers."

97. Jiryis, *Arabs in Israel*, 28–29.

98. See letter from AWC-Nazareth on February 23–24, 1950, ISA 56/G2201/28; and "AWC's Executive Committee presents powerful memo," *al-Ittihad*, August 6, 1950. The AWC was established in August 1945 and affiliated with the NLL. MAKI took control of the union in late 1948.

99. "Repetition of police attacks on Arab citizens in Wadi Nisnas," *al-Ittihad*, September 12, 1958.

100. Those who attempted to intervene were tried and jailed for not being able to pay the heavy fines imposed. On Tayyibe, see Baransi, "Story of a Palestinian," 14–16; and the exchange of letters in late 1953, ISA 102/GL17118/40. On beatings, secret interrogations, and acts of dog mauling carried out by Officer Avraham Yarkoni in Dayr Hanna and 'Arrabe, in the Upper Galilee, see Tawfiq Tubi to MoD Ben-Gurion, Question #204, April 10, 1951, in IDFA 1559/52–113. Elderly residents of Sakhnin, which neighbors the two villages, continue to tell stories of Yarkoni's brutality. Interviews in Sakhnin, July 13, 2002. See also note 62 above.

101. *Kol ha-'Am*, August 19, 1954, excerpted in ISA 56/G2220/31–33.

102. In 1955, the IDF's Chief of Staff wrote that because Israel was so narrow, the

entire country was a frontier. Dayan, "Israel's Border," 254. On the racialization of the frontier in Israeli nationalism, see Gordon, *Israel's Occupation*, 122; Weizman, *Hollow Land*, 57–64, 107; Kemp, "From Politics of Location," 75; and Yiftachel, "Territory as the Kernel," 215–248.

103. Morris, *Border Wars*, 99–117.

104. Allon, *Masakh shel hol*, 330; Lustick, *Arabs in the Jewish State*, 146; Ronit Matalon, "Intifada? Riffraff!" interview with Joshua Palmon, *Musaf ha-Arets*, June 30, 1989, 4–7.

105. On the personal efforts of Jewish settlers to block refugee return, and their support for military rule as a tool for holding on to their wartime land gains, see Morris, *Border Wars*, 123–144, 166; and Korn, "Good intentions," 119–125.

106. Peretz, "Arab Refugee Dilemma," 137–138; Jiryis, "Domination by the Law," 84–92.

107. Lustick, *Arabs in the Jewish State*, 129–130.

108. Forman and Kedar, "From Arab Land"; Abu Sitta, *Dividing War Spoils*.

109. Beinin, *Red Flag*, 69. On this theme, see Tolan, *Lemon Tree*; Kanafani, *Palestine's Children*; and Hoffman, *My Happiness*.

110. After the Triangle's annexation in 1949, the local governor banned cars from Tira from using the main access road to a nearby kibbutz to reach the Jewish town of Kfar Saba. He claimed that its members did not want the Tira residents to pass near them. In March 1957, the kibbutz's soccer team invited players from Tira to a match, expressing their opposition to the road closure and a desire for better relations with their neighbors. "The Jews want brotherhood with the Arabs," *al-Ittihad*, March 29, 1957.

111. See the MoM's second published circular, February 25, 1949, ISA 49/G304/57. See also Anonymous, "Notes on the Alstun article," February 8, 1951, ISA 130.15(2)/HZ2564/22; MoI/Mins, "Independence Day celebrations schedule in the minorities regions," May 1957, ISA 56/G2220/26; Benziman and Mansour, *Subtenants*, 38.

112. In *al-Ittihad*, see "Communist Party presents draft bill to cancel military rule," February 2, 1952; and "The spirit of 'Little Rock' in Israel—Safad is open to 'Jews' but forbidden to 'Arabs,'" January 24, 1958. See also Dror, "Emergency Regulations," 137.

113. Schmidt, *Foundations*, 314–320; Benziman and Mansour, *Subtenants*, 104–105; Saltman, "Mandatory Emergency Laws," 388, 392; Schwarz, *Arabs in Israel*, 88; Ozacky-Lazar and Bäuml, "Tahat shilton," 60–62.

114. On the claim of universal enforcement for foreign consumption, see "The Arabs in Israel," Government Press Division, June 24, 1951, ISA 56/G2220; and the MFA's regular bulletin, *Arabs in Israel*, in 1958 (12), 1966 (8), and 1968 (13). See also Kemp, "Dangerous Populations."

115. Dowty, "Emergency Powers," 39; Schmidt, *Foundations*, 321–326.

116. Dayan, "Israel's Border;" Ze'ev Schiff, "Jewish and Arab Writers Meet," *New Outlook*, January 1959, 61–62.

117. Lehrman, "Arabs of Israel"; Ben Shlomo, "Arab Village."

118. Meysels, *Israel in Your Pocket (Central Israel)*, II-94–95 (on Abu Ghosh) and

II-164–165 ("Sightseeing in these Arab villages of the *Little Triangle* is not encouraged by the authorities"), as well as the *Northern Israel* volume, I-29–30 and I-66.

119. See, for example, Goldstein, "Anti-Arab terror continues," on the arrest of several Jewish residents of the MAKI-affiliated kibbutz Yad-Hana after they attended a party hosted by their neighbors in Tayyibe.

120. The dominant Hebrew-language press made a fuss over marriages between Jewish women and Palestinian men in MAKI (Ya'acov Avi'el, "A Jewess from Nazareth," *Ma'ariv*, July 12, 1957). So did the Shin Bet. In 1965, the agency asked the police to prepare a list of names of "all Jewish women married to minorities men" in the Northern District. In late August, the Acre District Station submitted the names of twenty-five women, along with their ages, countries of origin, whether they had converted, current residence and religion, and the names of their husbands. Just over half of the couples lived in Acre and Haifa; the rest lived in the husbands' home villages. Seven of the women were born in Morocco, and five were born in Palestine; the rest were mostly from southeast Europe, Iraq, Egypt, Syria, and Turkey. Many, but not all, had converted to Islam. The report claimed that most had worked as prostitutes prior to their marriages, and that their husbands belonged to the "Acre underground," left undefined (ISA 79/L395/1). In 1968, one anthropologist estimated that there were only a few hundred such marriages (Rosenfeld, "Change"). On the isolation and punishment of Jewish women who have married Arab men in Israel and (since 1967) the Occupied Territories, see the documentary film *Forbidden Marriages in the Holy Land*. For a fictional account, see Mu'ammar, "al-Kamin" [The ambush], in *al-Mutasalilun*, 50–64.

121. Kook, "Changing Representations," 155–156.

122. Some officials worried about the wide listenership among Mizrahi Jews to *Sawt Isra'il* (Voice of Israel), the state's Arabic radio station (whose programming was designed largely to conduct propaganda over the border), as well as to broadcasts from Cairo, Damascus, Beirut, and Ramallah. The VoI staff considered playing more songs by the popular singer Fairuz, to counter the popularity of their Lebanese rivals, which in the late 1950s announced plans to play her music all day so as to appeal to Mizrahi listeners. See the October 25, 1956 report in ISA 43.04/A7224/38. On Fairuz, see clippings from Israel's *ha-Boker*, September 8, 1959; and Beirut's *Al-Hayat*, August 13, 1959, in ISA 130/HZ3742/7. See also Naji 'Ezer to MFA/Middle East, "Secret," March 22, 1960, ISA 43.04/G6343/1793. The Iraqi-born author claimed that because Mizrahi immigrants "loved to listen" to *Sawt Isra'il* and did so in higher numbers than "the minorities," they were disappointed that the station declined them the same opportunity to request "the Arab songs so beloved to them." See also Penslar, "Broadcast Orientalism," 182–200; and Pearlson, *Simhah gdolah*. On similar concerns raised at the turn of the century, see Campos, *Ottoman Brothers*, 201.

123. Michael, *Refuge*; Snir, "Iraqi-Jewish Writers"; Beinin, *Dispersion* and *Red Flag*, 163.

124. Copty, *Knowledge and Power*, 144, 285. The number of Jewish teachers in the

Arab school system peaked in 1956, when they comprised one quarter of the national faculty. In 1960 they comprised 70 percent of high school teachers. A majority were Iraqi immigrants. See *Statistical Abstracts of Israel*, 1959–1966; E. Simon, "Arab Teachers and Intellectuals in Israel: Facts, Remarks, and Impressions," *NER*, February–April 1959; ISA 71/G1733/145/1, 71/GL1404/1351–3, 71/GL1616/1351, 71/GL1223/145, and 79/L2251/53; and Histadrut Archives, IV-219–232.

125. Cooper, "Parting of the Ways," 29. See also Hopkins, "Rethinking Decolonization"; and Lewis, "Ruling Compassions."

126. Dubow, "Smuts"; Shepard, "Algeria"; de Lepervanche, "From Race to Ethnicity."

127. Lehrman, "Arabs of Israel," 528; Ben-Gurion, "'Al ha-mi'ut ha-'aravi"; Samuel, "Prospect," 462; Shalom, "Finally Meet," 63; interview with Nuzhat Katsav, former broadcaster on Israel's Arabic radio station and head of the Histadrut's Arab and Druze Women's Division.

128. Y. Arni, "Minorities Folklore Exhibition in Acre," *Hed ha-Hinukh*, October 1958, 15–16; Benziman and Mansour, *Subtenants*, chap. 3; Danin, *Tsiyoni be-khol tnai*, 373–413; Somekh, "Reconciling Two Great Loves"; Regev, "Present Absentee," 443. Palestinians complained about the hollow use of these terms both during and after military rule. In addition to Somekh, see Mahmud Darwish, "Geographic Judaization," *al-Ittihad*, October 14, 1966; Watad, "Coexistence"; and Shoufani, *Rihla fi al-rahil*, 80.

129. In the early 1940s, the Jewish Agency established a "neighborly relations" division, which organized settlers' visits to the homes of Arab villagers and exploited their existing friendships in order to gather intelligence and recruit informants. It also taught courses in Arabic language and culture to aspiring intelligence officers. Cohen, *Army of Shadows*, 178–179.

130. In a speech in August 1948 one governor in the Galilee expressed his hope that Arabs and Jews could "live together freely, regardless of religious or racial differences" (Hoffman, *My Happiness*, 179). In December 1948, the Foreign Ministry profiled the official of Moroccan-Jewish ancestry who headed the short-lived MoM as follows: "Bechor Shitrit, with his expansive and hospitable warmth, his leisureliness and his charm, is unmistakably a personality formed by the Orient. Even those who object on principle to the political representation of the 'racial' communities as such welcome the emergence into public life of so distinctive and colorful a figure" (Peled, "The Other Side," 87).

131. Anonymous, "Notes on the Alstun article," February 8, 1951, ISA 130.15(2)/HZ2564/22.

132. Ozacky-Lazar and Bäuml, "Tahat shilton," 4–7. Similarly, an MFA spokesperson told an American reporter in 1949 that economic equality between Arabs and Jews would "take time because the Arabs start so far behind" (Lehrman, "Arabs of Israel," 532).

133. During a debate on military rule at the Foreign Ministry in March 1953, one person argued that the restrictions imposed on Arabs were important because of their "primitive thinking and intellect" (Benziman and Mansour, *Subtenants*, 20). On the be-

lief among census officials that Arabs were incapable of appreciating science, see Leibler, "Establishing Scientific Authority," 232.

134. Quoted in Teller, "Arab Minority Problem," 556–557.

135. *Davar*, January 14, 1953.

136. Palmon to Eitan, MFA, December 19, 1949, ISA 102/GL17111/27.

137. Segev, *1949*, 67.

138. Polakow-Suransky, *Unspoken Alliance*, 20–21.

139. Reported years later in *al-Ittihad*, April 6, 1956. At a press conference before his departure, Malan spoke in Afrikaans to his listeners back home: "Israel's activities to till and preserve the land can serve as a model from which you in South Africa can learn. Shalom." See T. Liuta, "Malan departs with the greeting, 'Shalom,'" *Ma'ariv*, June 17, 1953.

140. Cockrell, "South African Bill," 514.

141. The first edition of the translation was advertised in *'Al ha-Mishmar* on December 2, 1951. Reprints were issued in 1954, 1958, and 1963.

142. Anderson, Paton, and Levin, *Avudim ben ha-kokhavim*. See a review in "Ze'akat ha-nidka'im" [Cry of the oppressed], *'Al ha-Mishmar*, May 15, 1953.

143. Rav Ipkha Mistabra [Rabbi to the contrary], "Za'aki erets ahuvah" [Cry, the beloved country], *Ma'ariv*, December 25, 1953. On Carlebach, see Beinin, "Forgetfulness," 15–16.

144. Azriel Carlebach, "You Can't Come to an Understanding," 1955, reprinted in 2002 by *Nativ*, the English-language online journal of the Ariel Center for Policy Research, a West Bank think tank that opposes a two-state solution: http://www.afsi.org/OUTPOST/2002FEB/feb9.htm. See also the introduction to an excerpt of "Cry the Beloved Country" in *Occupation Magazine*, n.d. http://www.kibush.co.il/show_file.asp?num=29121.

145. Rav Ipkha Mistabra, "Za'aki, erets ahuvah."

146. Ibid.

147. *Al-Ittihad*, June 18, 1950.

148. The "Crimes Against the State" law, which Ben-Gurion presented to the Knesset in late 1952, would have stripped the civil liberties of all citizens, including Jews, in the name of state security. A public outcry ensured its defeat in the Knesset. Dr. A. Y. Yaroslavsky, Chairman of the League for Human and Civil Rights in Israel, to Justice Minister Rosen et al., February 22, 1953, ISA 16/L597/16; Shlomo Nakdimon, "If there is a need to shoot, shoot!" *ha-Arets*, November 11, 2011.

149. "African workers die from poverty in gold mines," *al-Ittihad*, April 6, 1956.

150. Quoting, respectively, Ben Nahum, "Uproot the disease," and Hebrew University Professor Uriel Heyd, in 1952, in Kapeliuk, "Israel's Center for Oriental Studies." Heyd advocated studying Arab history in order "to constitute an 'école de générosité,' a preparation for mutual understanding among the nations, on the French pattern." See also Monroe, "Arab-Israel Frontier," 444.

151. Ihud Association Central Committee, "The Position of the Arabs in the State of Israel: Reply to Mr. Y. Palmon," *NER* (March 1953): 3–5.

152. Ben-Dor, "Merts 1948," 12–17.

153. Shamir, *Colonies of Law.*

154. Benziman and Mansour, *Subtenants*, 19–20; Almog, *Sabra*, 188–189; Beinin, *Red Flag*, 81–84; Rosenfeld, *Hem hayu falahim*, 71.

155. In *Ma'arakhot*, see, for example, Lt. Col. H. M. Baraus, "Eliminating ethnic riots inside walled cities," December 1945, 23–30, reprinted in the January 1955 issue; Maj. Gen. Sir Charles Gwen, "On the postwar 'police duties' of the British army," May 1946, 33–34; Major P. Moore, "Guerilla v. standing army—might and its weakness," November 1946, 25–29; "Internal security duties," January 1947, 59–60; M.M.K. Chertis, "A year as an intelligence officer in Palestine," March 1947, 58–61; Prof. E. G. Boring, "The use of psychology in war," March 1947, 48–52; Lt. Col. H. E. Crocker, "Facing the Indonesian guerilla," June 1947, 51–52; Louis H. Léoté, "Thoughts on colonial and semi-colonial wars," September 1949, 40; and Captain A.P.A. De Grasse, "Military rule over an unruly territory," January 1955, 216–219. Similar pieces reappeared after 1967.

156. Ben-Gurion, "Foreign Policy Speech to the Knesset," February 4, 1952, in *Rebirth*, 395–396.

157. Ben-Gurion, "Call of the Spirit," and "To America's Jewry," a speech delivered to an audience of American Zionists in Jerusalem on September 3, 1950, both translated in *Rebirth*, 414 and 538.

158. Ben-Eliezer, "State Versus Civil Society?" 373 and 374–375.

159. Dankner and Tartakover, *Efo hayinu*, 167 (on cowboys and Karl May) and 86 (on Tarzan and other comics); Eshed, *Komiks 'ivri.* On the idealization of cowboys before and after 1948, see Almog, *Sabra*, 99–101, 112–113, 135. On the circulation of Karl May dime novels, see Gitlis, *ha-Moshel ha-mekho'ar* (hereafter, *Ugly governor*). On children's literature more generally, see al-Asmar, *Hebrew Looking Glass.*

160. In 1949, a reporter from the (then liberal) American Jewish magazine *Commentary* introduced the "Bedouin chieftain" he met in the antechamber of the Beersheba governor's office as "a character out of a Hollywood version of [T. E. Lawrence's] Revolt in the Desert. . . . Six feet tall, flowing robes and desert head-dress, steel gray chin-whiskers, a coppery face like the Indian on a penny. He carried two bandoliers filled with bullets across his chest, two pistols in his sash, and a dagger in a silver sheath. A few respectful paces behind him staggered his small son, about nine years old, lugging a long carbine" (Lehrman, "Arabs of Israel," 528–529).

161. See Meysels' 1955 edition of *Israel in Your Pocket*, 315. Reprinted in the 1956 edition, I-49–50. On the German fascination with Native Americans, see Penny, "Elusive Authenticity." See Poiger, *Jazz*, 40–41, on the popular consumption of dime-novel Westerns among German youth in the late 1940s.

162. Morris, *Refugee Problem Revisited*, 473–490; Nazzal, *Palestinian Exodus.*

163. Meysels, *Israel in Your Pocket* (Northern Israel), I-66. For other examples, see also the tenth anniversary edition (1958), 49–50; and Comay, *Introducing Israel*. On the aerial bombing of Sa'sa and the expulsion of its surrendering residents, see 'Awawdah, *Dhakira la tamut*, chap. 13.

164. Feldman, "Refusing Invisibility."

165. In 1957, 32 percent of the population still could not read Hebrew. Limor, "Ta'arukhat he-'asor," 91–101. On tourism, see Ilyas, *Isra'il wa-l-siyaha*; Natan, "ha-Tse'adim"; and Bar-On, "Megamot."

166. Mikhael Assaf, "The military regime," *Davar*, April 4, 1952; and "Let's wisen up," *Beterem*, December 15, 1950, 48–50. For other complaints, see Tuvia Cohen, MoR Liaison to MoR, August 6, 1950; and Aharon Haim Cohen, Histadrut clerk in Nazareth, to Ben-Gurion, November 13, 1950, ISA 102/GL17111/27. In September 1951, the Shin Bet report confirmed that the Arab public had undertaken no attempt at sabotage. They had despaired of the "second round" for which Israeli leaders had accused them of praying lest it bring about popular Jewish revenge. Benziman and Mansour, *Subtenants*, 104–105.

167. Ben-Gurion, *War Diary*, November 10, 1948, 807–809. On the mysterious police murder of a man from Shafa 'Amr whose Temporary Residency Permit had expired, see IDFA 263/66–3936, especially the February 19, 1952 letter from his mother to the local governor, and the follow-up by Palmon the next day. See also letters from Palmon throughout 1949–1950, ISA 102/GL17118/40.

168. Quoting an undated Shin Bet report in reference to MAKI's success in channeling the popular outrage of Tayyibe residents in the southern Triangle over the regular, unprovoked beating of residents (to the point of hospitalization) and animal theft by a newly stationed Border Guard unit in the area in late 1953. For the first time since 1949, a reported two thousand villagers assembled in the public square, demanding the dissolution of the appointed local council and its replacement by a democratically elected body. They also sent petitions to Israel's president. The governor reprimanded the council despite its members' oath of loyalty to the regime and the letters of denunciation they sent to *ha-Arets* and *al-Yawm*. See the report, along with the petitions, press clippings, and a transcript of the formal MAKI inquiry to the police minister dated October 28, 1953, ISA 102/GL17118/40. See also *Kol ha-'Am* and *Davar*, November 9, 1953.

169. CSM minutes, April 12, 1950, IDFA 834/53–293. On the premier's advocacy for a modified "millet system," see Ben-Gurion, *War Diary*, November 10, 1948, 807–809. See also Peled, *Debating Islam*, 38; and "Other Side," 91.

170. MFA official, quoted in Firro, "Reshaping Druze Particularism," 40.

171. E. Mor, September 27, 1951, meeting, in IDFA 834/53–133.

172. In summer 1948, the IDF permitted the Druze to harvest their crops and bring supplies into their villages. It also provided health care to the families of volunteer recruits. Parsons, "Palestinian Druze" 86; and Parsons, *The Druze Between*.

173. Lehrman, "Arabs of Israel," 529; Firro, "Reshaping Druze Particularism," 42–43;

Pappe, *Ethnic Cleansing*, 188; Dagan and Kozviner, *Palhib*; Paul Kohn, "Minorities Help in Negev," *NER*, September–October 1960, viii–ix; Shafir and Peled, *Being Israeli*.

174. Firro, "Reshaping Druze Particularism," 42–43.

175. *Al-Ittihad*, March 8, 1955.

176. Cohen, *Good Arabs*, 159–164.

177. In 1960, Druze conscripts continued to receive less training, enjoyed fewer opportunities for advancement, and were always deployed far from their Galilee homes to the Negev. Their commander rejected their integration with Jewish conscripts partly because it would be harder to monitor them. Ben-Gurion, "'Al ha-mi'ut ha-'aravi."

178. See also Kanaaneh, *Surrounded*.

179. Stoler, *Carnal Knowledge*, 138, and "Sexual Affronts."

180. Assaf, "The terrible myth of the military government," *Beterem*, May 15, 1953.

181. In September 1951, Israel declared the military governor its representative (that is, the sole sovereign) in the territory under his jurisdiction. The Ministry of Defense also established the Military Government Department to take complaints, respond to permit requests, and liaise with state agencies and civil bodies. It instructed governors to avoid harming civilians or interfering in their humanitarian problems. Ozacky-Lazar and Bäuml, "Tahat shilton," 4–7; Bäuml, "Mapai Committee," 413–415.

182. *Selected Judgments*, 86–87.

183. Ibid., 89 and 87, respectively.

184. Ozacky-Lazar and Bäuml, "Tahat shilton," 58. See E. Mor, "Commander of the Military Government in the Occupied Territories," to MoI et al., March 21, 1950; and other letters, ISA 102/17115/24. Since 1948, Israel has defined the term *muhzak*, a derivative of the root "to hold," in different ways, including "occupied," "administered," and "disputed." The international laws of war do not recognize this distinction. Here I also follow Shenhav, "Worthless Flock," 262, 33n.

185. On the police's concern about Jewish settlers hiring "infiltrators" and "foreign Arabs" on their farms, see the memorandum by P. Dayan, head of the "Jewish Division" at the Investigations Branch, re: "Aid of Jews to infiltrators and Arabs of Occupied Territory," July 17, 1951, ISA 79/L2181/14.

186. In May 1956, the Military Government instructed the police to return Palestinians "from the reserves" (*ezore ha-syag*) who were known to be working in colonies in the Rehovot area, south of Tel Aviv. Regretfully, explained the security officer, if there were also workers there who were Arab residents "of the state," the most the bloc commander could do was "use [his] influence so that Jewish residents will not hire them." See his letter, May 13, 1956, ISA 79/L43/13. On the uncertainty of whether the Bedouin were "minorities in Israel" or "residents of the frontier" (*toshve ha-sfar*), see the November 9, 1948 MFA memo, "Minorities in Israel," ISA 130.15(02)/HZ2564/22. On the first MG Commander's refusal to assume jurisdiction over the village of Faradis because it was "within the state of Israel," see his September 23, 1948, letter, ISA 130.15(2)/HZ2564/11.

187. Assaf, "Let's wisen up."

188. Bäuml, "ha-Mimshal ha-tsva'i," 136–137.

189. Ozacky-Lazar and Bäuml, "Tahat shilton," 61–63.

190. Ibid., 4–7; Benziman and Mansour, *Subtenants*, 32; 37–38; Masalha, *Land Without a People*, xii–xiii.

191. See the MoM file "Return of Arabs to Jaffa," July–December 1948, ISA 49/ G306/106.

192. Lockman, *Comrades and Enemies*, 80–81.

193. Ibid.; Greenstein, "Palestinian Revolutionary," 32–35.

194. Lockman, *Comrades and Enemies*, 259.

195. Lockman, *Comrades and Enemies*, 268, 305–307; Beinin, *Red Flag*, 42–43; Budeiri, *Palestine Communist Party*, 129–144. The newspaper became biweekly in 1955.

196. Beinin, *Red Flag*, 24–25; Budeiri, *Palestine Communist Party*, 155–158.

197. See Budeiri, *Palestine Communist Party*, 158–160; and Turki, *Humat al-diyar*, 48–53.

198. Quoted in Budeiri, *Palestine Communist Party*, 161.

199. Beinin, *Red Flag*, 53. The ultra-Orthodox party Agudat Yisra'el was also non-Zionist.

200. Ibid., 51–55.

201. Lockman, *Comrades and Enemies*, 90. It is true that the MAPAI-dominated Histadrut had felt threatened enough by the PCP's union activities to work to undermine them. However, the largest percentage of votes the PCP won in the Yishuv's representative assembly was 8 percent. This occurred in 1925, an achievement the party was never able to repeat.

202. Beinin, *Red Flag*, 45–46.

203. Shortly after the Partition Resolution was announced, the PCP changed its name to the Communist Party of the Land of Israel (MAKEI), which resonated with Zionist biblical claims to Palestine. Leaders removed the words "Land of" (*Eretz*) just before their reunification with the NLL, thus becoming MAKI. Beinin, *Red Flag*, 46.

204. Beinin, *Red Flag*, 54.

205. In August 1948, a military intelligence report argued that the party's activities showed that it posed no threat to state security and had demonstrated its "loyalty" to the state. It was for this reason that the Labor Ministry recognized and briefly agreed to work with the labor exchange it established in Nazareth. This raised MAKI's influence in the city. Only after the Haifa meeting did Ben-Gurion identify MAKI as a "threat" and order the arrest of any Arab activists and trade unionists who had supported Partition. Dallasheh, "Nazarenes," 61 and 65; Cohen, *Good Arabs*, 42; Tuma [Touma], *Thalathin 'am* (hereafter, "Thirty years"); Beinin, *Red Flag*, 121–122; Nakdimon, "If there is a need."

206. Beinin, *Red Flag*. MAPAM opened its doors to Arabs in 1954.

207. Ibid., 123–124.

208. It is impossible to know what would have happened had young activists like Habibi and Tubi chosen a different path.

209. Interviews with Najla Abu Ra's and 'Amr 'Asfur.

210. Hoffman, *My Happiness*, 203–206.

211. MAPAM's *al-Mirsad*, its literary companion *al-Fajr*, and its small Arabic publishing house published the voices of some nationalists who did not want to affiliate themselves with MAKI, but it lasted only until 1962; Nassar, "Marginal as Central"; Hoffman, *My Happiness*, 223–225. See also Dallasheh, "Political Mobilization."

212. Bäuml suggests that the party's control of the cabinet, the major ministries, the Histadrut, and all national institutions rendered it effectively identical with the state. "Mapai Committee," 414.

213. Pappe, "Uneasy Coexistence," 643–644. Coercion by the military regime helped MAPAI's "Arab lists" win half of all Palestinian votes in the first Knesset elections. Although that number would drop over time, the party would continue to enjoy an electoral majority until military rule was lifted.

214. Jiryis, *Arabs in Israel*; Baruch, "Facing the 180,000."

215. Beinin, *Red Flag*, 142–143, 197–198.

CHAPTER 3

1. Bishara, *Fasl al-Maqal*, May 2003.

2. "Delineating Israeli citizenship on passports," June 14, 1949, *Cabinet Meeting Protocols*, vol. 5, ISA. For press coverage on the problem of Jewish travelers abroad, see *Ma'ariv*, November 21 and December 15, 1948, and April 21, 1949; *Davar*, December 13 and 21, 1948.

3. Rosenne, "Israel Nationality Law," 13–17; Bentwich, "Nationality." On the legal ambiguity of Mandate citizenship, see Feldman, "Difficult Distinctions." On race and citizenship in the British Empire, see Mongia, "Race, Nationality, Mobility"; and Paul, *Whitewashing Britain*.

4. They favored "Israel" over "Land of Israel" (*Erets Yisra'el*) to reflect the modern name of their state, and probably also because most still dreamed of conquering the rest of the Jewish lands of the Bible. Shelef, *Evolving Nationalism*.

5. In 1947, two-thirds of Palestine's population were Arab, the majority of them native-born. Most of the Jewish "third" were born elsewhere.

6. In 1948, for example, Ben-Gurion marveled at the ongoing Arab flight from Jerusalem: "There are no strangers, one hundred percent Jews," (quoted in Ben-Ami, *Scars*, 44–45). After the war he continued to describe the population as "alien" ("Israel Among the Nations," *Government Yearbook*, October 1952, reprinted in *Rebirth*, 493–495). Labor performed by Palestinian Arabs continued to be referred to as *avodah zara*, or "foreign" (Assaf, "Terrible myth").

7. MG, MFA, and MoM representatives all advised against Arab suffrage or, if this was politically unfeasible, for minimizing the territory from which Arabs could vote. See Minutes, September 12, 1948, ISA 49/G308/9.

8. Forman, "Historical Geography," 800; Kedar, "First Step," 150.

9. On the pursuit of "normalcy," see Agassi, *Liberal Nationalism*, 22.

10. Quoted in Segev, *1949*, 29. At the time, Sharett still went by the name Shertock.

11. Morris, *Birth*, 309–340; Golan, "Transformation." Some argue that this position was consolidated only in December 1948. Carmi and Rosenfeld, "The Time."

12. It cannot be overstated that, unlike the army, politicians who portrayed Palestinian return as suicidal for the Jewish state explained the threat primarily in political and economic (rather than security) terms. This changed only in the early 1950s, when some returnees came armed in response to Israel's free-fire policy along the borders. Korn, "Refugees to Infiltrators"; Morris, *Border Wars*, 118, 176.

13. Quoted in Cohen, *Good Arabs*, 68; and Gruber, *Israel Today*, 173, 177.

14. MFA official quoted in Bracha, "Unfortunate or perilous," 376.

15. Morris, *Righteous Victims*, 263; Piterberg, "Erasures."

16. Ben-Ami, *Scars*, 46.

17. Hoffman, *My Happiness*, 140–155.

18. Korn, "Refugees to Infiltrators."

19. Committee alongside the MG, August 29, 1948, ISA 130.15(2)/HZ2564/11; G. Zeid to MoM and MG, November 28, 1948, ISA 49/G302/110; and October 12 (letter) and November 9 (report), 1948, ISA 130.15(2)/HZ2564/22. Leibler and Breslau make a similar point in "The Uncounted."

20. *Davar*, April 22, 1949; and *Ma'ariv*, April 24, 1949; January 10, 1950; April 2, 1952.

21. Arendt, *Origins of Totalitarianism*, 296.

22. Leibler, "Statisticians' Ambition," and "Establishing Scientific Authority"; *Ma'ariv* and *Davar*, November 7–9, 1948.

23. On the brutality of Operation Hiram and the sectarian nature of the army's expulsions, see Morris, *Refugee Problem Revisited*, 473–492, 518; and Pappe, *Ethnic Cleansing*, 180–185.

24. Dr. Miuzam, Central Bureau of Statistics, to MFA, October 24, 1948, ISA 130.15(2)/HZ 2564/22.

25. Kamen, "After the Catastrophe I," 475–478; Korn, "Good intentions," 123–124. This amounted to 14 percent of all males in that age bracket. Roughly half of them were released between January and March 1949. On the detention of POWs in Jaffa and Nazareth "for no reason at all," and on the conditions in the camps, see the testimony of the Jaffa military governor in Pappe, *Ethnic Cleansing*, 200–207; Ben-Gurion, *War Diary*, October 9, 1948, 740.

26. Interview with Wasfiyya Salim Ramadan.

27. Ben-Gurion, *War Diary*, December 18, 1948, 882–884.

28. Zeid to Shitrit, MoM, and MGC E. Avner, November 28, 1948, ISA 49/G302/110; Y. Shim'oni, December 28, 1948, ISA 130.15(2)/HZ2564/22; Morris, *Border Wars*, 153–154.

29. The army also conducted its own counts, but they were inaccurate because of the constant population flux and the lack of systematic procedures. Ben-Gurion, *War Diary*, December 20, 1948, 888–889. For other local results, see the reports from the MoM (ISA 49/G301/110, 49/G302/110, 49/G1320/11), MFA (ISA 130.15[2]/HZ2564/22), and IDFA (IDFA 721/72–841, 100243/52–1, 100243/52–2). See also Kamen, "After the Catastrophe I," 444–447.

30. Mazzawi, *Palestine and the Law*, 83–84; Claude, *National Minorities*, 179. The decision marked the first time that UN members mobilized to block a state's admission to the organization. Liang, "Conditions of Admission." Six days later the UNGA passed Resolution 194 in support of the refugees' right to return to their homes. Quigley, "Displaced Palestinians."

31. Cuba and Lebanon were the only states to raise concerns about the Palestinians still inside Israeli-held territory during the December deliberations. Yet even they did not object when Israel's representative to the United Nations, Abba Eban, declared that despite the nullification of the Partition Plan (the result, he argued, of its rejection by the Arab side) Israel would protect "minority rights" by choice. Claude, *National Minorities*, 180–182; UNSC, *385th Meeting*.

32. Shim'oni, December 28, 1948, ISA 130.15(2)/HZ2564/22.

33. MGC E. Mor, Governors Meeting, September 27, 1951, IDFA 834/53–133.

34. On the murder of sixteen "infiltrating smugglers" after they refused arrest, see EG Governor E. Solts to MG, September 23, 1949, IDFA 721/72–843. On the demand for an investigation of the police shooting death of a Palestinian ID holder walking home at night, see MK Imil Habibi to Police Minister, *Divre ha-Knesset* 2, v. 13, December 5, 1952 and January 7, 1953.

35. Morris, *Border Wars*, 121–123. The Border Patrol was placed under police authority in 1953.

36. See eyewitness accounts in Shoufani, *Rihla fi al-rahil*; and Ibrahim, *Shajarat al-ma'arafa*, 133–134. See also Morris, *Border Wars*, 128–29, 157–162.

37. In Hebrew these pens were termed *mikhla'ot*. The sweep operation was adapted from the counterinsurgency tactic of "caging a village" that British troops developed in order to identify hiding Palestinian Arab rebels during their uprising from 1936 to 1939 (Ibrahim, *Shajarat al-ma'arafa*, 13). For descriptions of individual operations, see the Activities Reports and the Weekly Report on Sweeps in IDFA 721/72–841, 721/72–842, 721/72–843, 834/53–293, 263/66–3936, 1559/52–113, 171/65–8, and 171/65–27.

38. The first Military Government commander complained to the prime minister that "his main job was to protect Arabs from acts of revenge and looting" by his own staff (Pappe, "Uneasy Coexistence," 639–640). On the widespread vigilantism, urban home raids, desecration of holy sites, and "lust for theft" that permeated the army and

Jewish society in the summer and fall of 1948, see Lehrman, "Arabs of Israel," 531; Korn, "Good intentions," 134–136; Pappe, *Ethnic Cleansing*, 200–207 (208–212 on rape); and Morris, *1948 and After*, 190. On the murder of eighty civilians as well as incidents of rape and looting in Acre, see Torstrick, *Limits of Coexistence*, 54–55. In personal letters from the front, some soldiers attributed postconquest violence to victory drunkenness and revenge. Hazkani, "Religion for a Revolver."

39. This figure is a conservative estimate based on the archival records made available to me. One mid-January report counted nearly a thousand paperless residents of four Upper Galilee villages ("Population Census, 17–18 January 1949," n.d., ISA 49/G302/110). In April, a survey of four Nazareth-district villages with a total population of 5,899 indicated that more than 20 percent had not been counted. On 'Ilabun, Jish, Dayr Hanna, and al-Maghar, see Blum to MG, April 2, 1949, IDFA 721/72–841.

40. See *Davar*, December 14 and 28, January 11, 16, and 17.

41. Inaugurated in April 1949 and celebrated as "pioneer poverty," Israel's price controls and rations program were based on the ideal of the European welfare state but also on the need to guarantee basic nutrition to the population while allocating 25 percent of the national budget to defense. Officially it lasted for ten years, but compliance ended by early 1950. See Rozin, "Food"; Segev, *1949*, 296–323.

42. Red Cross and American Quaker volunteers distributed some food in the newly occupied territories through the summer of 1949, but the government ordered them not to feed returnees from Lebanon. Gallagher, *Quakers*, 121–122.

43. Palmon to MoJ Legal Advisor, September 2, 1949, IDFA 100243/52–6. 'Ilabun and al-Maghar residents protested, "We cannot leave [our] villages . . . or farm our lands because the military police, which waits along the road, arrests anyone without proof of ID" (*al-Ittihad*, May 23, 1949). See also *al-Ittihad*, September 4, 1949.

44. Palmon to Road Transportation Inspector, MG, MoI, et al., July 12, 1949, ISA 102/GL17114/19; and Palmon to MoI, September 1950, GL17100/28. Fewer than thirty thousand Palestinians were eligible to vote in the first election. Teller, "Arab Minority Problem."

45. Ibrahim, *Shajarat al-ma'arafa*, 133–134. On October 6, 1949, a Rame resident who forgot to bring his receipt on a walk to buy meat in a neighboring village was deported during a sweep there (*al-Ittihad*, November 13, 1949; see also April 23, 1950).

46. Five months after their January registration, the people of I'blin reported that they continued to lack any papers and were now paying a fee to get their rations. *Al-Ittihad*, June 5, 1949.

47. The authorities also eased the bureaucratic burden of those Arabs who opted to emigrate, so long as they returned their identity papers and signed a declaration stating that they were leaving on their own volition, renouncing all claims against the State of Israel (Weekly Security Report, April 1950, IDFA 834/53–293). From the government's perspective, this approach had only minimal success. By July 1951, only two thousand Pal-

estinians had left in this manner. In addition to the above report, see CSM, September 8, 1949, IDFA 721/72–842; and Benziman and Mansour, *Subtenants*, 58–59.

48. In ISA, see the June 21 and July 27, 1949, reports, 102/GL17116/10, and the July 13 report, 102/GL17116/11.

49. At least thirteen Galilee villages were not registered at all until September, and the census was still unfinished at the end of the year. Governor 'Amir to MGC, September 14, 1949, IDFA 721/72–841; Palmon, December 27, 1949, ISA 102/GL17114/12.

50. See complaint from residents of Tamra, near Haifa, to which registration clerks failed to return after turning up three hundred forms short. *Al-Ittihad*, June 5, 1949.

51. One third of some five thousand villagers in the Western Galilee were registered for the first time only in February 1950. Lishansky to MGC, February 24, 1950, IDFA 100243/52–1.

52. In November 1949, for example, one Kafr Yasif resident who managed to return without permission claimed he had been expelled even though his name was on the governor's list of former detainees who were still owed wages from the labor they had performed in the camp (*al-Ittihad*, November 27, 1949; for other cases see the paper's June 5 and November 13 issues). Already seven months earlier, the prime minister had promised to investigate these cases (Kamen, "After the Catastrophe I," 486–487). Many detainees later reported that camp officials offered them money and smooth transit to emigrate with their families. Interview with Wasfiyya Salim Ramadan.

53. Murqus, *Aqwa min al-nisiyan*.

54. Lishansky to MGC, August 28, 1950, IDFA 100243/52–6.

55. Novelist Hanna Ibrahim, hired as a temporary registration clerk in his native Bi'na, insists that many of those expelled during the January 6 and November 9, 1949, sweeps had been counted but had not yet received receipts. He recalls how the villagers sensed a "feeling of revenge" among the soldiers: "We began to sense that our mere presence as Arabs was what was bothering them." The town of Shafa 'Amr offers a case study on the sectarian implementation of the sweeps. In early 1949, nearly two hundred residents of the town returned home after leaving temporarily before the occupation in July 1948. At the time, the authorities had agreed to let the residents return and promised them IDs. By August 1951, registration officials had kept their promise only with the Christians in the group. It took several more months for the Muslim residents to obtain their IDs; the authorities yielded only after sustained pressure in the Knesset and letters from the residents' Jewish attorney. MK Tawfiq Tubi to MoD, April 13, 1951; Lt. Col. Stavy, June 21, 1951, IDFA 263/66–3936; Palmon's correspondence with Attorney Zvi Shapiro from 1950 to 1951, IDFA 263/66–604.

56. The night before the late October surrender of Majd al-Krum, roughly one-third of the village population fled to Lebanon; more fled to nearby forests on November 6 after Jewish troops executed nine residents. By the time the census clerks arrived three weeks later, many of those who had since fled had returned and were counted. Hundreds of others who had stayed put were also counted. In a sweep on January 9, the army de-

ported 355 of the 506 people it checked; locals reported that nearly all of them had been registered but had not received receipts. A reported 274 residents who claimed they had never left were expelled after a sweep in November. See Ibrahim, *Shajarat al-ma'arafa*, 133–134; Manna', "Majd al-Krum 1948"; *al-Ittihad*, November 13, 1949; Krasnansky to MG, November 8, 1949, IDFA 721/72–43. Revenge may have played a role here, because the village had a nationalist past (Morris, *Refugee Problem Revisited*, 478). On more cases of political retaliation in Mi'ilya, Rame, and the Eastern Galilee, see the autobiographical account of Shoufani, *Rihla fi al-rahil*, 46–56; M. Vardi to MoR/Christian Division, May 20, 1949, IDFA 721/72–841; and EG Governor to MG HQ, July 1949, IDFA 721–72/842.

57. In February 1950, for example, a sweep in 'Arrabe led to the expulsion of most of the (already once expelled) Hittin refugees living there. All of them had been registered in that village in May 1949 but were denied receipts so that the government could "clarify" their status. *Al-Ittihad* editors speculated that the government never issued IDs to them because they continued to insist on returning to Hittin (Avner, June 23, 1949, in IDFA 721–72/841; *al-Ittihad*, October 23, 1949, February 26, 1950.) A similar delay occurred in 'Ilabun, whose expelled, largely Catholic, residents received special permission to return from Lebanon as a way to reduce criticism from the Vatican. Even with their exceptional circumstances, they were refused registration by the authorities until August 1949 and IDs until 1951. Blum to MG, April 2, 1949, IDFA 721–72/841; Morris, *Birth*, 229–230; *Ma'ariv*, June 2, 1949; *al-Ittihad*, September 4, 1949.

58. *Al-Ittihad*, September 18, October 9 and 23, and December 4, 1949.

59. The best-known cases were in Iqrit and Bir'im (expelled November 5, 1948), Saffuriya (January 7, 1949), Ghabsiyya (February 1, 1950), and Majdal (June–October 1950). See MG Front to EG Governor, April 3, May 8, and June 14, 1949, IDFA 263/66–132; Morris, *Birth*, 241, and *1948 and After*, 323–347; Hoffman, *My Happiness*.

60. On the reported expulsion of a woman from al-Maghar who carried IDs for her and her children in order to deter her husband from returning, see Avner, June 23, 1949, IDFA 721/72–841. On August 14, 1949, *al-Ittihad* reported the expulsion to Gaza of a family of ID holders in Majdal.

61. The police counted a total of 3,181 returnees expelled in 1952; many of them were caught along the armistice lines rather than inside villages. See Morris, *Border Wars*, 177; and Masalha, *Land Without a People*. General harassment, unemployment, and separation from relatives also led more than four thousand nonreturnee Palestinians to leave by July 1951, a movement the government went out of its way to facilitate. Benziman and Mansour, *Subtenants*, 58–59.

62. In early 1953, the prime minister's advisor on Arab affairs, Joshua Palmon, announced that since 1948 Israel had "let in" (retroactively, for the most part) thirty-five thousand people to reunite with their families (*JTA*, January 31, 1953). My estimate of 30 percent excludes the number of Arabs ultimately counted in the Military Government districts by May 1949 (Jiryis, *Arabs in Israel*, 289). This falls in the middle of a range of

figures of "resettled infiltrators" and those who received retroactive permission to stay, two categories whose distinction is unclear. In late 1953, MG head Y. Shani believed that thirty thousand Palestinians had resettled in Israel by early 1949, and twenty thousand more had resettled since then (Morris, *Border Wars*, 39, 45n). In 1967, the government repeated the thirty-five thousand figure and noted that by 1961 these people accounted for 7 percent of the "non-Jewish minorities" (*Davar*, April 8, 1967). See also the undated report in IDFA 721/72–842 entitled "Military Government in the Administered Territories," July 1–October 24, 1949.

63. Abrams, "Notes."

64. Interviews in Sakhnin and ʿArrabe, August 3, 2002. See Shoufani, *Rihla fi al-rahil*, 46–56.

65. In 1949, see Western Galilee Intelligence Officer to Governor, June 10, IDFA 721/72–841; CSM, September 8; Lt. A. Ben Yosef to Governors, September 11, IDFA 721/72–842; CSM, September 16, IDFA 100243/52–6; Krasnansky to HQ, September 22, IDFA 721/72–843. See also Morris, *Border Wars*, 157–158.

66. Jewish settlers comprised just 12 percent of the region's population (Morris, *Refugee Problem Revisited*, 510).

67. In April 1949, for example, the American settlers of Kibbutz Saʿsa, near the Lebanon border, comprised just 20 percent of the five hundred people who worked in the confiscated olive groves owned by refugees over the armistice line. Lehrman, "Arabs of Israel," 527–528.

68. MoM, *ʿAl ha-Naʿaseh* 1, February 10, 1949, ISA 49/G304/57. In February 1949, the MoM reported that a "group of Jews" were coming to Abu Ghosh, near Jerusalem, to buy sheep, rice, sugar, and meat from smugglers who bought them in the West Bank and remitted the proceeds to refugees there. Years later, the police warned of "a growing problem in which Jews in need of cheap labor (and who are even in contact with smugglers) are encouraging the arrival of infiltrators due to the reduction in punishments the Courts are issuing. . . . We're trying to create new [civil] laws to try the[m] . . ." (September 9, 1951, ISA 79/L2181/14).

69. Krasnansky, October 7, 1949, IDFA 721/72–843.

70. Forged receipts were first reported in June 1949. See Auslander to Eastern Galilee, June 12, 1949, IDFA 263/66–132; and MGC to MoD, December 2, 1949, IDFA 721/72–843. In October 1950, Ben-Gurion estimated that "several thousand" people had managed to obtain permanent IDs by acquiring forged receipts (*al-Ittihad*, October 29, 1950), and in 1953, then PM Sharett noted in his diary that the "custom [of forgery] has resulted in a situation that, in some Arab villages, women have simply ceased to die" (Morris, *Border Wars*, 40, 49n). See also CSM, November 24, 1950; and Yektueli to Operations, December 11, 1950, IDFA 100243/52–6.

71. Ibrahim, *Shajarat al-maʿarafa*, 129. On weapons, see also Morris, *Refugee Problem Revisited*, 531.

72. Palmon's office reported on this phenomenon in September 1950 and issued new instructions that anyone without a civil ID must obtain prior permission from the authorities to get married (ISA 102/GL17100/28). The army did not hesitate to expel the paperless wives of men who carried IDs (*al-Ittihad*, June 26 and July 18, 1949).

73. Interview in Nazareth, November 14, 2001; AAA to MoR and MoH, August 1953 report, ISA 102/GL17100/28. This trend figures prominently in fictional accounts of the period. In Ilyas Khuri's epic novel *Bab al-Shams*, the protagonist Yunis regularly crosses into Israel to spend time and bear children with his wife, Nahila. During one of her pregnancies, when she begins to show, a military tribunal sentences her to three days of confinement for bearing the children of an infiltrator and refusing to reveal his whereabouts. "Do we need permission from the military governor to conceive?" she asks her interrogator. After her daughter is born, the clerk refuses to register the baby in the father's absence (286). The protagonist of Imil Habibi's sardonic 1969 novella, *al-Mutasha'il* (translated into English as *The Secret Life of Saeed, the Ill-Fated Pessoptimist*), chooses a different path. "Since I realized that birth control was proof of loyalty, we had no more children." Cited in Ghanem, "al-Mutafaqim," 17.

74. Governor 'Amir to MG HQ, September 9, 1949, IDFA 721/72–842.

75. In August 1949, a regulation designed to discourage potential hosts by requiring families to post a stiff bail for the release of their relatives only backfired. So many families were managing to collect the bail money and then applying for their relatives to obtain permanent residence that MG HQ issued instructions for governors to automatically reject any applications for people who had already returned. "We must stop accepting interventions and recommendations," urged MGC Mor (December 1, 1949, IDFA 834/53–293). See also Krasnansky, October 7, 1949; and Mor, October 10, 1949, IDFA 721/72–843.

76. In December, after little had changed, Governor 'Amir raised the penalties dramatically: fines, imprisonment, and even exile for the offenders, along with collective curfews and sieges on the communities in which returnees were found ('Amir to MGC, September 9, 1949, IDFA 721/72–842; and December 16, 1949, IDFA 834/53–293). Senior officials evidently approved his proposals but appear to have avoided bringing nuclear families to court (Morris, *Border Wars*, 159). As late as 1953, the police estimated that Palestinian citizens had sheltered some 745 returnees that year. Korn, "Political Control," 164.

77. Quoted in Teller, "Arab Minority Problem." The statistic comes from Dayan, "Israel's Border," 261.

78. Medical terms come from Khuri, *Bab al-Shams*, 63–64, and MGC Mor, Governors Meeting, September 27, 1951, IDFA 834/53–133, respectively. An estimated three to five thousand Palestinians were killed along the truce lines by 1956. The policy was prefigured by Chief of Staff Yigal Yadin's orders in June 1948 to prevent return "by every means." Southern Commander (and later PM) Yitzhak Rabin was one of its first proponents. Morris, *Border Wars*, 119, 125–133, 145–147.

79. In the summer of 1949, the army conducted a 2 A.M. raid in a Catholic boarding school in Haifa to expel the fifteen-year-old daughter of a city council member whose family had never left the city. Haifa's archbishop protested the failure of the police to consult with her parents beforehand as a "violation of family honor and public morality," and he warned that similar "tragedies" were "raising . . . doubts regarding the fate of Arabs in the state." Butrus Fakhuri, n.d., enclosed in Yetah to Haifa Police, August 23, 1949, ISA 56/G2201/28.

80. See, in *al-Ittihad*, "[Back and forth] between government agencies: wasting the hours of the day!" December 4, 1949; and the editorial on November 27, 1949. Similar complaints continued to appear nearly a year later, for example, in the August 6, 1950 issue.

81. This and the previous quote translated in MGC Avner, June 23, 1949, IDFA 721–72/841. The local commander replied that he had taken "disciplinary measures" in those cases where "small deviations from orders [not to harm residents] took place." Even so, he blamed the returnees for forcing his staff to do its job.

82. Ibid.

83. Quoting a discussion of a MAKI inquiry into two expulsions from Rame (*al-Ittihad*, April 4, 1949).

84. *Al-Ittihad*, August 21, 1949.

85. Quoted in the October 23 and November 13, 1949 issues, respectively. Over time, expressions of incredulity turned to cynicism as the regime's cruelty and capriciousness failed to change. By August 1950, editors were openly mocking the faith—actual or rhetorical—that fellow Palestinians continued to place in the word of the authorities. Thus they dismissed as "naive" a letter from a pregnant woman in Acre that begged the interior minister to bring home her deported returnee husband, whom she had married only after the governor assured them that he could stay (*al-Ittihad*, August 6, 1950).

86. *Al-Ittihad*, June 12 and 19, and July 3, 1949. Complaints included looting, the destruction of food and furniture, body searches of women, and depriving people of food and water.

87. Interviews with Odette Nimr, Samira Khuri, Nabiha Murqus, and Nimr Murqus. See also Murqus, *Aqwa min al-nisiyan*, 104–106; Ibrahim, *Sharajat al-ma'arafa*, 116; and Tuma, *Thirty years*, 86.

88. The military censor removed the details of some incidents (*al-Ittihad*, March 14 and April 4, 1949). MK Sayf al-Din al-Zu'bi, who ran on one of MAPAI's "Arab lists," also raised at least one question. See also Hofnung, *Democracy*, 81; and Kamen, "After the Catastrophe I," 486–487.

89. *Al-Ittihad*, August 14 and 21, 1949. On the seven Nahaf residents, see MG Activities Report, June 1, 1949, IDFA 721/72–841. Tubi subsequently met with the Western Galilee governor to present similar cases of "illegal expulsion" from six other villages. See *al-Ittihad*, September 18, October 9, and December 4, 1949; and Ibrahim, *Shajarat al-ma'arafa*, 113. See also the August 21 and September 4, 1949 issues.

90. *Al-Ittihad*, November 13 and 20, 1949. Military officials vehemently denied the charge. Mor to MoD, December 2, 1949, IDFA 721/72–843.

91. On foreign complaints, see Parlov to Commanders, December 1949, IDFA 834/53–293; and Governor 'Amir to MG, n.d., IDFA 721/72–843; Morris, *Border Wars*, 174–177; and Segev, *1949*, 61. In a rare moment of public discord, the interior minister admitted in September 1949 that he disagreed with the police minister's orders to expel paperless Palestinian women and children (*al-Ittihad*, September 4, 1949). Questions were also raised about female returnees who had obtained from their local governor papers that they believed to be registration receipts, as well as others whose bail had been guaranteed by communal leaders months earlier. See *al-Ittihad*, November 13, 1949 (on Majd al-Krum), September 17, 1949 (on Shafa 'Amr), and December 4, 1949 (on Haifa). The government also worked with allied deputies to bring criminal charges against anyone who provided any information about the campaign to the public (Bracha, "Unfortunate or perilous," 377–378).

92. Morris, *Border Wars*, 141–145.

93. *Ma'ariv*, June 2, 1949. Villagers were forced out in July 1948, and by the following January nearly half of the 960 residents had returned (Morris, *1948 and After*, 257–70; ISA 49/G307/46). MK Moshe Erem pleaded passionately that those deported were "not criminals or delinquents. . . . Our morals are being destroyed and this will not contribute to our security or . . . existence" (Bracha, "Unfortunate or perilous," 373, 377–378).

94. Quoted in Morris, *Border Wars*, 39. See also Lehrman, "Arabs of Israel," 527–528.

95. Hofnung, *Democracy*, 78; Korn, "Political Control," 164.

96. On working returnees from Saffuriya, see Hoffman, *My Happiness*, 183. By the end of 1953, still less than one-fifth of the Jewish population lived on farms, the total land mass cultivated was 12 to 15 percent lower than it had been before the war, and the production of several basic commodities had dropped to less than half of its pre-war levels. The reported unwillingness of Jewish farmers to do menial harvesting forced Israel to import much of its olive oil. Patterson, "Israel's Economic Problems."

97. In late 1948, Chief of Staff Yadin proposed the recruitment of expert Arab smugglers to rob returnees and serve as a human belt to block their return from Lebanon (Ben-Gurion, *War Diary*, December 20, 1948, 888–889). The police also planted informants among returnees in Jordan and Lebanon in order to ambush or simply kill them. Some informants, however, acted as double agents. In the south, Israel relied on Shaykh Sulayman Huzayl to control smuggling routes as well as food rations, and some worried about the power that agents like him had amassed. Cohen, *Good Arabs*, 82–99, 92–94, 192.

98. In some cases, the police and military operated their own smuggler rings for cattle and sheep. In IDFA 834/53–293, see Governors Meeting, January 1, 1950; MG Report on Security Situation, January 8–23, 1950; and Y. Safran, Jezreel Police, November 25, 1955.

99. In 1955, Saffuriya's former mayor was elected to one of MAPAI's "Arab lists"

after pressuring fellow town dwellers, now internal refugees, to end their land claims against the state—but not before securing IDs for many of his fellow Saffuriyans who had returned without permission (Hoffman, *My Happiness*, 179). Both Shitrit, the minister of minorities and minister of police, and MFA Sharett believed that Arabs who had arranged land sales during the Mandate should get special status. Cohen, *Good Arabs*, 22.

100. Cohen, *Good Arabs*, 76–77.

101. Morris, *Refugee Problem Revisited*, 321–322. On Palmon, see Gelber, "Druze and Jews," 232.

102. Morris, *Refugee Problem Revisited*, 318–320; *Ma'ariv*, June 2, 1949. Even MoM Shitrit, known for his "liberal" positions, viewed these minorities as "inherently friendlier to the state." Peled, "The Other Side," 91; Shenhav, "Worthless Flock," 262–263.

103. The army sent Kafr Bir'im residents to nearby Jish after refusing to allow them to resettle in their village. Morris, *Refugee Problem Revisited*, 479–480, 507–508.

104. Ben-Gurion, *War Diary*, November 25, 1948, 844–845.

105. On lobbying for the Zu'bi family, see Pappe, *Ethnic Cleaning*, 114. On a settler in Zikharon Ya'acov who exploited his former ties to Haganah intelligence to secure the release of detained returnees and procure temporary papers for them in exchange for their free labor in his vineyards, see P. Dayan, Police HQ/Investigations Branch/Jews Division, July 17, 1951, in ISA 79/L2181/14. See also Manna', "Majd al-Krum 1948."

106. Interview in 'Arrabe, July 13, 2002. In 1952, former Jewish National Fund agent Yosef Nahmani arranged entry papers for a Palestinian refugee in 'Ayn al-Hilwe camp so that he could resume tending Nahmani's orchards. Although barred from returning to his native Hittin, the man registered himself in a nearby village, added his children's names to his ID ledger, and then snuck back to Lebanon to smuggle them over the border (interview with Imm Hisham). Nahmani, for his part, continued to pursue the work of which he was proudest—purchasing Arab land for its exclusive use by Jews. Throughout the 1950s he pressured Arab citizens to sell their land or accept meager compensation after it had already been confiscated. He also repeatedly pressed the government to find new ways to encourage the Arabs of the Galilee to emigrate. On Nahmani, see Masalha, *Land Without a People*, 5; Morris, *1948 and After*, 159–211; Cohen, *Good Arabs*, 112; and the documentary film, *ha-Yomanim shel Yosef Nahmani*.

107. See, for example, March 30, 1950, in IDFA 100243/52–1; Haifa Police to National HQ, 26 January 1950, ISA 79/L139/23; Nehemias to Palmon, 13 July 1949, ISA 102/GL17115/30; Morris, *Border Wars*, 39–40. Palestinian recruits for work as informants were motivated by a variety of factors, including the fear of Jewish retaliation for their nationalist past, the hope of retrieving their land seized during the war, and—in the Triangle—resentment of the wartime plunder and rape conducted by Jordanian and Iraqi troops. Cohen, *Good Arabs*, 16.

108. Coordination Committee of Groups Operating in the Little Triangle, December 4, 1949, IDFA 834/53–293; and Krasnansky to the Western Galilee governor re: Nimr

al-Baba, November 16, 1949, IDFA 721/72–843. On the theft of a radio by a Bi'na resident suspected of securing his return from Syria by agreeing to work as an informant, see *al-Ittihad*, October 4, 1949. In April 1950, new rules required the Shin Bet to request in advance for their agents a set number of permits, which would be valid only in a specific location and for a few days at a time. Palmon to MGC, April 20, 1950, IDFA 100243/52–6. In the same file, see also CSM, April 12, 1950.

109. "Procedure for authorizing entrance of Arabs into Israel and for issuing IDs and TRPs," n.d., 1949, ISA 102/GL17114/12; Palmon to MG, June 12, 1949, ISA 102/GL17115/17.

110. On the MoM and its closure, see Korn, "Good intentions," 113–140.

111. Robson, *Colonialism and Christianity*; Cohen, *Army of Shadows*.

112. Palmon, then with the MFA, also opposed Arab suffrage. "Don't let them feel like citizens!" he proclaimed, lest they encourage the refugees to return and demand free movement and the restoration of their property. Ben-Gurion, *War Diary*, December 18, 1948, 882–884.

113. Quoted in Yektueli to Palmon, n.d. 1953, ISA 130.15/HZ2565/6 (emphasis added).

114. Attorney Mohamed Nimr al-Hawari is one of the most prominent Palestinians who returned in this manner in late 1949 or early 1950, although the hopes the regime placed in him were quickly dashed. Even before he abandoned his attempt to start a new political party in the mid-1950s, he returned to law and began to represent Palestinians in cases against land confiscation and MG abuse (see MG Security Report for January 8–23, 1950, IDFA 834/53–293; al-Hawari to MGC, December 16, 1950, ISA 56/G2201/28; al-Hawari, *Sirr al-Nakba*; and Cohen, *Good Arabs*, 53–58). On Israel's invitation to Bishop Ya'aqub Hanna to return from Lebanon to Rame following the failure of prior "strongmen" like al-Hawari, see *Ma'ariv*, August 21, 1952. Hanna had fled in 1948 after supporting the ALA in the Galilee. In March 1949 several of his relatives were expelled, reportedly on the pretext of trumped-up charges of weapons possession (Vardi to MoR/Christian Division, May 20, 1949, IDFA 721/72–841).

115. His nationalism did not prevent him from selling his own land. Cohen, *Good Arabs*, 47; Morris, *Refugee Problem Revisited*, 103–109, 321; "Anglo-American inquiry committee hears Palestinian government spokesman, church leaders," *JTA*, March 25, 1946.

116. *Al-Yawm*, May 4, 1949; *al-Ittihad*, September 4, 1949.

117. The overwhelming majority of Catholics from large depopulated Arab communities such as Tiberias, Safad, and Bassa were excluded. See the mutual pledges in their original Arabic, June 10, 1949, and Hakim's lists of proposed returnees in ISA 102/GL17114/20. The June agreement followed an earlier proposal from Hakim to "move" the Christian returnees out of the northern village of Tarshiha (already partly inhabited by Jewish settlers), conduct positive public relations abroad, and effectively "end the Christian affair" in exchange for the repatriation of five hundred families. See Barkai, MGC to MoD, May 30, 1949, in ibid.

118. Robson, *Colonialism and Christianity*.

119. The roughly fifty thousand Christians who became refugees during the war amounted to 35 percent of Palestine's overall Christian population and 7 percent of all Palestinian refugees. "Israel," Catholic Near East Welfare Association, available at http://www.cnewa.us/default.aspx?ID=1226&pagetypeID=8&sitecode=US&pageno=3.

120. During the first Knesset elections, MAKI won more than 50 percent of the votes in Nazareth, 22 percent in Haifa, 25 percent in Acre, and 25 percent each in the villages of Kafr Yasif and Shafa 'Amr. (Tuma, *Thirty years*, chap. 5). Before the war, the Greek Orthodox comprised the single largest Christian community in Nazareth (O'Mahony, "Palestinian Christians"). One reporter noted that Christians made up two-thirds of the town's population and that party "comrades wore their hammer and sickle badges to Church" (Lehrman, "Arabs of Israel," 526–527).

121. As in Hakim's deal, each person would have to pass a security clearance. They would also have to submit proof of former residence in the country, such as a marriage license or birth certificate. Tens of thousands of Family Reunification applicants were reportedly rejected because they had lost these documents during the war. Peretz, *Israel and the Palestine Arabs*, 50–57.

122. In fact, the Truman administration pressured Israel to take back more than two hundred thousand refugees. Little, *American Orientalism*, 269–272.

123. Sharett privately regretted Israel's inability to "uproot" the thirty thousand native villagers they found. Morris, *Birth*, 247–249.

124. Palmon was furious about the confusion and had to clarify repeatedly that they should delay the expulsion of no one but individual Greek Catholics who asked them first to contact Hakim. EG to MG, July 5, 1949, ISA 102/GL17114/20; Announcement, July 14, 1949, IDFA 721/72–842. See the July 1949 exchange between Palmon and MG, ISA 102/GL17115/30.

125. See letters from August 3, 1949 (ISA 102/GL17115/20) and July 23; August 16, 18, 21, and 31; and September 3, 1949, ISA 102/GL17115/30.

126. Mor to Police and Palmon, October 10, 1949, ISA 102/GL17114/18.

127. Hartglass to MoI/Director General and Hornstein, August 7, 1949, IDFA 100243/52–6 (emphasis added).

128. See the correspondence between Palmon and the MoJ Legislative Division director, September 2 and October 12, 1949, IDFA 100243/52–6.

129. For example, issuing orders against looting and violence, providing water and shade, and replacing the army with the civil police. M. Gordon (MG Operations), July 6, 1949; and CSM, August 8, 1949, both in IDFA 721/72–842; Governors Meeting, January 31, 1950, IDFA 834/53–293; Morris, *Border Wars*, 162. MGC Avner proposed that the MG take "a more remorseful [*harata nosefet*] path" (Memo to MoD and Chief of Staff, July 1, 1949, IDFA 721/72-842).

130. Another group of returnees at this time were discharged ALA recruits with nowhere to turn but to their families back home (Krasnansky, October 7, 1949, IDFA

721/72–843). On camp conditions, see Hoffman, *My Happiness*, 154–155; and Sayigh, *Palestinians*, 98–143.

131. See note 127.

132. CSM, October 13, 1949, IDFA 10024/52–6.

133. As tensions over Jewish immigration grew in the early twentieth century, Ottoman authorities required all foreign visitors to leave their passport at the border and carry a three-month temporary visa called the Red Note. Campos, *Ottoman Brothers*, 147.

134. CSM, September 8, 1949, IDFA 721/72–842.

135. Ibid. "We do not want to give them rights," explained Palmon in an earlier memo, "before we can testify to their character." Palmon to MoI/Registration, June 29, 1949, IDFA 100243/52–6; MG HQ to MoD et al., July 3, 1949, IDFA 721/72–842; CSM, August 8, 1949, IDFA 721/72–842; Palmon to MoJ/Counsel, September 2, 1949, IDFA 100243/52–6.

136. Y. Kisilov to S. Landman, October 1949, IDFA 721/72–843. See earlier formulations in CSM, August 8, 1949, IDFA 721/72–842; Palmon to MoJ and MoI, September 2, 1949, and an undated report in IDFA 100243/52–6.

137. See, *inter alia*, Lishansky to MG Branch/Operations, September 3, 1950, IDFA 100243/52–1; and Kisilov, MoI/General Administration to MoI/Mins, October 1949, IDFA 721/72–843. For earlier formulations, see CSM, August 8, 1949, IDFA 721/72–842; Palmon to MoJ and MoI legal advisors, September 2, 1949, IDFA 100243/52–6; and undated report in ibid.

138. Palmon to MoI/Registration, June 29, 1949, IDFA 100243/52–6; MG HQ to MoD, PMB, MoI/Immigration, July 3, 1949, IDFA 721/72–842; CSM, August 8, 1949, IDFA 721/72–842; Palmon to MoJ/Counsel, September 2, 1949, IDFA 100243/52–6. CSM, August 8, 1949, IDFA 721/72–842.

139. See reports from November 1949 through March 1950 in IDFA 100243/52–1, 100243/52–2, and 100243/52–6, and the TRP Committee's plan to review lists of fifty-four hundred military ID holders in the Galilee in December 1950 and January 1951 (Meeting, November 2, 1950, ISA 102/17114/17). In February 1950, nearly half of the nearly seventeen hundred Western Galilee villagers who were registered for the first time received TRPs instead of IDs. That figure jumps to 60 percent if we exclude the village of Abu Snan, where some 90 percent of the residents were Druze and Christian, and where most new registrants received civil IDs. Governors were required to indicate the religion of each TRP recipient in their reports. See also note 55 of this chapter.

140. N. Stavy, District Police Chief to E. Mor, MGC, January 10 and 22, 1950; EG to MGC, February 13, 1950; and A. Karmur to Stavy, January 22, 1950, in IDFA 100243/52–6; and Governors Meeting, January 3, 1950, IDFA 834/53–293. Meanwhile, MG staff and registration clerks blamed the police for obstructing the process. One report accused the Western Galilee police chief of repeated no-shows during the scheduled registrations

and noted that his Arab "informant stopped coming after he received his own ID . . ." (Lishansky to MGC, February 10, 1950, IDFA 100243/52–1).

141. Palmon to MoI et al., December 5, 1949; Palmon to MG HQ et al., December 6, 1949; E. Mor to Military Governors, December 22, 1949; Cpt. Y. Lavie to MoD et al., February 13, 1950; and Palmon to MG, May 2, 1950, all in IDFA 100243/52–6. See also Palmon to Police, December 10, 1949, ISA 102/GL17102/15. In IDFA 100243/52–1, see Palmon to MGC et al., February 21 and March 17, 1950; and Lishansky to MG Operations, September 3, 1950.

142. Bedouin registration in the south began only in June 1951. In IDFA 100243/52–3 see Officer N. Stavy to MG HQ, February 15, 1950; MGC to Negev Governor, February 22, 1950; and Y. Varbin to HQ et al., March 12, 1950. See also Palmon to MGC et al., February 19 and March 19, 1950, IDFA 100243/52–6; Meeting with Negev Governor, March 28, 1950, and CSM, April 12, 1950, both IDFA 834/53–293; Y. Marcus (MoI) to Palmon, February 19, 1950, and his March 13, reply, ISA 102/17114–12; Marcus, MoI, to MG, July 4, 1949, IDFA 721/72–842; and MG Negev, Minutes from Staff Meeting, June 25, 1951, IDFA 834/53–133.

143. In theory, local authorities were required to submit weekly reports on the details of each TRP they issued. See, for example, Governor Y. Tessler to MGC, January 14, 1950, IDFA 100243/52–2.

144. List issued in Shafa 'Amr, I'blin, and Tamra, November–December 1949, in IDFA 100243/52–1. Individual names and locales have been erased. The permits in this group lasted from several months to one year.

145. For example, Bakar (Tiberias) to Military Governor, July 25, 1950, IDFA 263/66–3936. The officer quotes a letter from the Safad District police chief, who recommended issuing a TRP and a fine to an eleven-year-old girl who was registered on her sister's military ID because their father had died. She was released from detention after she was discovered to have crossed into Lebanon for a brief stay with relatives. See also Officer Karmur to Galilee Governor, September 23, 1951, IDFA 263/66–3936.

146. Activist Nimr Murqus, who began teaching in Dayr al-Asad in 1952, recounts the expulsion of one of his pupils. The family of nine-year-old Nur al-Din had fled to Lebanon. Either left behind or having managed to return, he lived with his elderly grandparents and was hid repeatedly by his neighbors during sweeps. Ultimately the police found the boy and drove him to the border (Aqwa min al-nisiyan, 126–128).

147. In July 1950, a mother walked with her two young children from the West Bank to the central town of Ramle, where her husband (their father) was a registered resident. She was expelled three days later despite having immediately reported herself to the police, explaining that she was sick and had no means of supporting her family (al-Ittihad, August 6, 1950). In March 1952, three young women, including a young widowed mother of two, were expelled from Nazareth after returning to their families and reporting themselves to the authorities months—and in at least one case, more than

a year—earlier. Neither their formal requests to stay nor the intervention of Hakim's representative in the city helped. Hakim to Governor, January 24, 1952; and Governor to Tiberias Police, March 17, 1952, IDFA 263/66–3936.

148. Palmon to MoI/Director General and MoD, December 5, 1949, IDFA 100243/52–6; Palmon to MGC and Western Galilee Governor, February 21, and March 17, 1950, IDFA 100243/52–1.

149. CSM, March 22, 1950, IDFA 100243/52–6.

150. Another change was the prohibition against issuing any papers to a group classified as "political refugees." There would also be a new procedure for issuing IDs "to Arabs and other minorities (Armenians, Greeks, Iranians [Bahá'is], etc.) who entered with a permit from the [Interior Ministry's] Immigration Desk" but outside the family reunion framework. Palmon to MGC et al., May 9, 1950, IDFA 100243/52–6.

151. CSM, November 24, 1950, IDFA 100243/52–6.

152. One complaint raised in the Knesset pertained to hundreds of former POW camp detainees. As we saw earlier in the chapter, many of them were expelled during sweeps because registration clerks had failed to issue registration receipts to them upon their release. This group was also forgotten in the initial deliberations over TRP eligibility, leading to further post-sweep expulsions (Y. Lavie, MGC to MoD et al., February 13, 1950, IDFA 100243/52–6). On petitions from former Galilee detainees and protests for regular IDs, see al-Ittihad, November 20 and 27, 1949; December 4, 1949; and January 29, 1950.

153. Attorney Nimr al-Hawari to MGC in Jaffa, December 16, 1950, ISA 56/G2201/28.

154. I discuss the Absentee Property Law in Chapter Two.

155. ISA 130/HZ/2564/22. Their plight was well known. See the correspondence between local clergy, the MoI, and the CAP on November 1 and 28, 1949, ISA 56/G2201/28.

156. Murqus, Aqwa min al-nisiyan, 105–107. Farah managed to obtain the IDs in advance and then failed to burn the building.

157. Ibrahim, Shajarat al-ma'arafa, 113–114.

158. Interview with Fathiyya 'Awaysa.

159. Murqus, Aqwa min al-nisiyan, 107–108.

160. In 1951, one American reporter cynically alluded to the fiction of "coexistence" that Israel presented to international audiences: "Some glib publicists have tried to suggest to the world that photographs of Jewish and Arab notables sitting cross-legged and smiling over a common bowl of rice and lamb give a full account of the matter.... [E]veryone knows that it is infinitely more complex." Teller, "Arab Minority Problem," 557. On the Oslo years, see Stein, Itineraries in Conflict.

161. Military reports, personal memoirs, press accounts, and fictional depictions comprise a rich archive of the culinary politics that permeated relations between Palestinians under military rule and the Israeli officials who policed them. For examples of social realist portrayals in music, fiction, and film, see Revi'iyat Mo'adon ha-Te'atron, "Moshlim tsva'iyim"; Gitlis, Ugly governor; and the film, Wedding in Galilee.

162. Interview with Efrayim Ben-Natan, former Umm al-Fahm governor.

163. Benziman and Mansour, *Subtenants*, 103.

164. Governors Meeting, December 27, 1949, IDFA 834/53–293. In May 1950, *Yedi'ot Ahronot* covered a feast made for the chief of staff by southern tribal leader Shaykh Sulayman Huzayl (Cohen, *Good Arabs*, 210–213; see also note 97 of this chapter).

165. Translated letter from "Credible Informant" to MoI, April 1, 1950, ISA 56/G2201/28.

166. *Al-Ittihad*, May 14, 1950.

167. Ibrahim, *Shajarat al-ma'arafa*, 135–136. *Al-Ittihad* reported that similar abuses had occurred under Ottoman rule but without the goal of "systematically stripping the Arab residents of their citizenship" (Ibid).

168. *Al-Ittihad*, October 1, 1950. Two months earlier, rumors had circulated that anyone who did not pay the tax would lose his right to a blue ID (*al-Ittihad*, August 6, 1950).

169. Mohamed Sa'id al-Khatib al-Asadi, "Age 70," to MoI, December 31, 1950, ISA 56/G2201/28. His letter was typed in English. The matter was eventually forwarded for investigation to the local governor, who enjoyed good relations with the mukhtar and the other officials who reportedly had been bribed.

170. Governors Meeting, November 19, 1951, IDFA 834/53–133.

171. Shaykh Sulayman Huzayl was allowed to stay after 1948 because of his activity against Mufti Hajj Amin al-Husayni, who appropriated the leadership of the 1936–1939 Arab Revolt and of the national movement more generally. Huzayl also actively cooperated in the War on Return. In July 1949, *al-Ittihad* reported the expulsion of "a number of refugees" whom he had tricked into crossing the border and paying a thirty-guinea "government fee" in exchange for his promise to arrange their paperwork. In December 1949, the MGC reported that, unlike in the Galilee, unwanted return had been reduced in the south: "With the help of Arabs under our patronage [i.e., Huzayl], two infiltration paths have been closed off" (E. Mor, Weekly Security Report, December 6, 1949, IDFA 834/53–293; *al-Ittihad*, July 18, 1949). See also Cohen, *Good Arabs*, 213–216 and 221–222. Huzayl's close relationship with local settlers before 1948 was public knowledge. Shabtai Teveth, "Be'er Sheva Governor: Mikha'el ha-Negbi," *ba-Mahaneh*, June 9, 1949, 5, 13; Weigert, *My Life*, 95.

172. Near Acre, the village of Nahaf became notorious for the mafia-like rule of its mukhtar, who reportedly used the threat of the red IDs to coerce villagers into farming his land for no pay, abandoning commercial projects that competed with his own, ceasing all MAKI activity, and offering him "reward" money when they obtained the papers they were scheduled to receive anyway. See "Nahaf mukhtar dreams of return to the days of slavery and feudalism in the State of Israel," *al-Ittihad*, November 13, 1949, as well as the November 26 and December 24, 1950 issues. Cohen also discusses this in *Good Arabs*, 90–96.

173. "What's strange is that the authorities are taking people away on the basis of rumors [*wishaya*] which are proof of their so-called 'treason' and applying the 'law'—

expulsion—without trial or anything else . . . ," commented *al-Ittihad*'s editors. "Today the accusation of weapons possession has become the 'fashion' throughout . . . the Galilee. . . . [Here a large white space indicates censored material.] We denounce these acts which violate democracy and . . . all the declared laws of the state." See issue 23 (date cut off but likely March 14, 1949).

174. See anonymous letter, February 10, 1952; Landman, MoI/Mins, to MoI/Registration, March 10, 1952; reply from J. Khalil, March 19, 1952, all in ISA 56/G2215/10.

175. See the February 23, 1952 letter from "credible informant" to the "Informants Supervisor" urging the police to expel residents he deemed illegal (IDFA 263–66/3936); and another dated November 20, 1952, ISA 56/G2215/10.

176. The clerks also denied the charge, insisting that they had followed orders from Jerusalem by recording "144 infiltrators" without furnishing any of them with civil IDs or receipts. (They also rejected the mukhtar's claim, that some forty people in the group had been expelled *after* being registered on time.) Most of the returnees received military IDs and subsequently exchanged them for civil IDs. See anonymous letter, February 10, 1952; S. Landman, March 10, 1952, and J. Khalil, March 19, 1952, ISA 56/G2215/10.

177. See undated, handwritten letter and its Hebrew translation to the Eastern Galilee Governor, IDFA 263/66–3936, folder dated April 1950–June 1953.

178. Yektueli (AAA Office) to MFA, n.d. (1953), ISA 130.15/HZ 2565/6.

179. Quoting Ehud Sprinzak, who describes Ben-Gurion as "a stranger to liberal and constitutional traditions" ("Elite Illegalism," 183–184). See also Doron, "Judges," 593–594. The government was always suspicious of the High Court's interference and viewed it solely as a tool to bolster the state's identification with "enlightened, Western culture" (Lahav, "Supreme Court," 53).

180. *Ma'ariv*, July 1 and October 26, 1948, February 20 and April 24, 1949, April 2, 1952; *Davar*, April 22, 1949.

181. Quoting his February 20, 1950 speech to the Knesset, when the issue briefly resurfaced. Much of the public supported the constitution; Martin Buber imagined the document as a tool to fill the "empty shell" of the state with meaningful spiritual content, but the premier rejected this vision (Shamir, *Colonies of Law*, 155–156; see also Rozin, "Collective Identity," 251–254). The essence of the nation was shaped not by laws, the Old Man lectured, but by the army, the schools, and literature. What's more, what the people needed first was a "charter of duties," not rights, because the Yishuv had been "ingrained with scorn for the law" (Ben-Gurion, *Rebirth*, 363–380, esp. 375–376). Bolstering his opposition were the ultra-Orthodox deputies, who insisted that the Bible made a secular constitution superfluous. On this and Ben-Gurion's disdain for the rule of law, see Shapiro, "Le'an ne'elmu," 96–98; Sprinzak, "Elite Illegalism"; and Doron, "Judges," 593–594. It is likely that Ben-Gurion's desire to avoid defining Israel's borders and not be obstructed in the government's declaration of war also played a role (Tuma, *Thirty years*, chap. 7; Peleg, "Constitutional Order," 235–236).

182. *Ma'ariv*, November 21 and December 13 and 15, 1949; *Davar*, December 21, 1949.

183. On problems for Jewish travelers, see *Ma'ariv*, April 21 and November 21, 1949; and *Davar*, December 21, 1950. On the holdup of German reparations and a trade agreement with the United States, see *Ma'ariv*, January 21 and July 9, 1951.

184. Shim'oni to Yovel, New York Consulate, ISA 130.15(02)/HZ2564/22; *Davar*, December 13, 1950.

185. Warhaftig, *Hukah*, 137–149; Carmi, *Hok ha-shvut*, 21–23.

186. "Ata kofer be-khol ha-medinah." Quoted in Benziman and Mansour, *Subtenants*, 127. For the same reason, Ben-Gurion opposed linguistic equality for Hebrew and Arabic. Shahar, "Yisra'el ke-medinah du-horit."

187. Yanai, "Musag ha-ezrahut," 495–497.

188. Benziman and Mansour, *Subtenants*, 126. In a similar fashion, he told the British Peel Commission that "the Balfour Declaration is not our Bible. The Bible is our Balfour Declaration." Levinthal, "Case," 92.

189. Quoted in "Law of Return; Nationality Law," in Lorch, *Major Knesset Debates*, 611. Ben-Gurion believed that the law merely "reaffirmed" the historic right of Jews to settle in Israel. Hacohen, "Law of Return."

190. Doron, "Judges"; Israel First Knesset, "Debate on a Constitution," 96–102.

191. Ben-Gurion, "Law of Return; Nationality Law," 611. The Knesset rejected Tubi's reservation against treating Jewish immigrants on the same terms as native-born Jews and veteran settlers (*Davar*, July 6, 1950).

192. Ben-Gurion, "Law of Return (Second and Third Readings)," in Lorch, *Major Knesset Debates*, 621.

193. Ziv v. Gubernik, December 2, 1948, affirmed in Ahmed Shauki El Kharbutli v. MoD and others, January 3, 1949. Lauterpacht, *Annual Digest* 15: 7, and 16: 41–45.

194. *Davar*, July 11, 1950; *Ma'ariv*, July 13, 1950; Weiss, "Golem," 89–93.

195. Ben-Gurion, "Law of Return," 615. The commandment appears in Exodus 12:49.

196. Benziman and Mansour, *Subtenants*, 128.

197. *Davar* and *Ma'ariv*, July 4, 1950. Citizenship would also be granted automatically by marriage and by blood, that is, to all children with at least one citizen parent.

198. *Davar*, July 11, 1950; *Ma'ariv*, July 13, 1950. Palmon proposed that the law should openly differentiate between the rights of Arabs and the rights of Jews to enter the country. Benziman and Mansour, *Subtenants*, 127.

199. *Davar*, August 13, 1950, and November 12, 1951; *Ma'ariv*, January 21, March 6, and November 21, 1951.

200. CSM, July 19, 1950, IDFA 100243/52–6.

201. Some of the five hundred Majd al-Krum residents who received TRPs in May 1950 considered hiring Hanna Naqara to sue for civil IDs, but they backed down under pressure (Ibrahim, *Shajarat al-ma'arafa*, 267–278). At the time, few villagers were literate. Interview with Aziz Haidar.

202. On the High Court's "utilitarian approach to jurisprudence," see Lahav, "Supreme Court," 45–48. Judges were unsympathetic to anyone who had been expelled before having the chance to register, or who had left "voluntarily," for example, in fear after a massacre, or to study. They reasoned that the state had no obligation to aid anyone who had chosen to live in an enemy country. Bracha, "Unfortunate or perilous," 353–356, 358–369.

203. Quoted in Bracha, "Unfortunate or perilous," 349 and 365, respectively.

204. One procedural loophole that the Court sought to fill was the trend among returnees to petition for an injunction while they were still in exile and then cross into Israel once (and if) the Court accepted it. This pattern emerged after military authorities began to deport petitioners from the detention camps within days of their capture, before the judges ruled on whether to accept their petition (Lt. Col. Y. Bar to MG et al., October 9, 1949, IDFA 721/72–843). In 1951, Justice Ulshan proposed that the Court refuse to issue an injunction unless the plaintiff was physically located in the country, even if their prior expulsion had violated procedure (Bracha, "Unfortunate or perilous," 348, 379–80). Other judges complained about the laxity of the registration process (Ramati to Chief of Staff et al., October 3, 1951, ISA 102/GL17115–13). On the brutal conditions and use of forced labor in the camps, see Morris, *Border Wars*, 157–158.

205. Bracha, "Unfortunate or perilous," 356; Sprinzak, "Elite Illegalism"; Lahav, "Supreme Court."

206. Hofnung, *Democracy*, 80–86; Peretz, *Israel and the Palestine Arabs*, 112.

207. Jiryis, *Arabs in Israel*, 82. There may have been many more; these were only the files to which he was given access at the time.

208. Quoted in Bracha, "Unfortunate or perilous," 354.

209. Benziman and Mansour, *Subtenants*, 127.

210. Bracha, "Unfortunate or perilous," 345–356. Military prosecutors tried returnees on grounds of violating other provisions of the 1945 DERs (such as entering a closed zone without a permit or, less frequently, smuggling or weapons possession), but it was difficult for the tribunals to justify punishments beyond imprisonment or fines. For statistics on convictions and punishments, see Korn, "Pshi'a," 167–170. See also Morris, *Border Wars*, 154, 128n.

211. Although the DERs were technically outside the purview of judicial oversight, the Court assumed the right of review in line with other provisions of mandatory law. Peretz, *Israel and the Palestine Arabs*, 110–120.

212. Lauterpacht, "State Succession," 110–112. In 1923, the Lausanne Treaty established the principle that former Ottoman subjects would be considered "ipso facto nationals" of the successor states that replaced its territory (Bentwich, "Nationality," 97). This was consistent with the League of Nations principle that all populations were "nationals" of the territories they inhabited. Quigley, "Displaced Palestinians," 206.

213. Quoted in Mautner, "ha-Praklit ha-tsva'i ha-rashi," 169–170.

214. Naqara came of age during the crystallization of the Palestinian nationalist

movement. In the 1930s, the young graduate of Damascus University Law School began his career defending clients in Haifa's military court in cases involving land confiscation, arbitrary detention, and the death penalty. Naqara was at the courthouse in Acre on the day that Palestine's civil war reached Haifa in April 1948. Barred by British troops from returning home, he stayed until the city fell to IDF bombardment in May, when he joined thousands of others who fled by ship to Beirut. Armed with cash and determination, Naqara flew home from Cyprus in August. Israeli authorities detained him at the airport but were forced to release him after several months of lobbying on his behalf. Ibrahim, *Hanna Naqara*.

215. The Court based its ruling on the fact that the family had traveled there prior to the start of the civil war in December 1947, and that the boy had reported himself to the police when he arrived ("Important court decision," *al-Ittihad*, February 26, 1950; Murqus, *Aqwa min al-nisiyan*, 105). In December Naqara won another important case in a ruling that forced the interior minister to issue a civil ID to a boy who had been expelled two weeks after he was registered (but before receiving his receipt). Although the boy had returned on January 30, 1949, he missed the distribution of receipts. The police caught up with him only in July 1950 and were in the process of trying to expel him in October, when Naqara took up his case. The court ruled in his favor because his name and registration number were in the Population Registry (*al-Ittihad*, July 9, October 29, and December 10, 1950).

216. "These extensive powers given to the Military Government to systematically strip Arab residents of citizenship ... are spawning revulsion and denunciation, not only from the residents of Majd al-Krum but from all of the Arab and Jewish people in Israel" (*al-Ittihad*, May 14, 1950). See also the April 4, 1950 issue, which reported on a petition to the governor signed by a number of al-Maghar residents regarding the expiration of many TRPs after three months, exposing their holders to sweeps. The petitioners demanded "restoration of justice and the granting of civil IDs that they are owed."

217. *Al-Ittihad*, December 24, 1950. Five men still carried their detention certificates because they had never received receipts.

218. This decision was not a small matter, for most people "were used to going through connections rather than relying on courts" (Ibrahim, *Sharajat*, 267–268). The issue of the TRPs had already started to gain attention in the Knesset. On Tubi's inquiries and the local campaign, see *al-Ittihad*, August 6, September 3, October 1, and October 29, 1950.

219. Acre's military governor, for instance, threatened three residents with expulsion unless they agreed to accept their red ID. Y. Shvili (pronounced "Shwayli" in Arabic), the town's police chief, also intervened. One such leaflet stated that "even banishment is not worse than stripping a man of his citizenship and making him a refugee in his own homeland, subject to a worse fate" (Ibrahim, *Hanna Naqara*, 114–115, 137–138).

220. *Al-Ittihad* opined that Bi'na's victory was "a good sign for the rights of all citizens who carry the registration receipts to receive civil IDs and clear proof of the au-

thorities' retreat in the face of the villagers' unity and solidarity in the struggle for their rights." See the December 3 and 17, 1950 issues; on the subsequent Dayr al-Asad victory, see the December 24, 1950 issue.

221. Abu Khadr was the nickname for Acre's notorious police chief, Y. Shvili. Cited in Ibrahim, *Hanna Naqara*, 268–269, 275; Ibrahim, *Shajarat al-ma'arafa*, 141; and Murqus, *Aqwa min al-nisiyan*, 12–22. My translation tries to keep the spirit of the rhyme and rhythm of this *zajjal*—the poetic form in which the song was written. Bushnaq, "Folklore," 133.

222. Attorney General Shomron to MoD/MG re: Naqara's eighty clients, November 5, 1951, and the discussion of the government's "slim chances" in cases 104/51, 138/51, 192/51, 32/52, 236/51, 237/51, and 32/52, ISA 102/GL17115/13.

223. Yektueli to MFA, n.d. (1953), ISA 130.15/HZ2565/6.

224. Quoted in Avriel, PMB, to MoI, October 30, 1950, ISA 102/GL17115/29.

225. Ibrahim, *Hanna Naqara*, 133–134.

226. Palmon to PM's Military Secretary, August 2, 1951 (emphasis added); and Krasnansky to NCO, July 12, 1951, both in IDFA 263/66–3936.

227. See HCJ case 145/51, and Stavy to Attorney General, MG, and Palmon, January 1, 1952, in ISA 102/GL17115/13.

228. Emphasis added. Government Legal Advisor to PM, November 29 and December 25, 1951, ISA 74/G5593/4677; Conclusions from Governors Meeting, January 11, 1952, IDFA 405/54–146.

229. *Davar*, November 21, 1951; Peretz, *Israel and the Palestine Arabs*, 50–57.

230. *Ma'ariv*, November 21, 1951.

231. *Davar*, November 21, 1951.

232. *Al-Ittihad*, November 24, 1951.

233. *Davar*, April 2, 1952.

234. The general hostility to these objections peaked when Rustum Bustani took the podium. The Palestinian MAPAM deputy audaciously proposed that after Israel signed peace agreements with its neighbors, the state should grant the same homecoming and citizenship rights to Arab refugees that the Law of Return extended to Jewish immigrants. *Ma'ariv*, *Davar*, and *al-Ittihad*, November 21, 1951.

235. *Ma'ariv*, March 26, 1952.

236. *Davar*, March 26, 1952; April 19, 1952.

237. "On behalf of the Communist Party, Mikunis calls on 'all the patriotic forces and all Arab residents to unite in a shared struggle against the racist clauses of the Citizenship [*Jinsiyya*] Law,'" *al-Ittihad*, April 5, 1952. See also, "The story of the crane and the Israeli Nationality Law," April 12, 1952; and "The racist orientations and clauses in the Israeli Nationality Law," April 19, 1952. MK Tawfiq Tubi claimed that the government's figure of 5 percent contradicted its prior infiltration statistics (*Davar*, July 24, 1952). See also Benziman and Mansour, *Subtenants*, 128.

238. "Racist orientations," *al-Ittihad*, April 19, 1952. The language requirement was

dropped for anyone born before 1948 (*Ma'ariv*, April 2, 1952). See also Kretzmer, *Legal Status*, 35–48.

239. *Davar*, April 2, 1952.

240. "On behalf of the Communist Party," *al-Ittihad*, April 5, 1952. Another article ("Story of the crane," April 12) noted that the law was "inspired by the stagnated swamps of South Africa." One month later, Palestinian MAPAM deputy Rustum Bustani protested that unlike African Americans, who also faced "national terror" [*irhab qawmi*], Palestinians in Israel did not enjoy even the pretense of legal equality. "Tel Aviv meeting demands changes in Nationality Law and its conformity with Declaration of Independence" (*al-Ittihad*, May 24, 1952). For other comparisons, see *Davar*, March 26, 1952; and *Ma'ariv*, April 2, 1952.

241. See the full text at http://www.israellawresourcecenter.org/israellaws/fulltext/nationalitylaw.htm.

242. Rosenne, "Israel Nationality Law," 15.

243. On the MoI's pledge of nondiscrimination and his assurances that most Arabs would have "no difficulty" acquiring citizenship, see *Davar*, March 26, April 2 and 9, and August 13, 1952; *Ma'ariv*, April 2, 1952.

244. By contrast, Ben-Gurion broadcast this fact openly for Jewish audiences. In Israel's 1952 *Yearbook*, published shortly after the citizenship law went into effect, he repeated the refrain that "Jews and non-Jews have equal rights" while noting twice that the state was "identical neither with its land nor with its people" (*Rebirth*, 466, 489, 517).

245. In May, the MoI's legal advisor was reportedly forced to acknowledge that there were serious problems with the law. *Al-Yawm* editor Mikhael Assaf claimed that "only the naïve, fools, and demagogues and Israel haters can claim that [since 1948 there has been] one law and one legal system [that governs all people equally]." See "The Arabs and the Citizenship Law," *Davar*, July 4, 1952.

246. Two Jews were denied permanent residence during the first two decades of statehood. The first was a Romanian national wanted back home for multiple crimes. A small group of Jewish citizens lobbied in vain for the government to reverse its decision. The law also authorized the interior minister to revoke the citizenship of any resident who "obtained it by the wrong committee, was absent from the country for seven successive years, or . . . [who] worked out of disloyalty to the state of Israel" (Warhaftig, *Hukah*, 146–148).

247. Activists claimed that the children of Arab citizens who were studying abroad would also be denied. *JTA*, July 16, 1952; *al-Ittihad*, April 19, 1952.

248. Rosenne, "Israel Nationality Law," 7, 37–39.

249. Ibid. Margalith ("Enactment," 66) argued that the law was "as liberal a piece of legislation as existing conditions could produce." See also Moshe Tabor, "Citizenship," *Davar*, April 9, 1952; and Menahem Kapuliuk, "Response to M.A. [Mikhael Assaf]," *Davar*, July 17, 1952.

250. The first meeting was held in Haifa on April 7, 1952 (*al-Ittihad*, April 19, 1952). Even Archbishop Hakim reprinted the coverage of the protest meetings in his magazine, *al-Rabita*. Kapuliuk, "Response to M.A."

251. *Al-Ittihad*, April 19 and May 24, 1952; *Ma'ariv*, July 15–17, 1952; *Davar*, May 16, June 22, and July 14–15 and 17, 1952; *JTA*, July 17, 1952. Meetings were reportedly held in forty-two localities. Tuma, *Thirty years.*

252. *JTA*, July 16, 1952.

253. In November 1952, the High Court affirmed the ruling of a Tel Aviv district court that the new citizenship law would not only replace the 1925 British Ordinance but also permanently stripped Palestine's 1.5 million Arabs of their prior citizenship without offering them a new one. Goodwin-Gil, "Nationality and Statelessness."

254. Yarkoni (Police HQ) to Field Units, April 13, 1953, IDFA 263/66–3936; letters between Ben-Gurion (Police HQ) and Pereg (IDF/Operations), February 23 and March 15, 1954, IDFA 8/56–26. The MG also did not trust the Entry to Israel Law to do its work. Morris, *Border Wars*, 166.

255. There were some exceptions. See "Arab who spied for Israel requests injunction against his expulsion," *ha-Arets* and *Zmanim*, both January 6, 1955, ISA 102/GL17115–13. On thirty Nahaf residents who in 1955 were still awaiting the High Court's ruling on their expulsion orders, see Ibrahim, *Hanna Naqara*, 264–268.

256. The law defined an "infiltrator" widely as "a person who has entered Israel knowingly and unlawfully" and who at any time between November 29, 1947, and the time of his entry was a national of any of the seven Arab states that declared war on Israel in May 1948, visited or lived in any of those countries or in any part of Palestine outside of Israel, or "a Palestinian citizen or . . . resident without nationality or citizenship or whose nationality or citizenship was doubtful and who, during the said period, left his ordinary place of residence in an area which has become a part of Israel for a place outside Israel."

257. On the maximum punishments stipulated in the law as well as the specific clause against harboring, see Korn, "Refugees to Infiltrators," 7, 11–15; and Bracha, "Unfortunate or perilous," 353. In 1954, a seventy-five-year-old man was sentenced to two months in prison for harboring his son, whose presence the authorities had approved years earlier. His daughter-in-law, six months pregnant, received a three-month sentence. *Kol ha-'Am*, August 19, 1954.

258. In June 1952, a special committee was established to set guidelines for how to implement the citizenship law. They recommended that the interior minister push back the proof of continuous presence requirement by several months from 1948 and grant automatic status to TRP holders who had returned through the Family Reunification program but still lacked IDs. There is reason to believe that these recommendations were not approved. Central Council on Arab Affairs (CCAA) Meeting, June 24, 1952; CCAA to Immigration and Naturalization Services, July 23, 1952, ISA 102/GL17116/19.

259. See the inquiries on general problems and individual cases in *Divre ha-Knesset*, vol. 13, November 3, 1952, to March 26, 1953, esp. November 25, 1952; January 7 and 27, 1953; February 9, 1953; and March 11, 18, and 24–25, 1953. The government usually evaded these inquiries. The law that enabled deportation was repealed only in 1979, with the enactment of the Emergency Powers (Detention) Law. Hofnung, *Democracy*, 84.

260. Interview in Dabburiya, February 22, 2002.

261. Shahak, *Civil Rights*, 35; Jiryis, "Domination by the Law," 80–81. By the early 1960s, even the High Court was urging the government to interpret the law in a more "flexible and realistic" manner. *Davar*, January 12, 1962.

262. The Knesset signed the Convention but never ratified it. The amendment allowed stateless children to apply for automatic status during the five years following their eighteenth birthday so long as they had resided in Israel for five successive years prior to the date of their application, had not been convicted of security violations, and had not been imprisoned for five years or more. Another new clause authorized the interior minister to revoke the citizenship of anyone who committed a crime of state security, including illegally crossing the border to a neighboring Arab country. No such restrictions were imposed on Jewish children. Layish to Lubrani, January 14, 1964, in ISA 43.04/G6300/1033; IDFA 100243/52–6; *Davar*, December 6, 1966.

263. Quoting Justice Minister Shapira during the law's first reading in "Law of Return; Nationality Law," in Lorch, *Major Knesset Debates*, 613.

264. Forman and Kedar, "From Arab Land"; Kedar, "Legal Transformation."

265. Beinin, *Red Flag*, 196–197.

CHAPTER 4

1. Roughly 270 residents earned wages performing daily jobs for the army, the electric company, and the Custodian of Absentee Property. The Ministry of Health established a local medical clinic in December 1948. More than one hundred residents of Abu Ghosh were refugees from neighboring villages. See the reports of S. Yeshayahu, the Jerusalem district commissioner, in ISA 49/G307/46. The history of Abu Ghosh's cooperation with the Zionist movement remains fuzzy. The mukhtar dated this history to 1919, but a photo from April 1936 shows residents pledging their allegiance to the leadership of the Arab Revolt. See W. Khalidi, *Before Their Diaspora*, 198.

2. Egyptian troops left Bethlehem and Hebron for Gaza in May 1949, following the conclusion of the armistice agreement with Israel. Feldman, *Governing Gaza*.

3. Mahmud Rashid Abu Ghosh, May 7, 1949, ISA 49/G307/46.

4. As he explained to the foreign minister, residents of nearby Jewish colonies such as Kibbutz Kiryat Anavim credited the people of Abu Ghosh with protecting them during the war: "This police activity is likely to go public and tarnish the image of the authorities" (Yeshayahu, May 13, 1949, ISA 130.15(2)/HZ2564/22; and November 21, 1948, ISA 49/G307/46).

5. Morris, *Border Wars*, 164. More than one hundred villagers were expelled the following summer, on July 7, 1950.

6. Stoler, "Sexual Affronts," 531.

7. Al-Haj, *Education*, 103–108, 193; *Istiqlal.*

8. Bordieu, *Outline*, 237, 47n.

9. This idea was introduced most famously by Edward Said, first in "Zionism from the Standpoint of Its Victims" and again in "Burdens of Interpretation." More recently see LeVine, "Nation from the Sands," 31; and Halper, "Nishul."

10. Knesset, "Law of Independence Day," April 13, 1949.

11. Knesset, "Flag and Emblem Law," May 18, 1949, available at http://www.israellaw resourcecenter.org/israellaws/fulltext/flagandemblemlaw.htm. Anyone who "assaulted the honor" of the flag or failed to raise it on a required building faced up to one year in prison and a three hundred lira fine.

12. Excerpts from three speeches recorded on April 23, 1950, ISA 79/L121/16.

13. MGC Mor, Meeting Minutes, September 27, 1951, IDFA 834/53–133; Ighbariyya, *'Arayn al-thuwwar*, 82–83; Morris, *Birth*, 249. Twenty-eight-year-old Muhammad Abu Ra's was among those questioned. Decades later he recalled bitterly that he and other villagers had only damaged weapons, and in any event were denied the chance to fight. (Interview). See also the personal testimony of another Tayyiban in Baransi, "Story."

14. Baransi, "Story," 8.

15. Interviews with 'Amr 'Asfur and Najla Abu Ra's.

16. Triangle farmers also lost land on the Jordanian side of the armistice line. Still more was sold and confiscated after the annexation. Abu Sitta, *Financing Racism*, Appendix 2.

17. Baransi, "Story," 7–8; interviews in Tayyibe, 2002.

18. Interviews with Nimr Murqus, former Kafr Yasif mayor, and Zvi Elpeleg, former Triangle governor; Kanaana, "Survival Strategies;" Lustick, *Arabs in the Jewish State*, 193; Cohen, *Good Arabs*, 32–35, 79–81.

19. Hanokh, April 23, 1950, ISA 79/L121/16.

20. Faraj, April 23, 1950, in ibid.

21. In the initial years of statehood, the Ministry of Education's Arab Division routed out politically "suspect" teachers who had remained in the country. See Cpt. Y. Krasnansky, Security Officer, October 7, 1949, IDFA 721/72–843.

22. Late Ottoman and British ceremonies involving some of these elements were apparently not held in the countryside and of course not under the threat of mass expulsion. Halabi, "Transformation."

23. Interviews in Kafr Qasim and Jaljulya, 1998 and 2002; Morris, *Border Wars*, 431–434. On the recruitment of Palestinian police officers, see ISA 79/L29/9; Firro, *The Druzes*, 106; and Lustick, *Arabs in the Jewish State*, 231. Similar units were posted in the South.

24. "Speech for the Holiday of Victory," name illegible (my emphasis).

25. During the war, most Jaljulyans sought shelter with relatives in nearby Tulkarm, in the West Bank. Only a small group of young men stayed behind to defend the village. Interview, June 8, 2002.

26. Gibb and Kramers, *Encyclopaedia of Islam*, v. 5, 955–956; Sulaiman, *Palestine and Modern Arab Poetry*, 18–20. I thank Elliott Colla for helping me think through this poem.

27. Cohen, *Good Arabs*, 96.

28. Many villagers also resented Iraqi troops for stealing and harassing local women (interview with Isma'il 'Aqab Mahmud Budayr). General anger toward the King also appears in fiction from and about the period, such as Habibi, *Sudasiyat al-ayyam*. See also Shoufani, "Fall of a Village," 109–121; and Baransi, "Story."

29. Cohen, *Good Arabs*, 32–35.

30. Hawari, "Men;" Lustick, *Arabs in the Jewish State*, 204–205; Cohen, *Good Arabs*, 94, 233–239; Al-Haj and Rosenfeld, *Arab Local Government*, 1–8; Hoffman, *My Happiness*, 225–228.

31. Interview with Isma'il 'Aqab Mahmud Budayr.

32. For useful critiques, see O'Hanlon, "Recovering the Subject"; Asad, *Genealogies of Religion*; Cooper, "Conflict and Connection"; Prakash, "Subaltern Studies"; Mitchell, "Everyday Metaphors"; Kligman, *Politics of Duplicity*; and Wedeen, *Ambiguities of Domination*, 79. Wedeen emphasizes the ambivalent nature of public rituals, "the ways in which people are neither totally alienated nor totally inscribed" in the collective power relations they produce.

33. Sayer, "Everyday Forms," 373–375.

34. Across the road from the colony of Zikharon Ya'acov, Furaydis and Jisr al-Zarka were the only villages out of sixty-two that were left intact in the Tel Aviv-Haifa region (Morris, *Birth*, 132, and *1948 and After*, 257–284). The part of Bayt Safafa that remained on the Israeli side of the armistice line was similarly isolated in the southern Jerusalem region.

35. Jaffans were nonetheless reminded to carry their IDs. *Al-Yawm*, May 5, 1949.

36. On urban population figures, see Pappe, *Ethnic Cleansing*, 205; Lehrman, "Arabs of Israel," 523–524; and Torstrick, *Limits of Coexistence*, 52–53. Haifa's Arab population was similar in size to Jaffa's both before and after 1948.

37. Deringil, *Well-Protected Domains*, 20–24; Campos, *Ottoman Brothers*, 31–33.

38. *Al-Yawm*, May 3–5, 1949.

39. "Minorities celebrate Independence Day," *al-Yawm*, May 5, 1949.

40. Ibid. Other dates were specific to the Arab population: the first wave of POW releases, the debut of the POW newsletter, *al-Asir*, and the appointment of the "first Arab judge in Nazareth."

41. See, especially, the reprint of Akram Za'atar's article from the Beirut-based *al-Hayat*, and "How we fought," an article authored by "The New Generation" in *al-Yawm*, May 4, 1949.

42. S. Yeshayahu, MoI, to DCs, February 26, 1951, ISA 56/G2220/26.

43. Landman to DCs, April 23, 1951, in ibid.

44. Gideon Weigert, "The Arabs of Israel and the third Independence Holiday," *al-Yawm*, May 8, 1951.

45. These poems were written primarily by Iraqi Jewish immigrants, such as "Dawud Samih," who published "Fragrance of the anniversary" in *al-Yawm* on May 11, 1951. Not long after, nineteen-year-old David Semah joined a circle of opposition poets and began to publish in *al-Ittihad* and its literary supplement, *al-Jadid*. After Semah's political alliances shifted, *al-Yawm* replaced him with Iraqi-born Salim Sha'shu'a (born 1930), who composed annual holiday praise poems through the end of the decade (Snir, "Iraqi-Jewish Writers"). Some of the Iraqi and Egyptian Jews who ran Israel's Arabic radio station also used their pre-Hebraicized names or invented new ones in order to appear as Palestinians (interview with Nuzhat Katsav, former host of the station's program, the Women's Corner). Years later this practice was outted and attacked.

46. Karji Hizma, "Revelation of the holiday," *al-Yawm*, May 10, 1951, and the two-page chart entitled "Some of the state's achievements on the third anniversary," May 11, 1951.

47. "The third Independence Holiday," *al-Yawm*, May 10, 1951.

48. *Al-Yawm*, May 6–11, 1951.

49. Landman to DCs, May 8, 1951, ISA 56/G2220/26. He was also keen to find out how urban audiences would react to the newsreel his office had produced on the "changes in the lives of the state and the Arab residents."

50. MoM Shitrit in February 1949, quoted in Benziman and Mansour, *Subtenants*, 20–22.

51. See reports dated May 13 through June 1, 1951, ISA 56/G2220/26.

52. Ibid., Yetah to Landman, May 13, 1951.

53. Ibid., reports on Nazareth (May 14), Acre (May 15), and Jaffa, Ramle, and Lod (May 24).

54. Ibid., reports dated May 14–15, May 24, and June 5.

55. Ibid., Yetah to Landman, May 15, 1951.

56. On the Maluls, see Campos, *Ottoman Brothers*, 163, 229–230.

57. "The few individuals [who] ... found [the] need to celebrate" by waving a flag or offering "a few words of praise" were those who "were obliged to show up ... by virtue of their status or position." This and the other quotes in this paragraph come from Malul to Landman, MoI/Mins, June 5, 1951, ISA 56/G2220/26. See also Malul's prior letter to the Tel Aviv commissioner, May 24, 1951. His biography comes from my telephone interview with his sister, Esther Malul.

58. Al-Haj, *Education*.

59. The British modeled their approach to Palestinian communalism on their experience in India. Robson, *Colonialism and Christianity*, 48–54. On the late Ottoman Empire, see Makdisi, "Ottoman Orientalism."

60. Wedeen, *Ambiguities of Domination.*

61. Mitchell, "Limits of the State"; Abrams, "Notes."

62. Benziman and Mansour, *Subtenants*, 19. I quote here the authors' paraphrase of Meir. It is unclear whether she was speaking literally or figuratively.

63. Masalha, *Land Without a People*, 2. In a late 1950 meeting with fellow MAPAI deputies, Ben-Gurion discussed the possibility of exploiting another moment of war to expel the Palestinians who remained. They did not belong in Israel, he insisted, just as American Jews did not belong in the United States.

64. It is unknown how many of the young men showed up to call the army's bluff. Some likely hoped to secure a stable income. Pappe, "Uneasy Coexistence," 624–625. Some IDF officials believe this decision was a mistake. Moshe Elad, "Put Arabs in the IDF," *Haaretz*, July 24, 2012. See Jabareen, "Likrat gishot bikortiot," for a critique of the demand that Palestinian equality in Israel be contingent upon army service.

65. Peled, *Debating Islam*, 101–103.

66. Benziman and Mansour, *Subtenants*, 51. This idea had a precedent in the early twentieth century, when a small group of Jewish artists and writers held out "hopes for racial fusion" between Palestine's Jews and Arabs. Saposnik, "Europe and Its Orients."

67. Quoting an Education Ministry official in the early 1950s, in Copty, "Knowledge and Power," 144.

68. Benor, January 13, 1953, quoted in Peled, *Debating Islam*, 103.

69. Stoler, "Sexual Affronts"; Cooper and Stoler, *Tensions of Empire.*

70. Throughout the 1950s, the government undertook special preparations to make sure that new immigrant communities celebrated Independence Day with proper enthusiasm—sending them flags, radios, and a mobile theater to show films. Kook, "Changing Representations."

71. Quoted in Koenig, "East Meets West," 168. See Werner, "Black Jews," for other contemporary observations of the denigration of Yemenites and other Jews from the Arab world as "blackies" or "primitive Arabs," and their frequent relegation to hard labor or domestic service for middle-class Ashkenazi families.

72. "We are adjured to carry out a project of colonization far greater than all of the last seventy years," the prime minister warned in October 1951. "No mistake is more harmful or hazardous than to imagine that the hour of pioneering has passed" (Ben-Gurion, "Call of the Spirit," in *Rebirth*, 400–401, 414).

73. Rozin, *Rise of the Individual.*

74. Ben-Eliezer, "Nation-in-Arms," 264. The PM spoke of the 1951 election campaign as something that could "shape . . . a nation for the state, because there is a state but not a nation."

75. Ben-Eliezer, "Nation-In-Arms," *Israeli Militarism*, and "State Versus Civil Society?" The blurring of the lines between state and society dates to the Mandate era, when the Yishuv leadership worked to build an alternative state structure (Elam, *Executors*, 57;

Kimmerling, "State Building," *Clash*, 132–153, and "Between the Primordial and Civil"). Together, the MoD and MoE established the *Gadna* (military training) program in Israeli high schools in order "to instill militarism in the youth" (Hermann, "Pacifism," 135–136).

76. Lustick, "Zionism and the State," 128. In early 1950, the minister of education told an audience of teachers that their job was to help transform the society from a "nation of priests" to a "nation of soldiers." See also Simon, "Costs"; Almog, *Sabra*, 133–135; Hermann, "Pacifism," 129–136; Beinin, *Red Flag*, 12–14; Ben-Ami, *Scars*, 55–56; Kimmerling, *Clash*, 139; and Silberman, *Prophet*, 170.

77. Israel's first major operation took place in the West Bank village of Qibya on October 14, 1953. An estimated sixty-nine Palestinian civilians, of whom three-fourths were women and children, were killed when the IDF dynamited their homes under orders to carry out "maximal killing." Their village was targeted following the death of three civilians in a grenade attack on the colony of Yehud—not because the attackers had come from Qibya, but because Qibya had appeared in prior intelligence reports as a general guerilla base. According to UN statistics, Arab states suffered 496 casualties as a result of Israel's border attacks in the twenty months between January 1955 and October 18, 1956. This figure amounted to more than four times the number of Israeli casualties during the same period. It was also higher than Israel's reported figure of 443 deaths in its entire eight years of statehood (Cordier and Foote, *Public Papers*, 289). For more on Israeli casualties, see Morris, *Border Wars*, 99–101, 110–107, 253–271, 296–297, and 315–316; and W. Khalidi and Caplan, "1953 Qibya Raid."

78. Kemp, "Dangerous Populations"; Weizman, *Hollow Land*, 63–64.

79. Quoted in Weizman, *Hollow Land*, 63; and Beinin, "Israel at Forty," 437.

80. Quoted in Hermann, "Pacifism," 129.

81. On Palmon's argument with his colleagues about this question in advance of the first Knesset elections, see Ben-Gurion, *War Diary*, 882–884.

82. In 1949, one MFA labored to explain to an American reporter that although Arabic was the native tongue of the Palestinians who remained, "the Arabs" were not, in fact, "racially Arab." "In their time they were Canaanites, Romans, Greeks, Turks" (Lehrman, "Arabs of Israel," 532). On the history of this trope, see Abu El-Haj, *Facts on the Ground*, 36–38.

83. In early 1953, a MFA report lamented that "Arab attitudes" had failed to "improve" and that the population showed no evidence of "basic psychological change" (Benziman and Mansour, *Subtenants*, 20–22).

84. See the late-1950 debate between Mikhael Assaf and Avraham Sharon in "Let's Wisen Up" (see note 167, Chapter Two). Nearly four decades later, Palmon would reveal his "disgust" with the "idiotic" attempt of certain military governors to try to turn Arab schoolchildren into good Zionists by having them sing Polish Jewish songs. See his response to an op-ed by former governor Zvi Elpeleg in "What the Arabs sang," *ha-Arets*, July 21, 1989; and Ronit Matalon, "Intifada? Riffraff!" *Musaf ha-Arets*, June 30, 1989, 4–7.

85. In January 1953, the Jewish National Fund's Yosef Nahmani urged Ben-Gurion to appreciate that the concentration of 45 percent of the entire Arab citizenry in a "homogenous, continuous area" in the Western Galilee "will be a burden on us" and offered proposals to encourage families to leave. He repeated these proposals in July 1953 and December 1955. Masalha, "Galilee Without Christians," 203. See also the demographic alarms sounded by then retired Palmah commander Yigal Allon in *al-Ittihad*, April 4, 1954.

86. On the buildup to the elections, see Forman, "Military Rule"; and Dallasheh, "Nazarenes," 131–139.

87. *Al-Ittihad*, April 22, 1954, citing the *Jerusalem Post*, cited in Tuma, *Thirty years*, 161.

88. Their ratio was only slightly higher elsewhere in the north. Forman, "Historical Geography"; Assaf, "Terrible myth" (see note 180, Chapter Two).

89. Forman, "Military Rule," 348–350. The first twelve hundred dunams of city land were confiscated that June.

90. Unauthored policy briefing dated 1954, ISA 102/GL17111/27.

91. Quoted in Elam, *Executors*, 63.

92. *Kol ha-'Am*, August 19, 1954. See also Baransi, "Story."

93. Cohen, *Good Arabs*, 231–232.

94. James, "Whose Voice"; Dawisha, *Arab Nationalism*, 147.

95. See, for example, PMB, "Broadcasting in Arabic with special reference to the Voice of Israel's Arabic Service," October 1956, ISA 43.04/A7224/38.

96. Quoted in Copty, "Knowledge and Power," 152–153, 175.

97. Juhayna, *al-Ittihad*, July 13, 1956. Juhayna, who published a regular column, was the pseudonym of MAKI deputy Emile Habibi.

98. Nassar, "Marginal as Central," 336; Beinin, *Red Flag*, 141.

99. Quoted in Ben Nahum, "Uproot the disease!" (see note 92, Chapter Two).

100. A. Ben-Dor, "Do we want Arabs on our farms?" newspaper illegible, June 29, 1956, clipped in ISA 102/GL17111/27. The Arab Scouts movement faced tremendous resistance from the military regime, which intimidated its young recruits—who wanted work, an escape from the travel restrictions imposed on them, and in some cases a chance to meet Jewish peers—and harassed their families. The movement also quickly began to face accusations of acting as a disguise for employing Arab workers on the cheap. It fell apart in the early 1960s as a result of these problems, as well as due to the contradiction between its professed values and MAPAM's ongoing support for the color bar on land ownership. The movement's Jewish leaders told graduates who now wanted to establish their own agriculture cooperatives with the party's resources and support that their idea was "impractical" (Netzer and Raz, *Tnu'at ha-no'ar ha-'aravi*).

101. Landman to DCs, April 7, 1962, ISA 56/G2220/26.

102. "Arabs celebrate the holiday," *al-Yawm*, April 30, 1952.

103. See the April 4, 1955 proposal, correspondence on April 5 and 20, 1955, and meeting minutes on February 11, 1957, all in ISA 56/G2220/26.

104. Yetah to Landman, May 4, 1952, and MoI/Mins Report, April 1955, in ibid. (emphasis added).

105. In 1956, three thousand people reportedly came out to see Filfel al-Masri, an Egyptian Jewish band, at the reception hosted by the Tayyibe Local Council (al-Yawm, April 24, 1956). In many cases, the concerts headlined Palestinian and Arab Jewish members of the Histadrut musical institute, some of whom also played in the symphony of Israel's Arabic radio station, Sawt Isra'il (Voice of Israel). See al-Yawm, April 23, 1955; and Pearlson, Simhah gdolah.

106. For both positive and negative reports, see Yetah to Landman, May 4, 1952, and the monthly summaries from Landman's office from March through June 1956 and May 1957, ISA 56/G2220/26.

107. In al-Yawm, see "Nazareth celebrates Independence Day," April 22, 1953; and "Clear expressions of the holiday," April 28, 1955, according to which all Nazareth shops closed, Israeli flags flew above homes and public buildings, and "four thousand residents made a beeline for Afula to watch the military parade." At the Galilee governor's reception, six hundred representatives of local "organizations, associations, and sects" reportedly delivered their "good wishes" (April 27, 1955). See also al-Yawm's 1956 coverage on April 15, 23, and 24.

108. Even Arab prison inmates, most of whom were detained for violating military regulations for which only Palestinians could be prosecuted, were granted two "exceptional" visiting sessions for the occasion. Al-Yawm, April 15 and 24, 1956.

109. Al-Yawm, April 22–23, 1956. For its coverage of the state's "achievements," see also issues from April 21, 1952; April 19 and 22, 1953; April 5, 1954; and April 12–26, 1956.

110. One report noted the "absence of special enthusiasm" in Nazareth despite the school celebrations and the free movie screening to which residents were invited. The same year, no complaints were received when only Druze residents of the Galilee were allowed to leave their villages on the holiday. See the January, March–April, and May–June 1956 division reports of the MoI/Mins, ISA 56/G2220/26.

111. Samuel, "Prospect," 462. Emphasis in original.

112. This was true even for the Druze. In 1953, for example, the unit's commander opposed a proposal to integrate the Druze with Jewish units on the grounds that it would be harder to supervise them (Cohen, Good Arabs, 159–164). During the 1956 celebrations in Daliyat al-Karmil, the school children reportedly sang Israel's national anthem and saluted the army while the principal congratulated the villagers and "the Jewish people on the freedom and independence they have achieved" (Nathir Nijm Hassun, al-Yawm, April 22, 1956).

113. Wolfe, "Elimination of the Native," 396–397.

114. Nakhleh, "Two Galilees," 12. See also Jabareen, "Likrat gishot bikortiot"; and Bishara, "Israeli Arabs."

115. A number of people I met dismissed the fear factor. In Sakhnin, eighty-nine-year-old Imm Mahmud insisted that she attended the celebrations because the Israelis "did not bother us or treat us unjustly. They used to eat with us whatever we ate."

116. Hall, "Toad in the Garden," 44.

117. Interviews with Wasfiyya Salim Ramadan, Kamil Mahmud Salim, and Imm Hisham. Depopulated villages constituted an exception to the areas that Palestinians could visit freely on the holiday. This was particularly painful for internal refugees who wanted to visit the site of their former homes. 'Awawdah, *Dhakira la tamut*; Darwish, *Ordinary Grief*, 96–97.

118. Interview. The description of a similar scene in an unidentified village appears in Juhayna [Imil Habibi], *al-Ittihad*, July 13, 1956, clipped in ISA 56/G2220/31–33.

119. I heard a similar story in Kafr Yasif.

120. Interview. I heard similar recollections in Acre and Sakhnin.

121. Quoting Kamil Mahmud Salim, interview.

122. Tayyibe's unemployment rate was 30 percent until 1959. Haidar, *On the Margins*.

123. Interview.

124. Interview. He estimated that by the 1960s there were just 150 copies of *al-Ittihad* for ten thousand people.

125. Stoler, "Sexual Affronts," 531.

126. Interview.

127. Interview (emphasis added).

128. In 1952, pupils of Jaffa's Hasan 'Arafa elementary school sang the anthem on Israel's Arabic radio station. See the announcement in *al-Yawm*, April 28, 1952.

129. Interview. 'Adawi's father compared holiday events to the celebrations commemorating the former Syrian president, Hafiz al-Assad.

130. J. L. Benor, MoE/Arab Division Director, in May 1957, quoted in Copty, "Knowledge and Power," 281.

131. *Istiqlal.*

132. Tuma, *Thirty years*, 161; Al-Asmar, *To Be an Arab in Israel*, 75.

133. Al-Haj, *Education*; Copty, "Knowledge and Power"; Cohen, *Good Arabs*.

134. In 1961, fourteen hundred of the eighteen hundred Arab civil servants in Israel worked for the Education Ministry. The only other serious career paths open to Palestinians were the police force or the prison service, where they could work as guards. Jiryis, *Arabs in Israel*; Baransi, "Story," 22; S. Kanaana, "Survival Strategies."

135. Shammas, "At Half-Mast," 219.

136. Goldman to Dr. Malhi, MoH/Mins, 1951 (n.d.), ISA 56/G2220/7. At least three more films were made specifically for Arab audiences by 1957; many more were made for Jewish audiences and tourists. For descriptions, see *al-Yawm*, May 7, 1957, and MoI/

Mins, October 7, 1957, ISA 56/G2220/27. For official bulletins and material shipped abroad in English, French, and Spanish, see the MFA Information Department series entitled *The Arabs in Israel*, published in 1952 and 1955. (Two more were published in 1958 and 1961 respectively.) In *ba-Mahaneh*, see Yair Kotler, "Military Government in the Triangle," March 20, 1952; A. Lev, "Inauguration of the road in Tayyiba," October 29, 1953; Yosef Sivan, "The Druze Unit demonstrates its power," May 27, 1954, Y. Lavie, "Double holiday for the Druze," May 6, 1957; M. Naor, "From Nazareth to Tayyiba," August 21, 1957.

137. K. Menahem, "Nazareth: Birth pangs of a new municipality," *Davar*, July 2, 1954. The caption of a large photo of a peasant woman carrying a water jug on her head notes that the town continues to move to the "rhythm of the nineteenth century." The reporter fails to mention the municipality's heated struggle with the government over the right to control its own water supply. See Dallasheh, "Nazarenes," chap. 4.

138. Bäuml, "ha-Mimshal ha-tsva'i."

139. Quoted in Lustick, *Arabs in the Jewish State*, 171. By 1964 that figure rose to 65 percent. It excludes the land confiscated from returnees and internal refugees. See also Peretz, "Arab Minority"; *al-Ittihad*, December 18, 1954; Jiryis, *Arabs in Israel*, 130, 292; Kanaana, "Survival Strategies."

140. Jiryis, *Arabs in Israel*, 304–309; Rosenfeld, "Class Situation," 387.

141. Jiryis, *Arabs in Israel*, 33.

142. MoI/Mins, "Health services to the Arab population, 1949–1959," ISA 56/G2220/7; Bäuml, *Tsel kahol lavan*, 204–208.

143. On these cases, see ISA 56/G2220/31–33; '*Al ha-Mishmar*, November 28, 1955, "Democratic women's union collects hundreds of signatures condemning the death of children," *al-Ittihad*, July 24, 1956; and Hadawi, *Israel and the Arab Minority*, 12–14.

144. By 1957, only one-quarter of villages and towns and 46 percent of the population were represented by any local councils, much less elected ones, compared to 99 percent of Jews. Jiryis, *Arabs in Israel*, 310.

145. Haidar, *Social Welfare Services*, 10–20.

146. The *kuffiyya* is a checkered headscarf, usually black and white or red and white. On the demonization of Palestinian returnees as spies, saboteurs, and armed gangsters, see Gitlis, *Ugly governor*; Ibrahim, "al-Mutasalilun"; Mu'ammar, *al-Mutasalilun*; Dankner and Tartakover, *Efo hayinu*; and Dror, "Emergency Regulations," 138–139. Studies include Al-Asmar, *Hebrew Looking Glass*, 59–104; and Urian, "Emergence of the Arab Image."

147. Rhoda Kanaaneh argues that Israel's schools, courts, and health delivery systems all "attempt to produce subjects who are self-alarmed by their own existence." "In the Name of Insecurity," 63.

148. Palmon, quoted in *Davar*, January 14, 1953.

CHAPTER 5

Sections of this chapter first appeared in Shira Robinson, "Local Struggle, National Struggle: Palestinian Responses to the Kafr Qasim Massacre and Its Aftermath, 1956–1966," *IJMES* 35, no. 3 (August 2003): 393–416.

1. Three of the four were workers from Tayyibe, Jaljulya, and Kafr Barʿa who happened to be driving or returning home with residents of Kafr Qasim that day. The fourth was an eleven-year-old boy from Tayyibe who was shot and killed when he went out to buy cigarettes for his father.

2. *Al-Mirsad*, November 21, 1957; *al-Ittihad*, November 15 and 22, 1957.

3. Quoted in Ben Nahum, "Uproot the disease!" (see note 92, Chapter Two).

4. See Chapters Two through Four on police brutality and government neglect. On the failure to punish an officer who fatally shot a boy in Umm al-Fahm, see *al-Ittihad*, September 15, 1951. On the refusal to try soldiers who shot to death two ʿAra residents and injured five more during a Ramadan border reunion, see *al-Ittihad*, September 6, 1952. For other cases, see MK Habibi to MoP (*Divre ha-Knesset* 2, v. 13, December 5, 1952, and January 7, 1953); Hoffman, *My Happiness*, 241–246; and League of Arab States, *Persecution*, 18–21. Recognized war crimes committed during the 1948 war also went unpunished (Aviv Lavie and Moshe Gorali, "I saw fit to remove her from the world," *ha-Arets*, October 29, 2003). On the presidential pardon of Shmuel Lahis after he was sentenced by a military court to seven years for killing thirty-five Palestinians in Saliha and on his promotion to direct the Jewish Agency, see "No Stigma Attached."

5. Benziman and Mansour, *Subtenants*, 19–20; Almog, *Sabra*, 188–189; Beinin, *Red Flag*, 81–84; Rosenfeld, *Hem hayu falahim*, 71.

6. Ratner, "ha-Mimshal ha-tsvaʾi"; Ben-Shlomo, "Arab Village," v–xi; Savuray, "Our School and the Arab Question."

7. Greenberg, *Race and State*, 374.

8. Woodward, *Strange Career*, 81. On workers, see Kanaana, "Survival Strategies," 11–13; Rosenfeld, "Class Situation," 397–398; and Schiff, "Pros and Cons."

9. *Al-Mirsad*, July 19, 1956. On the demand of Jewish drivers and bus company clerks that Arab workers stand up so that Jewish passengers could sit in their seats, see *al-Ittihad*, March 15, 1955. In early 1957, MAKI's Hebrew-language *ha-ʿOlam ha-Zeh* conducted a poll of hundreds of Jewish schoolchildren ages six to thirteen about how they thought the government should "handle" the Arab minority. "Murder" was the response of 95 percent of them; the other 5 percent supported concentrating them in detention camps or deporting them to the Negev desert. See Elias Kusa to US President Eisenhower, March 12, 1957, in Hanna Naqara's private papers (thanks to Leena Dallasheh). On the desecration of seventy-three crosses in a Christian cemetery in Haifa on Good Friday in 1954, see Hadawi, *Israel and the Arab Minority*, 16.

10. Of the 180,000 Palestinians in Israel in 1953, just 240 were in public secondary schools and none were in university. In 1954–1955, there were still only 800 Palestinian

high school students (comprising 6.5 percent of the total high school population) and 72 students at university (Ammoun, *Discrimination in Education*, 90, 104–105). During the 1956-1957 academic year, Arabs comprised 11 percent of Israel's population but less than 1 percent of university students (Al-Haj, *Education*, 103–108, 193). On the regime's efforts to block university admission to qualified Arab students starting in the summer of 1954, see Cohen, *Good Arabs*, chap. 7.

11. Somekh, "Reconciling Two Great Loves," 10–11.

12. Hoffman, *My Happiness*, 215, 241. The only Jews who entered the town for recreational purposes were soldiers on Saturday night.

13. For more see Chapter Two.

14. See the lighthearted coverage of a military trial of curfew violators in Baqa al-Gharbiyya the day after the village celebrated Independence Day: Y. Lavie, "A thousand and one excuses," *ba-Mahaneh*, April 25, 1956, 6–7.

15. Shaul Hon, "The Green Berets [border guards] need encouragement," *Ma'ariv*, January 1, 1957. In April 1957, *ha-Arets* predicted that the accused guards would be treated ultimately as heroes, not criminals, regardless of the final verdict (Hadawi, *Israel and the Arab Minority*, 19–21). See also a letter to Ben-Gurion from Ron Shafi, a private citizen, about the injustice of bringing soldiers to trial for following orders (January 18, 1957, in KQLC Archive); and a letter from the Jewish Agency's Department of Youth Education which thanked the premier for his Knesset address and noted the staff's "depression [over the fact that] uniform wearing Jews of the Border Patrol could kill innocent human beings, especially children" (December 20, 1956, in KQLC Archive). For an overview of the media reaction, see Linenberg, "Parashat Kfar Kassem."

16. Israeli diplomats in the United States quickly appreciated the gravity of the international public relations problem caused by the massacre and urged the Foreign Ministry to emphasize the "success" of the government's response to it. See Natanel Lorch to Israeli Embassy in Washington, DC, and the MFA/Information Division, January 16, 1957.

17. Levey, "Rise and Decline."

18. Cordier and Foote, *Public Papers*, 289. Other targets of Israeli reprisal raids included the Burayj Refugee Camp (Gaza, August 28, 1953; foreign observers described "an appalling case of deliberate mass murder"), Qibya (West Bank, October 14, 1953), Nahalin (West Bank, March 28, 1954), Gaza City (February 28, 1955), and Khan Yunis (Gaza, August 31, 1955). On Qibya, see note 77, Chapter Four.

19. Shlaim, "Between East and West."

20. Kahin, Asian-African Conference, 76–85; Berger, "After the Third World?" 11–12. Contrary to conventional wisdom, Bandung neither produced nor convened to formulate a policy of nonalignment (Vitalis, "Midnight Ride").

21. Ben-Gurion had initially welcomed the Free Officers when they came to power in 1952, but the relationship quickly soured. Beinin, *Red Flag*, 166.

22. El-Khawas, "Africa and the Middle Eastern Crisis," 33–34; Kohn, "New Nation States," 96–97; Shlaim, "Between East and West"; Abadi, *Quest for Recognition*, xiv.

23. Rivkin, "Afro-Asian World."

24. The Columbo powers were Burma, Ceylon, India, Indonesia, and Pakistan. Fraser, "American Dilemma"; Mao, "When Zhou Enlai Met Gamal Abdel Nasser." See also the memoirs of the former Iraqi prime minister who headed the delegation to Bandung (Jamali, *Arab Struggle*).

25. Rivkin, "Afro-Asian World." Given Jordan's desire to hold onto the West Bank, its concession may have lain in its willingness to invoke UN Resolution 181 in the first place. More research is needed on this question.

26. Kahin, *Asian-African Conference*, 82.

27. Beinin, *Red Flag*, 154.

28. Kohn, "New Nation States," 98; Beinin, *Red Flag*, 153–154.

29. On Nasser's repeated confirmations of this position back in Cairo, see Beinin, *Red Flag*, 153. For a survey of the revisionist literature showing that Ben-Gurion turned down multiple peace feelers after 1948 because he felt that refugee repatriation and a return to the partition borders were too high a price to pay, see Shlaim, "Debate About 1948," 300–301.

30. Beinin, *Red Flag*, 173–190; Shlaim, "Debate About 1948."

31. Beinin, *Red Flag*, 168.

32. Ibid., 157–162; Yaqub, *Containing Arab Nationalism*, 39–85; Little, *American Orientalism*, 88–90, 272–276.

33. Nadelmann, "Black Africa," 186–187.

34. Excerpted from the October 1958 District Court judgment against Lt. Gabriel Dahan in Dalia Karpel, "Yes, we are from the same village," *ha-'Ir*, October 10, 1986.

35. Beinin, *Red Flag*, 194; Almog, *Sabra*, 133–135.

36. "When Ben-Gurion Told the Cabinet About the Kfar Kassem Massacre," *Haaretz*, March 28, 2001.

37. On the absence of post-massacre soul-searching among Jewish liberal intellectuals and others, see Elam, *Executors*, 58–59; Ozacky-Lazar, "Hitgabshut," 44; and al-Asmar, *To Be an Arab in Israel*, 51.

38. *Al-Ittihad*, December 18, 1956. Palestinian communists linked Kafr Qasim to Dayr Yasin long before the details of the former surfaced (*al-Ittihad*, November 16, 1956).

39. Unauthored policy briefing dated 1954, in ISA 102/GL17111/27.

40. This summary is based on Habibi, *Kafr Qasim*, 13–21; Jiryis, *Arabs in Israel*, 137–157; and Qahwaji, *Dhill al-ihtilal*, 158–162.

41. Benjamin Kol, whose platoon was posted to Jaljulya and refused to allow his soldiers to shoot, later said, "We had an explicit order to kill everyone after 5 P.M." (Dalia Karpel, "The massacre in Kafr Qasim: We did not shoot," *ha-Arets*, October 6, 2008).

42. Ibid.

43. Excerpted from the protocols of the military trial, courtesy of Ruvik Rosenthal. See also Rosenthal, *Kfar Kassem.*

44. Habibi, *Kafr Qasim,* 73–74.

45. Tawfiq Tubi, *Knesset Memorandum,* December 23, 1956. GH, copied from Yad Tabenkin Archive, Jewish-Arab Series, 35/6/2.

46. KQLC, *al-Dhikra al-arba'un,* 5 (hereafter, *Fortieth anniversary*). Most of the thirteen survivors feigned death or hid under a tree all night (Tubi, *Knesset Memorandum*).

47. Interviews with 'Adil Budayr, chair of Kafr Qasim's Commemoration Committee; Ibrahim Sarsur, local council chair; and Mustafa Rabi'a, in Jaljulya.

48. Looking back at the role MAKI played in bringing the truth of the massacre to the public, *al-Ittihad* editors frequently used the term "conspiracy of silence." See, for example, the October 27, 1959 issue.

49. "How can people from among us do such a thing?" he asked the Cabinet on November 11, 1956. "We have a wonderful army, but apparently there are incidents and circumstances in which people lose their minds" ("When Ben-Gurion Told the Cabinet"). See also Ozacky-Lazar, "Hitgabshut," 42.

50. "When Ben-Gurion Told the Cabinet."

51. Rosenthal, *Kfar Kassem;* Tom Segev, "If the Eye Is Not Blind nor the Heart Closed," *Haaretz,* October 29, 2006. Many Qasimis today insist that the massacre was planned. Because their village lies at the southern tip of the Little Triangle, they believe there was a plan to trigger a wave of panic to the north that would lead, through the domino effect, to the flight of the population to Jordan. They point out that on the day of the massacre, soldiers blocked all but the eastern edge of the village, thus permitting them only one direction in which to escape (KQLC, *Fortieth anniversary*). Some also believe that the army deliberately chose Kafr Qasim as the site of the crime in order to avenge the village's successful defense against Jewish forces in 1948, a victory that saved numerous villages to its north from destruction (interview with Ibrahim Sarsur).

52. Reprinted in *NER,* December 1956, 36.

53. Many sustained serious bullet wounds in more than one part of their body. Inside the hospital, some of the injured were warned by compassionate Jewish patients to claim they were soldiers who had been injured in Gaza. Others reported being subjected to verbal harassment by medical staff, who accused them of lying about the source of their wounds. Some became permanently disabled and were forced to stay there for weeks, months, and even a year. Interviews with 'Amr 'Asfur, Ibrahim Sarsur, Isma'il 'Aqab Mahmud Budayr, and Latif Dori. See also *'Al ha-Mishmar,* January 14 and 21, 1957; and Ihud Association to PM, January 22, 1957, in KQLC Archive.

54. On November 13, the Knesset speaker revoked MAKI MK Esther Vilenska's right to speak and ordered her words "Kafr Qasim incident" stricken from the record when she demanded more information. When her colleague Tawfiq Tubi tried again one week later, fellow deputies ordered him to "shut up" and accused him of "waging

war against the state." Interview with Tubi; see also *al-Ittihad*, November 27, 1956. On MAPAM's Latif Dori's hospital visit, see *'Al ha-Mishmar*, November 15, 1956; and interview with Latif Dori.

55. Keren, *Zichroni*, 68, 77; Shapiro, "Le'an ne'elmu," 98–101, and "Historical Origins"; Beinin, *Red Flag*; Rosenfeld, "Class Situation," 388.

56. Gershom Schocken, *ha-Arets* editor and deputy of the liberal Zionist Progressive Party, reportedly described the massacre as "worse than treason" (Sacco, *Footnotes in Gaza*, 397). The limited public dissent and later the claim of the border guards that they had merely been following orders led a few people to compare public apathy to the complicity of Germans during the Holocaust. This included the vocal members of the Ihud Association, which replaced the defunct binationalist Brit Shalom movement in 1942. Throughout the initial months following the massacre they sent numerous letters to the prime minister comparing the event to Nazi crimes as well as to Israel's own Dayr Yasin and Qibya massacres, and they accused the entire state and its "extreme militarism" of the crime. See some of their letters in *NER*, December 1956. See also Dan Ben Amotz, "I did not know," *Ma'ariv*, December 7, 1956; Segev, *Seventh Million*, 298–302.

57. *Ha-Kol 'al Kfar Kassem*, December 1956; Keren, *Zichroni*, 55–71.

58. Natan Alterman, "Thum ha-meshulash" [Triangle Zone], *Davar*, December 7, 1956. Alterman was the first Zionist poet to idealize the martyrdom of the Haganah's elite shock troops, formed in 1937 (Ben-Eliezer, *Israeli Militarism*, 24). His poem was an exception to the rest of MAPAI's coverage throughout the affair. Linenberg, "Parashat Kfar Kassem," 50–51.

59. Ben-Gurion, "Incident in the villages of the Triangle," Sitting 203 of the Third Knesset, December 12, 1956, reprinted in *NER*, December 1956, 35.

60. Ibid.

61. Levinthal, "Case," 46; Claude, *National Minorities*, 107–108; Lahav, "Supreme Court"; Agassi, *Liberal Nationalism*, 213; Carnegie Endowment, *Israel and the United Nations*, 30.

62. Simon, "Costs."

63. Hadawi, *Israel and the Arab Minority*, 19–21, citing the *Jewish Newsletter*, July 8, 1958.

64. Morris, *Border Wars*, 255–316. Indeed, the government spent November 1956 working to cover up its massacre of nearly four hundred Palestinians in the freshly occupied Gaza Strip. Sacco, *Footnotes in Gaza*.

65. Quoted in Elam, *Executors*, 61.

66. Karpel, "The massacre."

67. *'Al ha-Mishmar*, November 15, 1956. Other area schools were forced to close because it was too dangerous for teachers from nearby villages to travel to work. Copty, "Knowledge and Power."

68. *NER*, December 1956, 20; *al-Ittihad*, January 4, 1957.

69. Intelligence agents reported widespread fear in Nazareth (ISA 79/L53/24–5). Poet Rashid Husayn later wrote that he "felt a tremble flood my body as [my friend] spoke about Hitler's crime and the Kafr Qasim massacre" ("Endangered conscience," July 8, 1959, in *Kalam mu'zun*, 3.

70. *Al-Ittihad*, December 18, 1956; Habibi, *Kafr Qasim*, 7–9. Some of the accused were born in North Africa, and many in the public reduced their behavior to their backward cultural mentality and the discrimination they had faced as children. This was a common trope that the prime minister helped to create. Throughout the early 1950s he repeatedly denied the army's responsibility for the reprisal raids he sanctioned and blamed them instead on vigilante settlers who had either emigrated from the Arab world or survived the Holocaust. Kordov, *11 kumtot*, 175 and 191; Pappe, *Ethnic Cleansing*, 139.

71. See the letters housed in the KQLC Archives and ISA 56/G2215/22. The term *national oppression* appeared interchangeably with *racial discrimination* from the beginning of statehood. See, for example, *al-Ittihad*, November 15, 1948.

72. Mikhail Assaf, *Davar*, June 3, 1955; Jiryis, *Arabs in Israel*, 34. For critiques in the spring and summer of 1956, see Dalia Karpel, "As Good As It Gets," *Haaretz Magazine*, July 20, 2001, 26–29; *ha-Boker*, July 13, 1956.

73. Beinin, *Red Flag*, 161. That year MAKI won 4.5 percent of the electorate and six parliamentary seats. Palestinians remained only 30 percent of its base, but the party won 35 percent of their votes in the cities and 15.6 percent in the countryside. MAPAM voted against MAKI bills to end military rule in December 1955 and February 1956.

74. Jiryis, *Arabs in Israel*, 35.

75. Korn, "Good intentions," 113–119; Bäuml, "Military Government"; Kemp, "Dangerous Populations."

76. See the classified intelligence survey of the Jordanian press, August 1, 1956, in ISA 56/G2220/31–33.

77. Beinin, *Red Flag*, 196.

78. Ibid.

79. Yani Yani, Kafr Yasif Mayor to MoI Bar Yehuda, March 18, 1957, ISA 56/G2215/22. See their entire exchange in the same file. Poet and journalist Fouzi al-Asmar recalls that the massacre was a watershed in his political consciousness. "I spent much time talking about the incident to my friends, who were also greatly affected to varying degrees. We asked ourselves: 'What will happen next? When will our turn come?'" *To Be an Arab in Israel*, 51–52.

80. This per Hadawi, *Israel and the Arab Minority*, 12–14.

81. "Announcement to Arab citizens," January 4, 1957, ISA 56/G2215/22; Matthews, *Confronting an Empire*; Fleischmann, *Nation*; Kabha, "Palestinian Press"; Cohen, *Army of Shadows*; Swedenburg, *Memories of Revolt*.

82. The police set up special checkpoints as well as car and foot patrols throughout the Galilee to try to block participation in the memorial events, and they issued detailed

lists of who would be allowed into Nazareth. See "The strike in the territories of the military government, January 5–6, 1957," ISA 79/L53/24.

83. *Al-Ittihad*, January 4, 1957.

84. *Al-Ittihad*, January 8, 1957; correspondents offered detailed coverage of strikes in Nazareth, Acre, Haifa, Ramle, and the villages of Rame, 'Arrabe, Sakhnin, Sulam, Shafa 'Amr, Tayyibe, Tira, Tamra, Kafr Yasif, and Umm al-Fahm. The day before, *Davar* reported that the authorities in Nazareth had warned activists that the police would use "a strong hand against them" if they demonstrated.

85. *Al-Ittihad*, January 8, 1957.

86. Minorities Officer to Sasson Rashti (MoI/North), January 7, 1957, ISA 56/G2215/22.

87. Ibid. On police surveillance, see ISA 79/L174/7 and 79/L80/6.

88. Habibi's *Pessoptimist* brilliantly captures this experience of living under the constant watch of military authorities. He drew a direct link between the novel and the massacre (*Kafr Qasim*, 1).

89. See *Davar*, January 7, 1957, for a sharp rebuttal to this claim.

90. *Ma'ariv*, January 7, 1957; *al-Ittihad*, October 21, 1957; October 27, 1958; October 26, 1965.

91. See Chapter Two.

92. *Divre ha-Knesset*, January 9, 1957, 715.

93. Referring to the "anti-Israeli venom" spewed at the memorial events the day before and the claim that most Nazareth residents "refused to raise the barricades" as called upon to do so by the "inciters," *Davar* concluded on January 7 that "the Kafr Qasim affair is one thing; demonstrations and wild disturbances are another."

94. Ibid., and *al-Ittihad*, January 11, 1957. The "other parties" were MAPAM, which could not mount any serious public opposition due to its partnership in the coalition, and the "Arab lists" of MAPAI.

95. None of the Qasimis I met mentioned the strike as part of their narrative of the memorial struggle.

96. *'Al ha-Mishmar*, January 21, 1957; *al-Ittihad*, January 15 and 25, 1957.

97. Some relief arrived in April in the form of outside donations raised by the Nazareth chapter of MAKI's Union of Democratic Women, with a monthlong bazaar, an art fair, and a final dinner (*al-Ittihad*, February 26, March 15, and April 9, 1957). In March 1957, the Histadrut's fund for construction workers distributed IL 2,000 to each of the ten widows whose husbands had been members. *Davar*, March 11, and *Haqiqat al-Amr*, March 14, 1957.

98. *'Al ha-Mishmar* and *Davar*, November 18, 1957. Ben-Gurion's office claimed that it never received the final recommendations that the Zohar Commission claimed it sent the previous November. The premier likely feared that adopting the recommendations would reinforce the state's responsibility for the crime. See Zohar's furious letter on November 16, 1957, ISA 43/G5593/4674, and the government's denial of the request made

by Palestinian MAPAM deputy Yusif Khamis to review the commission's protocols, in an exchange between June and December 1957, KQLC Archive.

99. War damages entailed a one-time payment of IL 5,000 to each family of the deceased, IL 350 for each surviving dependent, and IL 300 to each of the wounded.

100. Other members included two prominent (Jewish) MAPAI members of the town council and two Palestinians close to the authorities. Interviews with Ibrahim Sarsur and 'Ali Salim Sarsur.

101. One person was reportedly threatened with deportation. Interview with Ibrahim Sarsur; *ha-Arets* and *Jerusalem Post*, November 18, 1957.

102. The consent forms summarizing the committee's findings were in Hebrew, which most of the families at that time could not read. See *al-Mirsad*, October 31, 1957; *ha-Arets*, November 10, 1957; and *'Al ha-Mishmar*, November 18, 1957.

103. The government accused MAKI of "exploiting the tragedy for political purposes." According to *al-Yawm* (October 27, 1957), "no one was responsible for the crime except those who committed it, and . . . residents of the village appreciated the strong response and sentiments expressed by the Jewish community."

104. *Al-Ittihad*, November 1, 1957; *al-Mirsad*, October 31, 1957; *ha-Boker*, October 30, 1957.

105. *Al-Ittihad*, November 1, 1957. Because the police would not allow *al-Ittihad*'s correspondent to enter the village, the newspaper had to rely on the account of one of the ceremony's participants.

106. *Al-Yawm*, October 30, 1957; ISA 56/G2217/22.

107. *Al-Ittihad*, November 1, 1957.

108. Born in Baghdad in 1909, Agassi was fluent in Arabic and edited *Davar*'s Arabic edition, *Haqiqat al-Amr*. Lockman, *Comrades and Enemies*, 197–198.

109. *Al-Ittihad*, November 1, 1957.

110. Shmuel Segev, "The race for Kafr Qasim," *ha-Arets*, November 10, 1957.

111. *ha-Arets*, November 22, 1957.

112. In the decades before statehood, Jewish settlers who attacked Palestinian farmers had taken advantage of the tradition to reduce the chance of reprisals and avoid having to stand trial. In 1954, the Jewish Agency arranged a sulha on behalf of the family of a Jewish guard who shot dead a young Palestinian boy who had gone to harvest the mallow his family had planted on their former land. Morris and Black, *Israel's Secret Wars*, 22; Hoffman, *My Happiness*, 241–246.

113. Even had the massacre been the result of a "work accident," the government would have been required to award villagers three to four times more than the sum the committee determined. In November, Ben-Gurion personally blocked the formation of the proposed interministerial commission by refusing to send a Defense Ministry representative to participate. *'Al ha-Mishmar*, November 18–19, 1957; *Jerusalem Post*, November 18, 1957.

114. Recalling the massacre of Jews near Jerusalem in 1929, the sulha's emcee, Avraham Shapira, declared, "Violence between the Jews and Arabs of this country did not start at Kafr Qasim, and violence breeds violence" (*Jerusalem Post*, November 22, 1957).

115. *ha-Arets*, November 21, 1957. See *Davar* and *'Al ha-Mishmar*, November 18, 1957, on the widespread rumors that the government sought to use the committee to end the trial.

116. KQLC, *Fortieth anniversary*, 37.

117. *La-Merhav* and *ha-Arets*, November 22, 1957; *Jerusalem Post*, November 21–22, 1957. See the bilingual invitation in ISA 56/G2215/13.

118. *Jerusalem Post*, November 22, 1957.

119. Official newsreels from the event, included in an episode of the 1998 Israeli documentary series *Tkuma* on Palestinian citizens, show the somber mood of the villagers who attended, some of whom remained on crutches or were otherwise disabled.

120. *Jerusalem Post*, November 21, 1957. This is a rather obvious reference to both MAKI and MAPAM, whose deputy Hanan Rubin was one of the Ihud Association lawyers. Hanan Rubin was also a Knesset member for that party. Rubin repeatedly insisted that his legal services on behalf of the families had no connection to his political work.

121. *ha-Arets*, November 21, 1957.

122. KQLC, *Fortieth anniversary*.

123. Habibi, *Kafr Qasim*, 61.

124. KQLC, *Fortieth anniversary*, 38.

125. Ibid., 36–37.

126. *Al-Ittihad*, November 1, 1957; *ha-Arets*, October 30, 1957.

127. Beinin, *Red Flag*, 194–198.

128. Danin, *Tsiyoni be-khol tnai*, 373–413. In January 1957, the Arab League's office in New York published its first systematic bulletin on Israel's record at the United Nations. The report included a detailed discussion of military rule and Israel's violations of both international human rights law and the minorities provisions of UN Resolution 181 (Sayegh, *Record of Israel*). The League's Washington, DC office opened in 1945, but the New York office opened only ten years later (*JTA*, March 4, 1955).

129. Nassar, "Affirmation and Resistance," 236–239, and "Marginal as Central," 341–343. In *al-Ittihad*, see, for example, "21 February lives on: Day of international struggle against colonialism and of standing in solidarity with the youth in the colonies," February 18, 1955; Editorial, "Eden's resignation, a lesson for Israel," January 11, 1957; Nicola Jabra, "The only way to get closer to the people of Asia is to support them in their struggle against colonialism," January 18, 1957; Editorial, "Our solidarity with the Algerian people," February 1, 1957; "A nation that oppresses another cannot be free," May 7, 1957; Saliba Khamis, "Persecution of the Arab people and the Ben-Gurion democracy," September 11, 1957. Part of the ferment emerged in response to Eisenhower's post-Suez campaign to isolate Nasser, who continued to insist on taking a neutralist stance in his foreign policy. For background, see Yaqub, *Containing Arab Nationalism*, 57–180.

130. Copty, *Knowledge and Power*, 152–153.

131. Ibid., 283.

132. Cooper, "Parting of the Ways"; Shepard, "Algeria"; Connelly, "Taking Off the Cold War Lens"; Berger, "After the Third World?"

133. In fact, *al-Ittihad* had been following these struggles almost from the start. On Kenya and South Africa, see, for example, "Conference of progressive organizations in South Africa denounces the 'Ghetto' Law and the Law of 'Illegal Organizations,'" June 4, 1950; Issam Abbasi, "What's happening in Kenya?" November 21, 1952; "Lights revealed on the truth of the disturbances in Kenya," May 29, 1953; "Negroes toil in 'the most miserable place on Earth,'" March 8, 1955; "The Nazism of this generation: Defining the races . . ." October 18, 1955; "Women burn their permits in the courtyard!" May 29, 1956; "The darkness of British colonialism," June 5, 1956. On the United States, see Editorial, "The garbage under the rug," October 6, 1951; Juhayna, "Ugly fascism," August 26, 1955; "Spotlight: Nonviolent struggle of the Negroes in America," March 2, 1956; "Bus struggle continues," March 26, 1956; "US Supreme Court states that the segregation between whites and Negroes is illegal," April 27, 1956; "'Little Rock' embodies white supremacy toward Negroes," October 1, 1957.

134. The first such vote came in October 1955, when Israel sided with France against the request by the FLN (Front de Libération Nationale, or National Liberation Front) for the UN to investigate the growing crisis in Algeria. In *al-Ittihad*, see "Colonialism suffers defeat at the United Nations," October 4, 1955; George Tubi, "February 21 is the day of solidarity against colonialism," February 21, 1956; "A nation that oppresses another cannot be free," January 11, 1957; Nicola Jabra, "The only way to get closer to the people of Asia is to support them in their struggle against colonialism," January 18, 1957; "Our solidarity with the Algerian people," February 1, 1957; "With colonialism and against the people's aspiration for freedom: Israeli government rejects the proposal of the Algerian Liberation Movement!" October 4, 1957. Israel began to supply the French with intelligence on Egyptian cooperation with the FLN in exchange for training Israeli helicopter pilots to combat guerilla infiltration from Gaza in the summer of 1955. On their mutual aid throughout the revolution, see Laskier, "Israel and Algeria"; and Abadi, "Algeria's Policy."

135. This was as true for the UN's postcolonial newcomers like Lebanon and India as it was for veterans like Britain and the United States. See Claude, *National Minorities*, 80–81, 146–174, 185, 192, and 209–210; Hiscocks, "Work of the United Nations"; Humphrey, "The United Nations Sub-Commission"; and Lauren, "Seen from the Outside," 29–32.

136. UN General Assembly Resolution 1514 (XV), "Declaration on the Granting of Independence to Colonial Countries and Peoples," 14 December 1960, available at http://www.un.org/en/decolonization/declaration.shtml.

137. Schwelb, "International Convention;" Irwin, "Apartheid on Trial."

138. Danin, *Tsiyoni be-khol tnai*, 373–413. After 1956, the staff ballooned from 6 to 120, and its airtime more than doubled from three hours to seven.

139. Nadelmann, "Black Africa," 186–194.

140. Cohen, *Good Arabs*, 187–193.

141. *JTA*, April 8, 1957. The same exemptions were granted to Circassian soldiers.

142. Firro, "Reshaping Druze Particularism," 44–45. This move was at least two years in the making, and one that some in the community had openly opposed ("Druze religion does not need definition or recognition," *al-Ittihad*, April 23, 1955). Soon thereafter the Circassians were also granted separate nationality status.

143. Cited in Forman, "Historical Geography," 812–813.

144. Dallasheh, "Nazarenes."

145. Quoted in Forman, "Military Rule," 350–351.

146. In *al-Ittihad*, see "On 'security' pretext the government imposes plan to 'Judaize' Nazareth," February 18, 1955; and "Nazareth will not become a new South Africa," March 22, 1957. On October 4, 1957, the paper reported that Arab movement restrictions in the city had intensified, most likely to block local resistance to the new colony. Editors called the "racial oppression" faced by town residents "more degrading" than Apartheid ("Nazareth's Judaization and the travel permits system").

147. The deadliest incident took place in Sandala, where fifteen children were killed when they stepped on a land mine (planted, presumably, in 1948) on the way home from school. Smaller explosions and stray bullets from nearby army shooting exercises killed and injured more children in Umm al-Fahm, al-Maghar, Sakhnin, ʿArrabe, and ʿArab al-Suʿad (Habibi, *Kafr Qasim*, 62). From 1956 to 1958, residents of several villages discovered additional bombs in schools, playgrounds, and churches. In light of the authorities' inaction, Jiryis (*Arabs in Israel*, 155) suggests that the bombs were planted deliberately as a new means of terrorizing the Arab population. See attorney Hanna Naqara's request to the interior minister on the anniversary of the massacre to support the Arab people's demands to punish the murderers and end all discrimination. The minister responded by rejecting the attorney's "waste of lies," accusing Naqara and his friends of working to spread "wasteful national hatred" (ISA 56/G2215/22; *al-Ittihad*, October 28, 1957).

148. Beinin, *Red Flag*, 196 (emphasis added). This wording was a compromise between more and less militant proposals.

149. Jiryis, *Arabs in Israel*, 30; *JTA*, July 10, 1957.

150. Bäuml, "Mapai Committee," 413–418.

151. Haidar, *Social Welfare Services*, 10–20. Nazareth alone had a 30 percent unemployment rate at the time.

152. Schwarz, "Israel's Arab Minority," 23–24.

153. Ratner, "ha-Mimshal ha-tsvaʾi."

154. That August witnessed an unprecedented boycott of Egged, the national bus company, by fifty workers in the Western Galilee. Activists accused the firm of prevent-

ing Arab passengers from alighting the bus on the Kafr Yasif-Amka route until all Jewish passengers found seats (*al-Ittihad*, August 23, 1957).

155. Somekh to MoI/Mins, October 3, 1957, ISA 56/G2220/27. See also the minutes from the September 30, 1957 meeting, ISA 62/G736/19. Six of the villages represented were populated exclusively by Druze or Circassians.

156. Quoting Meyer Weisgal, US chair of the international committee planning the celebrations, who attended the meeting in Haifa. See the file "Independence Week—Minorities 1957" and Hirschberg, MoR/Muslim and Druze Division to Weisgal, March 19, 1958, in ISA 62/G731/5.

157. AAA Divon to Peri, July 3, 1957, ISA 62/736/19; Divon to new subcommittee of civil and military Arabists established to coordinate with the World Committee, November 20, 1957; Landman to Divon, June 27, 1958; and the undated summary of activities through 1958 of the MoI/Mins, all in ISA 56/G2220/27. See also the local and regional celebration dates and sites (April 30–May 18), undated, ISA 62/G740/53. Copies of bilingual invitations are available in ISA 56/G2220/27.

158. Atallah Mansur, "Minority Exhibition in Acre," *New Outlook*, January 1959, 59–61.

159. Subcommittee meeting minutes, January 8, 1958; Y. Elisha, Information Office/Arab Department to Kafr Yasif Mayor Yani Yani, March 13, 1958, ISA 56/G2220/27. By 1957, less than one-third of Israel's 104 Palestinian locales were "represented" by any kind of body recognized by the Interior Ministry. Only half were democratically elected; military governors appointed the rest. In villages without a recognized council, the authorities worked with mukhtars and notables they deemed cooperative. At the time, 99 percent of the Jewish public enjoyed a political voice at the local level. Shalev, "Jewish Organized Labor," 107–108; Jiryis, *Arabs in Israel*, 220–226, 310; Ben-Porath, *Arab Labor Force*, 51–54; Schwarz, "Israel's Arab Minority," 23–27. Villages were instructed to submit detailed plans for their celebrations. See memos from Tamra and Baqa al-Gharbiyya as well as bilingual invitations to the celebrations from multiple villages in the Triangle and Galilee to the Interior Ministry in ISA 56/G2220/27.

160. Quoted in subcommittee meeting minutes, January 8, 1958, ISA 56/G2220/27. Outside Israel, the Arab League's Information Office helped to plant these seeds. Its first systematic bulletin on Israel's violations of international law, regional agreements, and the minorities' provisions of Resolution 181 (which the government deemed null because of its rejection by the Arab states one decade earlier) appeared in January 1957. Sayegh, *Record of Israel*.

161. Announcement, in English, in "Independence Week," ibid. In ISA, see meeting minutes, 62/736/19, and Y. Somekh, Haifa Minorities Officer to MoI/Minorities Division, 56/G2220/27, both dated October 3, 1957.

162. Palestinians had "frustrated the government's wishes . . . to forget the slaughtered people" (*al-Ittihad*, October 25, 1957).

163. *Al-Ittihad*, October 25, 1957.

164. *Al-Ittihad*, October 11, 1957.

165. Fu'ad Khuri, "Arab municipal and local councils," *al-Ittihad*, October 28, 1957.

166. *Al-Ittihad*, November 1, 1957. A total of eighteen people were arrested in Tayyibe, Umm al-Fahm, and Nazareth, including a twelve year-old boy.

167. See, for example, *ha-Arets* and *Davar*, October 30, 1957.

168. *Al-Ittihad*, November 1, 1957; *ha-Arets*, October 30, 1957.

169. Hoffman, *My Happiness*, 264.

170. Once comprising the majority of a thriving commercial and artisan center, Safad's historic Arab community fled in response to Haganah shelling in May 1948. Now populated only by Jews, the army also used the city as a temporary open prison to which it could banish "troublesome" Palestinian citizens. It was one of these banished citizens whom the defendants had gone to visit the day of their arrest.

171. "The spirit of 'Little Rock' in Israel: Safad is open to 'Jews' but forbidden to 'Arabs,'" *al-Ittihad*, January 24, 1958.

172. Afro-Asian People's Solidarity Organisation, 237. The Liberian delegate reportedly muted a stronger formulation of the final text. Levey, "Rise and Decline," 158–161.

173. Beinin, *Red Flag*, 216–217.

174. See, for example, "Israeli army blows up Ghabsiyya homes whose owners were dispersed. . . . Are our villages demolished for the sake of peace?" January 7, 1958; "On the anniversary of the Sinai withdrawal: Between 'the present' and the 'past,'" January 14, 1958.

175. Bäuml, "MAPAI Committee," 421–422.

176. A private casual gathering had occurred in Habibi's home in late January, but the Shin Bet offered no evidence for their claim. Beinin, *Red Flag*, 199–200. See also the Shin Bet report, "Minorities in Israel: Withdrawal of Arab MAKI activists from plan to establish a 'National Liberation Movement,'" February 26, 1958, in ISA 102/GL17013/9.

177. Fu'ad Khury, "City Council members: Beware of treason!" *al-Ittihad*, February 7, 1958.

178. *Al-Ittihad* reiterated this point in its April 15 and 22, 1958 editorials.

179. See clippings in a file entitled, "Self-determination for the Arabs," in ISA 102/GL17013/9.

180. The effort of Palestinian communists to maintain a united front and to reinforce their belief in "Arab-Jewish brotherhood" continued throughout the spring. For example, they condemned the authorities' refusal to allow Jewish activist Mordechai Caspi to attend what they called the largest open meeting in Nazareth's history. "They don't want Arabs to see any Jews except for military governors and uniformed cops." See "The people of Nazareth [push through] the police encirclement and demonstrate their solidarity with the Algerians and their support for their national rights," *al-Ittihad*, March 4, 1958. The following month, progressive Jewish attorneys in Tel Aviv hosted

Hanna Naqara for a lecture, "Discrimination against the Arab people in Israel in law and practice." See "Naqara lays bare to jurists the laws of land confiscation from peasants," *al-Ittihad*, April 4, 1958.

181. Juhayna, "Weekly column," *al-Ittihad*, March 21, 1958.

182. On the poetry of this period, see Nassar, "Affirmation and Resistance," especially 341–343.

183. "We are part of . . . Asia," attorney Hanna Naqara told the crowd before him in Haifa, "whether Ben-Gurion likes it or not" (Haifa correspondent, "Algerian solidarity meeting in Haifa," *al-Ittihad*, April 1, 1958).

184. "Tawfiq Tubi at popular meeting in Tamra," *al-Ittihad*, March 18, 1958. Also in the newspaper that spring, see Imil Tuma, "Is this big noise a sign?" February 21; Shmuel Mikunis, "On the campaign of incitement against the Israeli Communist Party," February 28; "The people of Nazareth [confront] the police encirclement and demonstrate their solidarity with the Algerians," and Editorial, "Does Ben-Gurion resist the rights of the Palestinian Arab people?" both March 4; and "'Arrabe is unafraid of police terror: Its people stand in solidarity with the Algerian people," March 7.

185. According to *ha-Arets*, the premier appointed the Rosen Commission because a growing number of Israelis saw it as a stain on the country's global image. On the Rosen Commission, which MAKI condemned as a charade to appease local and international opinion, see "Maneuver of appointing ministerial commission to examine the military government," *al-Ittihad*, March 21, 1958.

186. We must "hold on to our national dignity," implored one leaflet that MAKI distributed in the Triangle and that was reprinted in *al-Ittihad* on April 22, 1958. Editors urged readers to "expose the disgrace of the turncoats who fabricated the wishes of the people." See the April 25 and 29, 1958 issues.

187. See Ilyas Kusa's letter to the councils of Baqa al-Gharbiyya and a number of other villages planning region-wide celebrations, published on April 8, in *al-Ittihad*, and attached in Somekh to Landman, March 12, 1958, ISA 56/G2220/27. Kusa was a seasoned activist from the Mandate period. He advocated for Arabic language rights before and after 1948 (Suleiman, *Arabic, Self and Identity*, 24–30).

188. "They're competing . . . ," *al-Ittihad*, April 22, 1958.

189. Quoting *al-Ittihad*, April 25 and May 2, 1958, respectively.

190. Nimr Murqus, "Arab intellectuals are the sons of their people," *al-Ittihad*, April 18, 1958. Murqus was one of the few schoolteachers who identified himself by name during the boycott campaign.

191. *Al-Ittihad*, April 10, 1958.

192. The successful two-day strike of Rayna pupils reportedly convinced the principle to return the IL 70 that he had taken from the fund. *Al-Ittihad*, April 18, 1958.

193. Letter from Tayyibe, *al-Ittihad*, April 22, 1958.

194. On complaints from Nazareth, Shafa 'Amr, and Rame, see *al-Ittihad*, April 22,

1958. Criticism was also leveled at those planning to unveil two renovated mosques in Acre and Jaffa on the holiday, not least because the renovations had been paid for with stolen Islamic endowment funds. *al-Ittihad*, April 25, 1958.

195. *Al-Ittihad*, April 25, 1958.

196. *Al-Ittihad*, April 22, 25, and 29, 1958.

197. Rashid Husayn initially refused an order from the local governor responsible for his village, Musmus, to write a poem in honor of the holiday, but he changed his mind after his family was threatened. Husayn, *Kalam mu'zun*, 425–427. See also Ibrahim, "al-Dhikra al-'ashira."

198. See internal report of the MoI/Mins, dated April–June 1958, ISA 56/G2220/27.

199. *JTA*, May 1 and 2, 1958.

200. There is no agreement on the precise number of arrests. Jiryis (*Arabs in Israel*, 40–41) says that more than 350 people were arrested. At a cabinet meeting the following week, Minister of Police Bechor Shitrit cited a total number of 177 arrests. This included thirty-three people who were released immediately, twenty-two who were sentenced by the IDF Chief of Staff to three months in administrative detention, and ten banished by the military governor. See Israel Cabinet Protocols, May 11, 1958, ISA.

201. Quoting the April–June 1958 MoI/Mins report, cited in note 198.

202. Ibid. Reportedly ten thousand people visited the Druze village of 'Isfiyya and six thousand attended the celebration held at the Druze shrine of Nebi Shu'ayb. Regional celebrations were also held in the Galilee (at al-Maghar and Tamra) and the Triangle (Qalansuwa, Baqa al-Gharbiyya, and Tira). See also Government Information Office/Minorities to the World Committee of the Tenth Anniversary, April 12, 1958, ISA 62/G731/6, and *al-Yawm*'s descriptions of celebrations in Baqa al-Gharbiyya, Umm al-Fahm, and Tayyibe on April 30, May 5, and May 12, 1958. On tourists, see "Minorities' regional celebrations," April 1958, ISA 62/G731/6 and ISA 56/G2220/27. In May 1958, the agency estimated that a total of fifteen thousand tourists had visited Israel that spring. *al-Yawm*, May 8, 1958.

203. U. Oren, "Kfar Kassem celebrates the anniversary," *Ma'ariv*, May 16, 1958.

204. In early May, for example, a salon owner in Ramat Gan, near Tel Aviv, reportedly threw a Tayyibe resident out of his shop, declaring "Get out—we do not cut the hair of Arabs!" and "Your money is from Nasser," and hurling epithets against the Prophet Mohammed and all Arabs. When the man went to the local police station to report the incident, the officer on duty warned him to go home rather than face the officer's own insults. See "During the days of 'the celebrations,'" *al-Ittihad*, May 2, 1958, which also reported the story of two police officers who stopped a hitchhiker in the Galilee on the pretense of offering him a ride home and then told him they preferred his death. At a meeting in the late summer or early fall of 1958, members of the Ihud Association discussed an incident in which a group of military police stopped a bus en route from Nazareth to Haifa. Upon entering the bus they shouted, "All Arabs, get out!" and

then lined them up outside to check their papers. See Dr. H. Strauss, "Ta'arukhat folklor ha-mi'utim be-yisra'el," *NER* (October–November 1958): 27. For more in *al-Ittihad*, see "Repetition of police attacks on Arab citizens in Wadi Nisnas," September 12, 1958; and Mohammad Khass, "Pins," January 27, 1959, on reports of racist jokes told by a Tel Aviv high school teacher.

205. In *al-Ittihad*, see, for example, "Attack on Arab workers to force them to ride bus to their village standing," March 25, 1958; "Egged employee provokes workers from Umm al-Fahm" and Hanna Ibrahim, "The story behind the strike against the Egged busses," August 5, 1958; and "The racist tendencies of Egged employees almost led to clashes and a disaster causing the death of passengers," July 28, 1959. In November 1959, these tensions burst when workers from Shafa 'Amr threw rocks at an Egged bus and the police. Seventy-seven of them were later convicted in court. See Israel Police HQ, "Disturbances in Shafa 'Amr, November 8, 1959," in ISA 79/L431/7.

206. Tuma, *Thirty years*, 235. Of that group, ninety-four were eventually convicted and imprisoned, and sixteen were banished to Safad.

207. One factor that led to the ruling was the impression left by the files of at least ten other previously classified cases in which soldiers involved in the murder of Arab civilians claimed that they had been merely "following orders" (Aviv Lavie and Moshe Gorali, "I saw fit to remove her").

208. See Linenberg, "Parashat Kfar Kassem," and the compilation of editorials and letters to the editor in *Hoveh* 2, December 1959, in ISA 105/2214/293.

209. *Al-Ittihad*, October 21, 1958, and October 27, 1961. The top three officers found responsible for the crime—Shmuel Malinki, Gabriel Dahan, and Shalom Ofer—were sentenced to fifteen, fifteen, and seventeen years, respectively. Years later, they claimed that Ben-Gurion told them personally that they were being made into the sacrificial lambs of the state. Ofer claimed they were made to sign forms of secrecy upon their release. Karpel, "Yes, we are from the same village," and "The massacre."

210. MAKI Central Committee, *Kfar Kassem*; *al-Ittihad*, October 14, 1958.

211. Darwish, "He Who Kills Fifty Arabs Loses One Piaster," in *Ordinary Grief*, 75–95.

212. Dahan was appointed head of Arab Affairs in the mixed city of Ramle, but the opposition of several city council members forced him to resign months later. He then moved to Paris to live a more anonymous life selling Israeli bonds. Malinki was appointed chief of security at Israel's nuclear plant in Dimona. Ofer also received a job in security. Haim Levy, Malinki's company commander who directly oversaw Dahan but was in Jaljulya the night of the massacre and was never brought to trial, was later promoted to chief of Border Guard and Prison Systems. Habibi, *Kafr Qasim*, 75–78; Karpel, "The massacre."

213. Tawfiq Zayyad, "Lan nansa," *al-Ittihad*, October 28, 1960, cited in Nassar, "Affirmation and Resistance," 215.

214. Robinson, "Local Struggle."

215. Soon thereafter, several young men told a reporter from *al-Ittihad* that "you will still find many people who are scared of you [MAKI] and . . . some of the others." But they also expressed their outrage that Dahan had been released and then hired as the advisor on Arab affairs in Ramle. "He's in charge of security. The murder of our people [was seen] in the interests of security!" (*al-Ittihad*, October 28, 1960; see also the newspaper's October 31, 1961 and November 3, 1963 issues.) Until that year, villagers had been too frightened to do anything more than gather for intimate ceremonies at the mosque and place flowers on the tombstones of the slain. Interviews with 'Amr 'Asfur, 'Adil Budayr, Isma'il 'Aqab Mahmud Budayr, and 'Ali Salim Sarsur.

216. The public awareness campaign of activists like Hanna Naqara, who in January 1958 had reached out to Jewish lawyers to speak to them about the formal and informal mechanisms of discrimination faced by the Arab minority, also played a role in this process. "Naqara lays bare."

217. Jiryis, *Arabs in Israel*, 38–40; H. Baruch, "Facing the 180,000: How does the military government work?" *Davar*, August 1, 1958; *State Comptroller's Report on Security for Financial Year 1957/1958* (Jerusalem: Government of Israel, February 1959), cited in Jiryis (Ibid.)

218. Bäuml, "Military Government," 51.

219. Bäuml, "Yahaso shel ha-mimsad," provides the most detailed account of this shift in government attitudes to date.

220. Shalev, "Jewish Organized Labor," 107–110. The subordination of Arab labor to Jewish labor was maintained long after the permit system through a combination of local employment ordinances and housing bans that ensured that Palestinians would nearly always be the first to be dismissed during a downturn. Jiryis, *Arabs in Israel*, 220–226; Greenberg, *Race and State*, 376; Rosenfeld, "Class Situation," 387; Shalev, "Jewish Organized labor," 108–110; Shahak, *Civil Rights*.

221. Lauren, "Seen from the Outside;" Pearson, "Theorizing Citizenship;" Irwin, "Apartheid on Trial;" Schwelb, "International Convention."

222. Yigal Allon, who played a pivotal role in depopulating the Galilee in 1948, was particularly candid in warning his colleagues not to justify military rule on grounds that resembled excuses offered for racial segregation in South Africa and the American south. See *Masakh shel hol*, 321–326.

223. See, for example, Ze'ev Schiff, "If I were an Arab," *ha-Arets*, April 4, 1961, cited in Jiryis, *Arabs in Israel*, 253; Serge Groussard, "Israel, Ben-Gurion, and the Arabs," *Le Figaro*, January 5–6, 1962; "What do they want from this bloody provocation?" *al-Ittihad* editorial, January 23, 1962; and "Where is this freedom," *al-Ittihad* editorial, September 7, 1962.

224. This was one of the reasons Tawfiq Tubi attacked the station as "imperialist." See MFA/Middle East, "Voice of Israel Responses," July–December 1959, in ISA 130/HZ3742/6. On Sharpeville, see Mohammad Khass, "Pins," *al-Ittihad*, April 5, 1960. In April 1961, Ben-

Gurion's new advisor on Arab Affairs drew directly on the vocabulary of the apartheid regime to express his regret that "the Arabs [had not] remained hewers of wood." Schiff, "If I were an Arab."

225. See, for example, Hadawi, *Israel and the Arab Minority*.

226. See, for example, the November 10, 1960 letter from Jabbur Yusif Jabbur, mayor of Shafa 'Amr, and nine other Palestinian intellectuals and activists not associated with the Communist Party, included in a pamphlet published in October 1961 entitled "Violations of Human Rights in Israel," in "Items-in-Peacekeeping Operations-Middle East-general-public, correspondence (UNEF Withdrawal)," S-0861-0001-03-00001, 66-87, http://archives-trim.un.org/webdrawer/rec/423777. In the *New York Times*, see "Israel Ridicules Colonial Charge," October 18, 1960; and Tariq Jabri, "Malpractices Against Arabs of Israel Quite Similar to Apartheid," September 30, 1961.

227. *JTA*, November 8, 1961. "South Africa does not want to oppress," wrote President Verwoerd; "it wants to differentiate." Verwoerd reiterated the similarities between the two states in 1963, after Israel withdrew its diplomatic representative from South Africa. "So. Africa Jews Welcome Premier's Call Against Anti-Jewish Feelings," *JTA*, October 1, 1963.

228. F. Sayegh, *Information Paper*; El-Khawas, "Africa and the Middle Eastern Crisis." Not surprisingly, *al-Ittihad* closely monitored these developments. See, for example, Mohammad Khass, "Pins: On the racism of Israeli rulers," *al-Ittihad*, October 6, 1962; Tawfiq Tubi, "Government crisis in Israel caused by a stupid policy that should be changed," January 15, 1965; and Editors, "Israeli delegate opposes expulsion of South Africa from the World Health Organization! Yemeni delegate condemns discrimination in Israel," June 4, 1965.

229. Beinin, *Red Flag*, 224–225; Abu Sitta, *Financing Racism*.

230. Morris and Black, *Israel's Secret Wars*, 142, 166–167.

231. Bäuml, "ha-Mimshal ha-tsva'i," 147–149.

232. Quoted in ibid., 144–147.

233. Segev, *1967*.

CONCLUSION

1. Carter, *Palestine*. The quote is excerpted from Carter's comments on WNYC's Leonard Lopate Show, December 12, 2006. Pacifica's "Democracy Now" broadcast similar comments on November 30, 2006. See also Carter's op-ed, "Speaking Frankly About Israel and Palestine," *Los Angeles Times*, December 8, 2006.

2. For an overview, see Agbaria and Mustafa, "Two States for Three Peoples." On education, see Human Rights Watch, *Second Class*.

3. Adalah, "The Democratic Constitution."

4. On the comments from the board of the Israel Democracy Institute, see Isabel Kershner, "Noted Arab Citizens Call on Israel to Shed Jewish Identity," *New York Times*,

February 8, 2007. On evocations of war in *Haaretz*, see Moshe Arens, "Same Ends, Different Means," February 13, 2007; Meron Benvenisti, "Threats of the Future Vision," December 17, 2006; Avi Sagi and Yedidia Stern, "We Are Not Strangers in Our Homeland," March 23, 2007; and Avraham Tal, "This Means War," December 9, 2006. The term *joint homeland* comes from Adalah's "The Democratic Constitution."

5. Meron Benvenisti, "Threats of the Future Vision," *Haaretz*, December 17, 2006.

6. Yoav Stern, "Prime Minister's Office to Balad: We Will Thwart Anti-Israel Activity Even If Legal," *Haaretz*, March 16, 2007.

7. Ibid.

8. Wolfe, "Elimination of the Native," 398.

9. "New names added to blacklist," *al-Ittihad*, August 9, 1968.

10. See the amendment to the Basic Law: The Knesset—1958, available at http://www.knesset.gov.il/laws/special/eng/basic2_eng.htm/.

11. Cook, "Myth;" Kedar, "First Step."

12. Stein, *Itineraries in Conflict*.

13. A. Zohar, "Muhammad and Mustafa [don't] celebrate Independence Day," *Hed ha-Krayot*, May 4, 1990; "Tayyibe Local Council chair surprises the guests at the ceremony to make toasts: Calls to liberate the Land Day detainees on the occasion of Independence Day," *Davar*, April 27, 1990; "Poll: 28 Percent of Israeli Arabs Celebrate Independence Day: Report Shows Trend Toward Integration," *Jerusalem Post*, May 7, 1995 (see similar reports from *Ma'ariv*, *ha-Tsofeh*, and *Yedi'ot Ahronot*, May 7, 1995); "Most Arab residents of the state satisfied with ha-Tikva [Israel's national anthem]," *Koteret Hefa*, May 12, 1995; Amir Gilat, "Israeli Arabs threaten: We snort at the events of Independence Day," *Ma'ariv*, April 17, 1996; Orna Yosef, "I was home when the siren sounded, but I didn't stand," *Kol ha-'Emek ve-ha-Galil*, May 16, 1997. See also Azmi Bishara, "Getting Your Victims to Love You," *al-Ahram Weekly*, October 25, 2007, available at http://weekly.ahram.org.eg/2007/868/op1.htm.

14. Ozacky-Lazar and Ghanem, *Or Testimonies*; Dalal and Rosenberg, *October 2000*.

15. Robinson, "My Hairdresser;" Neve Gordon, "Where Are the Peacenicks?" *The Nation*, April 29, 2002; Gideon Levy, "Practicing Apartheid—and Proud of It," *Mail and Guardian*, November 2, 2012, available at http://mg.co.za/article/2012-11-02-00-practising-apartheid-and-proud-of-it. See also http://mada-research.org/en/political-monitoring-report/.

16. Vered Lee, "Love in the Time of Racism: The New, Dangerous Low in the Campaign to Stop Interracial Relationships," *Haaretz*, April 25, 2013, available at http://www.haaretz.com/weekend/magazine/love-in-the-time-of-racism-the-new-dangerous-low-in-the-campaign-to-stop-interracial-relationships; Dimi Reider, "Tel Aviv presents: municipal program to prevent Arab boys from dating Jewish girls," *Coteret*, February 24, 2010, available at http://coteret.com/2010/02/24/tel-aviv-presents-municipal-program-to-prevent-arab-boys-from-dating-jewish-girls/.

17. Also, after the interior minister—for the first time since 1952—used his power to revoke the citizenship of three Palestinians for their suspected role in these attacks. See *al-Sinnara* (Nazareth), August 9, 2002; and Mazal Mu'alem, "I'm not Israeli, says Arab stripped of citizenship," *Haaretz*, September 12, 2002.

18. Adalah, "News Update."

19. Reprinted from *Yedi'ot Ahronot* at www.Arabs48.com, June 26, 2005. See also Gideon Alon, "Family Reunification Pared Down for Palestinian Spouses," Haaretz, July 28, 2005.

20. 'Awawdah, *Dhakira la tamut; Ma'lul tahtafil bi-dimariha* [Ma'lul celebrates its destruction]. In *al-Ittihad*, see April 27, May 4, May 12, and May 16, 2001.

21. The United Nations did not issue sanctions against South Africa until 1962. Dubow, "Rhetoric of Race and Rights."

22. On the "salt water" or "blue water" thesis of decolonization, see Österud, "Narrow Gate"; Churchill, "Reinscription"; and Wolfe, *Corpus Nullius*, 131. On the precursors to the UN's decision to exclude landlocked indigenous minorities, see Anaya, *Indigenous Peoples*, 76; Kuntz, "Chapter XI," 108–109; Wright, "Recognition," 27–28; and Thornberry, "Self-Determination," 868–873.

BIBLIOGRAPHY

ARCHIVAL COLLECTIONS

Acre Municipal Archive, Acre
Israel Defense Forces and Defense Establishment Archives (IDFA), Givatayim
Givat-Haviva Research and Documentation Center (GH), Menashe
Histadrut Archives, Lavon Institute, Tel Aviv
Israel State Archives (ISA), Jerusalem

    Cabinet Meeting Protocols
    Committee for the Tenth Anniversary of the State of Israel (RG 62)
    Ministry of Education (RG 71)
    Ministry of Foreign Affairs, Middle East Division (RG 130)
    Ministry of Interior, Minorities Division (RG 56)
    Ministry of Interior, Ramle District (RG 85)
    Ministry of Justice (RG 74)
    Ministry of Minorities (RG 49)
    Ministry of Police (RG 79)
    Office of the Prime Minister's Advisor on Arab Affairs (RG 102)
    President's Papers (RG 105)
    Prime Minister's Bureau (RG 43)

Jewish National and University Library, Jerusalem
Kafr Qasim Municipal Archives
National Photo Collection, Israel Government Press Office (GPO)
Palestine Poster Project Archives (PPPA), http://www.palestineposterproject.org
Private Papers of Ruvik Rosenthal
United Studios of Israel, Herzliya

GOVERNMENTAL AND INTERGOVERNMENTAL PUBLICATIONS

Afro-Asian People's Solidarity Organisation. *Afro-Asian Peoples' Solidarity Conference: Cairo, December 26, 1957–January 1, 1958*. Moscow: Foreign Languages Publishing House, 1958.

Ammoun, Charles. *Study of Discrimination in Education*. Special Rapporteur of the Sub-committee on the Prevention of Discrimination. New York: United Nations, 1957.

Ben-Gurion, David. *Yoman ha-milhamah: Milhemet ha-'atsma'ut, 1947–1949* [War diary: The war of independence, 1947–1949], vol. 3. Tel Aviv: Israel Ministry of Defense, 1982.

Council of the League of Nations, Nineteenth Session. *Mandate for Palestine*. Geneva, August 12, 1922 (C. 529. M. 314. 1922. VI).

Divre ha-Knesset [Knesset proceedings]. Yerushalayim: Knesset, 1949.

Government of Palestine. *1925 Order in Council*, July 24, 1925.

Hope Simpson, John. *Palestine: Report on Immigration, Land Settlement and Development*, 1930, Cmd. 3686 at ch. III. London: His Majesty's Stationery Office.

Israel Law Resource Center, *Laws of the State of Israel*, 2007. Available at http://www.israellawresourcecenter.org.

Israel Ministry of Foreign Affairs, Information Department. *The Arabs in Israel*. Jerusalem: Israel Ministry for Foreign Affairs, 1952, 1955, 1958, 1961, August 1966, and March 1968.

Kohn, Yehuda Pinhas. *Hukah le-yisra'el: Hatsa'ah ve-divre hesber* [A constitution for Israel: A proposal and explanatory notes]. Tel Aviv: Government of Israel, 1949.

League of Arab States. *Report on the Persecution of the Arabs in Israel*. Cairo: League of Arab States, 1955.

Sayegh, Fayez A. *Record of Israel at the United Nations*. New York: Arab Information Center, 1957.

———. *The Arab-Israeli Conflict*. New York: Arab Information Office, 1964.

Selected Judgments of the Supreme Court of Israel 1954–1958. Edited by E. David Goitein. Jerusalem: Justice Ministry, 1963.

State of Israel. "Declaration of Independence." Available at http://www.knesset.gov.il/docs/eng/megilat_eng.htm.

Statistical Abstracts of Israel, 1959–1966. Tel Aviv: Central Bureau of Statistics, 1966.

United Nations, Department of Public Information. *Yearbook of the United Nations 1946–1947*. New York: United Nations, December 31, 1947.

United Nations General Assembly, Ad Hoc Committee on the Palestinian Question. *Memorandum by His Britannic Majesty's Government, Communicated from the United Kingdom Delegation to the United Nations*. October 2, 1947 (A/AC.14/8). Available at http://unispal.un.org/UNISPAL.NSF/0/16B8C7CC809B7E5B8525694B0071 F3BD.

United Nations General Assembly, Forty-Fifth Meeting. *Application of Israel for Admission to Membership in the United Nations* (A/818). May 5, 1949 (A/AC.24/SR.45). Available at http://unispal.un.org/UNISPAL.NSF/0/1DB943E43C280A26052565FA004D8174.

United Nations General Assembly, Second Session. Special Committee on Palestine. *Summary Record of the Eighth Meeting*, June 17, 1947. Available at http://unispal.un.org/unispal.nsf/9a798adbf322aff38525617b006d88d7/7651f1007d32b88e852575ad006 8ce3c?OpenDocument.

———. "Special Note by Sir Abdur Rahman," *Report Addendum 1*, October 3, 1947 (A/364

Add. 1). Available at http://unispal.un.org/UNISPAL.NSF/o/FB6DD3FoE9535815 852572 DDoo6CC607.

————. *Verbatim Records of the Nineteenth Meeting*, July 7, 1947 (A/364/Add.2 PV.19); *of the Thirtieth Meeting*, July 14, 1947 (A/AC.13/PV.30); *of the Thirty-Second Meeting*, July 15, 1947 (A/AC.13/PV.32); and *of the Thirty-Fifth Meeting*, July 17, 1947 (A/AC.13/PV.35). All available at http://unispal.un.org/unispal.nsf/udc.htm.

United Nations General Assembly, Third Session. *Summary Record of the 207th Plenary Meeting*, May 11, 1949 (A/PV.207). Available at http://unispal.un.org/UNISPAL.NSF/ 9a798adbf322aff38525617boo6d88d7/ob3ab8d2a7c0273d8525694b00726d1b?Open Document&Highlight=0,A%2FPV.207.

————. *Resolution 273: Admission of Israel to Membership in the United Nations*, May 11, 1949 (A/RES/273 [III]). Available at http://unispal.un.org/UNISPAL.NSF/o/83E8C2 9DB812A4E9852560E50067A5AC.

United Nations Security Council, Third Year. *385th Meeting*, December 17, 1948 (S/PV.385). Available at http://unispal.un.org/UNISPAL.NSF/9a798adbf322aff38525617boo6d88d 7/437dd877e349151b052566ce006d9189?OpenDocument&Highlight=0,S%2FPV.385.

NAMED INTERVIEWS

Muhammad 'Abd al-Raziq Adawi, Tur'an, February 21, 2002.

Abd al-Karim Abu Ra's, Tayyibe, June 9, 2002.

Muhammad Abu Ra's, Tayyibe, March 2, 2002.

Najla Abu Ra's, Tayyibe, March 3, 2002.

Najma and Zlaykha Abu Yunis, Sakhnin, July 13, 2002.

Nicola 'Aqlah, Nazareth, November 14, 2001.

Shukri 'Araaf, Mi'ilya, February 17, 2002.

'Amr 'Asfur, Kafr Qasim, September 6, 1998.

Fathiyya 'Awaysa, Nazareth, September 5, 2002.

Yusif Fadil Basyuni and Inshirah Sa'id, Nazareth, November 14, 2001.

'Adil Budayr, Kafr Qasim, September 7, 1998.

Isma'il 'Aqab Mahmud Budayr, Kafr Qasim, August 31, 2002.

Efrayim Ben-Natan, Afula, August 8, 2002.

Latif Dori, Tel Aviv, September 8, 1998.

Zvi Elpeleg, Tel Aviv, August 12, 2002.

Shlomo Gazit, Tel Aviv University, August 23, 2006.

Haim Hefer, Tel Aviv, September 3, 2002.

Aziz Haidar, Jerusalem, May 27, 2002.

Imm Hisham, 'Arrabe, August 3, 2002.

Imm Mahmud, Sakhnin, June 29, 2002.

Salim Kana'ane, 'Arrabe, August 3, 2002.

Nuzhat Katsav, Ramat Gan, February 14, 2002.

Ibtihaj Khuri, Acre, February 19, 2002.

Samira Khuri, Nazareth, November 15, 2001.
Esther Malul, telephone conversation, Tel Aviv, September 10, 2003.
Nabiha Murqus, Kafr Yasif, February 18, 2002.
Nimr Murqus, Kafr Yasif, February 18, 2002.
Eliahu Nawwi, Tel Aviv, November 27, 2001.
Odette Nimr, Nazareth, September 5, 2002.
Mustafa Rabi'a, Jaljulya, June 8, 2002.
Wasfiyya Salim Ramadan, Acre, July 11, 2002.
Ghazi Sa'di, Tira, August 31, 2002.
Zuhayra Sabbagh, Nazareth, August 15, 2001.
Kamil Mahmud Salim, Acre, July 11, 2002.
'Ali Salim Sarsur, Kafr Qasim, September 6, 1998.
Ibrahim Sarsur, Kafr Qasim, September 6, 1998.
Tawfiq Tubi, Haifa, September 17, 1998.
Misbah Amin Zayyad, Nazareth, November 15, 2001.
Wajih Zand, Mi'ilya, June 28, 2002.

MAGAZINES, NEWSPAPERS, AND NEWS DIGESTS

Arabic

Fasl al-Maqal (Nazareth)
Haqiqat al-Amr (Tel Aviv)
al-Hayat (Beirut)
al-Ittihad (Haifa)
al-Jadid (Haifa)
al-Mirsad (Tel Aviv)
al-Sinnara (Nazareth)
al-Yawm (Tel Aviv)

English

Al-Ahram Weekly (Cairo)
Atlantic Monthly
Commentary (New York)
Foreign Affairs (Washington, DC)
Haaretz (English translation of *ha-Arets*)
Harpers Magazine (New York)
Jerusalem Post
Los Angeles Times
New Outlook (Tel Aviv)
New York Times
Jewish Telegraph Agency (New York)
The Forward (New York)

Hebrew

'Al ha-Mishmar (Tel Aviv)

ha-Arets and *Musaf ha-Arets* (Tel Aviv)

ha-Boker (Tel Aviv)

ba-Mahaneh: 'Iton Hayyale Yisra'el (Tel Aviv)

ha-'Olam ha-Zeh (Tel Aviv)

Beterem (Tel Aviv)

Koteret Hefa (Haifa)

Koteret Rashit (Jerusalem)

Davar (Tel Aviv)

Hed ha-Hinukh (Tel Aviv)

Hed ha-Krayot (Haifa)

ha-Herut (Jerusalem)

ha-'Ir (Tel Aviv)

Kol ha-'Am (Tel Aviv)

Kol ha-'Emek ve-ha-Galil (Upper Nazareth)

Ma'ariv (Tel Aviv)

Ma'arakhot (Tel Aviv)

la-Merhav (Tel Aviv)

Mibifnim ('Ein Harod)

'Omer (Tel Aviv)

NER: Monthly for Political and Social Problems for Jewish Arab Rapprochement (Jerusalem)

ha-Tsofeh (Jerusalem)

Yedi'ot Ahronot (Tel Aviv)

FILM AND MUSIC

Ani Ahmad [I am Ahmad]. Directed by Ram Loevy and Avshalom Katz. Tel Aviv: Ram Loevy Communications, 1966.

Forbidden Marriages in the Holy Land. Directed by Michel Khleifi. London: Sindibad, in association with Sourat Films, the Jerusalem Film Institute, and the Peace Media Programme of the European Commission, 1996.

ha-Yomanim shel Yosef Nahmani [The diaries of Yossef Nachmani]. Directed by Dalia Karpel. Tel Aviv: Transfax, 2005.

Istiqlal [Independence]. Directed by Nizar Hassan. Tel Aviv: Keshet, 1994.

Ma'lul tahtafil bi-dimariha [Ma'lul celebrates its destruction]. Directed by Michel Khleifi. Brussels: Marisa, in association with Centre de l'Audiovisuel à Bruxelles, 1985.

Revi'iyat Mo'adon ha-Te'atron [Theater Club Quartet]. "Moshlim tsva'iyim" [Military governors]. In *Shire ha-Frere Jacques* [Songs of Frere Jacques]. Holon: ABCD Music, 1977.

Wedding in Galilee. Directed by Michel Khleifi. Bruxelles: Marisa Films, 1987.

OTHER WORKS

Aaronsohn, Ran. "Settlement in Eretz Israel—A Colonialist Enterprise? 'Critical' Scholarship and Historical Geography." *Israel Studies* 1, no. 2 (Fall 1996): 214–229.

Abu Sa'ad, Isma'el. "Forced Sedentarization, Land Rights and Indigenous Resistance: The Palestinian Bedouin in the Negev." In *Catastrophe Remembered: Palestine, Israel and the Internal Refugees*, edited by Nur Masalha, 113–141. London: Zed Books, 2005.

Abadi, Jacob. "Algeria's Policy Toward Israel: Pragmatism and Rhetoric." *Middle East Journal* 56, no. 4 (Autumn 2002): 616–641.

———. *Israel's Quest for Recognition and Acceptance in Asia: Garrison State Diplomacy.* London: Frank Cass, 2004.

Abdo, Nahla, and Nira Yuval-Davis. "Palestine, Israel and the Zionist Settler Project." In *Unsettling Settler Societies: Articulations of Gender, Race, Ethnicity, and Class*, edited by Daiva Stasiulis and Nira Yuval-Davis, 291–322. London: Sage, 1995.

Abrams, Philip. "Notes on the Difficulty of Studying the State." *Journal of Historical Sociology* 1, no. 1 (1988): 58–89.

Abu El-Haj, Nadia. *Facts on the Ground: Archaeological Practice and Territorial Self-Fashioning in Israeli Society.* Chicago: University of Chicago Press, 2001.

Abu Lughod, Ibrahim. "The Pitfalls of Palestiniology." *Arab Studies Quarterly* 34, no. 4 (1981): 403–411.

Abu Sitta, Salman. *Dividing War Spoils: Israel's Seizure, Confiscation of Sale and Palestinian Property.* London: Palestine Land Society, 2009.

———. *Financing Racism and Apartheid: Jewish National Fund's Violation of International and Domestic Law.* London: Palestine Land Society, 2005. Available at http:// www.plands.org.

Adalah—The Legal Center for Arab Minority Rights in Israel. "News Update: Adalah to Supreme Court: Freeze Implementation of Ban on Family Unification Law and Issue Urgent Decision on Petition Challenging Its Constitutionality." August 4, 2005.

Agassi, Joseph. *Liberal Nationalism in Israel: Towards an Israeli National Identity.* 1st English ed. Jerusalem: Gefen, 1999.

Agbaria, Ayman K., and Muhanad Mustafa, "Two States for Three Peoples: The 'Palestinian-Israeli' in the Future Vision Documents of the Palestinians in Israel." *Ethnic and Racial Studies* 35, no. 4 (April 2012): 718–736.

Al Haj, Majid. *Education, Empowerment and Control: The Case of the Arabs in Israel.* Albany: SUNY Press, 1995.

Al-Haj, Majid, and Henry Rosenfeld. *Arab Local Government in Israel.* Boulder, CO: Westview Press, 1990.

Allon, Yigal. *Masakh shel hol: Yisra'el ve-'arav ben milhamah le-shalom* [Curtain of sand: Israel and the Arabs between war and peace]. Tel Aviv: ha-Kibbutz ha-Meuhad, 1959.

Anaya, S. James. *Indigenous Peoples in International Law*, 2nd ed. New York: Oxford University Press, (1996) 2004.

Al-Asmar, Fouzi. *Through the Hebrew Looking Glass: Arab Stereotypes in Children's Literature*. New York: St. Martin's Press, 1986.

―――. *To Be an Arab in Israel*. London: Frances Pinter, 1975.

Almog, Oz. *The Sabra: The Creation of the New Jew*. Translated by Haim Watzman. Berkeley: University of California Press, 2000.

Anderson, Maxwell, Alan Paton, and Menashe Levin. *Avudim ben ha-kokhavim: Mahazeh bi-shete ma'rakhot* [Lost in the stars: A play in two acts]. Tel Aviv: Habimah, 1953.

Anderson, Perry. "Agendas for a Radical History." *Radical History Review*, no. 36 (September 1986): 32–37.

Anghie, Antony. "Colonialism and the Birth of International Institutions: Sovereignty, Economy, and the Mandate System of the League of Nations." *NYU Journal of International Law and Politics* 34, no. 3 (2002): 513–633.

Appadurai, Arjun. *Fear of Small Numbers: An Essay on the Geography of Anger*. Durham, NC: Duke University Press, 2006.

Arendt, Hannah. *The Origins of Totalitarianism*. San Diego: Harcourt, 1994 (1973).

Asad, Talal. *Genealogies of Religion: Discipline and Reasons of Power in Christianity and Islam*. Baltimore: Johns Hopkins University Press, 1993.

Avineri, Shlomo. "Theodor Herzl's Diaries as a Bildungsroman." *Jewish Social Studies* 5, no. 3 (1999): 1–46.

'Awawdah, Wadi'. *Dhakira la tamut: Shuhud 'ayan fatahu qulubihim wa-hajarat dhakiratihim li-yarwu ma jara lahum fi al-1948; 'am al-nakba* [Memory does not die: Eyewitnesses open their hearts and the chambers of their memory to recall what happened to them in 1948; the year of the catastrophe]. Haifa: al-Jalil li-l-Tiba'a wa-l-Tajlid, 2001.

Baer, Mark. *The Dönme: Jewish Converts, Muslim Revolutionaries, and Secular Turks*. Stanford, CA: Stanford University Press, 2009.

Baransi, Salih. "The Story of a Palestinian Under Occupation." *Journal of Palestine Studies* 11, no. 1 (August 1981): 3–30.

Bar-On, Raphael Raymond. "Megamot ba-tayarut le-yisra'el" [Trends in Israeli tourism]. In Klein, *ha-Milyon ha-sheni*, 40–47.

Bashar, Muhammad Amin. *Saffuriya: Tarikh hadara wa-turath* [Saffuriya: History, civilization, and heritage]. 2 vols. Nazareth: Maktab al-Nawras li-l-Inma' al-Tarbawi, 2000.

Bashkin, Orit. *The Other Iraq: Pluralism, Intellectuals and Culture in Hashemite Iraq, 1921–1958*. Stanford, CA: Stanford University Press, 2009.

Bäuml, Yair. "Mapai Committee for Arab Affairs: The Steering Committee for Construction of Establishment Policy Towards Israeli Arabs, 1958–1968." *Middle Eastern Studies* 47, no. 2 (March 2011): 413–433.

―――. "The Military Government." *Jadal* 1 (January 2009): 46–54.

―――. "ha-Mimshal ha-tsva'i ve-tahalikh bitulo, 1958–1968" [The military government on the Arabs in Israel and the process of its revocation, 1958–1968]. *ha-Mizrah he-Hadash* [The New East] 43 (2002): 133–156.

————. *Tsel kahol lavan: mediniyut ha-mimsad ha-yisra'eli ve-pe'ulotav be-kerev ha-ezrahim ha-'aravim; ha-shanim ha-me'atsvot, 1958–1968* [A blue and white shadow: The Israeli establishment's policy and actions among its Arab citizens; The formative years, 1958–1968]. Haifa: Pardes, 2007.

Beinart, Peter. *The Crisis of Zionism.* New York: Henry Holt, 2012.

Beinin, Joel. *The Dispersion of Egyptian Jewry.* Berkeley: University of California Press, 1998.

————. "Forgetfulness for Memory: The Limits of the New Israeli History." *Journal of Palestine Studies* 34, no. 2 (Winter 2005): 6–23.

————. "Israel at Forty: The Political Economy and Political Culture of Constant Conflict." *Arab Studies Quarterly* 10, no. 4 (1988): 433–456.

————. *Was the Red Flag Flying There? Marxist Politics and the Arab-Israeli Conflict in Egypt and Israel, 1948–1965.* Berkeley: University of California Press, 1990.

Ben-Ami, Shlomo. *Scars of War, Wounds of Peace: The Israeli-Arab Tragedy.* Oxford: Oxford University Press, 2006.

Ben-Dor, Yisrael. "Merts 1948: Dimuye ha-'aravim be-sh'at ha-shefel shel ha-yeshuv ha-yehudi be-milhemet ha-'atsma'ut" [March 1948: Images of Arabs at the low point of the Yishuv during the war of independence]. *Ruah Mizrahit* [Eastern Wind] 6 (April 2008): 12–17.

Ben-Eliezer, Uri. *The Making of Israeli Militarism.* Bloomington: University of Indiana Press, 1998.

————. "A Nation-in-Arms: State, Nation, and Militarism in Israel's First Years." *Comparative Studies in Society and History* 37, no. 2 (1995): 264–285.

————. "State Versus Civil Society? A Non-Binary Model of Domination Through the Example of Israel." *Journal of Historical Sociology* 11, no. 3 (1998): 370–396.

Ben-Gurion, David. "'Al ha-mi'ut ha-'aravi, ha-mi'ut ha-druzi ve-ha-mimshal ha-tsva'i: pirsum rishon mi-tokh yoman Ben Gurion" [The Arab minority, the Druze minority, and the military government: The first publication from Ben-Gurion's diary]. *'Iyunim ba-Tkumat Yisrael* [Studies in the Revival of Israel] 2 (1992): 449–454.

————. "Letter from David Ben-Gurion to His Son Amos, written October 5, 1937." Translated in *Journal of Palestine Studies* 41, no. 2 (Winter 2012): 245–250. Available at http://www.palestine-studies.org/files/B-G%20Letter%20translation.pdf.

————. *Rebirth and Destiny of Israel.* Edited and translated by Mordekhai Nurock. New York: Philosophical Library, 1954.

Ben-Porath, Yoram. *The Arab Labor Force in Israel.* Jerusalem: Maurice Falk Institute for Economic Research in Israel, October 1966.

Ben Shlomo, S. "The Arab Village." *NER* 12, nos. 7–8 (May–June 1961): v–xi.

Ben-Ze'ev, Efrat, and Edna Lomsky-Feder. "The Canonical Generation: Trapped Between Personal and National Memories." *Sociology* 43, no. 6 (2009): 1–19.

Bentwich, Norman. "Nationality in Mandated Territories Detached from Turkey." *British Yearbook of International Law* 97, no. 7 (1926): 97–109.

Benvenisti, Meron. *Sacred Landscape: The Buried History of the Holy Land Since 1948*. Berkeley: University of California Press, 2000.

Benziman, Uzi, and Atallah Mansour. *Dayare mishneh: 'Arviye yisra'el, ma'amadam ve-ha-mediniyut klapehem* [Subtenants: The Arabs of Israel, their status, and the policies toward them]. Jerusalem: Keter, 1992.

Berger, Mark T. "After the Third World? History, Destiny and the Fate of Third Worldism." *Third World Quarterly* 25, no. 1 (2004): 9–39.

Berkowitz, Michael. *Western Jewry and the Zionist Project, 1914–1933*. Cambridge: Cambridge University Press, 1997.

Bernstein, Deborah, and Shlomo Swirsky. "The Rapid Economic Development of Israel and the Emergence of the Ethnic Division of Labour." *British Journal of Sociology* 33, no. 1 (March 1982): 64–85.

Bishara, Azmi. "Israeli Arabs: Reading a Fragmented Political Discourse." *Al-Ahram Weekly*, February 5–11, 1998. Available at http://weekly/ahram.org.eg/1998/1948/363_bshr.htm.

———. "Jewishness Versus Democracy." *Al-Ahram Weekly*, October 28–November 3, 2004. Available at http://weekly.ahram.org.eg/2004/714/op63.htm.

Bordieu, Pierre. *Outline of a Theory of Practice*. 1st English ed. Cambridge: Cambridge University Press, 1999.

Boullata, Kamal, and Mirène Ghossein, eds. *The World of Rashid Hussein: A Palestinian Poet in Exile*. Detroit: Association of Arab-American University Graduates, 1979.

Bracha, Oren. "Safek miskenim, safek mesukanim: ha-mistanenim, ha-hok, ve-beit ha-mishpat ha-'elyon, 1948–1954" [Unfortunate or perilous: The infiltrators, the law and the High Court, 1948–1954]. *'Iyune Mishpat* [Tel Aviv University Law Review] 21, no. 333 (April 1998): 333–385.

Brower, Benjamin C. *A Desert Named Peace: The Violence of France's Empire in the Algerian Sahara, 1844–1902*. New York: Columbia University Press, 2009.

Brown, Wendy. *Regulating Aversion: Tolerance in the Age of Identity and Empire*. Princeton, NJ: Princeton University Press, 2008.

Bruegel, J. W. "The Right to Petition an International Authority." *International and Comparative Law Quarterly* 2, no. 4 (October 1953): 542–563.

Budeiri, Musa K. *The Palestine Communist Party, 1919–1948: Arab and Jew in the Struggle for Internationalism*. London: Ithaca Press, 1979.

Bushnaq, Inea. "Folklore." In *Encyclopedia of the Palestinians*, edited by Philip Mattar. New York: Facts on File, 2000.

Cagaptay, Soner. "Race, Assimilation and Kemalism: Turkish Nationalism and the Minorities in the 1930s." *Middle Eastern Studies* 40, no. 3 (May 2004): 86–101.

Campos, Michelle U. *Ottoman Brothers: Muslims, Christians, and Jews in Early Twentieth Century Palestine.* Stanford, CA: Stanford University Press, 2011.

Carmi, Na'ama. *Hok ha-shvut: Zkhuyot hagirah ve-gvulotehen* [The Law of Return: Immigration rights and their limits]. Tel Aviv: Tel Aviv University Press, 2003.

Carmi, Shulamit, and Henry Rosenfeld. "The Time When the Majority in the Israeli 'Cabinet' Decided 'Not to Block the Possibility of the Return of the Arab Refugees,' and How and Why This Policy Was Defeated." In *Land and Territoriality*, edited by Michael Saltman, 37–69. Oxford: Berg, 2002.

Carnegie Endowment for International Peace, and The Hebrew University. *Israel and the United Nations: Report of a Study Group Set Up by the Hebrew University of Jerusalem.* New York: Manhattan Publishing, 1956.

Carter, Jimmy. *Palestine: Peace Not Apartheid.* New York: Simon & Schuster, 2006.

Claude, Inis L. Jr. *National Minorities: An International Problem.* Cambridge, MA: Harvard University Press, 1955.

Cockrell, Alfred. "The South African Bill of Rights and the 'Duck/Rabbit.'" *Modern Law Review* 60, no. 4 (July 1997): 513–537.

Cohen, Hillel. *Army of Shadows: Palestinian Collaboration with Zionism, 1917–1948.* Translated by Haim Watzman. Berkeley: University of California Press, 2008.

———. *Good Arabs: The Israeli Security Agencies and the Israeli Arabs, 1948–1967.* Translated by Haim Watzman. Berkeley: University of California Press, 2009.

Comaroff, Jean, and John Comaroff. *Of Revelation and Revolution: Christianity, Colonialism, and Consciousness in South Africa.* 2 vols. Chicago: University of Chicago Press, 1991.

Comay, Joan. *Introducing Israel.* London: Methuen, 1962.

Conklin, Alice L. "Colonialism and Human Rights, a Contradiction in Terms? The Case of France and West Africa, 1895–1914." *American Historical Review* 103, no. 2 (1998): 419–442.

Connelly, Matthew. "Taking Off the Cold War Lens: Visions of North-South Conflict During the Algerian War for Independence." *American Historical Review* 105, no. 3 (June 2000): 739–769.

Cook, Jonathan. "The Myth of Israel's Liberal Supreme Court Exposed." *Middle East Report Online*, February 23, 2012. Available at http://www.merip.org/mero/mero 022312.

Cooper, Frederick. "A Parting of the Ways: Colonial Africa and South Africa, 1946–48." *African Studies* 65, no. 1 (2006): 27–43.

———. *Colonialism in Question: Theory, Knowledge, History.* Berkeley: University of California Press, 2005.

———. "Conflict and Connection: Rethinking Colonial African History." *American Historical Review* 99, no. 5 (December 1994): 1516–1545.

Cooper, Frederick, and Ann Laura Stoler, eds. *Tensions of Empire: Colonial Cultures in a Bourgeois World.* Berkeley: University of California Press, 1997.

Copty, Makram Izzat. "Knowledge and Power in Education: The Making of the Israeli Arab Educational System." PhD diss., University of Texas at Austin, December 1990.

Cordier, Andrew W., and Wilder Foote, eds. *Public Papers of the Secretaries General of the United Nations, 1956–1957.* New York: Columbia University Press, 1973.

Dagan, Sha'ul, and Avner Kozviner. *Palhib: Bedu'im ba-palmah bi-yme tashah* [The Hib Company: Bedouins in the Palmah in the days of 1948]. Haifa: Gestlit Haifa, 1993.

Dalal, Marwan, and Rina Rosenberg. *October 2000: Law and Politics Before the Or Commission of Inquiry.* Shafa'amr: Adalah—The Legal Center for Arab Minority Rights in Israel, 2003.

Dallasheh, Leena. "Nazarenes in the Turbulent Tide of Citizenships: Nazareth from 1940 to 1966." PhD diss., New York University, 2012.

———. "Political Mobilization of Palestinians in Israel: The al-Ard Movement." In *Displaced at Home: Ethnicity and Gender Among Palestinians in Israel,* edited by Rhoda Anne Kanaaneh and Isis Nusair, 21–38. Albany: SUNY Press, 2010.

Danin, Ezra. *Tsiyoni be-khol tnai* [A Zionist in all conditions]. Jerusalem: Hed Press, 1987.

Dankner, Amnon, and D. Tartakover. *Efo hayinu u-ma 'asinu: Otsar shnot ha-hamishim ve-ha-shishim* [Where we were and what we did: An Israeli lexicon of the 1950s and 1960s]. Jerusalem: Keter, 1996.

Darwish, Mahmud. *Journal of an Ordinary Grief.* Translated by Ibrahim Muhawi. Brooklyn, NY: Archipelago Books, (1973) 2010.

Davis, Uri. *Utopia Incorporated: A Study of Class, State, and Corporate Kin Control.* London: Zed Press, 1978.

Dawisha, Adeed. *Arab Nationalism in the Twentieth Century: From Triumph to Despair.* Princeton, NJ: Princeton University Press, 2004.

Dayan, Moshe. "Israel's Border and Security Problems." *Foreign Affairs* 33, no. 2 (January 1955): 250–267.

Deringil, Selim. *The Well-Protected Domains: Ideology and the Legitimation of Power in the Ottoman Empire, 1876–1909.* London: IB Tauris, 1998.

Doron, Gideon. "Judges in a Borderless State: Politics Versus the Law in the State of Israel." *Israel Affairs* 14, no. 4 (October 2008): 587–601.

Doumani, Beshara. *Rediscovering Palestine: Merchants and Peasants in Jabal Nablus, 1700–1900.* Berkeley: University of California Press, 1995.

Dowty, Alan. "Israel's First Decade: Building a Civic State." In Troen and Lucas, *Israel: The First Decade,* 31–50.

————. "The Use of Emergency Powers in Israel." *Middle East Review* 21, no. 1 (Fall 1988): 34–46.

Dror, Emmanuel. "The Emergency Regulations." In *The Other Israel: The Radical Case Against Zionism*, edited by Arie Bober, 134–144. Garden City, NY: Anchor Books, 1972.

Dubow, Saul. "Smuts, the United Nations and the Rhetoric of Race and Rights." *Journal of Contemporary History* 43, no. 1 (2008): 45–74.

Ehrlich, Avishai. "Israel: Conflict, War and Change." In *The Sociology of War and Peace*, edited by Colin Creighton and Martin Shaw, 121–142. London: MacMillan Press, 1987.

El-Khawas, Mohamed A. "Africa and the Middle Eastern Crisis." *ISSUE: A Quarterly Journal of Africanist Opinion* 5, no. 1 (Spring 1975): 33–42.

Elam, Yigal. *Memal'ei ha-pkudot* [The executors]. Jerusalem: Keter, 1990.

Eldar, Akiva, and Idith Zertal. *Adone ha-arets: ha-mitnahalim u-medinat yisra'el, 1967–2004* [Lords of the Land: The settlers and the State of Israel, 1967–2004]. Or Yehuda: Kineret, Zemorah-Bitan, Devir, 2004.

Elkins, Caroline. "Race, Citizenship, and Governance: Settler Tyranny and the End of Empire." In Elkins and Pedersen, *Settler Colonialism*, 203–222.

Elkins, Caroline, and Susan Pedersen, eds. *Settler Colonialism in the Twentieth Century: Projects, Practices, Legacies*. New York: Routledge, 2005.

Esber, Rosemarie M. *Under the Cover of War: The Zionist Expulsion of the Palestinians*. Alexandria, VA: Arabicus Books and Media, 2009.

Eshed, Eli. *Komiks 'ivri, perek 1: ha-shanim ha-rishonot* [Israeli comics, part 1: The early years, 1935–1975]. Holon: ha-Moze'on ha-Yisra'eli le-Karikatura u-le-Komiks, 2008.

Eyal, Gil. "Dangerous Liaisons Between Military Intelligence and Middle Eastern Studies in Israel." *Theory and Society* 31, no. 5 (October 2002): 653–693.

————. *The Disenchantment of the Orient: Expertise in Arab Affairs and the Israeli State*. Stanford, CA: Stanford University Press, 2006.

Falah, Ghazi. "How Israel Controls the Bedouin in Israel." *Journal of Palestine Studies* 14, no. 2 (Winter 1985): 35–51.

————. "Israeli Judaization Policy in Galilee and Arab Urbanization." *Political Geography Quarterly* 8, no. 3 (July 1989): 229–253.

————. "The 1948 Israeli-Palestinian War and Its Aftermath: The Transformation and De-Signification of Palestine's Cultural Landscape." *Annals of the Association of American Geographers* 86, no. 2 (June 1996): 265–285.

Farsoun, Samih. "Settler Colonialism and Herrenvolk Democracy." In *Israel and South Africa: The Progression of a Relationship*, edited by Abdelwahab M. Elmessiri and Richard P. Stevens, 13–21. New York: New World Press, 1976.

Feldman, Ilana. "Difficult Distinctions: Refugee Law, Humanitarian Practice, and the Identification of People in Gaza." *Cultural Anthropology* 22, no. 1 (February 2007): 129–169.

―――. *Governing Gaza: Bureaucracy, Authority, and the Work of Rule, 1917–1967*. Durham, NC: Duke University Press, 2008.

―――. "Refusing Invisibility: Documentation and Memorialization in Palestinian Refugee Claims." *Journal of Refugee Studies* 21, no. 4 (2008): 498–516.

Firro, Kais. *The Druzes in the Jewish State: A Brief History*. Leiden: Brill, 1999.

―――. "Reshaping Druze Particularism in Israel." *Journal of Palestine Studies* 30, no. 3 (Spring 2001): 40–53.

Fleischmann, Ellen L. *The Nation and Its "New" Women: The Palestinian Women's Movement, 1920–1948*. Berkeley: University of California Press, 2003.

Fodor's Modern Guides. *Israel 1967–1968*. New York: David McKay, 1968.

Forman, Geremy. "A Tale of Two Regions: Diffusion of the Israeli '50 Percent Rule' from the Central Galilee to the Occupied West Bank." *Law and Social Inquiry* 34, no. 3 (2009): 671–711.

―――. "Law and the Historical Geography of the Galilee: Israel's Litigatory Advantages During the Special Operation of Land Settlement." *Journal of Historical Geography* 32, no. 4 (October 2006): 796–817.

―――. "Settlement of Title in the Galilee: Dowson's Colonial Guiding Principles." *Israel Studies* 7, no. 3 (2002): 61–83.

―――. "Military Rule, Political Manipulation, and Jewish Settlement: Israeli Mechanisms for Controlling Nazareth in the 1950s." *Journal of Israeli History* 25, no. 2 (September 2006): 335–359.

Forman, Geremy, and Alexander (Sandy) Kedar. "From Arab Land to 'Israel Lands': The Legal Dispossession of the Palestinians Displaced by Israel in the Wake of 1948." *Environment and Planning D: Society and Space* 22, no. 6 (2004): 809–830.

Fraser, Cary. "An American Dilemma: Race and Realpolitik in the American Response to the Bandung Conference, 1955." In Plummer, *Window on Freedom*, 115–140.

Gallagher, Nancy. *Quakers in the Israeli-Palestinian Conflict: The Dilemmas of NGO Humanitarian Activism*. Cairo: American University in Cairo Press, 2007.

Gavison, Ruth. "Jewish and Democratic? A Rejoinder to the 'Ethnic Democracy' Debate." *Israel Studies* 4, no. 1 (1999): 44–72.

Gelber, Yoav. "Ben-Gurion and the Establishment of the IDF." *Jerusalem Quarterly* no. 50 (1989): 56–80.

―――. "Druze and Jews in the War of 1948." *Middle Eastern Studies* 31, no. 2 (April 1995): 229–252.

Ghanayim, Mahmud. *Maraya fi al-naqd: Dirasat fi al-adab al-filastini* [Window in criticism: Studies in Palestinian fiction]. Kafr Qara: Markaz Dirasat al-Adab al-'Arabi wa Dar al-Huda, 2000.

Ghanem, Farid. "al-Mutafaqim: The Pessoptimist, State Security, and the Exception-Rule in Legal Practice." *Adalah's Review: In the Name of Security* 4 (2004): 11–22.

Gibb, H.A.R., and J.H. Kramers, eds. *The Encyclopaedia of Islam: New Edition*. 5 vols. Leiden: Brill, 1986 (1960).

Ginat, Rami. "India and the Palestine Question: The Emergence of the Asio–Arab Bloc and India's Quest for Hegemony in the Post-Colonial Third World." *Middle Eastern Studies* 40, no. 6 (November 2004): 189–218.

Gitlis, Barukh. *ha-Moshel ha-mekho'ar: ha-emet 'al ha-mimshal ha-tsva'i* [The ugly governor: The truth about the military government]. Jerusalem: Ogdan, 1967.

Go, Julian. "The Provinciality of American Empire: 'Liberal Exceptionalism' and U.S. Colonial Rule, 1898–1912." *Comparative Studies in Society and History* 49, no. 1 (2007): 74–108.

Golan, Arnon. "The Transformation of Abandoned Arab Rural Areas." *Israel Studies* 2, no. 1 (Spring 1997): 94–110.

Goodwin-Gil, Guy. "Nationality and Statelessness, Residence and Refugee Status: Issues Affecting Palestinians." *Refugees Studies Center* (March 1990): 1–9. Available at http://repository.forcedmigration.org/show_metadata.jsp?pid=fmo:567.

Gordon, Neve. *Israel's Occupation*. Berkeley: University of California Press, 2008.

Gorenberg, Gershom. *The Unmaking of Israel*. New York: Harper, 2011.

Greenberg, Stanley B. *Race and State in Capitalist Development: Comparative Perspectives*. New Haven: Yale University Press, 1980.

Greenstein, Ran. "A Palestinian Revolutionary: Jabra Nicola and the Radical Left." *Jerusalem Quarterly* 46 (Summer 2011): 32–48.

———. *Genealogies of Conflict: Class, Identity, and State in Palestine/Israel and South Africa*. Hanover: Wesleyan University Press, 1995.

Gruber, Ruth. *Israel Today: Land of Many Nations*. New York: Hill and Wang, 1958.

Habibi, Emile. *The Secret Life of Saeed, the Ill-Fated Pessoptimist*. Translated by Salma Khadra Jayyusi and Trevor LeGassick. Columbia, LA: Readers International, 1985.

Habibi, Imil. *Kafr Qasim: al-Majzara—al-siyasa* [Kafr Qasim: The massacre—the politics]. Haifa: Arabesque, October 1976.

———. *Sudasiyat al-ayyam al-sittah: Riwayah min al-ard al-muhtallah* [Sextet of the six days: Novel from the occupied land]. Haifa: al-Ittihad, 1970 (1954).

ha-Kol 'al Kfar Kassem [Everything on Kafr Qasim]. Tel Aviv: n.p., December 1956.

Hacohen, Dvora. "The Law of Return as the Embodiment of the Link Between Israel and the Jews of the Diaspora." *Journal of Israeli History* 19, no. 1 (Spring 1998): 61–89.

Hadawi, Sami. *Israel and the Arab Minority*. New York: Arab Information Center, 1959.

Haidar, Aziz. *On the Margins: The Arab Population in the Israeli Economy*. London: Hurst, 1995.

———. *Social Welfare Services for Israel's Arab Population*. Boulder, CO: Westview Press, 1991.

Halabi, Awad Eddie. "The Transformation of the Prophet Moses Festival in Palestine:

From Local to Islamic and National Identity, 1856–1936." PhD diss., University of Toronto, 2004.

Hall, Stuart. "The Toad in the Garden: Thatcherism Among the Theorists." In *Marxism and the Interpretation of Culture*, edited by Cary Nelson and Lawrence Grossberg, 35–74. Urbana: University of Illinois Press, 1988.

Halper, Jeff. "Nishul (Displacement): Israel's Form of Apartheid." Paper presented at "A South African Conversation on Israel and Palestine," Institute for African Studies, Columbia University, September 20–21, 2002.

Hawari, Areen. "Men Under the Military Regime." *Adalah's Review* 4 (Spring 2004): 33–43.

al-Hawari, Nimr. *Sirr al-nakba* [Secret of the catastrophe]. Nazareth: Hakim Press, 1955.

Hazkani, Shay. "'The Jews of Israel Abandoned Their Religion for a Revolver': Israeli Soldiers Writing on the 'Jewish Nature' in the 1948 War." Paper presented at the annual meeting of the Association for Israel Studies Conference, Brandeis University, June 13–15, 2011.

Hermann, Tamar. "Pacifism and Anti-Militarism in the Period Surrounding the Birth of the State of Israel." *Israel Studies* 15, no. 2 (Summer 2010): 127–148.

Herzl, Theodor. *The Complete Diaries of Theodor Herzl*, edited by Raphael Patai. Translated by Harry Zohn. New York: Herzl Press, 1960.

Hiscocks, Richard. "The Work of the United Nations for the Prevention of Discrimination." In *Die Moderne Demokratie und ihr Recht: Modern Constitutionalism and Democracy*, edited by Gerhard Leibholz and Karl Dietrich Bracher, 713–728. Tübingen: Mohr, 1966.

Hoffman, Adina. *My Happiness Bears No Relation to Happiness: A Poet's Life in the Palestinian Century*. New Haven: Yale University Press, 2009.

Hofnung, Menachem. *Democracy, Law and National Security in Israel*. Hants, England: Dartmouth, 1996.

Hopkins, A. G. "Rethinking Decolonization." *Past and Present* 200 (August 2008): 211–247.

Human Rights Watch. *Second Class: Discrimination Against Palestinian Arab Children in Israel's Schools*. New York: Human Rights Watch, 2001.

Humphrey, John P. "The United Nations Sub-Commission on the Prevention of Discrimination and the Protection of Minorities." *American Journal of International Law* 62, no. 4 (October 1968): 869–888.

Husayn, Rashid. *Kalam mu'zun* [Measured words]. Nazareth: Committee for the Collection of Heritage of Rashid Hussein, 1982.

Hussain, Nasser. "Towards a Jurisprudence of Emergency: Colonialism and the Rule of Law." *Law and Critique* 10, no. 2 (May 1999): 93–115.

Ibrahim, Hanna, ed. *Hanna Naqara: Muhami al-ard wa-l-sha'ab* [Hanna Naqara: Attorney of the land and the people]. Acre: Dar al-Aswar, 1985.

Ibrahim, Hanna. "al-Dhikra al-'ashira" [The tenth anniversary]. In *Azhar bariyya* [Wild flowers], 2nd ed., 92–104. Beit Berl: Dar al-Nashr al-'Arabi, 2000. First published 1972 in Haifa by al-Ittihad.

———. *Shajarat al-ma'arafa: Dhikrayat shab lam yatagharab* [Tree of knowledge: Memories of a boy who was not exiled], 3rd edition. Acre: Dar al-Aswar, 1996.

———. "al-Mutasalilun" [The infiltrators]. *Al-Jadid*, April 1954, 19–25.

Ighbariyya, Taysir Khalid. *'Arayn al-thuwwar (Umm al-Fahm, 1935–1965): Safahat wataniya wa nidaliya yarwiha Muhammad Shraydi wa akharun* [Lion's den of the rebels (Umm al-Fahm, 1935–1965): Nationalist and struggling pages narrated by Muhammad Shraydi and others]. Haifa: T. K. Ighbariyya, 1988.

Ilyas, Sa'd. *Isra'il wa-l-siyaha* [Israel and tourism]. Beirut: PLO Research Center, 1968.

Irwin, Ryan. "Apartheid on Trial: Southwest Africa and the International Court of Justice, 1960-66." *The International History Review* 32, no. 4 (December 2010): 619–642.

Israel Knesset. "The Debate on a Constitution, February 1 and June 13, 1950." In *Israel in the Middle East: Documents and Readings on Society, Politics, and Foreign Relations, 1948–Present,* edited by Itamar Rabinovich and Jehuda Reinharz, 96–102. New York: Oxford University Press, 1984.

Jabareen, Hassan R. "Likrat gishot bikortiot shel ha-mi'ut ha-falastini: Ezrahut, le'umiyut, ve-feminizm ba-mishpat ha-yisra'eli" [Towards a critical Palestinian minority approach: Citizenship, nationalism, and feminism in Israeli law]. *Plilim: The Multi-Disciplinary Journal of Public Law, Society and Culture* 9 (2000): 53–93.

Jamali, Muhammad Fadil. "Arab Struggle: Experiences of Mohammed Fadhel Jamali." Unpublished thesis, 1974.

James, Laura M. "Whose Voice? Nasser, the Arabs, and 'Sawt Al-Arab' Radio." *Transnational Broadcasting Studies* 16 (2006): 17 paras. Available at http://www.tbsjournal.com/James.html.

Jiryis, Sabri. *The Arabs in Israel.* New York: Monthly Review Press, (1969) 1976.

———. "Domination by the Law." *Journal of Palestine Studies* 11, no. 1 (Autumn 1981): 67–92.

Ka Pakaukau. "Reinscription: The Right of Hawai'i to Be Restored to the United Nations List of Non-Self-Governing Territories." In *Islands in Captivity: The Record of the International Tribunal on the Rights of Indigenous Hawaiians,* edited by Ward Churchill and Sharon H. Venne, 303–321. Cambridge, MA: South End Press, 2002.

Kabha, Mustafa. "The Palestinian Press and the General Strike, April–October 1936: 'Filastin' as a Case Study." *Middle Eastern Studies* 39, no. 3 (July 2003): 169–189.

Kafr Qasim Local Council. *al-Dhikra al-arba'un li-majzarat Kafr Qasim: al-Majzara 'ala haqiqatiha* [The fortieth anniversary of the Kafr Qasim massacre: The massacre in its reality]. Kafr Qasim: Kafr Qasim Local Council, October 1996.

Kahin, George McTurnan. *The Asian-African Conference: Bandung, Indonesia, April 1955.* Ithaca: Cornell University Press, 1956.

Kamen, Charles. "After the Catastrophe I: The Arabs in Israel, 1948–51." *Middle Eastern Studies* 23, no. 4 (1987): 453–495.

———. "After the Catastrophe II: The Arabs in Israel, 1948–51." *Middle Eastern Studies* 24, no. 1 (1988): 68–109.

Kanaana, Sharif. "Survival Strategies of Arabs in Israel." *MERIP Reports* 41 (October 1975): 3–18.

Kanaaneh, Rhoda Ann. *Birthing the Nation: Strategies of Palestinian Women in Israel.* Berkeley: University of California Press, 2002.

———. "In the Name of Insecurity: Arab Soldiers in the Israeli Military." *Adalah's Review* 4 (Spring 2004): 57–65.

———. *Surrounded: Palestinian Soldiers in the Israeli Military.* Stanford, CA: Stanford University Press, 2008.

Kanafani, Ghassan. *Adab al-muqawama fi filastin al-muhtalla, 1948–1966* [Resistance literature in occupied Palestine, 1948–1966]. Beirut: Dar al-Adab, 1968.

———. *Palestine's Children: Returning to Haifa and Other Stories.* Translated by Barbara Harlow. Boulder, CO: Lynne Rienner, 2000.

Kapeliuk, Amnon. "Israel's Center for Oriental Studies." *New Outlook*, May 1960, 523–533.

Kauanui, J. Kēhaulani. "Colonialism in Equality: Hawaiian Sovereignty and the Question of U.S. Civil Rights." *South Atlantic Quarterly* 107, no. 4 (Fall 2008): 635–650.

Kayyali, A. W., ed. *Zionism, Imperialism and Racism.* London: Croom Helm, 1979.

Kedar, Alexandre S. "A First Step in a Difficult and Sensitive Road: Preliminary Observations on Qaadan v. Katzir." In *Postzionism: A Reader*, edited by Lawrence J. Silberstein, 148–164. Piscataway, NJ: Rutgers University Press, 2008.

———. "The Legal Transformation of Ethnic Geography: Israeli Law and the Palestinian Landholder 1948–1967." *NYU Journal of International Law and Politics* 33, no. 4 (2001): 923–1000.

Kemp, Adriana. "'Dangerous Populations': State Territoriality and the Constitution of National Minorities." In *Boundaries and Belonging: States and Societies in the Struggle to Shape Local Identities*, edited by Joel Migdal, 73–98. Cambridge: Cambridge University Press, 2004.

———. "From Politics of Location to Politics of Signification: The Construction of Political Territory in Israel's Early Years." *Journal of Area Studies* 6, no. 12 (1998): 74–101.

Kennedy, Dane. *Islands of White: Settler Society and Culture in Kenya and Southern Rhodesia, 1890–1939.* Durham, NC: Duke University Press, 1987.

Keren, Michael. *Zichroni v. State of Israel: The Biography of a Civil Rights Lawyer.* Lanham, MD: Lexington Books, 2002.

Khalidi, Rashid. *Palestinian Identity: The Construction of a Modern National Consciousness.* New York: Columbia University Press, 1997.

———. *Iron Cage: the Story of the Palestinian Struggle for Statehood.* Boston: Beacon Press, 2006.

Khalidi, Walid. *All That Remains: The Palestinian Villages Occupied and Depopulated by Israel in 1948*. Washington: Institute for Palestine Studies, 1992.

———. *Before Their Diaspora: A Photographic History of the Palestinians 1876–1948*. Washington, DC: Institute for Palestine Studies, 1991.

———. "Why Did the Palestinians Leave?" *Middle East Forum* 35, no. 7 (July 1959): 21–24, 35.

———. "Plan Dalet: Master Plan for the Conquest of Palestine." *Journal of Palestine Studies* 18, no. 1 (Autumn 1988): 4–33.

Khalidi, Walid, and Neil Caplan. "The 1953 Qibya Raid Revisited: Excerpts from Moshe Sharett's Diaries." *Journal of Palestine Studies* 31, no. 4 (Summer 2002): 77–98.

Khazzoom, Aziza. "The Great Chain of Orientalism: Jewish Identity, Stigma Management, and Ethnic Exclusion in Israel." *American Sociological Review* 23, no. 68 (August 2003): 481–510.

Khleif, Waleed, and Susan Slyomovics. "Palestinian Remembrance Days and Plans: Kafr Qasim, Fact and Echo." In *Modernism and the Middle East: Architecture and Politics in the Twentieth Century*, edited by Sandy Isenstadt and Kishwar Rizvi, 186–217. Seattle: University of Washington Press, 2008.

Khoury, Ilyas. *Bab al-Shams*. Beirut: Dar al-Adab, 1998.

Kidron, Peretz. "Truth Whereby Nations Live." In *Blaming the Victims: Spurious Scholarship and the Palestinian Question*, edited by Edward Said and Christopher Hitchens, 85–96. London: Verso, 2001 (1988).

Kimmerling, Baruch. "Between the Primordial and Civil Definitions of the Collective Identity: Eretz Israel or the State of Israel?" In Kimmerling, *The Israeli State and Society*, 262–282.

———. *Clash of Identities: Explorations in Israeli and Palestinian Societies*. New York: Columbia University Press, 2008.

———. ed. *The Israeli State and Society: Boundaries and Frontiers*. Albany: SUNY Press, 1989.

———. "Sociology, Ideology, and Nation-Building: The Palestinians and Their Meaning in Israeli Sociology." *American Sociological Review* 57, no. 4 (August 1992): 446–460.

———. "State Building, State Autonomy and the Identity of Israeli Society: The Case of the Israeli State." *Journal of Historical Sociology* 6, no. 4 (December 1993): 396–429.

———. *Zionism and Territory: the Socio-Territorial Dimensions of Zionist Politics*. Berkeley: University of California Press, 1983.

Klein, Haim, ed. *ha-Milyon ha-sheni: Ta'asiyat ha-tayarut ha-yisra'elit, 'avar—hoveh—'atid* [The second million: The Israeli tourism industry past—present—future]. Tel Aviv: Hotsa'at Amir, 1973.

Kligman, Gail. *The Politics of Duplicity: Controlling Reproduction in Ceausescu's Romania*. Berkeley: University of California Press, 1998.

Koenig, Samuel. "East Meets West in Israel." *Phylon: A Review of Race and Culture* 17, no. 2 (1956): 167–171.

Kohn, Yehuda Pinchas (Leo). "The Constitution of Israel." *Journal of Educational Sociology* 27, no. 8 (April 1954): 369–379.

———. "Israel and the New Nation States of Asia and Africa." *Annals of the American Academy of Political and Social Science* 324, no. 1 (July 1959): 96–102.

Kook, Rebecca. "Citizenship and Its Discontents: Palestinians in Israel." In *Citizenship and the State in the Middle East: Approaches and Applications*, edited by Nils Butchenson, Uri Davis, and Manuel Hassassian, 263–287. Syracuse, NY: Syracuse University Press, 2000.

———. "Changing Representations of National Identity and Political Legitimacy: Independence Day Celebrations in Israel, 1952–1998." *National Identities* 7, no. 2 (June 2005): 151–171.

Kordov, Moshe. *11 kumtot yerukot ba-din: Parashat Kfar Kassem* [Eleven green berets on trial: The Kafr Qasim affair]. Tel Aviv: A. Narkas, 1959.

Korn, Alina. "Kavanot tovot: Kavim li-dmuto shel misrad ha-mi'utim, 14 be-mai 1948–1 be-yuli 1949 [Good intentions: The short history of the Ministry of Minority Affairs, May 14, 1948–July 1, 1949]." *Katedrah le-Toldot Erets Yisra'el ve-Yeshuvah* 127 (April 2008): 113–140.

———. "Crime and Law Enforcement in the Israeli Arab Population Under the Military Government, 1948–1966." In Troen and Lucas, *Israel: The First Decade*, 659–679.

———. "Crime and Legal Control: The Israeli Arab Population During the Military Government Period (1948–66)." *British Journal of Criminology* 40 (2000): 574–593.

———. "From Refugees to Infiltrators: Constructing Political Crime in Israel in the 1950s." *International Journal of the Sociology of Law* 31 (2003): 1–22.

———. "Military Government, Political Control and Crime: The Case of the Israeli Arabs." *Crime, Law and Social Change* 34, no. 2 (September 2000): 159–182.

———. "Pshi'a: Status politi ve-akhifat hok: ha-mi'ut ha-'aravi be-yisra'el bi-tkufat ha-mimshal ha-tsva'i, 1948–1966" [Crime, political status and law enforcement: The Arab minority in Israel during military rule, 1948–1966]. PhD diss., Hebrew University, 1997.

———. "Rates of incarceration and main trends in Israeli prisons." *Criminal Justice* 3, no. 1 (2003): 29–55.

Kornberg, Jacques. "Theodore Herzl: A Reevaluation." *Journal of Modern History* 52, no. 2 (June 1980): 226–252.

Kostal, Rande W. "A Jurisprudence of Power: Martial Law and the Ceylon Controversy of 1848–51." *Journal of Imperial and Commonwealth History* 28, no. 1 (January 2000): 1–34.

———. *A Jurisprudence of Power: Victorian Empire and the Rule of Law.* Oxford: Oxford University Press, 2005.

Kramer, Paul. "Empires, Exceptions, and Anglo-Saxons: Race and Rule Between the

British and United States Empires, 1880–1910." *Journal of American History* 88, no. 4 (March 2002): 1315–1353.

———. "Power and Connection: Imperial Histories of the United States in the World." *American Historical Review* 116, no. 5 (December 2011): 1348–1391.

Krämer, Gudrun. "Moving Out of Place: Minorities in Middle Eastern Urban Societies, 1800–1914." In *Urban Social History of the Middle East, 1750–1950*, edited by Peter Sluglett, 182–223. Syracuse, NY: Syracuse University Press, 2008.

Kretzmer, David. *The Legal Status of the Arabs in Israel.* Boulder, CO: Westview Press, 1990.

Kumar, Radha. "The Troubled History of Partition." *Foreign Affairs* 76, no. 1 (January/February 1997): 22–34.

Kuntz, Josef L. "Chapter XI of the UN Charter in Action." *American Journal of International Law* 48, no. 1 (January 1954): 103–110.

Lahav, Pnina. "The Supreme Court of Israel: Formative Years, 1948–1955." *Studies in Zionism* 11, no. 1 (1990): 45–66.

———. "Tsedek ve-kibush: Eikh hitsdiku ha-amerikanim et mosad ha-ʿavdut ve-ma nilmad me-ha-historiah shelahem ʿal zo shelanu? [Justice and occupation: How did the Americans justify slavery and what can their history teach us about our own?] *Mehkare Mishpat: Ktav ʿEt shel ha-Fakulta le-Mishpatim* [Bar Ilan Law Studies: Journal of the Faculty of Law] 20, no. 2 (2004): 561–568.

Lake, Marilyn, and Henry Reynolds. *Drawing the Global Colour Line: White Men's Countries and the International Challenge of Racial Equality.* Cambridge: Cambridge University Press, 2008.

Landis, Joshua. "Syria in the 1948 Palestine War: Fighting King Abdullah's Greater Syria Plan." In Rogan and Shlaim, *The War for Palestine*, 178–205.

Laskier, Michael M. "Israel and Algeria Amid French Colonialism and the Arab-Israeli Conflict, 1954–1978." *Israel Studies* 6, no. 2 (Summer 2001): 1–32.

Lauren, Paul Gordon. "Seen from the Outside: The International Perspective on America's Dilemma." In Plummer, *Window on Freedom*, 21–43.

Lauterpacht, Hersch, ed. *Annual Digest and Reports of Public International Law Cases.* London: Butterworth: 1940–1955.

———. "State Succession—Effect Upon Nationality—The Law of Israel." In *International Law Reports.* Vol. 17, edited by Hersch Lauterpacht, 110–112. London: Butterworth, n.d., ca. 1953.

Lehrman, Hal. "The Arabs of Israel: Pages from a Correspondent's Notebook." *Commentary*, December 1949, 523–533.

Leibler, Anat E. "Establishing Scientific Authority–Citizenship and the First Census of Israel." *Tel Aviver Jahrbuch fuer deutsche Geschichte* (Goettingen) 31 (2007): 221–236.

———. "Statisticians' Ambition: Governmentality, Modernity, and National Legibility." *Israel Studies* 9, no. 2 (2004): 121–149.

Leibler, Anat, and Daniel Breslau. "The Uncounted: Citizenship and Exclusion in the Israeli Census of 1948." *Racial and Ethnic Studies* 28, no. 5 (September 2005): 880–902.

de Lepervanche, Marie. "From Race to Ethnicity." *Australian and New Zealand Journal of
Sociology* 16 (March 1980): 24–37.

Levey, Zach. "The Rise and Decline of a Special Relationship: Israel and Ghana, 1957–
1966." *African Studies Review* 46, no. 1 (April 2003): 155–177.

LeVine, Mark. "A Nation from the Sands." *National Identities* 1, no. 1 (1999): 15–38.

———. *Overthrowing Geography: Jaffa, Tel Aviv, and the Struggle for Palestine, 1880–
1948.* Berkeley: University of California Press, 2005.

Levinthal, Louis E. "The Case for a Jewish Commonwealth in Palestine." *Annals of the
American Academy of Political and Social Science* 240 (July 1945): 89–98.

Lewis, J. E. "The Ruling Compassions of the Late Colonial State: Welfare Versus Force, Kenya,
1945–1952." *Journal of Colonialism and Colonial History* 2, no. 2 (Fall 2001): 56 paras. Available at http://muse.jhu.edu/journals/journal_of_colonialism_and_colonial_history.

Liang, Yuen-Li. "Conditions of Admission of a State to Membership in the United Nations." *American Journal of International Law* 43, no. 2 (April 1949): 288–303.

Limor, Galia. "Ta'arukhat he-'asor: ha-ta'arukhah she-ne'elmah" [The tenth anniversary
exhibition: The exhibition that disappeared from history]. Master's thesis, Hebrew
University, 2002.

Linenberg, Ron. "Parashat Kfar Kassem bi-r'i ha-'itonut ha-yisra'elit" [The Kafr Qasim
affair in the view of the Israeli press]. *Medinah, Mimshal, ve-Yahasim Benle'umiyim*
2, no. 1 (1972): 48–64.

Little, Douglas. *American Orientalism: The United States and the Middle East since 1945,*
3rd edition. Chapel Hill: University of North Carolina Press, 2008.

Lockman, Zachary. *Comrades and Enemies: Arab and Jewish Workers in Palestine, 1906–
1948.* Berkeley: University of California Press, 1996.

———. "'We Opened Up the Arabs' Minds': Labour Zionist Discourse and the Rail-
way Workers of Palestine (1919–1920)." *Review of Middle East Studies* 5 (1992): 5–32.

Lorch, Natanel, ed. *Major Knesset Debates, 1948–1981.* 6 vols. Lanham, PA: University
Press of America, 1991.

Lustick, Ian. *Arabs in the Jewish State: Israel's Control of a National Minority.* Austin: University of Texas Press, 1980.

———. "Zionism and the State of Israel: Regime Objectives and the Arab Minority in
the First Years of Statehood." *Middle Eastern Studies* 16, no. 1 (January 1980): 127–146.

MAKI Central Committee. *Kafr Qasim: al-Majzara wa-l-'ibra* [Kafr Qasim: The massacre and the lesson]. Tel Aviv-Jaffa: Israel Communist Party, 1997.

———. *Kfar Kassem: 'uvdot ve-'eduyot 'al ha-tevah ha-ayom* [Kfar Qasim: Facts and testimonies on the terrible massacre]. Tel Aviv: MAKI Central Committee, December 1958.

Makdisi, Ussama. *The Culture of Sectarianism: Community, History and Violence in Nineteenth-Century Ottoman Lebanon.* Berkeley: University of California Press, 2000.

————. *Faith Misplaced: The Broken Promise of U. S.–Arab Relations, 1820–2001.* New York: Public Affairs, 2010.

————. "Ottoman Orientalism." *American Historical Review* 107, no. 3 (June 2002): 768–796.

Manela, Erez. *The Wilsonian Moment: Self-Determination and the International Origins of Anticolonial Nationalism.* New York: Oxford University Press, 2007.

Manna', 'Adil. "Majd al-Krum 1948: 'Amaliyyat tamshit 'adiya!!" [Majd al-Krum 1948: Ordinary sweeping operations!]. *al-Karmil* 55–56 (1998): 184–200.

Mao, Yufeng. "When Zhou Enlai Met Gamal Abdel Nasser: Sino-Egyptian Relations and the Bandung Conference." In *Bandung 1955: Little Histories*, edited by Derek McDougall and Antonia Finnane, 89–108. Caulfield, Australia: Monash University Press, 2010.

Margalith, Haim. "Enactment of a Nationality Law in Israel." *American Journal of Comparative Law* 2, no. 1 (Winter 1953): 63–66.

Marmorstein, Emile. "Rashid Husain: Portrait of an Angry Young Arab." *Middle Eastern Studies* 1, no. 1 (October 1964): 3–20.

Marx, Emanuel. *Bedouin of the Negev.* New York: Praeger, 1967.

Masalha, Nur. *Expulsion of the Palestinians: The Concept of "Transfer" in Zionist Political Thought, 1882–1948.* Washington, DC: Institute for Palestine Studies, 1992.

————. "A Galilee Without Christians? Yosef Weitz and Operation Yohanan, 1949–1954." In O'Mahony, *Palestinian Christians*, 190–222.

————. *A Land Without a People: Israel, Transfer, and the Palestinians 1949–1996.* London: Faber and Faber, 1997.

Masalha, Nur, ed. *Catastrophe Remembered: Palestine, Israel and the Internal Refugees: Essays in Memory of Edward W. Said (1935–2003).* London: Zed Books, 2005.

Matthews, Weldon. *Confronting an Empire, Constructing a Nation: Arab Nationalists and Popular Politics in Mandate Palestine.* London: I. B. Tauris, 2006.

Mautner, Menachem. "ha-Praklit ha-tsva'i ha-rashi ve-ha-yo'ets ha-mishpati la-memshala" [The military advocate general and the attorney general]. In *Sefer Shamgar— sipur haim* [The book of Shamgar: A life story], edited by Yuval Shani and Tova Olstein, 143–192. Tel-Aviv: Attorney's Bureau, 2003.

Mazower, Mark. "An International Civilization? Empire, Internationalism, and the Crisis of the Mid-Twentieth century." *International Affairs* 82, no. 3 (2006): 553–566.

————. "The Strange Triumph of Human Rights, 1933–1950." *Historical Journal* 47, no. 2 (June 2004): 379–398.

Mazzawi, Musa E. *Palestine and the Law: Guidelines for the Resolution of the Arab-Israel Conflict.* Reading, UK: Ithaca Press, 1997.

Medding, Peter. *The Founding of Israeli Democracy, 1948–1967.* New York: Oxford University Press, 1990.

Mendes-Flohr, Paul R., ed. *A Land of Two Peoples: Martin Buber on Jews and Arabs*. New York: Oxford University Press, 1983.

Meouchi, Nadine, and Peter Sluglett. *The British and French Mandates in Comparative Perspectives / Les Mandats Français Et Anglais Dans Une Perspective*. Leiden: Brill, 2004.

Meysels, F. Theodor, in collaboration with Lucian O. Meysels. *Israel in Your Pocket: A Ramblers' Guide*. Vol. 3 (Southern Israel). Tel Aviv: Ben Dor, 1955.

———. *Israel in Your Pocket: A Ramblers' Guide*. Vols. 1 (Northern Israel) and 2 (Central Israel), 3rd rev. and enlarged ed. Tel Aviv: Ben Dor, 1956.

———. *Israel in Your Pocket: A Ramblers' Guide*, 10th anniversary edition. Tel Aviv: Ben Dor, 1958.

Michael, Sami. *Refuge*. 1st English ed., translated by Edward Grossman. Philadelphia: Jewish Publication Society, 1988.

Mitchell, Timothy. "Everyday Metaphors of Power." *Theory and Society* 19, no. 5 (October 1990): 545–577.

———. "The Limits of the State: Beyond Statist Approaches and Their Critics." *American Political Science Review* 85, no. 1 (March 1991): 77–96.

Moleah, Alfred. "Violations of Palestinian Human Rights: South African Parallels." *Journal of Palestine Studies* 10, no. 2 (Winter 1981): 14–36.

Mongia, Radhika Viyas. "Race, Nationality, Mobility: A History of the Passport." In *After the Imperial Turn: Thinking With and Through the Nation*, edited by Antoinette Burton, 196–214. Durham, NC: Duke University Press, 2003.

Monroe, Elizabeth. "The Arab-Israel Frontier." *International Affairs* 29, no. 4 (October 1953): 439–448.

Morris, Benny. *The Birth of the Palestinian Refugee Problem, 1947–1949*. Cambridge: Cambridge University Press, 1987.

———. *The Birth of the Palestinian Refugee Problem Revisited*. Cambridge: Cambridge University Press, 2004.

———. *Israel's Border Wars, 1949–1956: Arab Infiltration, Israeli Retaliation, and the Countdown to the Suez War*. Oxford: Clarendon Press, 1993.

———. *1948 and After: Israel and the Palestinians*, 2nd ed. New York: Oxford University Press, 1994.

———. *Righteous Victims: A History of the Zionist-Arab Conflict, 1881–2001*. New York: Vintage, 2001.

Morris, Benny, and Ian Black. *Israel's Secret Wars: A History of Israel's Intelligence Services*. New York: Grove Weidenfeld, 1992.

Mu'ammar, Tawfiq. *al-Mutasalilun wa qisas ukhra* [The infiltrators and other stories]. Nazareth: al-Rabita, 1957.

Murqus, Nimr. *Aqwa min al-nisiyan: Risala ila ibnati 1* [Stronger than oblivion: A letter to my daughter, part 1]. Kafr Yasif: Nimr Murqus, 1999.

Nadan, Amos. *The Palestinian Peasant Economy Under the Mandate: A Story of Colonial Bungling*. Cambridge, MA: Harvard University Press, 2006.

Nadelmann, Ethan. "Israel and Black Africa: A Rapprochement?" *Journal of Modern African Studies* 19, no. 2 (June 1981): 183–219.

Nakhleh, Khalil. "The Two Galilees." *Arab World Issues: Occasional Papers*. Vol. 7. Belmont, MA: Association of Arab American University Graduates, 1982.

Naor, Moshe. "Israel's 1948 War of Independence as a Total War." *Journal of Contemporary History* 43, no. 2 (April 2008): 241–257.

Nassar, Maha Tawfiq. "Affirmation and Resistance: Press, Poetry and the Formation of National Identity Among Palestinian Citizens of Israel, 1948–1967." PhD diss., University of Chicago, 2006.

———. "Palestinian Citizens of Israel and the Discourse on the Right of Return, 1948–1959." *Journal of Palestine Studies* 11, no. 4 (Summer 2011): 45–60.

———. "The Marginal as Central: *al-Jadid* and the Development of a Palestinian Public Sphere." *Middle East Journal of Culture and Communication* 3, no. 3 (November 2010): 333–351.

Natan, Shmuel. "ha-Tse'adim ha-rishonim" [The first steps]. In Klein, *ha-Milyon ha-sheni*, 33–40.

Nazzal, Nafez. *The Palestinian Exodus from Galilee*. Beirut: Institute for Palestine Studies, 1978.

Netzer, Yehoshafat, and Tamar Raz. *Tnu'at ha-no'ar ha-'aravi ha-halutsi mi-yozmat mifleget ha-po'alim ha-me'uhedet* [The Arab pioneer youth, established by the United Workers Party]. Tel Aviv: Shiloah Institute for Middle Eastern and African Studies, Tel Aviv University, 1976.

"No Stigma Attached." *Journal of Palestine Studies* 7, no. 4 (1978): 143–145.

O'Hanlon, Rosalind. "Recovering the Subject: Subaltern Studies and Histories of Resistance in Colonial South Asia." *Modern Asian Studies* 22, no. 1 (1988): 189–224.

O'Mahony, Anthony, ed. *Palestinian Christians: Religion, Politics and Society in the Holy Land*. London: Melisende 1999.

———. "Palestinian Christians: Religion, Politics and Society in the Holy Land, c. 1800–1948." In O'Mahony, *Palestinian Christians*, 9–55.

Olund, Eric N. "From Savage Space to Governable Space: The Extension of United States Judicial Sovereignty over Indian Country in the Nineteenth Century." *Cultural Geographies* 9 (2002): 129–157.

Österud, Öyvind. "The Narrow Gate: Entry to the Club of Sovereign States." *Review of International Studies* 23, no. 2 (April 1997): 167–184.

Oz, Amos. *Under This Blazing Light*. Translated by Nicholas de Lange. Cambridge: Cambridge University Press, 1995.

Ozacky-Lazar, Sarah. "Hitgabshut yahase ha-gomlin ben yehudim le-'aravim bi-mdinat yisra'el: he-'asor ha-rishon, 1948–1958" [The crystallization of mutual relations between Arabs and Jews in the State of Israel: The first decade, 1948–1958]. PhD diss., University of Haifa, 1996.

Ozacky-Lazar, Sarah, and Yair Bäuml. "Tahat shilton ha-mimshal ha-tsva'i: Yahaso shel ha-mimsad la-ezrahim ha-'aravim be-yisra'el ba-shanim 1948–1967" [Under the rule of the military government: The establishment's relationship to the Arab citizens in Israel, 1948–1967]. Open University, Department of Academic Development n.p.

Ozacky-Lazar, Sarah, and As'ad Ghanem, eds. Or Testimonies: Seven Professional Assessments Submitted to the Or Commission. Givat Haviva Peace Research Institute Press, 2003.

Pandey, Gyanendra. "Can a Muslim Be an Indian?" Comparative Studies in Society and History 41, no. 4 (October 1999): 609–629.

Pappe, Ilan. Britain and the Arab-Israeli Conflict, 1948–51. London: Macmillan, 1988.

———. "An Uneasy Coexistence: Arabs and Jews in the First Decade of Statehood." In Troen and Lucas, Israel: the First Decade, 617–657.

———. The Ethnic Cleansing of Palestine. Oxford, UK: Oneworld, 2006.

Parsons, Laila. The Druze Between Palestine and Israel, 1947–49. New York: St. Martin's Press, 2000.

———. "The Palestinian Druze in the 1947–1949 Arab-Israeli War." Israel Studies 2, no. 1 (April 1997): 72–93.

Paton, Alan. Cry, the Beloved Country. Translated by Aharon Amir, 3rd edition. Tel Aviv: Am Oved, 1952.

Patterson, Gardner. "Israel's Economic Problems." Foreign Affairs 32, no. 2 (January 1954): 310–322.

Paul, Kathleen. Whitewashing Britain: Race and Citizenship in the Postwar Era. Ithaca, NY: Cornell University Press, 1997.

Pitts, Jennifer. "Empire and Democracy: Tocqueville and the Algeria Question." Journal of Political Philosophy 8, no. 3 (September 2000): 295–318.

Pearlson, Inbal. Simhah gdolah ha-lailah: Muzikah yehudit 'aravit ve-zehut mizrahit [A great joy tonight: Arab Jewish music and Mizrahi identity]. Tel Aviv: Resling, 2006.

Pearson, David. "Theorizing Citizenship in British Settler Societies," Ethnic and Racial Studies 25, no. 6 (November 2002): 989–1012.

Pedersen, Susan. "Settler Colonialism at the Bar of the League of Nations." In Elkins and Pedersen, Settler Colonialism, 41–59.

Peled, Alisa Rubin. Debating Islam in the Jewish State: The Development of Policy Toward Islamic Institutions in Israel. Albany: State University of New York Press, 2001.

———. "The Other Side of 1948: The Forgotten Benevolence of Bechor Shalom Shitrit and the Ministry of Minority Affairs." Israel Affairs 8, no. 3 (Spring 2003): 84–103.

Peled, Miko. "Torture: Read It in the Israeli Press." Electronic Intifada, April 4, 2007. Available at http://electronicintifada.net/content/torture-read-it-israeli-press/6844.

Peleg, Ilan. "Israel's Constitutional Order and Kulturkampf: The Role of Ben-Gurion." *Israel Studies* 3, no. 1 (Spring 1998): 230–250.

Penny, H. Glenn. "Elusive Authenticity: The Quest for the Authentic Indian in German Public Culture." *Comparative Studies in Society and History* 48, no. 4 (October 2006): 798–818.

Penslar, Derek J. "Broadcast Orientalism: Representations of Mizrahi Jewry in Israeli Radio, 1948–1967." In *Orientalism and the Jews*, edited by Ivan Davidson Kalmar and Derek J. Penslar, 182–200. Waltham, MA: Brandeis University Press, 2005.

Penvenne, Jeanne Marie. "Settling Against the Tide: The Layered Contradictions of Twentieth Century Portuguese Settlement in Mozambique." In Elkins and Pedersen, *Settler Colonialism*, 79–94.

Peretz, Don. "The Arab Minority of Israel." *Middle East Journal* 8 (Spring 1954): 139–154.

———. "The Arab Refugee Dilemma." *Foreign Affairs* 33, no. 1 (October 1954): 134–148.

———. *Israel and the Palestine Arabs*. Washington, DC: Middle East Institute, (1956) 1958.

Piterberg, Gabriel. "Domestic Orientalism: The Representation of 'Oriental' Jews in Zionist/Israeli Historiography." *British Journal of Middle Eastern Studies* 23, no. 2 (November 1996): 125–145.

———. "Erasures." *New Left Review*, July–August 2001, 31–46.

———. *The Returns of Zionism: Myths, Politics and Scholarship in Israel*. London: Verso, 2008.

Plummer, Brenda Gayle, ed. *Window on Freedom: Race, Civil Rights, and Foreign Affairs, 1945–1988*. Chapel Hill: University of North Carolina Press, 2003.

Poiger, Uta G. *Jazz, Rock, and Rebels: Cold War Politics and American Culture in a Divided Germany*. Berkeley: University of California Press, 2000.

Polakow-Suransky, Sasha. *The Unspoken Alliance: Israel's Secret Relationship with Apartheid South Africa*. New York: Pantheon, 2010.

Prakash, Gyan. "Subaltern Studies as Postcolonial Criticism." *American Historical Review* 99, no. 5 (December 1994): 1475–1490.

Qafisheh, Mutaz. "The International Foundations of Palestinian Nationality: A Legal Examination of Palestinian Nationality Under the British Rule." PhD diss., University of Geneva, 2007.

Qahwaji, Habib. *al-'Arab fi dhill al-ihtilal al-isra'ili mundhu 1948* [The Arabs in the shadow of Israeli occupation since 1948]. Beirut: PLO Research Center, 1972.

Quigley, John. "Displaced Palestinians and a Right to Return." *Harvard International Law Journal* 39, no. 1 (Winter 1998): 171–229.

Radzyner, Amihai. "A Constitution for Israel: The Design of the Leo Kohn Proposal, 1948." *Israel Studies* 15, no. 1 (Spring 2010): 1–24.

al-Rafiq Ramzi Khuri: al-Dhikra al-sanawiyya al-khamisa li-rahil [Comrade Ramzi Khuri: Commemorating the fifth anniversary of his passing]. N.p., 1994.

Ram, Uri. "The Colonization Perspective in Israeli Sociology." *Journal of Historical Sociology* 6, no. 3 (September 2003): 327–350.

Ratner, Yohanan. "ha-Mimshal ha-tsva'i" [The military government]. *Mibifnim*, August 1956–May 1957, 49–52.

Regev, Motti. "Present Absentee: Arab Music in Israeli Culture." *Public Culture* 7 (1995): 433–445.

Reichman, Shalom. "Partition and Transfer: Crystallization of the Settlement Map of Israel Following the War of Independence, 1948–1950." In *The Land That Became Israel: Studies in Historical Geography*, edited by Ruth Kark, 320–330. New Haven: Yale University Press, 1990.

Rivkin, Arnold. "Israel and the Afro-Asian World." *Foreign Affairs* 37, no. 3 (April 1959): 486–495.

Robinson, Jacob. *Palestine at the United Nations*. Washington, DC: Public Affairs Press, 1947.

Robinson, Shira. "Local Struggle, National Struggle: Palestinian Responses to the Kafr Qasim Massacre and Its Aftermath, 1956–1966." *International Journal of Middle East Studies* 35, no. 3 (August 2003): 393–416.

———. "My Hairdresser Is a Sniper." *Middle East Report* 223, Summer 2002: 48–49.

———. "The Problem of Privilege." *Middle East Report* (blog), March 22, 2012. Available at http://www.merip.org/problem-privilege.

Robson, Laura. *Colonialism and Christianity in Mandate Palestine*. Austin: University of Texas Press, 2011.

Rodrigue, Aron. "Difference and Tolerance in the Ottoman Empire," interview by Nancy Reynolds. *Stanford Humanities Review* 5, no. 1 (Fall 1995) 81–92.

Rogan, Eugene L., and Avi Shlaim, eds. *The War for Palestine: Rewriting the History of 1948*. Cambridge: Cambridge University Press, 2001.

Rosaldo, Renato. "Imperialist Nostalgia." *Representations* 26 (1989): 107–122.

Rosenfeld, Henry. "Change, Barriers to Change, and Contradictions in the Arab Village Family." *American Anthropologist* 70, no. 4 (August 1968): 732–752.

———. "The Class Situation of the Arab National Minority in Israel." *Comparative Studies in Society and History* 20, no. 3 (July 1978): 374–407.

———. *Hem hayu falahim: 'Iyunim ba-hitpathut ha-hevratit shel ha-kfar ha-'aravi be-yisra'el* [They were peasants: Studies of the social development of the Arab village in Israel]. Tel Aviv: Hakibbutz Hameuchad, 1964.

Rosenne, Shabtai. "The Israel Nationality Law 5712–1952 and the Law of Return 5710–1950." *Journal du Droit International* 81 (1954): 4–63.

Rosenthal, Ruvik. *Kfar Kassem: Eru'im ve-mitos* [Kafr Qasim: Myth and history]. Tel Aviv: ha-Kibbutz ha-Meuchad, 2000.

Rozin, Orit. *The Rise of the Individual in 1950s Israel: A Challenge to Collectivism.* Translated by Haim Watzman. Waltham, MA: Brandeis University Press, 2011.

———. "Food, Identity, and Nation-Building in Israel's Formative Years." *Israel Studies Forum* 21, no. 1 (Summer 2006): 52–80.

———. "Forming a Collective Identity: The Debate over the Proposed Constitution, 1948–1950." *Journal of Israeli History* 26, no. 2 (September 2007): 251–271.

Saada, Emmanuelle. "Race and Sociological Reason in the Republic: Inquiries on the Métis in the French Empire (1908–37)." *International Sociology* 17, no. 3 (2002): 361–391.

Saban, Ilan. "Hashpa'at bet ha-mishpat ha-'elyon 'al ma'amad ha-'aravim be-yisra'el" [The impact of the Supreme Court on the status of the Arabs in Israel]. *Mishpat u-Mimshal* 3 (1996): 541–569.

———. "Le'ahar ha-barbariot?" [In the aftermath of barbarism?] In *ha-Boker le-maharat: 'idan ha-shalom, lo utopyah* [The morning after: The era of peace, not utopia], edited by Meron Benvenisti and Nimrod Goren, 63–94. Jerusalem: The Harry S. Truman Research Institute, Hebrew University 2002.

Sacco, Joe. *Footnotes in Gaza.* New York: Henry Holt, 2009.

Sa'di, Ahmad H. "Afterword: Reflections on Representations, History and Moral Accountability." In *Nakba: Palestine, 1948, and the Claims of Memory,* edited by Ahmad H. Sa'di and Lila Abu Lughod. New York: Columbia University Press, 2007.

———. "Control and Resistance at Local-Level Institutions: A Study on Kafr Yasif's Local Council Under the Military Government." *Arab Studies Quarterly* 23, no. 3 (2001): 31–47.

Said, Edward W. "The Burdens of Interpretation and the Question of Palestine." *Journal of Palestine Studies* 16, no. 1 (Autumn 1986): 29–37.

———. *Orientalism.* New York: Pantheon, 1978.

———. *The Question of Palestine.* New York: Times Books, 1979.

———. "Zionism from the Standpoint of Its Victims." *Social Text* 1 (1979): 7–58.

Salamanca, Omar Jabary, Mezna Qato, Kareem Rabie, and Sobhi Samour, eds. *Past Is Present: Settler Colonialism in Palestine.* Special Issue of *Settler Colonial Studies* 2.1 (2012). Available at http://ojs.lib.swin.edu.au/index.php/settlercolonialstudies.

Saltman, Michael. "The Use of the Mandatory Emergency Laws by the Israeli Government." *International Journal of the Sociology of Law* 10 (1982): 385–394.

Samuel, Edwin. "The Prospect for Israel's Arabs." *Commentary,* May 1955, 458–462.

Saposnik, Arieh Bruce. "Europe and Its Orients in Zionist Culture Before the First World War." *Historical Journal* 49, no. 4 (2006): 1105–1123.

Savuray, Rachel. "Our School and the Arab Question." *NER* 11, nos. 10–11 (July–August 1960): vii–ix.

Sayer, Derek. "Everyday Forms of State Formation: Some Dissident Remarks on 'Hegemony.'" In *Everyday Forms of State Formation: Revolution and the Negotiation of Rule in Modern Mexico*, edited by Gilbert M. Joseph and Daniel Nugent, 367–377. Durham, NC: Duke University Press, 1994.

Sayigh, Rosemary. *Palestinians: From Peasants to Revolutionaries*. London: Zed Press, 1979.

Schaller, Dominik J., and Jürge Zimmerer. "Settlers, Imperialism, Genocide: Seeing the Global Without Ignoring the Local—Introduction." *Journal of Genocide Research* 10, no. 2 (2008): 191–199.

Schiff, Ze'ev. "The Pros and Cons of the Military Government." *New Outlook*, February 1962, 64–71.

Schmidt, Yvonne. *Foundations of Civil and Political Rights in the Occupied Territories.* Munich: GRIN, 2001.

Scholch, Alexander. *Palestinians over the Green Line: Studies on the Relations Between Palestinians on Both Sides of the Armistice Line Since 1967.* London: Ithaca Press, 1983.

Schreier, Joshua. "Napoléon's Long Shadow: Morality, Civilization, and Jews in France and Algeria, 1808–1870." *French Historical Studies* 30, no. 1 (Winter 2007): 77–103.

Schwarz, Walter. *The Arabs in Israel*. London: Faber and Faber, 1959.

———. "Israel's Arab Minority: Safeguarding Their Rights." *Commentary*, January 1958, 23–27.

Schwelb, Egon. "The International Convention on the Elimination of All Forms of Racial Discrimination." *The International and Comparative Law Quarterly* 15, no. 4 (October 1966): 996–1068.

Sebba, Leslie. "Sanctioning Policy in Israel: An Historical Overview." *Israel Law Review* 30, no. 3–4 (1996): 234–275.

Segev, Tom. *1949: The First Israelis*. First Owl Books ed. New York: Henry Holt, 1998.

———. *1967: Ve-ha-arets shintah et paneha* [Israel in 1967: And the country changed its face]. Jerusalem: Keter, 2005. Translated by Jessica Cohen as *1967: Israel, the War, and the Year That Transformed the Middle East*. New York: Henry Holt, 2007.

———. *One Palestine, Complete: Jews and Arabs Under the British Mandate.* New York: Owl Books, 2000.

———. *The Seventh Million: The Israelis and the Holocaust.* Translated by Haim Watzman. New York: Hill and Wang, 1993.

Seikaly, Sherene. "Meatless Days: Consumption and Capitalism in Wartime Palestine 1939–1948." PhD diss., New York University, 2007.

Shafir, Gershon. *Land, Labor and the Origins of the Israeli-Palestinian Conflict, 1882–1914.* Berkeley: University of California Press, (1989) 1996.

———. "Settler Citizenship in the Jewish Colonization of Palestine." In Elkins and Pedersen, *Settler Colonialism*, 41–57.

Shafir, Gershon, and Yoav Peled. *Being Israeli: The Dynamics of Multiple Citizenship.* Cambridge: Cambridge University Press, 2002.

Shahak, Israel. "Civil Rights in Israel Today." In *Israeli League for Human and Civil Rights*

(The Shahak Papers), edited by Adnan Amad, 29–46. Beirut: Near East Ecumenical Bureau for Information and Interpretation and the Palestine Research Center, 1973.

Shahar, Yoram. "Yisra'el ke-medinah du-horit: ha-yishuv ha-'ivri ve-ha-tnu'ah ha-tsiyonit be-hatsharat ha-'atsma'ut" [Israel as a state with two parents: The Yishuv and the Zionist movement in the declaration of independence]. *Zmanim* 99 (2007): 32–45.

Shalev, Michael. "Jewish Organized Labor and the Palestinians: A Study of State/Society Relations in Israel." In Kimmerling, *The Israeli State and Society*, 93–133.

Shalom, Zaki. "Ben-Gurion and Tewfik Tubi Finally Meet (October 28, 1966)." *Israel Studies* 8, no. 2 (Summer 2003): 45–69.

Shamir, Ronen. *The Colonies of Law: Zionism and Law in Early Mandate Palestine.* Cambridge: Cambridge University Press, 2000.

Shammas, Anton. "At Half-Mast—Myths, Symbols, and Rituals of the Emerging State: A Personal Testimony of an 'Israeli Arab.'" In *New Perspectives on Israeli History: The Early Years of the State*, edited by Laurence J. Silberstein, 216–224. New York: New York University Press, 1991.

Shapira, Anita. *Land and Power: The Zionist Resort to Force, 1881–1948.* Translated by William Templer. New York: Oxford University Press, 1992.

———. "Politics and Collective Memory: The Debate over the 'New Historians' in Israel." *History and Memory* 7, no. 1 (Spring/Summer 1995): 9–40.

Shapiro, Yonatan. "Le'an ne'elmu ha-tnu'ot ha-liberaliyot ve-ha-re'ayon ha-liberali be-yisra'el?" [Where have the liberal movements and the liberal idea in Israel gone?]. *Zmanim* 14 (1996): 92–101.

———. "The Historical Origins of Israeli Democracy." In *Israeli Democracy Under Stress*, edited by Ehud Sprinzak and Larry J. Diamond, 65–79. Boulder, CO: Lynne Reiner, 1993.

Shelef, Nadav. *Evolving Nationalism: Homeland, Identity, and Religion in Israel, 1925–2005.* Ithaca, NY: Cornell University Press, 2010.

Shenhav, Shaul R. "A Worthless Flock with No Shepherd: Bechor Shalom Shitrit's Representation-Based Approach to Political Crisis Resolution." *Israel Affairs* 12, no. 2 (April 2006): 253–267.

Shenhav, Yehouda. "The Jews of Iraq, Zionist Ideology, and the Property of the Palestinian Refugees of 1948: an Anomaly of National Accounting." *International Journal of Middle East Studies* 31, no. 4 (November 1999): 605–630.

Shepard, Todd. "Algeria, France, Mexico, UNESCO: A Transnational History of Antiracism and Decolonization, 1932–1962." *Journal of Global History* 6, no. 2 (July 2011): 273–297.

Shlaim, Avi. "Israel and the Arab Coalition in 1948." In Rogan and Shlaim, *The War for Palestine*, 79–103.

———. "Israel Between East and West, 1948–1956." *IJMES* 36, no. 4 (November 2004): 657–673.

———. "The Debate About 1948: A Review Essay." *International Journal of Middle East Studies* 27, no. 3 (August 1995): 287–304.

———. *The Iron Wall: Israel and the Arab World*. New York: W. W. Norton, 2001.

Shoufani, Elias. "The Fall of a Village." *Journal of Palestine Studies* 1, no. 4 (1972): 109–121.

Shufani, Ilyas. *Rihla fi al-rahil: Fusul min al-dhakira . . . lam taktamul* [Journey in exodus: Chapters from an incomplete memory]. Beirut: Dar al-Kunuz al-Adabiyya, 1994.

Silberman, Neil Asher. *A Prophet from Amongst You—The Life of Yigael Yadin: Soldier, Scholar and Mythmaker of Modern Israel*. Reading, MA: Addison-Wesley, 1993.

Simon, Ernst. "The Costs of Arab-Jewish Cold War: Ihud's Experiment in Moral Politics." *Commentary*, September 1950, 256–262.

Simpson, A. W. Brian. *Human Rights and the End of Empire: Britain and the Genesis of the European Convention*. Oxford, UK: Oxford University Press, 2002.

Slyomovics, Susan. *The Object of Memory: Arab and Jew Narrate the Palestinian Village*. Philadelphia: University of Pennsylvania, 1998.

Snir, Reuven. "Iraqi-Jewish Writers in Israel in the 1950s." *Prooftexts* II, no. 2 (1991): 153–173.

Somekh, Sasson. "'Reconciling Two Great Loves': The First Jewish-Arab Literary Encounter in Israel." *Israel Studies* 4, no. 1 (1999): 1–21.

Sorek, Tamir. *Arab Soccer in the Jewish State: The Integrative Enclave*. Cambridge: Cambridge University Press, 2007.

Sprinzak, Ehud. "Elite Illegalism in Israel and the Question of Democracy." In *Israeli Democracy Under Stress*, edited by Ehud Sprinzak and Larry J. Diamond, 173–198. Boulder: Lynne Rienner, 1993.

Stein, Rebecca L. *Itineraries in Conflict: Israelis, Palestinians, and the Political Lives of Tourism*. Durham, NC: Duke University Press, 2008.

———. "From Shmaltz to Sacrilege: Commemorating Israel After Rabin." *Middle East Report* (Summer 1998): 43–45.

———. "Traveling Zion: Hiking and Settler-Nationalism in Pre-1948 Palestine." *Interventions: International Journal of Postcolonial Studies* 11, no. 3 (2009): 334–351.

Stern, Mordechai. *Ila al-'arab: al-Idhtihad al-mudhtahadin fi isra'il* [To the Arab: The oppressed in Israel]. Tel Aviv: al-Quwa al-Thalitha, 1959.

Sternhell, Zeev. *The Founding Myths of Israel: Nationalism, Socialism and the Making of the Jewish State*. Princeton: Princeton University Press, 1998.

Stoler, Ann Laura. *Carnal Knowledge and Imperial Power: Race and the Intimate in Colonial Rule*. Berkeley: University of California Press, 2002.

———. "Imperial Formations and the Opacities of Rule." in *Lessons of Empire: Imperial Histories and American Power*, edited by Craig Calhoun, Frederick Cooper, and Kevin W. Moore, 48–60. New York: New Press, 2006.

———. "On Degrees of Imperial Sovereignty." *Public Culture* 18, no. 1 (2006): 125–146.

———. "Sexual Affronts and Racial Frontiers: European Identities and the Cultural

Politics of Exclusion in Colonial Southeast Asia." *Comparative Studies in Society and History* 34, no. 3 (1992): 514–551.

Sulaiman, Khalid A. *Palestine and Modern Arab Poetry*. London: Zed Books, 1984.

Suleiman, Yasir. *Arabic, Self and Identity: A Study in Conflict and Displacement*. New York: Oxford University Press, 2011.

Sussman, Joel. "Law and Judicial Practice in Israel." *Journal of Comparative Legislation and International Law* 32, no. 3/4 (1950): 29–31.

Swedenburg, Ted. *Memories of Revolt: The 1936–1939 Rebellion and the Palestinian National Past*. Minneapolis: University of Minnesota Press, 1995.

Tarazi, Monica. "Planning Apartheid in the Naqab." *Middle East Report* 253 (Winter 2009): 32–36.

Taylor, Charles. "The Dynamics of Democratic Exclusion." *Journal of Democracy* 9, no. 4 (1998): 143–156.

Teller, Judd L. "Israel Faces Its Arab Minority Problem: The Native =Within Its Gates." *Commentary*, December 1951, 556–557.

Thompson, Elizabeth F. *Colonial Citizens: Republican Rights, Paternal Privilege, and Gender in French Syria and Lebanon*. New York: Columbia University Press, 2000.

———. *Justice Interrupted: The Long Struggle for Constitutional Government in the Middle East*. Cambridge: Harvard University Press, 2013.

Thornberry, Patrick. "Self-Determination, Minorities, Human Rights: A Review of International Instruments." *International and Comparative Law Quarterly* 38, no. 4 (October 1989): 867–889.

Tolan, Sandy. *The Lemon Tree: An Arab, a Jew, and the Heart of the Middle East*. New York: Bloomsbury, 2006.

Torstrick, Rebecca L. *The Limits of Coexistence: Identity Politics in Israel*. Ann Arbor: University of Michigan Press, 2000.

Townshend, Charles. "Martial Law: Legal and Administrative Problems of Civil Emergency in Britain and the Empire, 1800–1940." *Historical Journal* 25, no. 1 (March 1982): 167–195.

Trakhtenberg, Graciella. "ha-Mizrah ve-ha-hevra ha-yisra'elit" [The East and Israeli society]. In Zalmona, *Kadima*, 33–45.

Troen, S. Ilan, and Noah Lucas, eds. *Israel: The First Decade of Independence*. New York: SUNY Press, 1995.

Tuma, Imil. *Thalathin 'am 'ala al-Ittihad: Yawmiyyat sha'ab* [Thirty years of *The Union*: Diary of a people]. Haifa: Arabesques, 1974.

Turki, Khalid. *Humat al-diyar* [Guardians of the homeland]. Haifa: Khalid Turki, n.p., n.d., ca 2011.

Urian, Dan. "The Emergence of the Arab Image in Israeli Theatre, 1948–1982." *Israel Affairs* 1, no. 4 (Summer 1995): 101–127.

Veracini, Lorenzo. "'Emphatically Not a White Man's Colony': Settler Colonialism and the Construction of Colonial Fiji." *Journal of Pacific History* 43, no. 2 (2008): 189–205.

———. *Settler Colonialism: A Theoretical Overview*. Basingstoke: Palgrave Macmillan, 2010.

Vitalis, Robert. "The Midnight Ride of Kwame Nkrumah and Other Fables of Bandung (Bandoong)." *Humanity* 4, no. 2 forthcoming.

Warhaftig, Zorah. *Hukah le-yisra'el: Dat u-medinah* [A Constitution for Israel: Religion and State]. Jerusalem: Mesilot, 1988.

Watad, Muhammad. "Coexistence." *New Outlook*, September/October 1970, 68–73, 76.

Watenpaugh, Keith. "Cleansing the Cosmopolitan City." *Journal of Social History* 30, no. 1 (February 2005): 1–25.

Wedeen, Lisa. *Ambiguities of Domination: Politics, Rhetoric, and Symbols in Contemporary Syria*. Chicago: University of Chicago Press, 1999.

Weigert, Gideon. *My Life with the Palestinians*. Omer: Jerusalem Times, 1997.

Weis, Paul. "The United Nations Convention on the Reduction of Statelessness, 1961." *International and Comparative Law Quarterly* 11, no. 4 (October 1961): 1073–1096.

Weiss, Yfaat. "The Golem and Its Creator, or How the Jewish Nation-State Became Multiethnic." In *Challenging Ethnic Citizenship: German and Israeli Perspectives on Immigration*, edited by Daniel Levy and Yfaat Weiss, 82–104. New York: Berghahn Books, 2002.

Weitz, Eric D. "From the Vienna to the Paris System: International Politics and the Entangled Histories of Human Rights, Forced Deportations, Civilizing Missions." *American Historical Review* 113, no. 5 (2008): 1313–1343.

Weizman, Eyal. *Hollow Land: Israel's Architecture of Occupation*. London: Verso, 2007.

Weizmann, Chaim. *Trial and Error: The Autobiography of Chaim Weizmann*. New York: Harper, 1949.

Werner, Alfred. "Black Jews of Israel." *Negro Digest* (July 1951): 52–57.

White, Benjamin. *The Emergence of Minorities in the Middle East: The Politics of Community in French Mandate Syria*. Edinburg: Edinburg University Press, 2011.

Wolfe, Patrick. "*Corpus Nullius:* The Exception of Indians and Other Aliens in US Constitutional Discourse." *Postcolonial Studies* 10, no. 2 (March 2007): 127–151.

———. "History and Imperialism: A Century of Theory, from Marx to Postcolonialism." *American Historical Review* 102, no. 2 (April 1997): 388–402.

———. "Race and Racialisation: Some Thoughts." *Postcolonial Studies* 5, no. 1 (April 2002): 51–62.

———. "Settler Colonialism and the Elimination of the Native." *Journal of Genocide Research* 8, no. 4 (December 2006): 387–409.

Woodward, C. Vann. *The Strange Career of Jim Crow*, 3rd revised edition. New York: Oxford University Press, 2002 (1955).

Wright, Quincy. "Recognition and Self-Determination." *Proceedings of the American Society of International Law at its Annual Meeting* 48 (April 22–24, 1954): 23–37.

Yanai, Natan. "Musag ha-ezrahut bi-tfisato shel David Ben Gurion" [David-Ben Gurion's concept of citizenship]. *'Iyunim Bi-Tkumat Yisrael* 4 (1994): 494–504.

Yaqub, Salim. *Containing Arab Nationalism: The Eisenhower Doctrine and the Middle East.* Chapel Hill: University of North Carolina, 2004.

Yiftachel, Oren. "'Ethnocracy' and Its Discontents: Minorities, Protests, and the Israeli Polity." *Critical Inquiry* 26, no. 4 (2000): 725–756.

———. "Territory as the Kernel of the Nation: Space, Time and Nationalism in Israel/Palestine." *Geopolitics* 7, no. 2 (2002): 215–248.

Young, Iris Marion. "Polity and Group Difference: A Critique of the Ideal of Universal Citizenship." *Ethics* 99, no. 2 (January 1989): 250–274.

Yuval-Davis, Nira. "Nationalism and Racism." *Cahiers de recherche sociologique* 20 (1993): 183–202.

Zalmona, Yigal, ed. *Kadima: ha-mizrah be-omanut yisra'el* [To the east: Orientalism in Israeli art]. Jerusalem: Israel Museum, 1998.

———. "Mizrahah! Mizrahah? 'Al ha-mizrah be-omanut yisra'el" [Eastward! Eastward? Orientalism in Israeli art]. In Zalmona, *Kadimah*, 47–93.

Zayyad, Tawfiq. *al-Sira al-dhatiyya* [Autobiography]. Nazareth: Muwassassat Tawfiq Zayyad, n.p.

Zilber, Ya'acov. "'Naki me-'aravim!' amar Ben Gurion," ['Clean of Arabs!' said Ben-Gurion]. *'Iton 77* [Newspaper 77], October 1985, 336–338.

Zureik, Elia. *The Palestinians in Israel: A Study of Internal Colonialism.* London: Routledge and Kegan Paul, 1979.

INDEX

Italic page numbers refer to material in illustrations.

Arab convictions, 215n82; racial enforcement of, 48; stepped up enforcement in mid-1950s, 66; in War on Return ("Infiltration"), 97, 101, 244n210
Defense of the Realm Act (DORA), 34
Dirty war, 45
Divon, Shmuel, 138–39
Druze: Border Guard in Little Triangle, 120–21; in IDF Minorities Unit, 56–57, 142, 142–43, 222n172, 223n177; in Independence Day celebrations, 130; Jewish Agency courts, 20; Palestinians described as, 50; public services for, 149; recognized as nationality, 177, 269n142; support for return of, 82; Temporary Residency Permits for, 238n139; in tenth anniversary of Israeli statehood celebrations, 273n202

Eban, Abba, 36–37
Egged bus boycott, 186–87, 269n154, 274n205
Eisenhower, Dwight, 159, 267n129
Elpeleg, Zvi, 250n18, 254n84
Enclosed zone (syag; reservations; reserves), 32, 39
Entry into Israel Law, 71, 109
Equality: Ben-Gurion and, 164; contradiction with illiberal measures to ensure Jewish colonization, 80; in Declaration of Independence, 99, 164, 167; High Court defers to security experts on matters of, 156–57; High Court rulings acknowledge incompatibility of Zionism with, 196; intensifying struggle for racial, 176; Jewish liberal elite's ambivalence about, 195; versus keeping Arabs divided, 139; Khalil on, 125; MAKI demands for full, 140, 183; as mere casing, 152; Palestinian citizens

test limits of Israel's commitment to, 78; Palestinians acquire civil but not structural, 193, 198; in proposed constitution, 97–98; security rationales for depriving to Palestinians, 134; sovereignty versus, 59–67
Eshkol, Levy, 191–92
Ethnic cleansing, 1, 23, 35, 46, 156, 164, 184
Exceptionalism, 7

al-Fahum, Yusif, 93
Family Reunification program, 84–86, 237n121
Farah, Nicola, 92
Faraj, Faraj, 119–21
Filfel al-Masri, 256n105
Future Vision documents, 194

Galilee, 32, 142, 166, 187; Absentee Property Law's effect on, 47; Arabs banned from Jewish colonies in, 150; citizenship law and, 106–7; dearth of Jewish settlers in, 46, 77; division into Palestinian ghettos, 39; Druze in, 56; dual sovereignty in, 58; Egged boycott in, 186–87, 269n154, 274n205; eligibility to vote in, 51; Family Reunification program in, 85; first Israeli census in, 229n49; harboring illegal returnees in, 78, 232n76; Independence Day celebrations in, 127–28, 141, 256n107; Israeli conquest of Central, 30, 35; Israeli occupation of, 64, 73; Jewish settlements in, 177–78; Judaizing Central, 138; Kafr Qasim massacre protests in, 167–70, 176, 264n82; Khuri on colonization of, 181; land mine explosions and military shooting exercises in, 178, 269n147; MAKI on Israeli withdrawal from, 64; MAKI solidarity gathering in, 184; medical care in

Israel Defense Forces (IDF): Arab
recruits, 134; *ba-Mahaneh* magazine,
142, *142*; cross-border raids, 136–37,
157, 254n77, 260n18; forced conversion
to Judaism rejected by, 134; free-fire
policy, 81; in Kafr Qasim massacre,
160, 162; Minorities Unit, 56–57, *142*,
142–43; settlement department, 138;
Special Commando Unit, 101, 136–37;
in transforming individual Jews in
Israelis, 135–36
Israeli Communist Party. *See* MAKI
(Communist Party of Israel)
Israeli Independence Day: boycott of
tenth anniversary of, 182–88; coercion
of Palestinian participation in, 140–48,
253n70; commemorating the *nakba* on,
197; compared to *sulha* at Kafr Qasim,
154; continued hunt for Palestinian
affinity regarding, 196; disruptions
to, 180; early ceremonies, 116–26; first
anniversary, 127; institutionalization
of celebrations, 143; *Istiqlal* (film), 147;
key objective of celebrations, 131–32;
lack of open resistance on, 152; Law of
Independence Day, 116–17; measuring
Arab participation, 126–33; personal
memories of, 117, 119–23, 125–26, 143–46,
161, 250n13; photos of, 129, 132–33, 145,
147; police response to boycott of, 188;
spectacles of sovereignty at, 114–15;
third anniversary, 128
al-Ittihad (newspaper): on abuses of
War on Return ("Infiltration"), 79–80,
233n85; on Ben-Gurion teaching
racial discrimination, 53; on bribes to
organize tenth anniversary of Israeli
statehood celebrations, 184–85; British
revoke license of, 62; closed down temporarily for incitement, 109; establishes

presence in Galilee and coastal cities,
61; on Hittin refugees, 230n57; on Kafr
Qasim massacre, 153–54, 167, 170; Little
Triangle cut off from, 118; on Palestinians and peoples of Asia and Africa,
182; references to National Liberation
League disappear from, 64; Semah
publishes in, 252n45; smuggling copies
of, 144; on strike during tenth anniversary of Israeli statehood celebrations,
181; on struggles for independence and
racial equality, 176, 268n133; villagers
smuggle, 65

Jabbur, Jabbur Yusif, 276n226
Jaffa, 30, *32*, 62, 127; "Arabs of the state"
in, 59; Independence Day celebrations
in, 127, 131, 257n128; National Liberation League in, 63; repatriation requests
from former residents, 82
Jaljulya, *32*; during 1948 war, 251n25; Independence Day celebrations in, 117–25
Jerusalem, *32*; Dayr Yasin massacre, 31,
33, 210n8, 263n56; flight from, 225n6;
Independence Day celebrations in, *145*;
MAKI on Israeli withdrawal from, 64;
1929 massacre of Jews near, 267n114
Jerusalem Post (newspaper), 156, 173–74
Jewish Agency: DERs opposed by, 35;
divide-and-rule strategy of, 56; Druze
connections of, 56; establishment of, 16;
in Judaizing Central Galilee, 138; King
Abdullah negotiates with, 25; MAPAI
dominates, 63; "neighborly relations"
division, 219n129; Palestinian nationalism opposed by, 20; preparations for
war before the UN partition vote, 25;
in racialization of Palestinians, 18, 53;
unified communist party as threat to,
63; in UNSCOP hearings, 21

Stanford Studies in Middle Eastern and Islamic Societies and Cultures

Joel Beinin, *Stanford University*

Juan R.I. Cole, *University of Michigan*

Laura Bier, *Revolutionary Womanhood: Feminisms, Modernity, and the State in Nasser's Egypt*
2011

Samer Soliman, *The Autumn of Dictatorship: Fiscal Crisis and Political Change in Egypt under Mubarak*
2011

Rochelle A. Davis, *Palestinian Village Histories: Geographies of the Displaced*
2010

Haggai Ram, *Iranophobia: The Logic of an Israeli Obsession*
2009

John Chalcraft, *The Invisible Cage: Syrian Migrant Workers in Lebanon*
2008

Rhoda Kanaaneh, *Surrounded: Palestinian Soldiers in the Israeli Military*
2008

Asef Bayat, *Making Islam Democratic: Social Movements and the Post-Islamist Turn*
2007

Robert Vitalis, *America's Kingdom: Mythmaking on the Saudi Oil Frontier*
2006

Jessica Winegar, *Creative Reckonings: The Politics of Art and Culture in Contemporary Egypt*
2006

Joel Beinin and Rebecca L. Stein, editors, *The Struggle for Sovereignty: Palestine and Israel, 1993–2005*
2006